Philip H. Pfatteicher

Festivals and Commemorations

HANDBOOK TO THE CALENDAR IN LUTHERAN BOOK OF WORSHIP

AUGSBURG Publishing House • Minneapolis

MANUFACTURED IN THE UNITED STATES OF AMERICA

For my mother and father
in memoriam

May they be numbered with the saints
in glory everlasting.

Contents

Alphabetical List of Names and Festivals

Agricola, Michael—*April 10*
Aidan—*June 9*
All the Choirs (with Annunciation)—
March 25
All Saints' Day—*November 1*
Ambrose—*December 7*
Anatolius (with Watts)—
November 25
Andrew—*November 30*
Andrew of Crete (with Watts)
November 25
Andrewes, Lancelot (with Donne)—
March 31
Annunciation—*March 25*
Anselm—*April 21*
Ansgar—*February 3*
Antony (with Benedict)—*July 11*
Aquinas, Thomas—*March 7*
Athanasius—*May 2*
Augustine of Hippo—*August 28*
Bach, Johann Sebastian—*July 28*
Barclay, Robert (with Fox)—
January 13
Barnabas—*June 11*
Bartholomew—*August 24*
Basil the Great—*June 14*
Bede—*June 9*
Benedict of Nursia—*July 11*
Berggrav, Eivind—*January 14*
Bernard of Clairvaux—*August 20*
Birgitta of Sweden—*July 23*
Bonhoeffer, Dietrich—*April 9*
Boniface—*June 5*
Bunyan, John—*August 31*
Campanius, John (with Jensen)—
February 20
Calvin, John—*May 27*
Catherine of Siena—*April 29*
Chrysostom, John—*September 13*
Clare (with Francis of Assisi)—
October 4

Clement of Rome—*November 23*
Clement of Alexandria (with
Watts)—*November 25*
Columba—*June 9*
Confession of St. Peter—*January 18*
Coversion of St. Paul—*January 25*
Copernicus—*May 24*
Cranach, Lucas (with Duerer)—
April 6
Cyril—*February 14*
Donne, John—*March 31*
Dorcas—*January 27*
Duerer, Albrecht—*April 6*
Dunstan—*May 19*
Eckhart, Meister (with Catherine)—
April 29
Edwards, Jonathan—*March 22*
Egede, Hans (with Ziegenbalg)—
February 23
Eliot, John—*May 21*
Elizabeth of Hungary and
Thuringia—*November 17*
Epiphany—*January 6*
Erik—*May 18*
Euler, Leonhard—*May 24*
Falckner, Justus (with Jensen)—
February 20
Fedde, Elizabeth—*February 25*
Fliedner, Theodor—*October 4*
Flierl, Johann (with Francis
Xavier)—*December 3*
Fortunatus, Venantius (with
Watts)—*November 25*
Fox, George—*January 13*
Francis of Assisi—*October 4*
Frumentius (with Onesimos)—
June 21
Gerhardt, Paul—*October 26*
Germanus (with Watts)—
November 25
Gregory the Great—*March 12*

Gregory of Nazianzus—*June 14*
Gregory of Nyssa—*June 14*
Groote, Gerard (with Catherine)—
April 29
Gruenewald, Matthias (with Duerer)
—*April 6*
Grundtvig, N. F. S.—*September 2*
Guetzlaff, Karl (with Francis
Xavier)—*December 3*
Hammarskjold, Dag—*September 18*
Handel, George Frederick—*July 28*
Hauge, Hans Nielsen—*March 29*
Heermann, Johann—*October 26*
Henry—*January 19*
Herbert, George—*March 1*
Heyer, J. C. F.—*November 7*
Hilary (with Athanasius)—*May 2*
Holy Cross—*September 14*
Holy Innocents—*December 28*
Hus, Jan—*July 6*
Ignatius of Antioch—*October 17*
Irenaeus—*June 28*
James the Elder—*July 25*
James of Jerusalem—*October 23*
James the Less—*May 1*
Jensen, Rasmus—*February 20*
Jerome—*September 30*
John—*December 27*
John the Baptist—*June 24*
John Chrysostom—*September 13*
John XXIII—*June 3*
John of the Cross—*December 14*
Joseph—*March 19*
Joseph the Hymnographer (with
Watts)—*November 25*
Jude—*October 28*
Justin Martyr—*June 1*
Juusten, Paavali (with Agricola)—
April 10
Kagawa, Toyohiko—*April 23*
Kierkegaard, Søren—*November 11*
King, Martin Luther, Jr.—*January 15*
Knox, John (with Calvin)—*May 27*
Landstad, Magnus (with Wallin)—
June 30
Las Casas, Bartholome de—*July 17*

Lawrence—*August 10*
Lazarus—*July 29*
Livingstone, David (with
Schweitzer)—*September 4*
Loehe, Wilhelm—*January 2*
Louis (see Olav)—*July 29*
Luke—*October 18*
Luther, Martin—*February 18*
Lydia—*January 27*
Maass, Clara—*August 13*
Mark—*April 25*
Martha—*July 29*
Martin of Tours—*November 11*
Martyrs of Japan—*February 5*
Martyrs of Lyons (with
Irenaeus)—*June 28*
Mary the mother of Jesus—*August 15*
Mary of Bethany—*July 29*
Mary Magdalene—*July 22*
Matthew—*September 21*
Matthias—*February 24*
Melanchthon, Philipp—*June 25*
Merswin, Rulman (with
Catherine)—*April 29*
Methodius—*February 14*
Michael—*September 29*
Michaelangelo—*April 6*
Monica—*May 4*
Morrison, Robert (with Francis
Xavier)—*December 3*
Muhlenberg, Henry Melchior—
October 7
Munk, Kaj—*January 5*
Name of Jesus—*January 1*
Neale, John Mason—*July 1*
Nicholas—*December 6*
Nicolai, Philipp—*October 26*
Nightingale, Florence—*August 13*
Nommensen, Ludwig—*May 23*
Olav—*July 29*
Olga—*July 15*
Onesimos Nesib—*June 21*
Passavant, William A. (with
Fliedner)—*October 4*
Patrick—*March 17*
Paul—*June 29*

Penn, William (with Fox)—
January 13
Perpetua—*March 7*
Peter—*June 29*
Petri, Laurentius—*April 19*
Petri, Olavus—*April 19*
Philip—*May 1*
Phoebe—*January 27*
Polycarp—*February 23*
Presentation of the Augsburg
Confession—*June 25*
Presentation of our Lord in the
Temple—*February 2*
Prudentius, Aurelius Clemens (with
Watts)—*November 25*
Reformation Day—*October 31*
Ruotsalainen, Paavo (with
Agricola)—*April 10*
Ruysbroek, John (with Catherine)
April 29
Scholastica (with Benedict)—*July 11*
Schuetz, Heinrich—*July 28*
Schwartz, Christian Frederik (with
Ziegenbalg)—*February 23*
Schweitzer, Albert—*September 4*
Seattle—*June 7*
Sedulius, Coelius (with Watts)—
November 25
Sergius—*September 25*
Silas—*January 26*
Skrefsrud, Lars Olsen—*December 11*
Sieveking, Amalie (with Fedde)
February 25
Simon—*October 28*
Söderblom, Nathan—*July 12*
Stephen—*December 26*
Suso, Henry (with Catherine)—
April 29

Synesius of Cyrene (with Watts)—
November 25
Takawambpait, Daniel (with Eliot)
—*May 21*
Tauler, John (with Catherine)—
April 29
Taylor, Hudson (with Francis
Xavier)—*December 3*
Teresa (Theresa) of Avila—
December 14
Theodolph of Orleans (with
Watts)—*November 25*
Thomas—*December 21*
Thomas a Kempis (with
Catherine)—*April 29*
Thomas Aquinas—*March 7*
Timothy—*January 26*
Titus—*January 26*
Torkillus, Reorus (with Jensen)—
February 20
Tranovsky, Juraj—*May 29*
Tyndale, William—*October 6*
Visitation—*May 31*
Vladimir—*July 15*
Wallin, Johan Olov—*June 30*
Watts, Isaac—*November 25*
Wesley, Charles—*March 2*
Wesley, John—*March 2*
von Westen, Thomas (with
Ziegenbalg)—*February 23*
Willibrord (with Boniface)—*June 5*
Winkworth, Catherine—*July 1*
Woolman, John (with Fox)—
January 13
Xavier, Francis—*December 3*
Ziegenbalg, Bartholomaeus—
February 23
Zinzendorf, Nicolaus (with the
Wesleys)—*March 2*

Preface

Proper acknowledgement of all the people and sources which have contributed to a book of this kind is impossible.

The primary resources have been the Roman Catholic calendar, lectionary, and *Liturgy of the Hours;* and also the *Book of Common Prayer* (1979), together with *Lesser Feasts and Fasts* (revised edition, 1973) of the Episcopal Church. In addition, the *Evangelische Namenkalendar* published by the Lutheran Church in Germany in 1962 and 1966 has encouraged the enrichment of the calendar.

Correspondence from several people has been helpful in establishing dates and biographical details. The Lutheran Human Relations Association of America provided information concerning Native Americans; Loren Bliese, Gustav Aren, and the Evangelical Church Mekane Yesus in Ethiopia all helped in gathering material on Onesimos; E. Theodore DeLaney helped establish the date of the death of Tranovsky; the Alumnae Association of the Lutheran Medical School of Nursing in Brooklyn provided information about Elizabeth Fedde.

But most of all, this work owes an enormous debt to Charles A. Ferguson. His knowledge of church history and his unpublished manuscript *The Communion of Saints. A Calendar of Lutheran Commemorations* have been of great help in the creation of the calendar in the *Lutheran Book of Worship* and in the writing of many of the biographies in this book.

A work such as this which attempts to distill twenty centuries of Christian history is obviously liable to errors of both fact and judgment. For these no one can be held accountable but me.

PHILIP H. PFATTEICHER
East Stroudsburg, PA
All Saints' Day 1979

Introduction

Traditionally, the Christian calendar is of two parts. There is first of all the "temporal cycle" from Advent through Pentecost and beyond. It is the yearly commemoration of the redemptive acts of God, who in Christ was reconciling the world to himself. There is secondly the "sanctoral cycle," the commemoration of selected exemplars of the faith. Thus the acts of God in Christ are brought to an individual focus in particular lives. Both the actions and their application are essential dimensions of the proclamation of the Christian faith: there is the work of God in Christ and there is the work of the Spirit in his people. If only the acts of God are proclaimed, the result can be a rarified proclamation of historical and theological truths; if only the lives of the saints are celebrated, the result can be mere hero-worship. The observance of both cycles of the calendar together insures that the acts of God will be related to individual, everyday life and that ordinary life will be seen as capable of proclaiming the Gospel. So the Gospel is brought down to daily living, and daily living becomes the work of God.

The temporal cycle of the Christian calendar is familiar to Lutherans. They have throughout their history carefully observed the seasons of the church year. The sanctoral cycle is less familiar. For more than four centuries the Lutheran churches have retained the days of certain biblical saints—the Apostles and the Evangelists—on their calendars, together with Reformation Day and the commemoration of certain other occasions (Annunciation, Visitation, Presentation, Conversion of St. Paul). The days went unobserved and even unnoticed in many congregations, but the days were nonetheless retained on the calendar and listed in the service books.

The calendar of a church is an important reflection of the way that church perceives itself and its history. The usual Lutheran calendar gave the impression that nothing worth attention happened in the long dark ages between biblical times and 1517 when the Gospel was heard again through the Reformers and that then the curtain descended once more and since the Reformation there has been nothing worthy of celebration.

11

Such a restricted calendar was of course a reaction against the situation in the sixteenth century, for at the time of the Reformation the list of saints had become enormous and obscured the basic outline of the temporal cycle. The list of saints was not only long, with many saints appointed for each day of the year, but the list was also a curious collection of people, ranging from such universally-beloved figures as Francis of Assisi, to those who were notable for having done odd things such as St. Bavo, who forsook his wealth and went to live in a hollow tree, and those who may even have been fictitious such as Philomena, Barbara, and George.

The Reformers, in an effort to prune this over-abundant growth, drastically simplified the calendar of saints, and in the course of time only certain days with biblical warrant remained: the days of the Twelve Apostles and the Four Evangelists, together with a few other biblical people and events. But some important New Testament people such as the Virgin Mary, Barnabas, and Timothy were not generally included.

Despite the relatively conservative approach of the Lutheran Reformers, a popular understanding holds that "Lutherans do not have saints." (See, for example, the article on "Saint and Saints" in the *Encyclopedia of the Lutheran Church.*) Yet the Augsburg Confession and its Apology make clear that such is not the case and that Lutheran churches do indeed remember the lives of the saints.

It is also taught among us that saints should be kept in remembrance so that our faith may be strengthened when we see what grace they received and how they were sustained by faith. Moreover, their good works are to be an example for us, each of us in his own calling (Article XXI).

The Apology (Article XXI) recognizes a three-fold honor which is to be paid to the saints: thanksgiving for their lives, strengthening our faith in the abounding grace of God, and imitating their faith and other virtues.

The Apology, moreover, acknowledges that the angels pray for us and that the saints in heaven pray for the church in general. But invocation of the prayers of the saints is questioned as "something uncertain" since one cannot know from Scripture that the saints hear individual requests for prayers, and "prayer without faith is not prayer."

Definitions of "Saint"

The phenomenon of saintliness is widespread in the religions of the world and is not peculiar to Christianity. The English language, however, is very nearly unique in having a separate word "saint" (from the Latin *sanctus,* holy) as a title for particular people. Most languages simply use the word "holy" as an adjective and as a title, e.g. "Holy Stephen."

In the New Testament, "saint" is a word applied to all believers, all who have been made holy by being baptized into the body of Christ and filled with the holy and sanctifying Spirit. It is important to remember, however, that the number of Christians in those years was not large, and that membership in the church involved a deliberate choice and often a distinct risk, even of one's life. The church therefore could see itself collectively as separate from the world. The church (that is, people; there were not yet buildings or a hierarchy) was holy; the world was not.

As the church grew, the situation changed. Quite early in Christian history the word "saint" took on a more restricted use, for within the growing body of believers certain people of exemplary piety and goodness stood out: those who mirrored most clearly the new life of grace and faith. These were "saints" within the "holy nation" of the church, those who were seen as signs of the destiny of each member of the church. What they were already, all Christians were called to become and by the grace of God would one day be. God's people are "called to be saints" (Rom. 1:7; 1 Cor. 1:2). Saintliness in these passages is not so much a present condition as a vocation to which one is called, a goal toward which one strives. Moreover, one is summoned to become like those exemplars of grace and goodness. It is in this restricted sense that the word "saint" has continued to be used. In fact, it could be argued that calling all Christians "saints," following certain New Testament practices, can be unrealistic and even misleading in a church which now embraces most of the population and includes on its membership rolls a variety of merely nominal Christians who join a church for status, prestige, convenience, and other unworthy reasons.

In any case, the Lutheran Confessions accept both the more inclusive and the narrower definitions of "saint." Both have to do with the idea of separation—a people set apart from the nations and individuals who stand out among the holy people. The Augsburg Confession in Article VIII says, ". . . the Christian church . . . is nothing else than the assembly of all believers and saints. . . ." Here "saint" is used in the sense of "believer." But in Article XXI, quoted above, ". . . saints should be kept in remembrance so that our faith may be strengthened . . . ," "saint" is used in the narrower sense of an exemplary witness to the grace of God. Since both definitions are rooted in Scripture, the Lutheran church has generally accepted both the inclusive definition and the restrictive definition and used them side by side.

After the lifetime of Jesus, as time went by and as generations of Christians began to pass, the restrictive definition of "saint" as one who manifested clearly and compellingly the new life came to be applied only to those who had died. When the Apostle Paul wrote "to all the saints who are at Philippi," he addressed living believers in the Gospel. When the later church spoke of "saints" it meant departed witnesses to the Gospel. To some, it is surprising that church calendars list for commemoration, usually on the day of their death, certain Christians who have died. But the church knows better. Death does not silence those whom it claims, and the dead can speak with a powerful and commanding voice. The author to the Hebrews remarked, "Abel . . . died, but through his faith he is still speaking" (Heb. 11:4). In "Little Gidding" T. S. Eliot observes more explicitly,

> And what the dead had no speech for, when living,
> They can tell you, being dead: the communication
> Of the dead is tongued with fire beyond the language of the living.

The dead, whose lives in this world have been completed, speak with a force that those who are still living here with potential and possibility before them cannot achieve. Of the dead we know a whole story, the beginning and the ending. The story of the living is as yet inconclusive. The church therefore remembers the dead and listens to their testimony, for departed believers, especially those whose witness to the goodness of God has been exemplary, by the wholeness of their life and example can instruct and encourage those members of the church whose work is not yet done.

The Development of a Calendar of Commemorations

The first to be commemorated on Christian calendars were the martyrs, for their faithful witness ("martyr" means witness) even to death made a deep impression on the young church. The martyrs followed in the steps of Christ to the end and imitated him in death as well as in life. In the New Testament itself, the martyrs are singled out for special honor (Rev. 6:9-11; 17:6). In *The Apostles' Creed in the Light of Today's Questions* (Westminster, 1972), Wolfhart Pannenberg says that the phrase in the creed, "the communion of saints," originally meant not the coming together of believers but rather communion with the martyrs who already partake of salvation in heaven and communion in the sacraments, particularly the Eucharist, and that both understandings of *sancta*—the martyrs and the sacraments—"must be viewed as having equally primal force" (p. 149), since both link Christians with eternal salvation. The church commemorated the martyrs on the day of their bravest witness—their death—which was seen as the day of their birth into heaven. (See the reading for Polycarp.)

A category of "confessors," those who boldly endured persecution but who survived, was soon added to the list of those worthy of special remembrance by the church. The names of women and men then began to proliferate according to their popularity, and local observances varied widely. There was not for many centuries a universal, commonly agreed upon list, nor was there a prescribed procedure for adding names. The development of the calendar became largely haphazard.

Saints' legends grew as the list of heroes increased. Such legends are a kind of folklore, and their growth testifies to the international character of such tales. Stories from Greek mythology and even from the life of the Buddha are not uncommon patterns for the legends of Christian saints. Certain actions keep repeating themselves; at least nine saints, for example, have been credited with silencing the croaking of frogs. Wonders abound. St. Fursey and St. Isaac both spoke before they were born; St. Rumwold died when he was three days old, but he had already recited a profession of faith and had preached a sermon. There are moreover Gothic tales of sado-masochism. St. Agatha had her breasts ripped off; St. Lucy had her eyes gouged out.

It is small wonder that the Reformers rejected such legends and sometimes with them the whole cult of the saints from which they grew.

Yet one extreme begets another, and in rejecting the fantastic legends and the invocation of the saints, the wholesome examples of the saints were often lost and the knowledge of the church and its tradition shriveled. But now in the twentieth century, the Lutheran church has expanded its calendar, and the Episcopal Church has done the same in the 1979 *Book of Common Prayer*, The Roman Catholic Church has meanwhile greatly simplified its calendar of saints. The result is a notable convergence of approach in the three churches.

The Value of a Calendar of Commemorations

The calendar of commemorations is a kind of genealogical exploration of who one's spiritual ancestors have been. It is a way of encouraging people to examine the personal stories of certain women and men to learn of the richness and the potential of human life lived by the grace of God in Jesus Christ. A study of the calendar is at once a course in theology, church history (and sometimes political history as well), spirituality, and prayer.

Such a calendar can convey something of the breadth of Christian history and provide a richly assorted variety of the young and old, learned and ignorant, people of action and contemplatives, whose common denominator is simply that the grace of God worked mightily within them. In certain remarkable ways they have shown the world something of the greatness of God revealed in Jesus Christ and in our lives as well, and for that they are remembered with thanksgiving.

In *The Seven Storey Mountain* (New York; NAL, 1948), Thomas Merton wrote of the joy of discovering a new hero of the faith:

It is a wonderful experience to discover a new saint. For God is greatly magnified and marvelous in each one of His saints: differently in each individual one. There are no two saints alike: but all of them are like God, like Him in a different and special way. In fact, if Adam had never fallen, the whole human race would have been a series of magnificently different and splendid images of God, each one . . . showing forth His glories and perfections in an astonishing new way (p. 346).

So those who are remembered stretch our imagination and fire our hope.

There is a sense in which the people commemorated gratefully by the church are a consolation to us. In their holiness they do not forsake their humanity. They are people not unlike ourselves, who made it successfully through this life and its trouble, disappointments, frustration, pettiness. They have human failings and shortcomings. Phyllis McGinley wrote:

For the wonderful thing about saints is that they were *human*. They lost their tempers, got hungry, scolded God, were egotistical or testy or impatient in their turns, made mistakes and regretted them. Still they went on doggedly blundering toward heaven. *(Saint-Watching* [New York: Viking, 1969], 5-6.)

It is a consolation to know that the great people of God were—like us— not always entirely likeable, for as the Apology to the Augsburg Confession reminds us (Article IV), all saints have sin. Justified by grace, which they receive through faith, believers are nonetheless in this life still sinners.

In another sense, however, the saints are most unlike us. It has been said of Simone Weil:

She had an eye for pride, for vanity, for greed, for the corruptions of the mind and the soul and the heart, a spirit in the tradition of the saints, who were never meant to be glorified on this earth and who indeed were meant in a way to hector us and drive us to the very despair that in turn creates a kind of rage: Who is this person? What does she want of us? (Robert Coles, quoted in the *New York Times,* Oct. 11, 1975.)

The existence of saints is discomforting, for they are a constant reminder that we must never be content with this world but must press on toward the kingdom. They are a living judgment upon our small and satisfied lives. And because they are after all not so different from us, they urge us to follow their path.

The saints, then, are not characterized by a negative goodness of abstinence and rejection but rather by a drive toward wholeness, a total personal integrity which is rooted in a more than human achievement. Theirs has been a life of prayer and love and sacrifice, of charity perfected in suffering.

This holiness of wholeness has been expressed in astonishingly different ways and forms. The calendar is a most diverse collection of women and men, for as John the Scot observed, "There are as many unveilings of God (Theophanies) as there are saintly souls" *(De Divisione Naturae,* IV, 7). Rigid doctrinal tests are thus rendered impossible if a calendar is to suggest something of this richness and diversity of the revelation of God through the lives of his people. There are those who are dismayed to find Lutherans remembering George Fox (whose followers do not celebrate the sacraments) and not commemorating the seventeenth-century teachers of Lutheran orthodoxy —Martin Chemnitz, James Andreae, and John Gerhard. The inclusion of John Calvin, to some the rival from the Reformed churches, has raised some eyebrows. The calendar, as well as church history, however, urges us to remember not only those with whom we are comfortable because they are "our kind" and speak our language, but also those bristly souls who by their contrary opposition to what we find familiar and acceptable require us to reconsider the very nature of the Christian faith—George Fox challenging us not to take the church building (the "steeple house" as he called it) nor the ministry overly seriously; Catherine of Siena telling the pope to return from Avignon to Rome.

We are thus urged by the calendar to listen to new and unaccustomed voices with their insistent challenges that impel us to grow in our faith and knowledge of the nature of the church and God's ways with his world. In the evangelical tradition, the saints are remembered not so that they may hear us but that we may once again hear them.

A calendar of commemorations ought to expand our understanding of the size and extent of the church. For the church is larger than the individual congregation, larger than the denomination, larger even than the whole church on earth. It includes also all those who have gone before us in faith and whom we recall by remembering selected examples of that vast throng. In our praise of God, we join "with angels and archangels and with all the company of heaven" as the older language had it (the phrase is now simply "with the church on earth and the hosts of heaven," but the meaning is the same), "rejoicing in the fellowship of all the saints," we "commend ourselves, one another, and our whole life to Christ, our Lord" as the litany in Evening Prayer sings. Such remembering and rejoicing in the support of the cloud of witnesses who surround us is an important part of Christian life.

The Commemorations in the *Lutheran Book of Worship*

The calendar of commemorations in the *Lutheran Book of Worship* seeks to present a balanced reflection of the richness of Christian history. To emphasize the continuity of the tradition, no century is left without a witness. (Paul preached at Lystra, "In past generations God allowed all the nations to walk in their own ways; yet he did not leave himself without a witness. . . ." Acts 14:17.) The emphasis clearly falls on the first five centuries and on the time since the Reformation, and some of the centuries, to be sure, are obviously thin—notably the sixth through the fifteenth. But nonetheless, the continuity of the faith, even through the dark ages, is set forth.

The witnesses suggested for commemoration have distinguished themselves by conspicuous service within the Christian tradition, broadly understood. So, for example, some at the fringes of the church such as Hammarskjöld are included and some, like Gandhi, who made notable contributions to human society, are excluded.

Moreover, this calendar, following the tradition of the western church, excludes people of the Old Testament from specific commemoration. The Orthodox churches of the East include Old Testament people on their calendar. (St. Elijah the prophet is remembered on July 20, for example.) A proposal in the Episcopal Church to observe a day in commemoration of the "Holy Men and Women of the Old Testament" on November 8, the octave of All Saints' Day, was not preserved in the *Proposed Book of Common Prayer,* for this suggestion was perceived to be a kind of tokenism.

The women and men suggested for commemoration are not only ecclesiastics and those who have served the church organization. Also included are some who in various ways—by their service of society, by their creations, by their discoveries—sought to open humanity's eyes to the beauty and manifold grace of God.

The date chosen for a commemoration is normally—in accordance with the usual tradition of the church—that of the person's death, the "heavenly birthday." This practice has been followed even when it has meant doubling up commemorations on four occasions: February 23, March 7, July 29, and October 4. On certain other days related figures are gathered for a joint commemoration, such as the companions of St. Paul on January 26 and on January 27 the women who ministered with the Apostles. This practice also allows for certain emphases such as artists (April 6), church musicians (July 28), teach-

ers of science (May 24) and helps to avoid an unnecessary prolifera-
tion of dates.

In a few cases (e.g. Basil, June 14; John Chrysostom, September
13; Ambrose, December 7), the commemoration is not on the date
of the person's death. The date chosen instead in each case has the
support of both tradition and the revisions of the calendars of the
Episcopal and Roman Catholic Churches.

Using the Calendar

The calendar of festivals and commemorations invites creative use
by congregations, families, and individuals. Congregations should be
encouraged to make use of some of the days as a way of learning
about Christian history and their own tradition. Since many find this
a new experience, some specific plan should be devised to encourage
increasing familiarity with the calendar and its opportunities to enrich the devotional life of the congregation.

1. Determine to observe the principal festivals of the year which
fall on weekdays: Christmas Day, the Epiphany, Ascension Day.
These days can provide additional opportunities for worship, especially for those who find Sunday worship difficult or impossible to
share because of their schedule. The observance of these days should
normally include a festive celebration of the Holy Communion.

2. From the calendar of lesser festivals and commemorations select
certain representative days for special emphasis:

   a) a day for the Apostles (e.g. Peter and Paul, June 29);
   b) a day for the Evangelists (the day of the evangelist whose gos-
      pel forms the basis for that year in the lectionary cycle—Mat-
      thew, Year A, September 21; Mark, Year B, April 25; Luke, Year
      C, October 18);
   c) a day for the martyrs (e.g. Stephen, December 26, connecting
      his birth into heaven with the birth on earth of Christ; or Poly-
      carp, February 23);
   d) a day for the one for whom the congregation is named (e.g.
      Paul, John, Timothy);
   e) a day for one representing the ethnic character of the congre-
      gation;
   f) when appropriate, the day of the one for whom the city is
      named (e.g. Seattle, Francis, Monica, Augustine).

Schedule a service for each of these days, Morning or Evening Prayer perhaps. (Is it too much to attempt both?) Make the congregation aware of the day and its meaning by announcements, emphasis in the schools of the church, mailings, congregational calendars, posters, banners, exhibits. Send greetings and even a gift to any local churches that may be named for the person being celebrated. Provide the people of the parish with biographical data, readings, lessons, prayers for use at home, so that even those who cannot attend the service may share in the religious observance of the day.

3. Seek ways to expand upon this basic list, especially in times of special devotion: Advent, Lent, Easter. Encourage the congregation to study the lives, contributions, and work of the people whose days fall during these times. Again, provide biographical sketches, readings, lessons, prayers for use in families and in private. A congregational committee, or several ad hoc committees, one for each season, could be appointed to promote and plan and oversee the observance of these days. Seek a variety of appropriate celebrations. If the one commemorated was a poet, consider a festival of poetry reading; if a playwright, a dramatic presentation; if a hymnwriter, a festival of hymns (perhaps of one ethnic or national character); if a painter, an art exhibit; if a social worker, a social action project.

When two commemorations fall on the same day, a congregation may choose which of the two to observe, depending on local circumstances. The other person is remembered by using the appropriate collect after the prayer of the day. This practice of using a "memorial collect" may also be followed when a commemoration falls on a Sunday, since the Day of Resurrection always takes precedence over commemorations. The commemoration may also be noted in the prayers of intercession.

Using this Book

The following pages present a biography of each person commemorated in the calendar. To each, a brief bibliography is appended to guide further investigation. Occasionally, biographies are added of additional people who might appropriately be remembered with the one whose name appears on the calendar. So, for example, the Martyrs of Lyons might be remembered with Irenaeus, since Irenaeus was chosen Bishop of Lyons after the persecution of 177 in which the martyrs died. The biographies serve as background study in preparation for the observance of the commemoration. They may also serve as the basis for a sermon and may be excerpted in a congregational newsletter or service folder.

It is an ancient custom, when remembering worthy people of the past, that those commemorated should speak on their feast days. They can often address us through a reading from something they have written. If they have been hymnwriters, they can address us through the Hymn of the Day. In those cases where no appropriate writing is available for the reading, a selection from another writer is provided. The reading is often further instruction in the life and work of the one commemorated and can serve as a supplement to the biography. Moreover, the reading can be used following the reading of the scriptural lessons (especially in Morning or Evening Prayer) as an additional lesson. It may serve as a brief homily for the day. It may also be used as a devotional reading in private prayer.

In choosing the readings for the days of the calendar, the readings in the Roman Catholic *Liturgy of the Hours* were taken into account. When such readings (or part of them) were especially appropriate and theologically and devotionally acceptable, they were incorporated into this book. Those days that have the same reading appointed in this book and in the Roman Catholic liturgy are:

Birgitta (July 23)
Boniface (June 5)
Francis of Assisi (October 4)
Gregory the Great (March 12)
John Chrysostom (September 13)
John of the Cross (December 14)
Joseph (March 19)
Justin (June 1)
Lawrence (August 10)
Martin (November 11)
Monica (May 4)
Mary Magdalene (July 22)
Patrick (March 17)
Francis Xavier (December 3)

Moreover, the reading appointed in this book for the commemoration of Bartholomaeus Ziegenbalg is, in the Roman Catholic Office, appointed for the day of St. Ansgar (February 3).

Some of the readings, it should be noted, use masculine nouns and pronouns in a generic sense, a practice which we have come to realize is exclusive and to many undesirable. In certain cases this use has not been altered because of copyright restrictions or because of the nature of the text. Users of this book may choose to change these words for public use.

When a day is observed by the Roman Catholic and/or the Episcopal Church, those propers are provided in parallel columns for comparative study. The prayers of the Roman Catholic liturgy may suggest a phrase or an idea which may be of value to those who write the intercessions for the Eucharist or daily prayer. Many of these prayers may be used intact by evangelical Christians.

The prayers of the Episcopal Church, although the style of language may seem somewhat foreign to many Lutherans, can also help those who write prayers for the Eucharist and can serve as additional collects for services such as Morning and Evening Prayer. Occasionally, one of these prayers may replace the prayer provided in the *Lutheran Book of Worship* to prevent repetition and to give variety.

Sometimes the Lutheran prayer from the "common" (a set of propers that commemorate people who share a common attribute, such as martyrdom) proper for a commemoration is slightly altered to make it more specific for the particular day (e.g., February 3, October 4). The prayers for the Festivals are unchanged.

In *Lesser Feasts and Fasts* the Episcopal Church appoints two Psalms, one "especially suitable at the Entrance of the Ministers" and the other "especially suitable between the lessons." The provision of a proper entrance Psalm may be of special interest to Lutherans who seek occasionally to use a Psalm rather than a hymn as the entrance song.

The Scripture lessons suggested in the Roman Catholic or Episcopal calendars can be used to provide variety for those congregations that observe many of the days of the calendar, so that the same readings from the Lutheran "common" need not be used over and over again. These alternate possibilities can also serve as additional readings for private devotion.

The Roman Catholic lectionary has a long list of readings appropriate for the several "commons" from which two or three are to be selected for the Eucharist. Occasionally, specific lessons are suggested as especially appropriate for a particular day, and these are given in this book.

Sometimes the lessons of the Lutheran "common" are altered in this book to bring them into conformity with those of the other churches and to make the readings more specifically appropriate. When this is done, the changes are printed in italics.

The Hymn of the Day is by the person commemorated when such a hymn is available. If it is not, a hymn appropriate to the nation where that person's contribution was made or a hymn appropriate to the work of the person is selected. Occasionally when it seems appropriate an alternate hymn is suggested from the *Service Book and Hymnal* or *The Lutheran Hymnal* or *Worship Supplement*. Sometimes the name of a hymn tune is related to the person commemorated.

Suggestions or prayers are made to guide those who are responsible for writing or choosing prayers for a service. The suggestions are intended to make the calendar of commemorations relevant to a variety of concerns. They are not to be considered exhaustive. Other additional prayers may be locally appropriate.

The indication of the proper Preface for the day which is given in the Episcopal list can help guide those who plan the services. The Preface specified in the Ministers Edition of the *Lutheran Book of Worship* for the Lesser Festivals is indicated here also, and an appropriate Preface for the Commemorations is suggested. For example, the Epiphany Preface is appropriate for Missionaries.

The commemoration of exemplars of the faith always finds its proper focus in Christ, who works through his holy people and whose Spirit lives in them. It is therefore fitting that this book and the year begin with the holy name of JESUS.

THE NAME OF JESUS

In 153 B.C., January 1, the beginning of the month immediately following the winter solstice, was accepted by the Roman Empire as the beginning of the year. Previously, March 1 had been observed as New Year's Day; later, in the sixth century A.D., March 25, the Annunciation, was adopted throughout Christendom as the beginning of the year. In 1582 Gregory XIII reformed the calendar and restored the beginning of the year to January 1. The adoption of the new date spread slowly. It was not accepted in England and America until 1752.

In the pagan world, New Year's Day was a time of widespread license. For some centuries, therefore, the Christian church gave no liturgical notice to the day whatever. "I see you have come here," St. Augustine is reported to have said to the crowds in church on January 1, "as if we had a feast today." When the church noted the day at all, it was kept as a day of fasting and penitence; church attendance being seen as an antidote to participation in pagan revels. In a sermon for this day, Augustine said, "During these days when they revel, we observe a fast in order to pray for them." In the year 633, the Fourth Council of Toledo in Spain prescribed a strict fast and abstinence for January 1, and it became a day of such solemnity that "Alleluia" was omitted from the liturgy as it was during Lent. Throughout the church in these centuries there were repeated prohibitions against participation by Christians in the revels of the new year.

In the seventh century, however, probably under Pope Boniface IX (615), January 1 was made a church holiday, called simply "The Octave of the Lord" in imitation of the eighth day of Easter and of the Epiphany. Since the celebration of the new year could not be suppressed, the church did as it has often done and transformed the pagan holiday into a church festival. The appointed place (the "station") of the pope's mass that day was the church of St. Mary beyond the Tiber, the oldest Roman church dedicated to the Mother of the Lord; and so the day became connected with Mary, and the old Roman calendars call the day "The Feast of St. Mary." It is in a sense the oldest feast of Mary in the Western Church. The new

Roman Catholic calendar echoes the ancient name and calls the day "Octave of Christmas: the Solemnity of Mary, the Mother of God."

The celebration of the Circumcision began about the middle of the sixth century in Gaul. This celebration is not mentioned in the Eastern church before the eighth century, and it became established in Rome in the ninth century. This newer commemoration soon overshadowed the Octave of Christmas and came to be combined with the Octave in the name of the day: "The Circumcision of our Lord and the Octave of the Nativity."

In the middle ages, the day also came to be associated with devotion to the Holy Name of Jesus, since the brief Gospel (Luke 2:21) reported both the circumcision and the giving of the name. In 1530 the Franciscan Order received permission to celebrate the Name of Jesus as a separate festival on January 14. In 1721 the Feast of the Holy Name was fixed by Pope Innocent XIII on the Second Sunday after the Epiphany; in 1914 Pius X set the festival on the Sunday between January 1 and 6 or on January 2 if no Sunday occurred. That practice is now suppressed, and propers are provided for a votive mass of the Holy Name which can be celebrated whenever convenient and desired.

Certain Eastern rites kept the celebration of the Holy Name on January 1. In England, the Sarum rite kept the feast of the holy Name on August 7, a day which appears on some modern Anglican calendars as "St. Saviour" (i.e., the holy Savior). In the old *Book of Common Prayer*, January 1 is called simply "The Circumcision of Christ"; in the 1969 *Book of Common Prayer* the day is called "The Holy Name of our Lord Jesus Christ." There had been objection to the former title and particularly to the former collect, which asked for "the true circumcision of the spirit," since they made of circumcision a quasi-sacrament, and ritual circumcision has never been practiced in the church. Lutheran calendars retained the medieval association of the Circumcision and the Name of Jesus, and so the title has read in most Lutheran books (e.g., *Common Service Book*, the *Lutheran Hymnal*, and the *Service Book and Hymnal*.)

The office hymn for the Feast of the Holy Name, "Jesu dulcis memoria," ascribed to Bernard of Clairvaux, is still sung in English as "Jesus, the very thought of you," "O Jesus, joy of loving hearts," and "O Jesus, king most wonderful."

Reading

(From *Worship* by Evelyn Underhill.)

Eastern Catholicism . . . has . . . a technique . . . of a simple and beautiful kind, for the production and deepening of that simple, inclusive, and continuous act of communion with God, that humble "prayer of the heart," which is the substance of its mystical worship. This technique, so simple that it is within the compass of the humblest worshipper, yet so penetrating that it can introduce those who use it faithfully to the deepest mysteries of the contemplative life, consists in the unremitting inward repetition of the Holy Name of God; usually in the form of the so-called "Jesus-prayer"—"Lord Jesus Christ, Son of God, have mercy upon me!" This prayer has a unique place in the spiritual life of Orthodoxy. All monastic rules of devotion, and spiritual direction given by monks to the pious laity, aim at its development. It carries the simple and childlike appeal of the devout peasant, and the continuous self-acting aspiration of the great contemplative.

It can, when needful, replace the Divine Office and all other prayers; for it is of universal validity. The power of this prayer does not reside in its content, which is simple and clear (it is the prayer of the publican) but in the holy Name of Jesus. The ascetics testify that in this Name there resides the power of the Presence of God. Not only is God invoked in it, but He is already present in this invocation . . . thus the Name of Jesus present in the human heart communicates to it the power of that deification which the Redeemer has bestowed on us.

. . . "The light of the Name of Jesus pours through the heart, to irradiate the universe," a foretaste of that final transfiguration in which "God shall be all in all."

Evelyn Underhill, *Worship* (New York: Harper, 1937), 273-275. Used by permission.

Propers

ROMAN

God our Father,
may we always profit
by the prayers
of the Virgin Mother
Mary,
for you bring us life
and salvation
through Jesus Christ
her Son
who lives and reigns
with you and the
Holy Spirit,
one God, for ever
and ever.

(Text from the English translation of the Roman Missal © 1973, International Committee on English in the Liturgy, Inc. All rights reserved.)

Numbers 6:22-27
    Psalm 67:2-3, 5-6, 8
Galatians 4:4-7
Luke 6:16-21

LUTHERAN

Eternal Father, you gave your Son the name of Jesus to be a sign of our salvation. Plant in every heart the love of the Savior of the world, Jesus Christ our Lord, who lives and reigns with you and the Holy Spirit, one God, now and forever.

Numbers 6:22-27
    Psalm 8
Romans 1:1-7
    or Philippians 2:9-13
Luke 2:21

EPISCOPAL

Eternal Father, you gave to your incarnate Son the holy name of Jesus to be the sign of our salvation: Plant in every heart, we pray, the love of him who is the Savior of the world, our Lord Jesus Christ; who lives and reigns with you and the Holy Spirit, one God, in glory everlasting.

(Text from the Book of Common Prayer [Proposed], copyright 1977 by Charles Mortimer Guilbert as Custodian of the Standard Book of Common Prayer. All rights reserved. Used by permission.)

Exodus 34:1-8
    Psalm 8
Romans 1:1-7
Luke 2:15-21
Preface of the Incarnation

Hymn of the Day: "O Jesus, joy of loving hearts" (356)

Prayers: for grace to receive Jesus as Savior
for reverence of the holy name of Jesus
for the new year

Preface: Christmas

Color: White

Johann Konrad Wilhelm Loehe, Pastor, 1872

Wilhelm Loehe was born at Fuerth 21 February 1808. His father died in 1816, and the boy seems to have led a lonely childhood.

He attended C. L. Roth's gymnasium in Nurenberg and in 1826 entered the University of Erlangen to study theology. There he came under the influence of Christian Krafft, a Reformed professor and preacher, and there he also discovered the Lutheran Confessions. Following his study at Erlangen, Loehe went to Berlin for further study.

From 1831-1837 Loehe served in a number of places, and in 1837 he became pastor at Neuendettelsau, an insignificant village in Bavaria. His efforts to obtain a city parish failed, and he remained for the rest of his ministry in Neuendettelsau raising the village to international prominence. Although Loehe was born and reared in the city, he seems to have adapted well to rural life and was able from this little parish to influence church life on five continents.

Loehe was an ideal parish pastor, who got on well with all classes of people, and who in the parish was able to make practical application of his studies, particularly those of the Confessions and of the liturgy. He developed an understanding of the Holy Communion as the center of the congregation's life from which flowed liturgical renewal and social service. He combined a high view of the ministry, which he viewed as not dependent on the congregation's call but as transmitted from Christ himself through ordination, with an emphasis on the importance of the role of the laity in worship and missionary activity at home and abroad.

Loehe's missionary interest is seen in his pastoral concern (beginning in 1841) for Lutherans who emigrated to America. He solicited funds through periodicals, and he sent books and other necessary commodities. He was instrumental in sending "emergency pastors" to North America to serve the settlers and to convert the Indians. Loehe's emissaries assisted in the founding of the Synod of Ohio (although he withdrew support in 1845 because of the Synod's differences over theology and the use of English). With congregations established by C. F. W. Walther, Loehe's groups formed the Missouri Synod at Fort Wayne, Indiana in 1846. Loehe wrote the spiritual and secular regulations for a series of German colonies that were being established in Michigan—Frankenmuth, Frankenlust, Frankentrost, Frankenhilf. In 1853 Loehe's people moved into Iowa, and in the following year, joined by others from Neuendettelsau, established the Evangelical Lutheran Synod of Iowa and Other States. Moreover, his Neuendettelsau Foreign Mission Society sent pastors not only to North America but also to Brazil, the Ukraine, Australia, and New Guinea.

But Loehe's interest was not only in missions. In 1849 he founded the deaconess motherhouse in Neuendettelsau which became the center of social and educational service in schools, hospitals, and allied agencies. He also struggled with the territorial church in Bavaria to give it a clear confessional basis. His relations with the church were strained for several years between 1848 and 1852, but at length the conflict was resolved. He died January 2, 1872, at the age of sixty-three.

In short, Loehe was a remarkable advocate of confessional, devotional, missionary Lutheranism. The chapel at Wartburg Seminary in Dubuque, Iowa, is dedicated to his memory.

There is no biography of Loehe in English.

Reading

(From a statement by Wilhelm Loehe.)

What do I want? I want to serve. Whom do I want to serve? The Lord—in the person of his poor suffering children. And what is my reward? I serve neither for reward nor thanks, but out of gratitude and love; my reward is that I am permitted to serve. And if I perish in doing so? If I perish, I perish, said Esther, who, after all, did not know him who for love of me perished and who will not let me perish. And if I grow old in this service? Then my heart shall flourish like the palm tree, and the Lord will satisfy me with grace and mercy. Therefore, without anxiety I walk in peace.

Wilhelm Loehe in *Minister's Prayerbook*, ed. and trans. John Doberstein (Philadelphia: Muhlenberg Press, 1959), p. 218. rev. P.H.P.

Propers: Pastors (with the prayer "Heavenly Father. . . .")

Hymn of the Day: "Lord, whose love in humble service" (423)

Prayers: for truth
for doctrinal purity
for missionary concern at home and abroad
for a deeper understanding of the Holy Communion

Color: White

January 5

Kaj Munk, Martyr, 1944

Kaj Petersen was born 13 January 1898 in Maribo, Lolland, Denmark. His father was a tanner. His parents died before he was six, and he was adopted by the Munk family, his cousins, and took their name as his own. He has left a tender tribute to his adoptive mother upon the occasion of her death, in his sermon for the Sixth Sunday after Easter, collected in *By the Rivers of Babylon.* The boy was tutored privately by Oscar Geismar, a poet and literary critic. Although his family was poor, they were able to send him to Nykøbing University, Falster, so that he could become a pastor. While there he came under the influence of the work of Kierkegaard.

Munk was ordained in 1924 and became pastor at Vedersø, one of the smallest parishes in Denmark. It was his only parish. He married a local woman, and they had five children. He was influenced by the two strains of Danish devotion, Grundtvigianism and the evangelical fervor of Indre Mission. Munk was respected and loved by his people, and when he suggested that he ought to resign his parish to devote himself to his writing, the parishioners urged him to stay and called an assistant to help with the pastoral work. For a time in the 1930s Munk had admired Hitler and Mussolini, but after the occupation of Denmark by German forces during World War II, his powerful sermons drew masses to the resistance, and his own resistance became so outspoken that his plays were banned.

He wrote his first play, *Pilatus* (published 1938), as a schoolboy. Munk, an exponent of religious drama with a strong sense of theater, revived "heroic" Shakespearean and Schillerian drama with writing of a passionate intensity. His three best plays are *En Idealist*, 1928 (in English translation, *Herod the King*, 1955), which was panned by the critics when it was first staged in Copenhagen; *Ordet*, 1932 (English translation, *The Word*, 1955), a miracle play set among the peasants of Jutland; and *Han Sidder ved Smeltedigeln*, 1938 (English translation, *He Sits at the Melting Pot*, 1944), a drama of Hitler's Germany, attacking the persecution of the Jews.

Because of his outspoken resistance, Munk was arrested in the fall of 1943, but was released at Christmas. On the night of January 4, 1944, Munk was taken from his vicarage by the Gestapo. His body was found the next day in a ditch near Hørbylunde on the main road to Silkeborg. He had been shot through the head. More than four thousand people defied Nazi orders and attended his funeral at Vedersø.

Kaj Munk is commemorated not only for his own bold witness to the faith but also as a symbol of the many thousands who bravely but with less attention resisted Nazi tyranny. A popular telling of the stories of the heroes is found in John Oram Thomas, *The Giant Killers. The Story of the Danish Resistance Movement 1940-1945* (London: Michael Joseph, 1975). Munk's *Five Plays*, with a preface and English translations was published in 1953. His sermons have appeared in English as *Four Sermons* and *By the Rivers of Babylon*. A brief biography is appended to each volume. *Kaj Munk—Playwright, Priest, and Patriot* ed. R. P. Keigwin appeared in 1944.

Reading

(From a sermon for New Year's Day by Kaj Munk.)

Do not trust too much in the preachers. As a rule they are poorly paid. They are brought up as humanists. They have forgotten—or never learned—what Christianity is. They have imbibed lo-o-o-ve with the bottle milk in the cradle. In a world of men they too often plead the cause of the effeminate. They "abstain from politics." They preach peace at any price for the uplift of the devil, who rejoices to see evil develop in peace. The Scriptures do not say: When your neighbor is smitten on one cheek it is your duty to hold him so that he may be smitten on the other cheek also. Do not trust the preachers until they wake up and remember that they are servants of the whole gospel, and of the Prince of Peace who came not to bring peace but a sword; of Him who forgave Peter and permitted Judas to hang himself; of Him who was meek and humble of heart and yet drove the sacrilegists from the temple courts.

And do not trust the majority, which likes to take things easy and therefore is easy to please. . . . Do not trust the great neglected masses. I believe that the heart of the nation is strong, but it has become encased in fat. . . .

This is what our old nation needs; a rejuvenating power, God's rejuvenating strength, that a new people may come forth, which is yet the old, worthy sons of the fathers. The gospel will have to teach the Danish nation to think as a great people; to choose honor rather than profit, freedom rather than a well paid guardianship; to believe in the victory of the spirit of sacrifice; to believe that life comes out of death, and that the future comes out of giving oneself;—in short, faith in Christ. What would it profit a people if it gained all the advantages of the world, but lost its soul?

The cross in our flag—it is long since we realized that it stands for something, and we have forgotten that now. And yet it is the cross that characterizes the flags of the North.—We have come to church —the few of us who go to church, and we have heard about the cross, about Christ's example of suffering, and Christ's words about self-denial and struggle. We have thought that this was all to be taken in a spiritual sense, and that it did not pertain to our time. We thought we were Christians when we sat in church and sang Amen. But No, No! We are Christians only when we go out into the world and say No to the devil, renounce all his works and all his ways, and say Yes to the Holy Spirit.

Lead us, thou cross in our flag, lead us into that Nordic struggle where shackled Norway and bleeding Finland fight against an idea which is directly opposed to all our ideas. Lead old Denmark forth to its new spirit. Not by the grace of others, or by their promises, shall Dannebrog again become a free banner. For freedom only God can give; and he gives it only to those who accept its responsibilities.

Lead us, cross in our flag, forward toward unity with other flags of the cross. With honor and liberty regained, the old Denmark in the young North—that vision looms before us this New Year's Day. We who have the vision will give ourselves to its realization. We promise we will. May God hear our vow and add His Amen!

Kaj Munk, *Four Sermons*, trans. J. M. Jensen (Blair, NE: Lutheran Publishing House, 1944), pp. 27, 30-32.

Propers: Martyrs

Hymn of the Day: "Thy strong Word did cleave the darkness (233)

Prayers: for strength to follow Christ into the world
for those under persecution
for all who resist tyranny
for the theater: writers, actors, audiences, and all who
produce and perform drama

Color: Red

THE EPIPHANY OF OUR LORD

After Easter and Pentecost, each of which has Jewish antecedents, the Epiphany is the oldest festival in the church year. It too has ancient sources.

Both Christmas and Epiphany are related to pagan solstice festivals. In Egypt in 1996 B.C., the winter solstice occurred on January 6, and there was a night festival on January 5-6 celebrating the birth of the god Aenon (Osiris) from Kore the virgin. The waters of the Nile, it was thought, acquired miraculous powers and turned to wine that night. There came into existence, at least in the East, a Christian festival which echoed the ancient solstice festival and which was called "the Holy Day of Lights" or "the Day of Holy Lights," commemorating the manifestation of God in the birth and baptism of Jesus.

By the time Alexandria was founded in 331 B.C., the winter solstice occurred on December 25. In A.D. 274 the emperor Aurelian introduced the Festival of the Unconquered Sun, and early in the fourth century, we find in Rome the first evidence of a Christian celebration of the birth of Christ on what is now Christmas Day. It was a deliberate transformation of the pagan feast on December 25 into a Christian celebration of the birth of the unconquered Sun of Righteousness, who, unlike the sun, "knows no setting."

With the spread of Christmas as the celebration of Christ's birth, Epiphany was, in the West, coming to be associated with the visit of the Magi, probably because of the transfer of the relics of the Magi from Constantinople during the fifth century. The *Excerpta et Collectanea* associated with the Venerable Bede gives the number of the Magi as three and supplies their names as well as a fanciful description of each and a symbolic interpretation of the gift each brought:

> The Magi were the ones who gave gifts to the Lord. The first is said to have been Melchior, an old man with white hair and a long beard . . . who offered gold to the Lord as to a king. The second, named Gaspar, young and beardless and ruddy-complexioned . . . honored him as God by his gift of incense, an offering worthy of divinity. The third, black-skinned and heavily bearded, called Balthasar . . . by his gift of myrrh testified to the Son of Man who was to die.

This description has influenced the portrayal of the Magi ever since.

In the East, the Magi were commemorated as a feature of the celebration of the birth of Christ on December 25, and January 6 was observed as the commemoration of the baptism of Jesus. Then, to the mysteries of the Magi and the Baptism, a third was added—the first miracle at Cana (perhaps to counter the worship of Aenon-Osiris-Dionysus: Jesus supplies the true wine, which surpasses the claims of paganism). These several themes are gathered in the antiphon to the Benedictus in the Roman Catholic daily prayer for Epiphany:

> Today the Bridegroom claims his bride, the Church, since Christ has washed away her sins in the waters of the Jordan;
> the Magi hasten with their gifts to the royal wedding; and the wedding guests rejoice, for Christ has changed water into wine, alleluia.

The oldest name for this feast, still used by the Orthodox churches, seems to have been "Theophany," suggesting the origin of the day as a commemoration of the Incarnation as the revelation of God. In the Graeco-Roman world, a state visit of a king or emperor to a city in his realm, especially when he showed himself publicly to the people, was called an epiphany. In the East, the Epiphany of Christ has always had a more theological and less historical or commemorative character, so the baptism rather than the birth of Christ was selected as the event to illustrate the doctrine of the manifestation of God to the world in Jesus Christ.

Raymond E. Brown. *The Birth of the Messiah.* Garden City, NY: Doubleday, 1977.
A. A. McArthur. *The Evolution of the Church Year.* London: SCM, 1953.

Reading

Journey of the Magi

'A cold coming we had of it,
Just the worst time of the year
For a journey, and such a long journey:
The ways deep and the weather sharp,
The very dead of winter.'
And the camels galled, sore-footed, refractory,
Lying down in the melting snow.
There were times we regretted
The summer palaces on slopes, the terraces,
And the silken girls bringing sherbet.
Then the camel men cursing and grumbling
And running away, and wanting their liquor and women,
And the night-fires going out, and the lack of shelters,
And the cities hostile and the towns unfriendly
And the villages dirty and charging high prices:
A hard time we had of it.
At the end we preferred to travel all night,
Sleeping in snatches,
With the voices singing in our ears, saying
That this was all folly.

Then at dawn we came down to a temperate valley,
Wet, below the snow line, smelling of vegetation,
With a running stream and a water-mill beating the darkness,
And three trees on the low sky,
And an old white horse galloped away in the meadow.
Then we came to a tavern with vine-leaves over the lintel,
Six hands at an open door dicing for pieces of silver,
And feet kicking the empty wine-skins.
But there was no information, and so we continued
And arrived at evening, not a moment too soon
Finding the place; it was (you may say) satisfactory.

All this was a long time ago, I remember,
And I would do it again, but set down
This set down
This: were we led all that way for
Birth or Death? There was a Birth, certainly,
We had evidence and no doubt. I had seen birth and death,
But had thought they were different; this Birth was
Hard and bitter agony for us, like Death, our death.
We returned to our places, these Kingdoms,
But no longer at ease here, in the old dispensation,
With an alien people clutching their gods.
I should be glad of another death.

Propers

ROMAN	LUTHERAN	EPISCOPAL
Father, you revealed your Son to the nations by the guidance of a star. Lead us to your glory in heaven by the light of faith.	Lord God, on this day you revealed your Son to the nations by the leading of a star. Lead us now by faith to know your presence in our lives, and bring us at	O God, by the leading of a star you manifested your only Son to the peoples of the earth: Lead us, who know you now by faith, to your presence, where we may

ROMAN	LUTHERAN	EPISCOPAL
We ask this through our Lord Jesus Christ, your Son, who lives and reigns with you and the Holy Spirit, one God, for ever and ever.	last to the full vision of your glory, through your Son, Jesus Christ our Lord, who lives and reigns with you and the Holy Spirit, one	see your glory face to face; through Jesus Christ our Lord, who lives and reigns with you and the Holy Spirit, one God, now and for ever.

ROMAN	LUTHERAN	EPISCOPAL
Isaiah 60:1-6		
Psalm 72:2, 7-8, 10-13	God, now and forever.	Isaiah 60:1-6, 9
Ephesians 3:2-3a, 5-6	Isaiah 60:1-6	Psalm 72
Matthew 2:1-12	Psalm 72	*or* Psalm 72:1-2, 10-17
	Ephesians 3:2-12	Ephesians 3:1-12
	Matthew 2:1-12	Matthew 2:1-12
		Preface of the Epiphany

Hymn of the Day: "O morning star, how fair and bright" (76)

Prayers: for the nations
      for seekers of wisdom
      for the spirit of humility and reverence
      for those who bring offerings to God

Preface: Epiphany

Color: White

The Light Service at the beginning of Evening Prayer is especially appropriate for the Epiphany, recalling the First Lesson.

A useful custom is a procession to the crib with children dressed and crowned as the kings, bearing symbolic gifts for the Christ child —gold (or money), incense (perhaps just a stick or a cone of incense to be burned in his honor), a cross or other sign of his death. A star on a staff might replace the processional cross for this service.

George Fox, Renewer of Society, 1691

George Fox, a weaver's son, was born in July 1624 in the village of Drayton-in-the-Clay (now Fenny Drayton), Leicestershire, England. He was apprenticed for a time to a shoemaker; he may have also been a shepherd. There is little evidence that he had any formal education, yet he read extensively.

His religious background seems to have been Puritan, but he found this not entirely satisfying. At the age of eighteen he left home on a religious quest. During his search he experienced several "openings" as he called them in his *Journal,* which he thought corrected traditional concepts of faith and life in English religion. He went beyond the Puritan reaction to the forms of the established church, and after long and intense struggle, he arrived at the central belief of his life, that God speaks inwardly and directly to a person's heart. Finding no comfort in the church and receiving no help from its ministers, he became a wandering preacher, proclaiming the God-given inward light as the real source of authority above creeds and even above Scripture itself.

He travelled on foot, preaching in the Midlands and then in the northern counties of England. Local congregations were established by Fox and by other itinerant men and women preachers who called themselves "Publishers of the Truth." Fox had most success first in Westmoreland and later in Lancashire, Yorkshire, and London. His radical views and his peculiar habits (wearing a leather suit, sitting in hollow trees, refusing to take his hat off to anyone) provoked derision and hostility. He was beaten, stoned, put in the stocks, imprisoned. Between 1649 and 1673 he was jailed eight times. Nevertheless, he persisted and gained a considerable following, not only among the poor and uncultured, but also among people of wealth and distinction such as William Penn, who left an important summary of Fox's character. A man of enormous yet attractive self-confidence, Fox covered England with his influence and generated a new sense of morality. Tradesmen of this persuasion were universally respected for their integrity.

The restoration of the monarchy in 1660 led to special legislation and action against the "Quakers" as they were derisively nicknamed.

Fox encouraged the local groups of his followers to organize into
regular monthly and quarterly business meetings, and this became
the permanent pattern of church government for "the Society of
Friends." Not until the toleration Act of 1689 were the Quakers
accepted legally.

In 1669, after his return from a missionary trip to Ireland, Fox
married Margaret Fell, one of his early converts. She was the widow
of Judge Thomas Fell of Swarthmore Hall, Ulverston, Lancashire. It
was in this house that Fox lived from time to time in the years following. From 1671-1673 he visited the British colonies in the Carib-
bean and North America, especially Maryland and Rhode Island,
strengthening communities of Friends there. He also saw firsthand
the horrors of the slave trade, and upon his return to England he
founded the abolitionist movement. In 1677 and 1684 he journeyed
to Holland and northern Europe.

Fox died on the thirteenth of January (or as the Friends style it,
First Month), 1691 and was buried in the Friends' burial ground near
Bunhill Fields.

George Fox contributed to the renewal of the church by calling into
question its pride and self-satisfaction. But perhaps his greatest contribution is to the renewal of society in two principal ways—complete
religious toleration and the equality of everyone before the law.

The Journal of George Fox, ed. Thomas Elwood, intro. by William Penn,
    1694.
———. ed. John L. Nickalls, Cambridge, 1952.
Rufus M. Jones, *George Fox. Seeker and Friend*. New York: Harper, 1930.
Vernon Noble, *The Man in Leather Breeches*. New York: Philosophical
    Library, 1953.
Harry Emerson Wildes, *The Voice of the Lord*. Philadelphia: University of
    Pennsylvania Press, 1965.

With George Fox, three others of the Society of Friends might
fittingly be remembered. **William Penn** was born in 1644, the son of
a Cromwellian admiral who had become rich and powerful. He was
a quiet, introspective child, naturally drawn to the teachings of
George Fox, perhaps the first person of means, learning, and high
social standing to join the Quakers. He took the teaching of George
Fox and combined it with the work of a French theologian Moise
Amyraut, who had argued that God's laws live in the hearts of people

and that one learns them by listening to the voice of conscience, and popularized it through tracts and pamphlets, printed secretly and disseminated widely. He, like the others in the movement, was often imprisoned. He obtained the 45,000 square miles of Pennsylvania from Charles II in 1682 and regarded his colony there as a "holy experiment." Steadfastly committed to democratic principles, he established free public education in his commonwealth as well as chartering a private school, worked for better food and housing, regarded women as the equals of men, and established religious freedom. He suffered two strokes and lived out his last years in England in frail health. He died there 30 July 1718.

Harry Emerson Wildes, *William Penn.* New York: Macmillan, 1974.

Robert Barclay was the foremost theologian of the Society of Friends and, with William Penn, was the movement's most influential writer. He was born 23 December 1648 and was educated at the Roman Catholic Scottish College at Paris. He joined the Society of Friends in 1667. His humanitarian and his pacifist precepts are still followed, but his most important writing was *An Apology for the True Christian Divinity: Being an Explanation and Vindication of the People called Quakers* (Latin 1676, English 1678). This became the standard statement of Quaker doctrine and set forth fifteen propositions against both the Roman Catholic and the Protestant positions, affirming that neither the church nor Scripture could claim ultimate authority, but that both church and Scripture are secondary to the work of the Holy Spirit.

He was often imprisoned for his beliefs. He travelled through Germany and Holland advancing his views and upon his return home won the friendship of the Duke of York (later James II) who helped him obtain a patent to settle New Jersey. In 1683 Robert Barclay was himself governor of eastern New Jersey. He returned to his native Scotland, where he died 3 October 1690 at his estate in Aberdeen.

M. C. Cadbury, *Robert Barclay.* London, 1912.

John Woolman, judged by Elton Trueblood to be "the most highly respected Quaker who has ever lived," is a notable exemplar of ethical living. Born in 1720, he lived in Mount Holly, N.J., near Philadelphia, and worked as a tailor. He travelled widely as an itinerant minister.

He vigorously attacked slavery and roused the conscience of the Quakers against it and through them the whole western world. He refused to pay taxes to support the French and Indian War. He practiced and taught simple living both for individual and for social good, to the extent of giving up his store when business got too brisk and became an encumbrance. He sought to experience himself the hardships of slaves, seamen, and Indians so that he might "have a quick and lively feeling of the afflictions of my fellow creatures." John Woolman was one who radiated love and humility and who exemplified the sensitivity of the Quaker conscience and their steadfastness of purpose. His *Journal* (1774) is a classic of devotion and of literature; it begins with the sentence, "I have often felt a motion of love to leave some hints in writing of my experience of the goodness of God." John Woolman died of smallpox 7 October 1772.

Phillips P. Moulton, ed. *The Journal and Major Essays of John Woolman.* Oxford, 1971.

*

Reading

(From the journal of George Fox.)

After I had received that opening from the Lord, that to be bred at Oxford or Cambridge, was not sufficient to fit a man to be a minister of Christ, I regarded the priests less, and looked more after the dissenting people. Among them I saw there was some tenderness; and many of them came afterwards to be convinced, for they had some openings. But as I had forsaken the priests, so I left the separate preachers also, and those called the most experienced people; for I saw there was none among them all that could speak to my condition. And when all my hopes in them and in all men were gone, so that I had nothing outwardly, to help me, nor could tell what to do; then, O then, I heard a voice which said, "There is one, even Christ Jesus, that can speak to thy condition." When I heard it, my heart did leap for joy. Then the Lord let me see why there was none upon earth that could speak to my condition, namely, that I might give him all the glory. For all are concluded under sin, and shut up in unbelief, as I had been, that Jesus Christ might have the pre-eminence, who enlightens, and gives grace, faith, and power. Thus when God doth work, who shall let it? This I knew experimentally. My desires after the Lord grew stronger, and zeal in the pure knowledge of God, and of Christ alone, without the help of any man, book, or writing. For though I read the Scriptures that spake of Christ and of God, yet I knew him not by revelation, as he did who hath the key did open, and as the Father of life drew me to his Son by his Spirit. The Lord led me gently along, and let me see his love, which was endless and eternal, surpassing all the knowledge that men have in the natural state, or can get by history or books.

Thus in the deepest miseries, in the greatest sorrows and temptations that beset me, the Lord in his mercy did keep me. I found two thirsts in me; the one after the creatures, to have got help and strength there; and the other after the Lord the Creator, and his Son Jesus Christ; and I saw all the world could do me no good. If I had had a king's diet, palace and attendance, all would have been as nothing; for nothing gave me comfort but the Lord by his power. I saw professors, priests, and people, were whole and at ease in that condition which was my misery, and they loved that which I would have been rid of. But the Lord did stay my desires upon himself, from whom my help came, and my care was cast upon him alone. Therefore, all wait patiently upon the Lord, whatsoever condition you be in; wait in the grace and truth that comes by Jesus; for if ye do so, there is a promise to you, and the Lord God will fulfill it in you. Blessed are all they indeed that do indeed hunger and thirst after righteousness, they shall be satisfied with it. I have found it so, praised be the Lord who filleth with it, and satisfieth the desires of the hungry soul.

Passages from the Life and Writings of George Fox Taken from His Journal (Philadelphia: Friends Book Store, 1881), 18-20.

Propers: Renewers of Society
        First Lesson 1 Kings 19:9–13

Hymn of the Day: "Dear Lord and Father of mankind" (506)

Prayers: for seekers after truth
        for those in prison

for the outcast and those out of step with society
for equal justice for all

Color: White

The commemoration of George Fox, together with others of the Society of Friends, is an appropriate occasion to make generous use of silence in the service—after the Psalms, after the readings, at other times—and to instruct the congregation in the meaning and value and practice of silence. It is not necessarily a private activity, and the silence of an assembly of believers is a corporate act in which all share.

Most of us are uncomfortable with silence. We require sound around us continually and are therefore unaccustomed to silence in a service. We assume, when there is silence, that someone has missed a cue, and we feel very awkward. Those who lead worship need to allow a long time for meditation: there will be a lot of coughing and restlessness which suggest that people have had enough, but in fact the silence has not yet begun. Wait until all the restlessness ceases, and then the silence begins. In time a congregation will be able to move into silence more easily, naturally, and quickly. But it takes practice and patience.

Eivind Josef Berggrav, Bishop of Oslo, 1959

Eivind Berggrav was born October 25, 1884, in the port city of Stavanger, in the southwestern part of Norway. He was the son of the Bishop of Hamar, Otto Jensen. The name Berggrav, taken by the son, is thought to mean "mountain diggers," for his ancestors, like Luther's, were miners in Thuringia. They were invited to Norway in 1624 to work the Kongsberg silver mines. Eivind Berggrav first planned a career in engineering, but he was drawn to the ministry and received his master's degree in theology in 1908. Nonetheless, for ten years following his graduation he served as an editor of a local newspaper, studying the psychology of religion and wrestling with his own vocation. He also served as a teacher in a folk school in Eidsvoll, 1909-1914, and as headmaster of Holmestrand Teachers' College, 1914-1915. He studied at Oxford and Cambridge in 1914 and in Berlin in 1916. Finally, in 1919 he was ordained by the Church of Norway and became the pastor of a rural parish, Hurdal, near Oslo. In 1925 he became a prison chaplain in Oslo, and while there he earned his doctorate from the University of Oslo for his work *The Threshold of Religion*. In 1928 he was elected Bishop of Tromsø in northern Norway, a diocese of fishermen, fur trappers, and seamen, which reached to the land of the Lapps. In 1937 he was made Bishop of Oslo and Primate of Norway.

In May 1940, the Nazis invaded the country, and Berggrav was named one of the negotiators to determine the Nazi intentions. He withdrew from the commission after two days, refusing to offer a compromise to the Germans. With the six other bishops of Norway he led the opposition to the Nazi edicts and insisted on the right of clerical confidence, noninterference in the spiritual province of the church, and the rights of the Jews. Berggrav consolidated a united church front against the Nazis and wrote declarations and confessional documents in the *Kirchenkampf* (church struggle).

On February 1, 1942 Vidkun Quisling was appointed the head of the Nazi-controlled government. Bishop Berggrav, deprived by Quisling of the title of bishop and designated "an ordinary private person", was put under house arrest on Maundy Thursday (April 2). In protest, all the bishops and 797 of the 861 priests of the Church of Norway resigned their offices at Easter. Berggrav was then imprisoned on the charge of instigating rebellion and then placed again under house arrest (reportedly at the direction of Adolf Hitler because of reports of widespread public unrest). An underground church was formed to continue religious life independent of the Quisling regime. Berggrav, in disguise was able to meet with the church. In April, 1945, he escaped and remained in hiding in Oslo until the liberation of Norway shortly afterward.

After the war, in the reorganization of the church, he recommended a more active participation by lay people in the affairs of the church. He was a leader in the World Council of Churches from its founding in 1948 and in the Lutheran World Federation. Ill health forced him to resign his bishopric in 1950. He died January 14, 1959.

Berggrav published many books in the area of the psychology of religion: *Soldier Life and Religion* (1915), *The Threshold of Religion* (1925), *Religious Feelings* (1928), *The Prisoner's Soul* (1928), *Body and Soul* (1933). His *Biblical History* and his edition of Luther's *Small Catechism* have been widely used in schools in Norway. He also published *When the Fight Came* (1945) about his war experiences, *Church Order in Norway* about the reorganization of the church, and *Man and State,* a study of basic ethical questions. He translated into English a hymn by Peter Dass, "Mighty God, to thy dear name be given" which appeared in the *Service Book and Hymnal* (357).

Odd Godal. *Eivind Berggrav. Leader of the Christian Resistance.* London: SCM, 1949.
Alex Johnson. *Eivind Berggrav. God's Man of Suspense* tr. K. Jordhelm with H. Overholt. Minneapolis: Augsburg, 1960.

Reading

(From Eivind Berggrav, *Man and State,* written secretly while under house arrest by the Nazis.)

It cannot be denied that revolt is Christian. Nor is it enough to say that one must only turn in cases of necessity to revolt with arms or without. When men are mutiny-minded they can insist that a case of necessity exists every time something opposes their own wishes. That is why it is a good thing that revolt or mutiny always involves great outward risk. For one who is subject to an authoritative conscience, however, there is an ever greater risk—the judgment of God.

Christianity has always maintained that a willingness *to suffer* is a practical test in these matters of whether we are rightly related to God. Christianity has therefore designated as absolutely sinful any mutiny based solely on personal desire. At this point the Christian church must preach uncompromising obedience. Here Paul and the *Epistle to the Romans* are in complete agreement with the popular Lutheran interpretation. The Christian must even be willing to suffer considerable injustice against himself. If opposition to those in power is necessary it should be on the ground that *others* have suffered unduly and on the presupposition that such action would bring still more suffering to oneself. Thomas Aquinas says, "To bear with patience the evil which is committed against one is a sign of perfection. To be patient, however, with the evil which is done to others, is a sign of imperfection—yea, it is a sin."

It must be remembered, however, that suffering can be a dangerous test if one takes as one's starting point the natural desire to want to get off cheap. In that case the possibility of suffering would restrain one from undertaking anything. That's why it is equally important to make the Christian's burning challenge to withstand all unrighteousness the criterion. Where God's orders are trodden underfoot and the right of one's fellow man to live is threatened at the very outset, there the Christian must be. willing to go the way of *sacrifice,* even if it involves revolt against illegal authority. Keeping in touch with the conscience of one's fellows, i.e., with the corporate conscience, will constitute the greatest controlling factor. At a time of decision Cromwell said to his followers, "I charge you, Christians, to search your hearts and to consider whether you may not have erred."

But if conscience is rooted in God then a social matter is *also* God's concern. It is inappropriate for a Christian to say that the freedom of the church or of God's Word is not yet directly threatened and we ought not take suffering and strife upon ourselves just for the sake of "secular matters." There are no such things as "secular matters" for a Christian conscience. The moment that God calls on him to assume them they are God's concern as far as he is concerned. This is the explanation of that fact that the two expressions "to suffer for Jesus' sake" and "to suffer for righteousness' sake" stand side by side in the Sermon on the Mount. The moment conscience has received its orders and is willing to accept suffering and sacrifice, the thing becomes more than social. It then signifies covenant relationship with God.

The words on John Knox's tombstone are a challenging note about the strongest radical guaranty in this life: "Here lies the man who never feared the face of any man."

Man and State, tr. George Aus (Philadelphia: Muhlenberg, 1951) 282-284.

Propers: Pastors

Hymn of the Day: "Bow down your ear, almighty Lord" (286) *or*

"Mighty God, to thy dear Name be given" *(SBH*
357; see *LBW* 244)

Prayers: for those under persecution
for those who resist tyranny
for those in prison
for those who explore relationships between religion and
    culture
for colleges and schools.

Color: White

Martin Luther King Jr., Renewer of Society, Martyr, 1968

Martin Luther King Jr., who led the first mass civil rights movement
in the United States, was born January 15, 1929 in Atlanta, Georgia.
An exceptional student, he entered Morehouse College in Atlanta at
the age of fifteen under a special program and earned his B.A. in
1948. His earlier interest in medicine and law gave way to a decision
to enter the ministry. He entered Crozer Theological Seminary, Ches-
ter, Pennsylvania, where he studied Gandhi's philosophy of nonviolence. King was elected president of the student body and graduated
from the seminary in 1951. He then went to Boston University where
he met Coretta Scott who was a student at the New England Con-
servatory of Music. They married in 1953. King received the Ph.D.
from Boston University in 1955. He became pastor of the Dexter Ave-
nue Baptist Church in Montgomery, Alabama, and while he was there
a group decided to challenge racial segregation on public buses. On
December 1, 1955, Mrs. Rosa Parks refused to give up her seat on a
bus to a white passenger and was arrested for violating the city's
segregation law. The Montgomery Improvement Association was
formed, and King was named leader. His home was dynamited and
his family was threatened, yet he held fast. In a year desegregation
was accomplished.

To capitalize on the success in Montgomery, King organized the

Southern Christian Leadership Conference in 1957, which gave him a base of operation and a national platform.

In 1960 he moved to Atlanta as co-pastor of Ebenezer Baptist Church with his father. In October 1960 he was arrested for protesting the segregation of the lunch counter of a department store in Atlanta. The years 1960-1965 marked the height of his influence. Although not always successful, the principle of nonviolence aroused the interest and allegiance of many blacks and whites. In the spring of 1963 he was arrested in a campaign in Birmingham, Alabama to end the segregation of lunch counters. The police had turned fire hoses and dogs on the demonstrators and brought the incident to national attention. Some of the clergy of the city had issued a statement urging the citizens not to participate in the demonstrations, and King responded eloquently in his *Letter from Birmingham Jail.*

On August 28, 1963 two hundred thousand people marched on Washington in a peaceful assembly at the Lincoln Memorial and heard King's emotional and prophetic "I have a dream" speech. The Civil Rights Act passed later that year authorized the federal government to enforce the desegregation of public accommodations and outlawed discrimination in publicly owned facilities and in employment. Also in 1964 Martin Luther King was awarded the Nobel Prize for Peace for his application of the principle of nonviolent resistance in the struggle for racial equality.

King broadened his concern to include not only justice between the races but justice between nations as well. In January 1966 he condemned the Vietnam War and the attack was renewed on April 4, 1967 at Riverside Church in New York and on April 15 at a huge rally for peace.

King had planned a Poor People's March on Washington but interrupted his plans in the Spring of 1968 to travel to Memphis, Tennessee in support of striking sanitation workers. On April 4 he was shot and killed by a sniper while standing on the balcony of a motel where he was staying.

By his eloquent and often prophetic preaching, Martin Luther King, Jr., called the United States to a new commitment to the ideal of justice, while at the same time consistently resisting the temptation to violence, even when provoked. Struggling against two sides at once—the status quo on the one hand and racial revolution on the other—he taught by word and example the value of what he liked to call "redemptive suffering," bringing the crucifixion into relation to modern society. He spoke God's word to a complacent nation, moving it toward the realization of the kingdom of God.

The birthday of Martin Luther King has been made a holiday in several places in the United States, and for this reason his commemoration in the Lutheran calendar is kept on January 15, rather than on the day of his death, April 4. That date remains an alternate possibility for his commemoration.

Daniel L. Lewis. *Crusader Without Violence.* New York: Praeger, 1970. C. Eric Lincoln, ed. *Martin Luther King, Jr.* New York: Hill & Wang, 1970. Alan F. Westin and Barry Mahoney. *The Trial of Martin Luther King.* New York: Crowell, 1975.

Reading

(From *Letter from Birmingham Jail* by Martin Luther King Jr., April 16, 1963.)

. . . I, along with several members of my staff, am here because I was invited here. I am here because I have organizational ties here.

But more basically, I am in Birmingham because injustice is here. Just as the prophets of the eighth century B.C. left their villages and carried their "thus saith the Lord" far beyond the boundaries of their home towns, and just as the Apostle Paul left his village of Tarsus and carried the gospel of Jesus Christ to the far corners of the Graeco-Roman world, so am I compelled to carry the gospel of freedom beyond my own home town. Like Paul, I must constantly respond to the Macedonian call for aid.

Moreover, I am cognizant of the interrelatedness of all communities and states. I cannot sit idly by in Atlanta and not be concerned about what happens in Birmingham. Injustice anywhere is a threat to justice everywhere. We are caught in an inescapable network of mutuality tied in a single garment of destiny. Whatever affects one directly, affects all indirectly. Never again can we afford to live with the narrow, provincial "outside agitator" idea. Anyone who lives inside the United States can never be considered an outsider anywhere within its bounds.

My friends, I must say to you that we have not made a single gain in civil rights without determined legal and nonviolent pressure. Lamentably, it is an historic fact that privileged groups seldom give up their privileges voluntarily. Individuals may see the moral light and voluntarily give up their unjust posture; but, as Reinhold Niebuhr has reminded us, groups are more immoral than individuals.

We know through painful experience that freedom is never voluntarily given up by the oppressor; it must be demanded by the oppressed. Frankly, I have yet to engage in a direct-action campaign that was "well timed" in the view of those who have not suffered unduly from the disease of segregation. For years now I have heard the word "Wait!" It rings in the ear of every Negro with a piercing familiarity. This "Wait" has almost always meant "Never." We must come to see, with one of our distinguished jurists, that "justice too long delayed is justice denied."

We have waited for more than 340 years for our constitutional and God-given rights. The nations of Asia and Africa are moving with jetlike speed toward gaining political independence, but we still creep at horse-and-buggy pace toward the gaining of a cup of coffee at a lunch counter. Perhaps it is easy for those who have never felt the stinging darts of segregation to say, "Wait." But when you have seen vicious mobs lynch your mothers and fathers at will and drown your sisters and brothers at whim; when you have seen hate-filled policemen curse, kick and even kill your black brothers and sisters; when you see the vast majority of your twenty million Negro brothers smothering in an airtight cage of poverty in the midst of an affluent society; when you suddenly find your tongue twisted and your speech stammering as you seek to explain to your six-year-old daughter why she can't go to the public amusement park that has just been advertised on television, and see tears welling up in her eyes when she is told that Funtown is closed to colored children, and see ominous clouds of inferiority beginning to form in her little mental sky, and see her beginning to distort her personality by developing an unconscious bitterness toward white people; when you have to concoct an answer for a five-year-old son who is asking: "Daddy, why do white people treat colored people so mean?"; when you take a cross-country drive and find it necessary to sleep night after night in the uncomfortable corners of your automobile because no motel will accept you; when you are humiliated day in and day out by nagging signs reading "white" and "colored"; when your first name becomes "nigger," your middle name becomes "boy" (however old you are) and your last name becomes "John," and your wife and mother are never given the respected title "Mrs."; when you are harried by day and haunted by night by the fact that you are a Negro, living constantly at tiptoe stance never quite knowing what to expect next, and plagued with inner fears and outer resentments; when you are forever fighting a degrading sense of "nobodiness"—then you will understand why we find it difficult to wait. There comes a time when the cup of endurance runs over, and men are no longer willing to be plunged into the abyss of despair. I hope, sirs, you can understand our legitimate and unavoidable impatience.

Martin Luther King Jr., *Why We Can't Wait* (New York: Harper and Row, 1964) 78-79, 82-84.
The letter was written in response to a published statement by eight Alabama clergymen, the "sirs" of the last sentence.

Propers: Renewers of Society
　　　　　First Lesson: Amos 5:21-24

Hymn of the Day: "Judge eternal, throned in splendor" (418)
　　　　　　　　　or "Lift every voice and sing" (562)

Prayers: for peace
　　　　　for social justice
　　　　　for grace to learn that voluntary suffering can be redemptive
　　　　　for a quickening of the national conscience

Color: Red

January 18

THE CONFESSION OF ST. PETER

The martyr deaths of Peter and Paul are commemorated jointly on June 29. Paul has a festival of his own marking his conversion (January 25), which is the conclusion of the Week of Prayer for Christian Unity. It has seemed logical, therefore, to celebrate a festival of St.

Peter and to set it at the beginning of that week, in this way including the week officially on the calendar of the church. The Week of Prayer for Christian Unity is thus set between the two great apostles of Christianity—Peter and Paul. Moreover, the two represent in a way two faces of biblical tradition: Peter, the apostle to the Jews, represents the Mosaic tradition of law, and Paul, the Apostle to the Gentiles, represents the Abrahamic tradition of faith.

Since the fourth century there had been a festival of Peter, called "the Chair of Peter," which honored both Peter as the head of the Roman church as well as his *cathedra* ("chair") of episcopal authority and focus of church unity founded upon the leader of the twelve apostles. The Roman Catholic Church observes this feast now on February 22, the older date, but because it often falls in Lent many churches had moved the celebration to January 18.

The Episcopal Church has taken this feast with its Gospel of Peter's confession that Jesus is "the Christ, the Son of the living God" and set it at the beginning of the Week of Prayer for Christian Unity. The Lutheran calendar has followed that suggestion and has given the week of prayer a standing in the calendar that no other church has done.

Oscar Cullmann. *Peter: Disciple, Apostle, Martyr.* Philadelphia: Westminster, 1953.
E. J. Goodspeed. *The Twelve.* New York: Holt, Rinehart, Winston, 1957.
John Lowe. *St. Peter.* New York: Oxford, 1956.
Daniel William O'Connor. *Peter in Rome. The Literary, Liturgical, and Archaeological Evidence.* New York: Columbia University Press, 1969.
Peter in the New Testament ed. Raymond E. Brown, Karl P. Donfried, John Reumann. Minneapolis and New York: Augsburg and Paulist, 1973.

Reading

(From *Peter: Disciple, Apostle, Martyr* by Oscar Cullmann.)

. . . during the lifetime of Jesus Peter did not show himself a "rock" at all; on the contrary, his human weakness was very striking. The scene at the Sea of Gennesaret gives a concrete illustration of Peter's character. He is impulsive and enthusiastic; in the first burst of enthusiasm, he does not hesitate to throw himself into the sea when Jesus calls him, but his courage soon fades and fear grips him. So, too, he is the first to confess loudly his loyalty to his Master, but he is the first one who will deny him in the hour of danger. And yet, so one assumes, precisely this character, with its notable contradictions, makes Peter appear as the disciple with special psychological fitness to be the "rock" among the other disciples. The exuberant enthusiasm, the fiery zeal of this disciple are said to be in fact the human qualities that are necessary to deserve such a title of honor. His instability and weakness are said to be only the dark side of these qualities.

Nevertheless, it is hardly possible to give a psychological basis for the unique position of Peter and for the giving to him of this name. Indeed, we should not ask at all why Jesus singled him out as "rock" instead of choosing another disciple. According to our sources, we can only confirm the fact of this distinction.

Probably, however, it is also a mistake to say that the representative position of the disciple Peter and the qualities mentioned were derived only from the giving of the name. We can hardly say that only by this act did he become conscious that in his person he represented, so to speak, the totality of the disciples, even during the earthly life of Jesus. Again we can only state *the fact:* Peter lets us see clearly everything that the call to discipleship involves in human weakness and privilege.

Oscar Cullmann, *Peter: Disciple, Apostle, Martyr.* Trans. Floyd V. Filson (New York: Meridian, 1958) 31-32. Second Revised Edition. Copyright © 1962 SCM Press, Ltd. Published in the U.S.A. by The Westminster Press, 1962. Used by permission.

Propers

ROMAN	LUTHERAN	EPISCOPAL
(February 22) All-powerful Father, you have built your Church on the rock of Saint Peter's confession of faith. May nothing divide or weaken	Almighty God, you inspired Simon Peter to confess Jesus as the Messiah and Son of the living God. Keep your Church firm on the rock of this faith, that in unity and peace it may pro-	Almighty Father, who inspired Simon Peter, first among the apostles, to confess Jesus as Messiah and Son of the living God: Keep your Church steadfast upon the rock of this faith, so that in unity

ROMAN	LUTHERAN	EPISCOPAL
our unity in faith and love. Grant this through our Lord Jesus Christ, your Son, who lives and reigns with you and the Holy Spirit, one God, for ever and ever.	claim one truth and follow one Lord, your Son, our Savior Jesus Christ, who lives and reigns with you and the Holy Spirit, one God, now and forever.	and peace we may proclaim the one truth and follow the one Lord, our Savior Jesus Christ; who lives and reigns with you and the Holy Spirit, one God, now and for ever.

ROMAN	LUTHERAN	EPISCOPAL
1 Peter 5:1-4 Psalm 23 Matthew 16:13-19	Acts 4:8-13 Psalm 18:1-6, 17-20 1 Corinthians 10:1-5 Matthew 16:13-19	Acts 4:8-13 Psalm 23 1 Peter 5:1-4 Matthew 16:13-19 Preface of Apostles

Hymn of the Day: "How sweet the name of Jesus sounds" (345) (to the tune *St. Peter*)

Prayers: for the unity of the church
for clarity and boldness in the church's preaching
for reconciliation between the Roman and non-Roman churches

Preface: Apostles

Color: White

January 19

Henry, Bishop of Uppsala, Missionary to Finland, Martyr, 1156

Henry, or Henrik as he is called throughout Scandinavia, was born in England early in the twelfth century. He became bishop of Uppsala in Sweden in 1152 and is generally known as St. Henry of Uppsala. In the first dated event in the history of Christianity in Finland,

Henry accompanied Eric, the king of Sweden, on an expedition to the Finns in 1155 which was intended both to Christianize the people and to bring them under firmer control of the Swedish crown. After the king returned, Bishop Henry remained and began the organization of the church. In January of the following winter (1156), Bishop Henry was slain with an axe on frozen Lake Köyliö by a Finnish farmer named Lalli (=Lawrence). The generally accepted version of St. Henry's death is that Lalli was a murderer who had been censured by the bishop and disciplined by the church. There is also a Finnish folk ballad which tells the story that Lalli slew Henry out of resentment for his wife's selling provisions to the bishop and that he was punished in turn by God for his act.

Henry was not the first to preach the Gospel among the Finns, but this missionary martyr bishop was the effective founder of the church in Finland, although full outward Christianization of Finland was not completed until the appointment of a Finn, Magnus, as bishop of Abo (= Turku) in 1291. Henry's body was buried in Nousainen, north of Turku, and within a few years Henry was commemorated on the date of his death.

At the beginning of the thirteenth century, the first bishop of Finland, Thomas (d. 1248), also English-born, transferred the see from Nousainen to Koroinen, an old trading center close to Turku. A little later it was transferred again to the new Turku, where a cathedral —the most impressive building in medieval Finland—was built before the end of the thirteenth century. The church was closely related to the cult of St. Henry, who by then had come to be regarded as the patron of Finland.

St. Henry is not on the Episcopal or the general Roman Catholic calendar.

T. Borenius. *Archaeological Journal* 87 (1930) 340-358.

Reading

(From *Imitation of Christ.*)

What do you seek here, since this world is not your resting place? Your true home is in Heaven; therefore remember that all the things of this world are transitory. All things are passing, and yourself with them. See that you do not cling to them, lest you become entangled and perish with them. Let all your thoughts be with the Most High, and direct your humble prayers unceasingly to Christ. If you cannot contemplate high and heavenly things, take refuge in the Passion of Christ, and love to dwell within His Sacred Wounds. For if you devoutly seek the Wounds of Jesus and the precious marks of His Passion, you will find great strength in all troubles. And if men despise you, you will care little, having small regard for the words of your detractors.

Christ himself was despised by men, and in His direst need was abandoned by his friends and acquaintances to the insults of His enemies. Christ was willing to suffer and to be despised; and do you presume to complain? Christ had enemies and slanderers; and do you expect all men to be your friends and benefactors? How will your patience be crowned, if you are not willing to endure hardship? Suffer with Christ, and for Christ, if you wish to reign with Christ.

Had you but once entered perfectly into the Heart of Jesus and tasted something of his burning love, you would care nothing for your own gain or loss; for the love of Jesus causes a man to regard himself very humbly. The true, inward lover of Jesus and the Truth, who is free from inordinate desires, can turn freely to God, rise above self, and joyfully rest in God.

Thomas a Kempis, *Imitation of Christ*, II, 1 trans., Leo Sherley-Price (Baltimore: Penguin, 1952), 68-69. Copyright © Leo Sherley-Price, 1952. Reprinted by permission of Penguin Books Ltd.

Propers: Missionaries (or Martyrs)

Hymn of the Day: "Lost in the night do the people yet languish" (394)

Prayers: for the Church of Finland
       for faithfulness
       for zeal in preaching the Gospel
       for the unity of the church

Color: Red

THE CONVERSION OF ST. PAUL

Paul's conversion to Christianity was of such decisive importance for the young Church that the story of his conversion is told three times in Acts (9:1-22; 22:3-21; 26:9-20), and Paul himself makes mention of this experience three times in his letters (Gal. 1:11-16; 1 Cor. 9:1-12; 15:3-11). The risen Lord had appeared to Saul, and that dedicated enemy of the church submitted himself totally to the lordship of Christ.

The origin of the observance of the Conversion of St. Paul is obscure. The commemoration seems to have begun in Gaul, as contrasted with the Festival of SS. Peter and Paul, which began in Rome. In the fourth-century martyrology of St. Jerome, the day is called the "translation" of St. Paul, which suggests that the day may have begun as a celebration of the anniversary of the moving of the relics of St. Paul to his basilica outside Rome. The day does not seem to have been generally observed until about the twelfth century. It is not observed in the East.

The festival was particularly popular in northern Europe, and this, in addition to its biblical basis, perhaps accounts for the retention of the day on both Lutheran and Anglican calendars. The day was traditionally of lower rank than the feasts of the Apostles, however, and in England it was retained on the calendar only with some difficulty.

The day marks the conclusion of the Week of Prayer for Christian Unity.

Lucas Grollenberg. *Paul*. Philadelphia: Westminster, 1979.
Robert Jewett. *A Chronology of Paul's Life*. Philadelphia: Fortress, 1978.
Ernst Käsemann. *Perspectives on Paul*. Philadelphia: Fortress, 1979.
Leander E. Keck. *Paul and His Letters*. Philadelphia: Fortress, 1978.
Samuel Sandmel. *The Genius of Paul*. Philadelphia: Fortress, 1979.
Krister Stendahl. *Paul Among Jews and Gentiles*. Philadelphia: Fortress, 1975.

Reading

(From *The Word of God and the Word of Man* by Karl Barth.)

We all know the curiosity that comes over us when from a window we see the people in the street suddenly stop and look up—shade their eyes with their hands and look straight up into the sky toward something which is hidden from us by the roof. Our curiosity is superfluous, for what they see is doubtless an aeroplane. But as to the sudden stopping, looking up, and tense attention characteristic of the people of the Bible, our wonder will not be so lightly dismissed. To me personally it came first with Paul: this man evidently sees and hears something which is above everything, which is absolutely beyond the range of my observation and the measure of my thought. Let me place myself as I will to this coming something that in enigmatical words he insists he sees and hears, I am still taken by the fact that he, Paul, or whoever it was who wrote the Epistle to the Ephesians, for example, is eye and ear in a state which expressions such as inspiration, alarm, or stirring or overwhelming emotion, do not satisfactorily describe. I seem to see within so transparent a piece of liturature a personality who is actually thrown out of his course by seeing and hearing what I for my part do not see and hear—who is, so to speak, captured, in order to be dragged as a prisoner from land to land for strange, intense, uncertain, and yet mysteriously well-planned service.

And if ever I come to fear lest mine is a case of self-hallucination, one glance at the secular events of those times, one glance at the widening circle of ripples in the pool of history, tells me of a certainty that a stone of unusual weight must have been dropped into deep water somewhere—tells me that, among all the hundreds of peripatetic preachers and miracle-workers from the Near East who in that day must have gone along the same Appian Way into imperial Rome, it was this one Paul, seeing and hearing what he did, who was the cause, if not of all, yet of the most important developments in that city's future.

Karl Barth, *The Word of God and the Word of Man* tr. Douglas Horton Boston: Pilgrim Press, 1928) 62-63. Used by permission of Peter Smith.

Propers

ROMAN	LUTHERAN	EPISCOPAL
God our Father, you taught the gospel to all the world through the preaching of Paul your apostle. May we who celebrate his conversion to the faith follow him in bearing witness to your truth. We ask this through our Lord Jesus Christ, your Son, who lives and reigns with you and the Holy Spirit, one God, for ever and ever.	Lord God, through the preaching of your apostle, Paul, you established one Church from among the nations; as we celebrate his conversion, we pray that we may follow his example and be witnesses to the truth of your Son, Jesus Christ our Lord, who lives and reigns with you and the Holy Spirit, one God, now and forever.	O God, by the preaching of your apostle Paul you have caused the light of the Gospel to shine throughout the world: Grant, we pray, that we, having his wonderful conversion in remembrance, may show ourselves thankful to you by following his holy teaching; through Jesus Christ our Lord, who lives and reigns with you, in the unity of the Holy Spirit, one God, now and for ever.

ROMAN	LUTHERAN	EPISCOPAL
Acts 22:3-16 Psalm 117 Mark 16:15-18	Acts 9:1-22 Psalm 67 Galatians 1:11-24 Luke 21:10-19	Acts 26:9-21 Psalm 67 Galatians 1:11-24 Matthew 10:16-22 Preface of the Apostles

Hymn of the Day: "O Spirit of the living God" (388)

Prayers: for the unity of the church
        for renewal of faith
        for preachers of the Gospel
        for opening our eyes to see beyond this world

Preface: Apostles

Color: White

Timothy, Titus, and Silas

Two of these three disciples are linked with St. Paul in the address of 1 Thessalonians 1:1.

Timothy is described by Paul as a "brother" (1 Thess. 3:2) and was apparently converted by Paul when Paul first visited Lystra in Asia Minor (1 Cor. 4:17; 1 Tim. 2:2, 18; 2 Tim. 1:2). Timothy's father was a Greek; his mother, Eunice (according to Acts 16:1-3, a Jew), was the daughter of a Christian, Lois (2 Tim. 1:5). St. Paul had Timothy circumcised so that he would be acceptable to the Jews as well as the Gentiles. Timothy first appears in the New Testament as a young associate of Paul and Silas (Silvanus) at Corinth. He went with Paul to Philippi and then to Beroea, where he remained alone for a time, rejoining Paul again in Athens. Paul then sent Timothy back to the Thessalonian church to strengthen their faith during a time of persecution. Timothy returned to Paul at Corinth with a report of their steadfastness (1 Thess. 1:6-9).

Timothy was apparently the bearer of Paul's letter to Corinth, and 1 Corinthians 16:10-11 urges the Corinthians to put the emissary at ease, as if he were somewhat shy. While at Corinth, Timothy preached the same message as had Paul and Silas (1:19), but the problems of that church remained.

Because his father was a Gentile, Timothy was sent to strengthen Gentile churches, for he seemed to have their confidence (Phil. 2:20-22). Paul seems to have sent his young companion ahead to prepare for Paul's visit to Macedonia and Achaia and later to Jerusalem. According to Hebrews 13:23 he was imprisoned and then freed.

There is no genuine information about Timothy in ancient non-biblical sources. John Damascene says that Timothy, the first bishop of Ephesus, witnessed Mary's assumption. According to tradition, Timothy was beaten and stoned to death in A.D. 97 under Nerva because he opposed heathen worship, and in 356 his supposed remains were moved to Constantinople by Constantine. His feast day in the Greek and Syrian churches is January 22. Timothy's feast day in the West had been January 24, but the Episcopal and Roman Catholic churches now commemorate him with Titus on January 26, remembering these two companions of St. Paul immediately after the celebration of Paul's conversion.

Timothy had delivered First Corinthians. The bearer of Second Corinthians is **Titus,** who seems to be Paul's new deputy. He plays an important role in the Corinthian correspondence from this point on. Titus is not mentioned in Acts, but he is frequently referred to in Paul's letters. He was born of Gentile parents (Gal. 2:3), and was perhaps a native of Antioch, since he was in the delegation from Antioch to Jerusalem (Acts 15:2; Gal. 2:1-3), and he may have been converted by Paul (Titus 1:4). He and a companion were sent to Corinth after First Corinthians had been sent there, because of reports Paul had received about that troublesome church. The mission was a delicate one. Paul had expected to meet Titus at Troas (2 Cor. 2:12-13), but instead Titus met him in Macedonia with good news (7:6, 13-14), and he returned to Corinth with Second Corinthians (8:6, 13, 23).

The Epistle to Titus gives the information that Titus had been left on Crete to oversee the organization of the churches there. Titus' mission to Dalmatia (Yugoslavia) is alluded to in 2 Timothy 4:10. Tradition says that Titus lived in Crete and died there at the age of 93. His head was later transferred from Gortyna to St. Mark's in Venice after the invasion of the Saracens in 823. Ancient sources provide no further information.

In the writings of Paul, Titus is pictured as vigorous, resourceful, decisive, efficient, zealous; yet with it all of a kindly disposition. In the Pastoral Letters a rather different character is drawn. Titus there needs to be reminded to exercise his authority (Titus 2:15). This clear difference in characterization is a primary reason why many think that the Pastoral Letters are pseudonymous.

Titus' feast day in the Greek and Syrian churches is August 25. In the West it had been January 4, but was then transferred to February 6 by Pius IX to avoid a conflict with what was then (January 4) the octave of the Holy Innocents. On the new Roman calendar Titus is remembered with Timothy on January 26.

Silas (as he is called in Acts; in the epistles he is called Silvanus, his Latin and Hellenistic name, which resembles his Armenian name, Saul) was a leader in the church at Jerusalem who was sent with

Paul to tell the Christians of Antioch of the decision of the Jerusalem Council concerning Gentile Christians. Paul chose Silas to replace John Mark on the second missionary journey when Mark and Barnabas left, and so Silas was one of the first Christian missionaries on the continent of Europe. Paul and Silas were imprisoned together at Philippi, and Silas was with Paul during the riot at Thessalonica. He was then sent away to Beroea and remained there when Paul went on to Athens. He rejoined Paul at Corinth. When Paul left Corinth, Silas remained, and this seems to be the end of the relationship between the two. Silas is not mentioned again.

Silas-Silvanus was probably the Silvanus who delivered First Peter (5:12); some say he was the author of First Peter or at least the amanuensis. Legend says that he was bishop of Corinth and that he died in Macedonia. His traditional feast day in the West has been July 13.

Reading

(From Wilhelm Loehe.)

Among the means which the church uses to save souls, preaching stands first. It is the means by which those are called who stand afar off, and those who have been called are rendered steadfast in their calling and election. In preaching, the church does not aim to support the holy Word by human art, but the chief matter is not to hinder its power and operation and not to impose upon the Word any kind or manner of operation which does not befit it.

The preacher proclaims salvation in Christ Jesus with the consciousness that it is not what he does, but the noble contents of the Word itself that must separate souls from the world and bring them near to God. Of course the preacher believes and therefore speaks, and it is a detestable contradiction to preach and yet not to believe; but a true preacher will not try to recommend the truth by imparting his faith and experience; that would be only to recommend himself; rather he seeks to bring his people to say with the Samaritans: "Now we believe, not because of your saying; for we have heard him ourselves, and know that this is indeed the Christ, the Saviour of the world."

An upright preacher does not purposely withdraw himself, nor does he purposely make himself prominent, but he comes with the Word and the Word comes with him; he is a simple, faithful witness of the Word, and the Word witnesses to him; he and his Word appear like one thing. All his preaching is based upon holy peace. Even when he rebukes, and zeal for God's house eats him up, it is not the wrath of the restless world, but the wrath of the unapproachable God of peace, that burns within him. It is not he that speaks, but the Lord speaks in him and through him, and his execution of his office is worthy of the Lord.

Wilhelm Loehe, *Three Books Concerning the Church* tr. Edward T. Horn (Reading, Pa.: Pilger Publishing Co., 1908) 181 f. rev. P.H.P.

Propers

ROMAN

God our Father, you gave your saints Timothy and Titus the courage and wisdom of the apostles: may their prayers help us to live holy lives and lead us to heaven, our true home. Grant this through our Lord Jesus Christ, your Son, who lives and reigns with you and the Holy Spirit, one God, for ever and ever.

LUTHERAN

God of grace and might, we praise you for your servants Timothy, Titus, and Silas, to whom you gave gifts to make the good news known. Raise up, we pray, in every country, heralds and evangelists of your kingdom, so that the world may know the immeasurable riches of our Savior, Jesus Christ our Lord.

EPISCOPAL

Almighty God, who called Timothy and Titus to the work of evangelists and teachers, and made them strong to endure hardship: Strengthen us to stand firm in adversity, and to live soberly and righteously in this present time: that with sure confidence we may look for the blessed hope and glorious appearing of our great God and Savior Jesus Christ, who lives and reigns with you and the Holy Spirit, one God now and forever.

ROMAN	LUTHERAN	EPISCOPAL
2 Timothy 1:1-8 or Titus 1:1-5 Common of Pastors	Isaiah 62:1-7 Psalm 48 *2 Timothy 2:1-10* Luke 24:44-53	Psalm 111 2 Timothy 2:1-10 or Titus 2:11-15 Psalm 112:1-9 John 10:1-10 Preface of Pentecost

Propers: Missionaries

Hymn of the Day: "Spread, oh, spread, almighty Word" (379)

Prayers: for the hesitant
for reconciliation
for mixed marriages

Color: White (or red for Timothy)

January 27

Lydia, Dorcas, and Phoebe

Lydia was Paul's first convert in Macedonia and Europe. He met her, a woman from Thyatira in Asia Minor (it was a Lydian city; her name may originally have been an adjective), at Philippi. She is described in Acts 16:11-40. St. Paul does not refer to her. She sold purple-dyed goods—an occupation which required considerable capital. She was therefore probably well-to-do. (Both Philippi and Thyatira were famous for their dyeing.) After her baptism she invited Paul and his companions to stay in her house, which relieved Paul of the necessity of earning his support, as was his custom elsewhere. St. Paul had a special love for the church at Philippi as shown in his letter to that church; Lydia's help was doubtless a cause of this special relationship.

Dorcas or Tabitha (the name means "gazelle" and was a favorite name among both Greeks and Jews) was a Christian woman from Joppa, a friend and helper of the poor. When she died, Peter restored her to life (Acts 9:36-43)—the first of such miracles by an Apostle. The miracle won many believers for the church. Dorcas is called a "disciple" in a feminine form of the word that is applied only to her in the New Testament. The Dorcas Societies of church women devoted to good works are named for her.

Phoebe (her name means "bright" or "radiant") was a deaconness at the church at Cenchreae, the east seaport of Corinth. The word translated "deaconness" might perhaps be better translated "patronness" or "helper," for Paul (2 Cor. 11:23; Col. 1:23, 25) does not mean that he is a *deacon* when he applies a similar word to himself. Nonetheless, Phoebe by her work and her service became the inspiration for the more regular order of deaconesses that was to emerge in the church. In Romans 16:1-2, Paul commends her to the Roman church upon her move there, and this fact that she was free to travel suggests that she was perhaps a widow. Her specific service that earned her the title of "helper" or "deaconness" was perhaps her willingness to stand by foreigners in their uncertainties.

Reading

(From *Light of Christ* by Evelyn Underhill.)

There are two sides to every vocation: unconditional giving of self to the call of God—"Here I am, send me!"—and the gift of power which rewards the total gift of self to God. In Christ's life we see these two movements in perfect balance. How humbly He submitted to the Will of the Father, totally absorbed in His business, and to the tests, pressure, suffering that came through circumstances; and yet how, though never in His own interest and never apart from His love and pity for man, there is always the Power to intervene, save, mould, defeat opposition, transform even the humble accidents of life. In all men and women of prayer deeply united to God that double state exists too. That handing of self over and the mysterious power that somehow acts through self in consequence—the right word said, the right prayer prayed. But only in proportion to the self-effacement. The power of course is God's, not ours. One hears people say, "He (or she) is simply wonderful!" Not at all! He or she is the self-emptied channel of the only Wonderful—the Mighty God, the Everlasting Father. When we give ourselves to Him without reserve we become points of insertion for the rescuing spirit of Love. We are woven into the Redeeming Body so that we may provide more and more channels for God.

Evelyn Underhill, *Light of Christ* (London: Longman's 1945), 74-75.

Propers: Saints

Hymn of the Day: "Lord, speak to us that we may speak" (403)

Prayers: for the poor
for foreigners in a strange land
for deaconesses

Color: White

THE PRESENTATION OF OUR LORD

This feast brings the celebration of Christmas to an end, and by the Gospel's prophecy that a sword will pierce the soul of the Mother of Jesus the day looks ahead to the crucifixion. It is therefore a bridge between the Nativity and the Passion. In origin, the Presentation of Jesus in the temple by his parents is a festival of the Lord (called by the Armenians "The coming of the Son of God into the Temple"), but it is also the occasion of the purification of the Virgin Mary in accordance with the requirements of the Law.

In the Eastern churches, where the feast originated, the day is called *Hypapante*, "the Meeting" (of Christ with Simeon, and, by extension, of God with his people). The day was observed in Jerusalem at the end of the fourth century and was introduced in Constantinople by the Emperor Justinian in 542. In the West, the day seems first to appear in the sacramentaries of Gelasius (seventh century) and of Gregory (eighth century), where it was called the Purification of Mary. Pope Sergius (d. 701) seems to have introduced the practice of a procession with lighted candles on this date (as well as on the other Marian feasts), and the procession, somewhat incongruously, was in its origins a penitential rite (down to modern times violet vestments were worn for this part of the ceremonies of the day).

In the Gospel, Simeon sings that the infant Christ is "a light to lighten the Gentiles," and so the procession shows the entrance of the true light into the world and the gradual illumination of the world by him. St. Sophronius (died ca. 638) in a sermon for the Presentation exhorts his congregation:

. . . Everyone should be eager to join the procession and to carry a light.

Our lighted candles are a sign of the divine splendor of the one who comes to expel the dark shadows of evil and to make the whole universe radiant with the brilliance of his eternal light. Our candles also show how bright our souls should be when we go to meet Christ.

. . . So let us all hasten together to meet our God.

(Oratio de Hypapante 6, 7. From the English translation of the Office of Readings © 1974 by the International Commisson for English in the Liturgy, Inc. All rights reserved.)

Sometime after the introduction of the procession, the custom arose of blessing all the candles to be used during the year on this festival of light (called "Candlemas" in England). This day is the appropriate time for candlelight services marking the conclusion of the celebration of the forty days of Christmas.

Because the Presentation is the conclusion of the celebration of Christmas, the Preface appointed in the *Lutheran Book of Worship* is the Preface for Christmas, which can easily be related to the Gospel for the day, although the Preface for Epiphany with its reference to light is also appropriate.

Throughout Europe, February 2 was considered a portentous day for weather forecasting, and the American custom of observing Groundhog Day is but an extension of that custom.

Reading

(From *The Light of the World* by Jaroslav Pelikan.)

The cleansing power of the light had penetrated the darkness in the coming of Christ. Those who had received it and had been cleansed by it no longer lived in darkness, but had become "children of light." . . . They knew what Christ was because they experienced what Christ did in them and to them. The illumination in which they now lived showed that the radiance had shone in them. And the radiance, in turn, pointed beyond itself to the light with which it was one. As the church contemplated what the light had brought and as it worshipped the source of its own being, its illumination reflected his light. The church viewed itself and its world differently because the illumination had come in Christ. It viewed God differently too, because his personal radiance had brought the illumination that transformed and healed every human vision. The gift of this salvation, accomplished by God the light in Christ the radiance, Athanasius found represented in the image of light, as confessed by the psalmist: "In thy light do we see light."

Over the darkling world the demonic powers had drawn a veil, to keep men from realizing that this was still God's world. But God had pierced the veil by coming in Christ, who was "light from light" and the very radiance of the Father. By him God had saved and illumined his darkling world, "to give light to those who sit in darkness and in the shadow of death."

Jaroslav Pelikan, *The Light of the World. A Basic Image in Early Christian Thought* (New York: Harper, 1962) 91-92, 110. Used by permission.

Propers

ROMAN	LUTHERAN	EPISCOPAL
All-powerful Father, Christ your Son became man for us and was presented in the temple. May he free our hearts from sin and bring us into your presence. We ask this through our Lord Jesus Christ, your Son, who lives and reigns with you and the Holy Spirit, one God, for ever and ever.	Blessed are you, O Lord our God, for you have sent us your salvation. Inspire us by your Holy Spirit to see with our own eyes him who is the glory of Israel, and the light for all nations, your Son, Jesus Christ our Lord.	Almighty and everliving God, we humbly pray that, as your only-begotten Son was this day presented in the temple, so we may be presented to you with pure and clean hearts by Jesus Christ our Lord; who lives and reigns with you and the Holy Spirit, one God, now and for ever.

ROMAN	LUTHERAN	EPISCOPAL
Malachi 3:1-4 Psalm 24:7-10 Hebrews 2:14-18 Luke 2:22-40 (22-32)	1 Samuel 1:21-28 Psalm 84 Hebrews 2:14-18 Luke 2:22-40	Malachi 3:1-4 Psalm 84 or 84:1-6 Hebrews 2:14-18 Luke 2:22-40 Preface of the Epiphany

Hymn of the Day: "In his temple now behold him" (184)

Prayers: for the illumination of the darkness of the world
for the aged
for those who wait patiently for salvation
for those who have become mothers

Preface: Christmas

Color: White

Ansgar, Archbishop of Hamburg, Missionary to Denmark and Sweden, 865

Ansgar (or Anskar), the Frankish missionary to Scandinavia, often called "the Apostle of the North," was born in 801 near Amiens. He became a monk of the Benedictine monastery of Corbie nearby and later transferred to the monstery of New Corbie on the Weser River. He was a man of great personal piety, and he combined an eager desire to explore new lands with an unusual organizing ability.

At the beginning of the ninth century the church was just starting its efforts to spread the gospel to Scandinavia, and the founding of the bishopric of Hamburg in 804 was one of the first important steps in this direction. The first actual missionary venture was in 826 and was connected with the attempt of the newly-converted King Harald of Denmark to regain his throne. Harald was unsuccessful in his political aim, and Ansgar, who went along with him as a missionary, also met with little success, although he established contact with merchants and travelers from Scandinavia.

In the summer of 829, a group of merchants from the trading town of Birka in Sweden asked the emperor, Louis the Pious, to send a Christian mission, and again Ansgar was chosen. During the long trip northward, Ansgar and his companions were attacked by Viking pirates and robbed, arriving in Birka almost penniless. King Bjorn and the local authorities gave permission to preach the new faith and to establish a church. Most of the Christians there seem to have been slaves who had brought their faith with them, but a few Swedes were converted and baptized. Among them was the king's bailiff in Birka, who at his own expense built a church—the first Christian church in all of Scandinavia. After a year and a half of work, St. Ansgar returned home.

In 831 Ansgar was appointed Abbot of Corbie and Archbishop of Hamburg, with the idea that this would be the base for missionary operations in Scandinavia as opportunities arose. For the next thirteen years Ansgar preached and organized missions in northern Germany and Scandinavia. He participated in the consecration of Gotbert, the first bishop for Sweden. In 845, however, the Vikings destroyed the city of Hamburg by fire, and sweden and Denmark relapsed into paganism. In 848 Ansgar was made Archbishop of the combined sees of Bremen and Hamburg, and he began the restoration of his missions in Denmark. His patient work led to small success, but after his death on February 3, 865, in Bremen, practically all that he had accomplished in Scandinavia was lost, and three centuries passed before the Christianization really resumed.

St. Ansgar was a prophetic figure, and the church in Scandinavia honors his memory. He is often portrayed with a fur collar on his bishop's vestments, holding a church in his hand. He is respected by Scandinavian Lutherans, especially the Danes, and numerous churches, societies, and educational institutions are dedicated to his memory. There are about a dozen Lutheran churches in North America named for him.

Adam of Bremen, *History of the Archbishops of Hamburg-Bremen*, tr. F. J. Tschan. New York: Columbia University Press, 1959.
Rimbert, *Anskar*, tr. C. H. Robinson. London, 1921.

Reading

(From *Imitation of Christ.*)

When God bestows spiritual comfort, receive it with a grateful heart; but remember that it comes of God's free gift, and not of your own merit. Do not be proud, nor over joyful, nor foolishly presumptuous; rather, be the more humble for this gift, more cautious, and more prudent in all your doings, for this hour will pass, and temptation will follow it. When comfort is withdrawn, do not immediately despair, but humbly and patiently await the will of Heaven; for God is able to restore to you a consolation even richer than before. This is nothing new or strange to those who know the ways of God, for the great Saints and Prophets of old often experienced these changes.

I have never found anyone, however religious and devout, who did not sometimes experience a withdrawal of grace, or feel a lessening of devotion. And no Saint has ever lived, however highly rapt and enlightened, who did not suffer temptation sooner or later. For he is not worthy of high contemplation who has not suffered some trials for God's sake. Indeed, the temptation that precedes is often a sign of comfort to follow. For heavenly comfort is promised to those who have been tried and tempted. "To him who overcomes," says God, "I will give to eat of the Tree of Life."

Thomas a Kempis, *Imitation of Christ,* II, 9, tr. Leo Sherley-Price (Baltimore: Penguin, 1952) 79-80. Copyright © 1952, Leo Sherley-Price. Reprinted by permission of Penguin Books Ltd.

Propers

ROMAN	LUTHERAN	EPISCOPAL
Father, you sent Saint Ansgar to bring the light of Christ to many nations. May his prayers help us to walk in the light of your truth. We ask this through our Lord Jesus Christ, your Son, who lives and reigns with you and the Holy Spirit, one God, for ever and ever.	God of grace and might, we praise you for your servant Ansgar, to whom you gave gifts to make the good news known to the people of Scandinavia. Raise up, we pray, in every country, heralds and evangelists of your kingdom, so that the world may know the immeasurable riches of our Savior, Jesus Christ our Lord.	Almighty and everlasting God, we thank you for your servant Anskar, whom you called to preach the gospel to the people of Scandinavia. Raise up in this and every land, heralds and evangelists of your kingdom, that your Church may make known the immeasurable riches of our Savior Jesus Christ, who lives and reigns with you and the Holy Spirit, one

ROMAN	LUTHERAN	EPISCOPAL
(Text from the English translation of the Roman Missal © 1973, International Committee on English in the Liturgy, Inc. All rights reserved.)		God, now and for ever. *(Text from Lesser Feasts and Fasts, Revised Edition, copyright 1973 by Charles Mortimer Guilbert as Custodian of the Standard Book of Common Prayer. All rights reserved. Used by permission.)*

Common of Pastors (for Missionaries)	Common of Missionaries
	Isaiah 62:1-7
	Psalm 48
	Romans 10:11-17
	Luke 24:44-53
		Common of a Missionary I
		  Psalm 96:1-7
		  Isaiah 52:7-10
		  Psalm 96:8-13
		  Acts 1:1-9
		  Luke 10:1-9
		  Preface of Pentecost

Hymn of the Day: "O Christ, our light, O Radiance true" (380)

Prayers: for courage and resolution in the face of defeat
       for the church in Sweden
       for the church in Denmark

Preface: Epiphany

Color: White

February 5

The Martyrs of Japan, 1597

Christianity was brought to Japan by Francis Xavier and spread with remarkable success. The rapid advance, however, led to resentment and opposition on the part of the native Buddhists and Shintoists. There was suspicion of the methods of the missionaries which involved mass conversions, and there was rivalry between the several religious orders. These suspicions, coupled with a fear of foreign invaders, resulted in increased persecution of Christians. In 1597, twenty-six Christians—six European Franciscan missionaries, three Japanese Jesuits, and seventeen Japanese laymen, three of whom were young boys—were killed by a kind of crucifixion at Nagasaki. They were raised on crosses and then stabbed with spears. Within a year, more than one hundred thirty churches were burned. After a time, the persecution subsided, but in 1613 it broke out again, and by 1630 what was left of Christianity in Japan was driven underground. Nonetheless, the faith was preserved, although the church in Japan was without clergy until the missionaries returned at the end of the nineteenth century.

The first victims of the persecution, the twenty-six martyrs of 1597, were canonized by the Roman Catholic church in 1862. Paul Miki, a Japanese Jesuit priest, is the most celebrated of the martyrs; the Roman calendar calls the commemoration "Paul Miki and his Companions" (although it is observed on February 6 since February 5 is St. Agatha's Day). The Franciscan missionaries were led by a Spanish priest, Peter Baptist. One of the laymen was a Korean, Leo Karasuma.

The Nippon Sei Ko Kai (the Holy Catholic Church of Japan), which is affiliated with the Anglican communion, adopted this commemoration in its calendar of 1959 as an inclusive festival of all those who have given their lives for the Christian faith in Japan. The Episcopal Church in the United States has also included the day on its new calendar.

C. R. Boxer, *The Christian Century in Japan, 1549-1650.* Berkeley: University of California Press, 1951.

O. Cary. *A History of Christianity in Japan.* 2 vols. 1909.

Reading

(From *Imitation of Christ.*)

Be assured of this, that you must live a dying life. And the more completely one dies to self, the more one begins to live to God. No one is fit to understand heavenly things unless he is resigned to bear hardships for Christ's sake. Nothing is more acceptable to God, and nothing more salutary for yourself, than to suffer gladly for Christ's sake. And if it lies in your choice, you should choose rather to suffer hardships for Christ's sake, than to be refreshed by many consolations; for thus you will more closely resemble Christ and all His Saints. For our merit and spiritual progress does not consist in enjoying such sweetness and consolation, but rather in the bearing of great burdens and troubles.

Had there been a better way, more profitable to the salvation of mankind than suffering, then Christ would have revealed it in His word and life. But He clearly urges both His own disciples and all who wish to follow Him to carry the cross, saying, "If any will come after me, let him deny himself, and take up his cross and follow Me." Therefore, when we have read and studied all things, let this be our final resolve: "that through much tribulation we must enter the Kingdom of God" (Acts 14:22).

Thomas a Kempis, *Imitation of Christ*, II, 12, tr. Leo Sherley-Price (Baltimore; Penguin, 1952) 88-89. Copyright © 1952, Leo Sherley-Price. Reprinted by permission of Penguin Books Ltd.

Propers

ROMAN

(February 6)
God our Father,
source of strength for
all your saints,
you led Paul Miki and
his companions
through the suffering
of the cross
to the joy of eternal
life.
May their prayers
give us the courage
to be loyal until death
in professing our
faith.
We ask this through
our Lord Jesus
Christ, your Son,
who lives and reigns
with you and the
Holy Spirit,
one God, for ever and
ever.

(Text from the English translation of the Roman Missal © 1973, International Committee on English in the Liturgy, Inc. All rights reserved.)

Common of Martyrs
or Galatians 2:19-20
Matthew 28:16-20

LUTHERAN

Gracious Lord, in every age you have sent men and women who have given their lives for the message of your love. Inspire us with the memory of those martyrs for the gospel in Japan whose faithfulness led them in the way of the cross, and give us courage to bear full witness with our lives to your Son's victory over sin and death; through Jesus Christ our Lord.

Common of Martyrs:
Ezekiel 20:40-42
Psalm 5
Revelation 6:9-11
Mark 8:34-38

EPISCOPAL

Almighty God, by whose grace and power your holy martyrs in Japan triumphed over suffering and despised death: Grant, we pray, that enduring hardship and waxing valiant in fight, we may with the noble army of martyrs receive the crown of everlasting life; through Jesus Christ our Lord, who lives and reigns with you and the Holy Spirit, one God, now and for ever.

(Text from Lesser Feasts and Fasts, Revised Edition, copyright 1973 by Charles Mortimer Guilbert as Custodian of the Standard Book of Common Prayer. All rights reserved. Used by permission.)

Common of a Martyr
III: Psalm 69:18-22
Jeremiah 15:15-21
Psalm 69:31-36
1 Peter 4:12-19
Mark 8:24-28
Preface of Holy Week

Hymn of the Day: "Have no fear, little flock" (476)
　　　　　or "Savior, sprinkle many nations" (*SBH* 312)

Prayers: for the church in Japan
　　　　for boldness to confess Christ
　　　　for the spirit of Christ to forgive our enemies

Preface: All Saints

Color: Red

Cyril, Monk, 869; and Methodius, Bishop, 885; Missionaries to the Slavs

These brothers, known as "the Apostles of the Slavs," were two of seven children of a wealthy and scrupulously orthodox family.

Cyril, as he is known, was born in 827 at Thessalonica, Greece, and was named Constantine. He was educated at Constantinople and became a noted professor of philosophy there about 850. After a time, he withdrew to the monastic life in Bithynia, not far from Methodius, his older brother. In 850 Emperor Michael III sent the brothers on a religious and diplomatic mission to the Khazars, a Tartar people who lived northeast of the Black Sea. On the journey the brothers found what were considered to be the relics of Clement of Rome.

Upon their return in 863, the brothers were sent as missionaries to Moravia, in response to a request by Prince Rostislav in order to counteract the expanding power of the German bishops in his lands. In Moravia Cyril took an interest in the vernacular language and invented an alphabet, Glagolitic, in order to translate the Gospels and the liturgy into Slavonic. The Cyrillic alphabet (modern Russian), from Greek capital letters, is based on this work. His interest in the vernacular was opposed by the Western clergy in Moravia who recognized only the three languages of Pilate's sign above the cross of Jesus: Hebrew, Latin, and Greek. Cyril journeyed to Rome and was there received by Pope Hadrian II in 867, and the pope confirmed Cyril's Slavonic translations. Cyril had been in poor health for some time, and at Rome, February 14, 869, fifty days after taking the monastic habit and the name Cyril by which he is known, he died at the age of 42. He had given the pope the supposed relics of St. Clement and so was buried in the basilica of San Clemente. Until the revision of the Roman calendar after Vatican II, his feast day in the West had been July 7. In the East his commemoration is May 11.

Cyril's older brother **Methodius** was born about 825 and attained high rank in his province of Macedonia before he withdrew to a monastic life. In 863 he went with Cyril to Moravia. After Cyril's death, Pope Hadrian made Methodius Archbishop of Sirmium, and Methodius returned to the Slavic mission field for sixteen more years. He encountered violent opposition from the German bishops and even from his own suffragan, despite the reconfirmation of his liturgy by Pope John VIII in 879. Methodius died April 6, which was Tuesday in Holy Week 885, in his cathedral church. Opposition to the work of the two brothers continued even after their deaths, and their followers scattered, spreading with them the spiritual, liturgical, and cultural work of the brothers.

The Slovaks, Czechs, Croats, Serbs, and Bulgars all revere the memory of Cyril and Methodius as founders of their alphabet, translators of their liturgy, and builders of the foundation of their literature, as well as heralds of the gospel in their land.

Francis Dvornik, *The Slavs: Their Early History and Civilization.* Boston: American Academy of Arts and Sciences, 1956.
Z. R. Dittrich. *Christianity in Greater Moravia.* Groningen, 1962.

Reading

(From a letter by Martin Luther to Philipp Melanchthon, January 13, 1522.)

Now let me deal with the "prophets."

In order to explore their individual spirit, too, you should inquire whether they have experienced spiritual distress and the divine birth, death, and hell. If you should hear that all [their experiences] are pleasant, quiet, devout (as they say), and spiritual, then don't approve of them, even if they should say that they were caught up into the third heaven. The sign of the Son of Man is then missing, which is the only touchstone of Christians and a certain differentiator between the spirits. Do you want to know the place, time, and manner of [true] conversations with God? Listen: "Like a lion he has broken all my bones"; "I am cast out from before your eyes"; "My soul is filled with grief, and my life has approached hell." The [Divine] Majesty (as they call it) does not speak in such a direct way to man that man could [actually] see it; but rather, "Man shall not see me and live." [Our] nature cannot bear even a small glimmer of God's [direct] speaking. As a result God speaks through men [indirectly], because not all can endure his speaking. The angel frightened even the Virgin, and also Daniel. And Jeremiah pleads, "Correct me [O Lord] but in just measure," and, "Be not a terror to me." Why should I say more? As if the [Divine] Majesty could speak familiarly with the Old Adam without first killing him and drying him out so that his horrible stench would not be so foul, since God is a consuming fire! The dreams and visions of the saints are horrifying, too, at least after they are understood. Therefore examine [them] and do not even listen if they speak of the glorified Jesus, unless you have first heard of the crucified Jesus.

Luther's Works vol. 48, Letters I, trans. Gottfried G. Krodel (Philadelphia: Fortress, 1963) 365, 366-367. Used by permission.

Propers

ROMAN	LUTHERAN	EPISCOPAL
Father, you brought the light of the gospel to the Slavic nations through Saint Cyril and his brother Saint Methodius. Open our hearts to understand your teaching and help us to become one in faith and praise. Grant this through our Lord Jesus Christ, your Son,	God of grace and might, we praise you for your servants Cyril and Methodius, to whom you gave gifts to make the good news known to the Slavic people. Raise up, we pray, in every country, heralds and evangelists of your kingdom, so that the world may know the immeasurable riches of our Savior, Jesus Christ our Lord.	Almighty and everlasting God, we thank you for your servants Cyril and Methodius, whom you called to preach the gospel to the Slavic people. Raise up in this and every land heralds and evangelists of your kingdom, that your Church may make known the immeasurable riches of our Savior Jesus Christ, who lives and reigns with

ROMAN	LUTHERAN	EPISCOPAL
who lives and reigns with you and the Holy Spirit, one God, for ever and ever.		you and the Holy Spirit, one God, now and for ever.

ROMAN — *(Text from the English translation of the Roman Missal © 1973, International Committee on English in the Liturgy, Inc. All rights reserved.)*

EPISCOPAL — *(Text from Lesser Feasts and Fasts, Revised Edition, copyright 1973 by Charles Mortimer Guilbert as Custodian of the Standard Book of Common Prayer. All rights reserved. Used by permission.)*

ROMAN	LUTHERAN	EPISCOPAL
Common of Pastors (for Missionaries) *or* Saints	Common of Missionaries Isaiah 62:1-7 Psalm 48 Romans 10:11-17 Luke 24:44-53	Common of a Missionary I: Psalm 96:1-7 Isaiah 52:7-10 Psalm 96:8-13 Acts 1:1-9 Luke 10:1-9 Preface of Pentecost

Hymn of the Day: "God, my Lord, my strength" (484)

Prayers: for those under persecution and attack
   for the Slavic churches
   for linguists and translators
   for respect for the past and openness to the future

Preface: Epiphany

Color: White

February 18

Martin Luther, Renewer of the Church, 1546

Martin Luther was born November 10, 1483, in Eisleben, Saxony, of peasant stock. He was baptized the following day, which was St. Martin's day, and was given the name of that saint. His intellectual abilities were evident early, and his father planned a career for him in law. After attending schools in Mansfeld, Magdeburg, and Eisenach, Luther at the age of eighteen entered the University of Erfurt, where he completed his master's examination in 1505 and began the study of law. His real interest lay elsewhere, however, and on July 17, 1505 he entered the local Augustinian monastery. He was ordained a priest April 3, 1507 and a month later he celebrated his first mass in the presence of friends and his father, who had disapproved of his son's entrance into the monastery.

Luther had seen his first Latin Bible in the school at Magdeburg, and at the monastery, with the encouragement of his superiors, he continued his study of the Scriptures. He helped with the instruction of novices in the order and served as a teaching assistant in moral philosophy at the new University of Wittenberg. In 1510 he made a trip to Rome for the Augustinian order. There, like St. Francis and others before him, he was shocked by the laxity and worldliness of many of the clergy.

In October 1512 Luther received his doctorate in theology, and shortly afterward he was installed as a professor of biblical studies at the University of Wittenberg. His lectures on the Bible were popular, and within a few years he made the university a center of biblical humanism. As a result of his theological and biblical studies he called into question the practice of selling indulgences or remissions of the punishment to be undergone in purgatory. On the eve of All Saints' Day, October 31, 1517, he posted on the door of the castle church in Wittenberg, as was the custom, the notice of an academic debate on indulgences, listing ninety-five theses for discussion. Luther's theses spread rapidly throughout Germany and other parts of Europe. As the effects of the theses became evident, the pope called upon the Augustinian order to discipline their member. After a series of meetings, political maneuvers, and attempts at reconciliation, Luther, at a meeting with the papal legate in 1518, refused to recant, and in debate with John Eck he was forced to admit that some of his views were not in accord with the official doctrines of the church.

Up to this time Luther had attempted to reform the church from within, but it was now clear that a break was inevitable and on June 15, 1520 the pope issued a bull which gave Luther sixty days in which to recant. Many schools burned Luther's books, and he retaliated by burning a copy of the papal bull and books of canon law. He was excommunicated on January 3, 1521, and the Emperor Charles V summoned him to the meeting of the Imperial Diet at Worms. There Luther resisted all efforts to make him recant, insisting that he had to be proved in error on the basis of Scripture. The Diet was divided in its judgments, but it finally passed an edict calling for the arrest of Luther. Luther's own prince, the Elector Frederick of

Saxony, however, had him spirited away and placed for safekeeping in his castle, the Wartburg.

Here Luther translated the New Testament into German and began the translation of the Old Testament. In March 1522 Luther returned to Wittenberg against the wishes of the prince in order to settle the disturbed situation of the churches there, which were under the disruptive leadership of Andreas von Karlstadt. Luther preached a series of eight famous sermons in which he restored order to the community and set the lines of the Reformation.

He then turned his attention to the organization of worship and education. He introduced congregational singing of hymns, composing many himself, and he issued model orders of service in Latin (*Formula missae*, 1523) and, for more general use, in German (*Deutsche Messe*, 1526). In 1529 he published his large and small catechisms for instruction in the faith and also a series of sermons. During the years from 1522 to his death, Luther wrote a prodigious quantity of books, letters, sermons, and tracts. The recent American edition of his works is in fifty-five large volumes, and that does not include everything that he wrote.

On June 13, 1525 Luther married Katherine von Bora, one of a number of nuns rescued from the cloister of Nimbschen in 1523. The couple had six children, and with his wife's aunt, Lena, eleven nieces and nephews, and constant company of students and visitors, Luther's household was a busy center of fellowship and discussion. At the dinner table the famous "Table Talk" was recorded by various guests and later published.

In 1546 Luther was called to Eisleben to mediate in a family quarrel among the princes of Mansfeld, and after resolving the quarrel, Luther died there in the town of his birth on February 18. Thousands of people came to the service for the great reformer, and his body was interred in the Castle Church in Wittenberg on February 22.

Lutherans have named many churches, colleges, and societies after Luther, and in North America there are more than seventy-five churches named for him. There are monuments to Luther in many cities. The most famous is the one at Worms in which Luther rests his hand on the Bible and is surrounded by likenesses of earlier reformers and his protectors and friends.

Events in Luther's life have been commemorated on various dates. The anniversary of the posting of the ninety-five theses has become the Festival of the Reformation on Lutheran calendars and is also observed by some other Christian churches. The four hundredth anniversary of his birth was the occasion of a great celebration in 1883. Many Lutheran communities have remembered Luther on the day of his death; on the centennial in 1646 the day was observed particularly in Wittenberg and Erfurt, and later the observance became more widespread.

Paul Althaus. *The Theology of Martin Luther.* Philadelphia: Fortress, 1966.
Roland Bainton. *Here I Stand. A Life of Martin Luther.* New York and
    Nashville: Abingdon, 1950.
Gerhard Ebeling. *Luther: An Introduction to His Thought.* Philadelphia:
    Fortress, 1970.
E. G. Schwiebert. *Luther and His Times.* St. Louis: Concordia, 1950.

Reading

(From Luther's *Preface to the Complete Edition of Luther's Latin Writings* [Wittenberg, 1545].)

I had indeed been captivated with an extraordinary ardor for understanding Paul in the Epistle to the Romans. But up till then it was not the cold blood about the heart, but a single word in chapter 1 [:17], "In it the righteousness of God is revealed," that had stood in my way. For I hated that word "righteousness of God," which, according to the use and custom of all the teachers, I had been taught to understand philosophically regarding the formal or active righteousness, as they called it, with which God is righteous and punishes the unrighteous sinner.

Though I lived as a monk without reproach, I felt that I was a sinner before God with an extremely disturbed conscience. I could not believe that he was placated by my satisfaction. I did not love, I hated the righteousness of God who punishes sinners, and secretly, if not blasphemously, certainly murmuring greatly, I was angry with God and said, "As if, indeed, it is not enough, that miserable sinners, eternally lost through original sin, are crushed by every kind of calamity by the law of the decalogue, without having God add pain to pain by the gospel and also by the gospel threatening us with his righteousness and wrath!" Thus I raged with a fierce and troubled conscience. Nevertheless, I beat importunately upon Paul at that place, most ardently desiring to know what St. Paul wanted.

At last, by the mercy of God, meditating day and night, I gave heed to the context of the words, namely, "In it the righteousness of God is revealed, as it is written, 'He who through faith is righteous shall live.'" There I began to understand that the righteousness of God is that by which the righteous lives by a gift of God, namely, by faith. And this is the meaning: the righteousness of God is revealed by the gospel, namely, the passive righteousness with which merciful God justifies us by faith, as it is written, "He who through faith is righteous shall live." Here I felt that I was altogether born again and had entered paradise itself through open gates. There a totally other face of the entire Scripture showed itself to me. Thereupon I ran through the Scriptures from memory. I also found in other terms an analogy, as, the work of God, that is, what God does in us, the power of God, with which he makes us strong, the wisdom of God, with which he makes us wise, the strength of God, the salvation of God, the glory of God.

And I extolled my sweetest word with a love as great as the hatred with which I had before hated the word "righteousness of God." Thus that place in Paul was for me truly that gate to Paradise.

Luther's Works vol. 34 Career of the Reformer IV ed. Lewis W. Spitz, trans. Lewis W. Spitz, Sr. (Philadelphia: Muhlenberg, 1960) 336-337. Used by permission.

Propers: Renewers of the Church
       or Reformation Day

Hymn of the Day: "Lord, keep us steadfast in your Word" (230)

Prayers: for the continual cleansing of the church
       for an ever-new discovery of the good news of God
       for the unity of the church

Color: White

Rasmus Jensen, the First Lutheran Pastor in North America, 1620

In the spring of 1619, King Christian IV of Norway and Denmark sent an expedition consisting of two ships, the *Unicorn* and the *Lamprey* and sixty-four men to North America to search for the Northwest Passage to India. The chaplain of the expedition was Rasmus Jensen who became the first Lutheran pastor in the New World. Little is known of his life; he may perhaps have been from the parish of Aarhus. The expedition was under the leadership of the most travelled and experienced officer in the Danish navy, Jens Munk (Munck), who was born June 3, 1579 and who died June 23, 1628. The ships left Denmark on May 9, touched the coast of Greenland, reached the American shore on July 8, crossed Hudson Bay, naming the area Nova Dania, and landed at the mouth of a river on the Western shore of Hudson Bay at what is now Churchill, Manitoba. Locked in ice for the long winter, the explorers made the first settlement of Lutherans in America. The captain wrote in his journal:

On the 24th of December, which was Christmas Eve, I gave the men wine and strong beer, which they had to boil afresh, for it was frozen at the bottom; so they had quite as much as they could stand, and were very jolly, but no one offended another with as much as a word.

The Holy Christmas Day we all celebrated and observed solemnly, as a Christian's duty is. We had a sermon and Mass; and, after the sermon, we gave the priest an offertory, according to ancient custom, each in proportion to his means. There was not much money among the men, but they gave what they had; some of them gave white fox-skins, so that the priest got enough wherewith to line a coat. However, sufficiently long life to wear it was not granted to him.

During all the Holy Days, the weather was rather mild; and, in order that the time might not hang on hand, the men practised all kinds of games; and whoever could imagine the most amusement was the most popular. The crew, most of whom were, at that time, in good health, consequently had all sorts of larks and pastimes; and thus we spent the Holy Days with the merriment that was got up.

The foreboding which shadows Munk's narrative was fulfilled, and soon most of the members of the crew, attacked by scurvy, died.

On the 23rd of January, died one of my two mates, Hans Brock by name, who had been ill, in and out of bed, for nearly five months. On the same day, it was fine weather and beautiful sunshine; and the priest sat up in his berth and gave the people a sermon, which sermon was the last he delivered in this world. . . .

On the 20th of February, in the evening, died the priest, Mr. Rasmus Jensen aforesaid, who had been ill and had kept his bed a long time. . . .

On the 14th of April, there was a sharp frost. On that day, only four, besides myself, had strength enough to sit up in the berth and listen to the homily for Good Friday.

The 16th of April was Easter Day. Then died Anders Oroust and Jens, the cooper, who had been ill and in bed a long time; and, as the weather was fairly mild, I got their bodies buried. On the same day, I promoted my captain of the hold to be skipper, although he was ill, in order that he might assist me somewhat, as far as his strength allowed, because I was myself then quite miserable and abandoned by all the world, as everybody may imagine.

Munk himself had become deathly sick, but eventually recovered. With the last two surviving sailors he set sail in July in the smaller of the two vessels, the *Lamprey*, and reached Norway in September and arrived in Copenhagen on Christmas Day 1620. He published a diary of his voyage in Danish in 1624. An English translation appeared in 1897. It is a moving and melancholy account of hardship, death, and bravery.

A memorial to the expedition has been erected at Port Churchill.

After this disheartening experience in Canada, Danish missionary activity was concentrated in India and in the Virgin Islands. By 1656 a Lutheran pastor, the second in the New World, Magister Lauritz Anderson Rhodius, was ministering to the tobacco-producing islands of the West Indies; and Kjeld Jensen Slagelse on January 8, 1665 became the pastor at St. Thomas, in the Virgin Islands where a strong Lutheran tradition has been maintained. He died in June 1672.

Danish Arctic Expeditions 1605 to 1620. Book II.—The Expedition of Captain Jens Munk. ed. C. C. A. Gosch. Published by the Hakluyt Society, n.p., 1897.

Hansen, Thorkild. *The Way to Hudson Bay. The Life and Times of Jens Munk.* trans. James McFarlane and John Lynch. New York: Harcourt, Brace, World, 1965.

Lutheran Church Review, vol. 17, pp. 55-63.

Three other pastors associated with the founding of the church in North America might also be remembered on this day. **Reorus Torkillus** was the first Lutheran pastor to organize a congregation in North America. He arrived in 1639 at Fort Christina (Wilmington, Delaware). His ministry there was brief; he died September 7, 1643.

John Campanius, 1646 on Tinicum Island in the Delaware River below Philadelphia, built the first Lutheran church building in America. Campanius arrived in the New World with Governor John Printz in 1643. Among the twenty-eight articles of instruction from the crown was this directive:

26. Above all things, the governor shall see to it that divine service be zealously performed according to the Unaltered Augsburg Confession, the Council of Uppsala, and the ceremonies of the Swedish church. . . .

Campanius was in America from 1643-1648 and did missionary work among the Delaware Indians, translating the *Small Catechism* into their language. The Swedes dealt justly and peacefully with the Indians, whom they regarded as the "rightful lords" of the land. Campanius died in Sweden, September 17, 1683, at the age of eighty-two.

Justus Falckner (1672-1723) was the first Lutheran pastor ordained in America (November 24, 1703). The service of ordination at Gloria Dei ("Old Swedes") Church in South Philadelphia showed the international character of Lutheranism, Falckner, a Halle-trained German, was ordained by Andrew Rudman, who was apparently acting as suffragan of the Archbishop of Uppsala, to serve the Dutch Lutherans in New York. The elaborate ordination service included Swedish vestments and featured an organ, an orchestra, and a men's choir singing Latin. Falckner, sensing a mission wherever Lutherans settled, extended his ministry from Albany, New York, to the Raritan valley in New Jersey. He is remembered for his stirring hymn, "Rise, O children of salvation." The date and place of his death are unknown.

Reading

(From *The Cost of Discipleship* by Dietrich Bonhoeffer.)

Happy are they who have reached the end of the road we seek to tread, who are astonished to discover the by no means self-evident truth that grace is costly just because it is the grace of God in Jesus Christ. Happy are the simple followers of Jesus Christ who have been overcome by his grace, and are able to sing the praises of the all-sufficient grace of Christ with humbleness of heart. Happy are they who, knowing that grace, can live in the world without being of it, who, by following Jesus Christ, are so assured of their heavenly citizenship that they are truly free to live their lives in this world. Happy are they who know that discipleship simply means the life which springs from grace, and that grace simply means discipleship. Happy are they who have become Christians in this sense of the word. For them the word of grace has proved a fount of mercy.

Dietrich Bonhoeffer, *The Cost of Discipleship* rev. ed., trans. R. H. Fuller and Imgard Booth (New York: Macmillan, 1963) 60. Copyright © 1959 SCM Press, Ltd. Used by permission.

The selections from the journal of Jens Munk given in the biography of Jensen are also an appropriate reading.

Propers: Pastors

Hymn of the Day: "Unto the hills around do I lift up" (445)

Prayers: for the church in Canada
      for faithful pastors and chaplains
      of thanksgiving for those who planted the church on these
        shores.

Color: White

Polycarp, Bishop of Smyrna, Martyr, 156

Polycarp was born about the year 70. He was a disciple of St. John the Apostle, became bishop of Smyrna (modern Izmir, Turkey), and is a connecting link between the apostolic age of the church and the Christian life of the second century. He was a close friend of Ignatius of Antioch, and it was probably at Polycarp's request that Ignatius wrote his famous epistles to various churches in Asia Minor and to Polycarp himself.

Polycarp has only one surviving work, his *Epistle to the Philippians,* which many believe is actually composed of two letters, one written about 115 enclosing Ignatius' epistles and the other written about 135 to warn the Philippian church against the spreading Marcionite heresy, a dualistic faith which rejected the Old Testament and distorted orthodox doctrines. Polycarp's *Epistle* was still read in the churches at the time of St. Jerome, but it was not included in the canon of the New Testament.

During much of his life Polycarp was in many ways the leading figure of Christianity in Asia Minor, and he was referred to with great respect and affection by Irenaeus and Ignatius. As a very old man Polycarp went to Rome to discuss the problem of the dating of Easter—a vexing problem for the early church. After his return to Smyrna he died a martyr's death in 155 or 156 at the age of eighty-six. The commemoration of his death is the first saint's day whose observance is attested in the history of the church; a reliable story of his martyrdom is given in the eye-witness account, the *Martyrdom of Polycarp.*

After some Christians had been thrown to the lions, Polycarp was called before the proconsul, and, when he refused to give divine honors to the emperor and confessed himself a Christian, he was condemned to death. Since the games were over he could not be thrown to the lions, as he fully expected, but was instead burned alive. The *Martyrdom of Polycarp* places his death on February 23, and the Eastern churches have commemorated him on that date. From the eighth century the Western church observed his day on January 26, but the new Roman calendar has moved the commemoration to January 23, as has the Episcopal church.

Reading

(From *The Martyrdom of Polycarp*.)

. . . there was a great tumult on hearing that Polycarp had been arrested. Therefore, when he was brought before him, the proconsul asked him if he were Polycarp. And when he confessed that he was, he tried to persuade him to deny [the faith], saying, "Have respect to your age"—and other things that customarily follow this, such as "Swear by the fortune of Caesar; change your mind; say 'Away with the athiests!'"

But Polycarp looked with earnest face at the whole crowd of lawless heathen in the arena, and motioned to them with his hand. Then groaning and looking up to heaven, he said, "Away with the athiests!"

But the proconsul was insistent and said: "Take the oath, and I shall release you. Curse Christ."

Polycarp said: "Eighty-six years I have served him, and he never did me any wrong. How can I blaspheme my King who saved me?"

And upon his persisting still and saying, "Swear by the fortune of Caesar," he answered, "If you vainly suppose that I shall swear by the fortune of Caesar, as you say, and pretend that you do not know who I am, listen plainly: I am a Christian. But if your desire to learn the teaching of Christianity, appoint a day and give me a hearing."

The proconsul said, "Try to persuade the people."

But Polycarp said, "You, I should deem worthy of an account; for we have been taught to render honor, as is befitting, to rulers and authorities appointed by God so far as it does us no harm; but as for these, I do not consider them worthy that I should make a defense to them."

But the proconsul said: "I have wild beasts. I shall throw you to them, if you do not change your mind."

But he said: "Call them. For repentance from the better to the worse is not permitted us; but it is noble to change from what is evil to what is righteous."

And again [he said] to him, "I shall have you consumed with fire, if you despise the wild beasts, unless you change your mind."

But Polycarp said: "The fire you threaten burns but an hour and is quenched after a little; for you do not know the fire of the coming judgment and everlasting punishment that is laid up for the impious. But why do you delay? Come, do what you will."

And when he had said these things and many more besides he was inspired with courage and joy, and his face was full of grace, so that not only did it not fall with dismay at the things said of him, but on the contrary, the proconsul was astonished, and sent his own herald into the midst of the arena to proclaim three times: "Polycarp has confessed himself to be a Christian."

. . . Straightway then they set about him the material prepared for the pyre. And when they were about to nail him also, he said: "Leave me as I am. For he who grants me to endure the fire will enable me also to remain on the pyre unmoved, without the security you desire from the nails."

So they did not nail him, but tied him. . . .

And when he had . . . finished his prayer, the men attending the fire lighted it. And when the flame flashed forth, we saw a miracle, we to whom it was given to see. And we are preserved in order to relate to the rest what happened. For the fire made the shape of a vaulted chamber, like a ship's sail filled by the wind, and made a wall around the body of the martyr. And he was in the midst, not as burning flesh, but as bread baking or as gold and silver refined in a furnace. And we perceived such a sweet aroma as the breath of incense or some other precious spice.

At length, when the lawless men saw that his body could not be consumed by the fire, they commanded an executioner to go to him and stab him with a dagger. And when he did this [a dove and] a great quantity of blood came forth, so that the fire was quenched and the whole crowd marveled that there should be such a difference between unbelievers and the elect.

So later we took up his bones, more precious than costly stones and more valuable than gold, and laid them away in a suitable place. There the Lord will permit us, so far as possible, to gather together in joy and gladness to celebrate the day of his martyrdom as a birthday, in memory of those athletes who have gone before, and to train and make ready those who are to come hereafter.

From *Early Christian Fathers* Vol. 1, The Library of Christian Classics, newly translated and edited by Cyril C. Richardson, 152-155. Published in the U.S.A. by The Westminster Press. Used by permission.

Propers

ROMAN	LUTHERAN	EPISCOPAL
God of all creation, you gave your bishop Polycarp the privilege of being counted among the saints Who gave their lives in faithful witness to the gospel. May his prayers give us the courage to share with him the cup of suffering and to rise to eternal glory. We ask this through our Lord Jesus Christ, your Son, who lives and reigns with you and the Holy Spirit, one God, for ever and ever.	Gracious Lord, in every age you have sent men and women who have given their lives for the message of your love. Inspire us with the memory of those martyrs for the Gospel like your servant Polycarp whose faithfulness led them in the way of the cross, and give us courage to bear full witness with our lives to your Son's victory over sin and death; through Jesus Christ our Lord.	Almighty God, who gave to your servant Polycarp boldness to confess the Name of our Savior Jesus Christ before the rulers of this world, and courage to die for this faith: Grant that we may also be ever ready to give a reason for the hope that is in us, and to suffer gladly for the sake of our Lord Jesus Christ, who lives and reigns with you and the Holy Spirit, one God, for ever and ever.

(Text from the English translation of the Roman Missal © 1973, International Committee on English in the Liturgy, Inc. All rights reserved.)

(Text from Lesser Feasts and Fasts, Revised Edition, copyright 1973 by Charles Mortimer Guilbert as Custodian of the Standard Book of Common Prayer. All rights reserved. Used by permission.)

Common of Martyrs
or Pastors
or Revelation 2:8-11

Common of Martyrs
Ezekiel 20:40-42
Psalm 5
Revelation 2:8-11
Mark 8:34-38

Psalm 146:1-5
Revelation 2:8-11
Psalm 119:153-160
Matthew 20:20-23
Preface of Holy Week

Hymn of the Day: "How firm a foundation, O saints of the Lord" (507)

Prayers: for a life of devotion
for boldness to witness to the faith
for courage to follow Christ, even to death
for faithfulness to the apostolic tradition

Preface: All Saints

Color: Red

92

Bartholomaeus Ziegenbalg, Missionary to India, 1719

Bartholomaeus Ziegenbalg was born in Pulsnitz, a little town in Saxony on June 10, 1682, the son of poor, devout parents. As a child he showed his great ability in school work and music. He studied at the University of Halle, then the center of the pietistic movement in the Lutheran church under the influence of A. H. Francke. In 1705 Ziegenbalg responded to the call of King Frederik IV of Denmark to take the gospel to India. On July 9, 1706 Ziegenbalg and his associate Heinrich Plütschau arrived in Tranquebar on the southeast coast of India—the first Protestant missionaries to that country.

Despite the hostility of the local Danish authorities as well as the Hindu religious leaders, Ziegenbalg and Plütschau carried on their work, baptizing their first Indians on May 12, 1707. In 1712 a printing press was set up, and Ziegenbalg published important studies on the Tamil language and wrote voluminously on Indian religion and culture. Several of his manuscripts, including *The Genealogy of the Malibar Gods*, were sent to Halle, but they were never printed. His translation of the New Testament into Tamil (1715) was revised by a successor, Johann Fabricius and is still in use. The Church of the New Jerusalem built and dedicated by Ziegenbalg and his associates in 1718 is still being used today.

During his brief lifetime (he died when he was 36) Ziegenbalg had to endure poor health, the lack of support from the church, opposition of the civil authorities, and many misfortunes. The Copenhagen Mission Society, with the admirable goal of not making the new church a transplanted European Christianity, wanted its missionaries simply to preach the gospel and not to involve themselves in other matters. Ziegenbalg insisted, however, that the care of souls also implies a concern for the physical and mental welfare of the people and that such service is implicit in the preaching of the gospel.

The low point of Ziegenbalg's life was a period of four months, 1708-1709, spent is a stifling prison cell on the charge that by converting the Indians he was stirring up rebellion. The last three years of his life, however, were full of joy: his marriage in 1716, the arrival of a new and friendly governor, the publication of his New Testament, and the founding of a seminary to train native clergy. His cooperation with the Anglican Society for the Propagation of Christian Knowledge was one of the first ecumenical ventures. He died in Madras on February 23, 1719, leaving as his monument a Tamil dictionary and grammar, a Tamil translation of the New Testament and the Old Testament as far as Ruth, some thirty-two tracts on Christian doctrine and duties, two church buildings, the seminary, and a community of 250 baptized Christians.

The work of the Ziegenbalg mission later declined and was in part taken over by Anglican missionaries, but it was the inspiration for missionary efforts elsewhere in the world, and it led indirectly to the flourishing Tamil-speaking Lutheran churches of India today. Dr. Rajah B. Manikam, the first Indian bishop of the Tamil Evangelical Lutheran Church, was consecrated in Tranquebar in 1956 during the year of celebration of the 250th anniversary of Ziegenbalg's arrival in India.

E. Bayreuther. *Bartholomaeus Ziegenbalg*. Madras, 1955.
C. B. Firth. *An Introduction to Indian Church History*. Madras, 1961.
E. A. Lehmann. *It Began at Tranquebar*. Madras, 1955.

Christian Frederik Schwartz (1726-1798), probably the most influential worker in the Tranquebar Mission after Ziegenbalg, might also be remembered on this day. He involved himself in the political affairs of his people and was extraordinarily influential, respected for his integrity and loved for his saintliness. He spent 48 years in India. His work was notably ecumenical (the English made him a chaplain in Trichinopoly), yet he remained a faithful Lutheran. He died on February 12, 1798.

Another important early Lutheran missionary, also sponsored by the Copenhagen Mission Society, is **Hans Egede,** the Apostle of Greenland. He was born in 1686 in Norway. After studying theology in Denmark, he was a pastor for a time in Norway, but he was increasingly fascinated by the story of the Norse settlers of Greenland, from whom there had been no reports since the fifteenth century. After rebuffs by his bishop and by the King of Denmark, he raised money himself, bought a ship, and arrived in Greenland in 1721. He was disappointed to find only Eskimos and not a trace of a Scandinavian settlement. With his wife, **Gertrud Rask,** he began missionary work there nonetheless. The mission made slow progress. It met competition with the arrival of Moravian missionaries in 1733 and from an epidemic of smallpox. The selfless service of Gertrud Rask and her husband made a deep impression on the Eskimos, however, and the work showed more promise. Rask died in 1735, and in the following year Egede returned to Denmark to train missionaries. His son Poul carried on the work in Greenland. Egede died November 5, 1758.

Yet another Lutheran missionary sent out by the Copenhagen Mission Society was **Thomas von Westen,** the Apostle to the Lapps. He died April 9, 1727.

Reading

(From the decree on the missionary activity of the Church of the Second Vatican Council)

Every disciple of Christ is responsible in his own measure for the spread of the faith, but Christ the Lord is always calling from among his followers those whom he wills, so that they may be with him and be sent by him to preach to the nations.

Those whom God calls must answer his call in such a way that, without regard for purely human counsel, they may devote themselves wholly to the work of the Gospel. This response cannot be given except with the inspiration and strength of the Holy Spirit.

The person who is sent enters into the life and mission of him who emptied himself, taking the nature of a slave. He must be ready therefore to be true to his vocation for life, to deny himself, renouncing all that he had before, and to become all things to all men.

In preaching the Gospel to the nations he must boldly proclaim the mystery of Christ, whose ambassador he is, so that in Christ he may have the courage to speak as he ought, and not be ashamed of the scandal of the cross. He must follow in the footsteps of his Master, who was gentle and humble of heart, and reveal to others that his yoke is easy and his burden light.

By a life that is truly according to the Gospel, by much endurance, by forbearance, by kindness and sincere love, he must bear witness to his Lord, even, if need be, by the shedding of his blood.

He will pray to God for strength and courage, so that he may come to see that for one who experiences great hardship and extreme poverty there can be abundant joy.

Propers: Missionaries
      Second Lesson: Revelation 21:1-4

Hymn of the Day: "Your Kingdom come, O Father, to earth's
      remotest shore" (384)

Prayers: for the church in India
      for schools and orphanages
      for those who seek to understand new and different cultures
      for those in weak health
      for a spirit of understanding, acceptance, and support
        for new work in the church

Color: White

Those who desire to commemorate Polycarp on this date might transfer the commemoration of Ziegenbalg and others to the date of Ziegenbalg's arrival in India (July 9) or of his first baptisms (May 12) or to the date of the death of Egede (February 12) or of von Westen (April 9).

February 24

ST. MATTHIAS, APOSTLE

Nothing is known for certain of the life of Matthias except for the story of his selection to replace Judas Iscariot, as recorded in the Second Lesson, Acts 1:15-26. After the Ascension, when about a hundred and twenty of the followers of Jesus met in the upper room, Peter asked the group to choose a replacement for Judas, the betrayer of the Lord. Two witnesses of the resurrection were suggested, a certain Joseph Barsabbas and Matthias. Tradition has included both among the seventy sent out by Jesus, but neither is mentioned elsewhere than in Acts 1. After prayer, the choice was left to the casting of lots, and Matthias became the twelfth apostle. St. Paul (1 Cor. 15:5–6) refers to a resurrection appearance of Jesus to "the Twelve"; Origen thought that this number included Matthias.

There has been some confusion in the apocryphal literature between Matthias and Matthew. Clement quotes a second-century Gospel of Matthias, now lost. A sixth-century "Acts of Andrew and Matthias (Matthew)" relates that the land of the cannibals fell to Matthias as the sphere of his missionary activity; an Old English poem *Andreas* tells the tale. There are stories of Matthias preaching in Judea and in Ethiopia, and one tradition asserts that he met his death in Colchis, near modern Georgia in the Caucasus. All the traditions at least agree that he was a martyr for the faith. His feast day was one of the last of the apostles' days to be added to the calendar, not dating back before the eleventh century. One reason for the late establishment of his feast day is that St. Paul was thought to have been the one chosen to replace Judas and to restore the complement of twelve.

The reason for the traditional date of February 24 is not known. In the new Roman calendar, St. Matthias' Day is moved to May 14 to avoid conflict with Lent and to place the commemoration in the Easter season, emphasizing Matthias' role as a witness to the resurrection. The Episcopal Church retains the traditional Western date. Matthias' Day is celebrated on August 9 in the Eastern churches.

Reading

(From Luther's "Lectures on Galatians.")

. . . Christ wanted no one to be made an apostle by men or the will of men but as the result of a call from Him alone. For this reason the apostles did not dare elect Matthias; they gained his appointment from heaven in answer to their prayer. And it was from heaven that God called Paul himself and made him an apostle, in particular through the voice of the Holy Spirit. "Set apart for Me," He says, "Paul and Barnabas for the work to which I have called them." Thus Paul boasts in Rom. 1:1f. that he was set apart for the Gospel of God, inasmuch as he himself, together with Barnabas, was set apart for the uncircumcised and the Gentiles, while the rest of the apostles were sent to those who were circumcised.

Note also that Paul makes the name "apostle" so emphatically expressive of an office and of dignity that he uses it as a participle and says "an apostle, not from men," which means "sent, not from men". . . . All these facts aim to make you see with what care Christ has established and fortified His church, lest anyone rashly presume to teach without being sent by Him or by those who He has sent. For just as the Word of God is the church's first and greatest benefit, so, on the other hand, there is no greater harm by which the church is destroyed than the word of man and the traditions of this world. God alone is true, and every man a liar. Finally, just as David once left behind all the means by which Solomon was to build the temple, so Christ has left behind the Gospel and other writings, in order that the church might be built by means of them, not by human decrees.

Martin Luther, "Lectures on Galatians" trans. Richard Junguntz, in *Luther's Works* vol. 27, p. 165. © 1964 Concordia Publishing House. Used by permission.

Propers

ROMAN	LUTHERAN	EPISCOPAL
(May 14) Father, you called Saint Matthias to share in the mission of the apostles. By the help of his prayers may we receive with joy the love you share with us and be counted among those you have chosen. We ask this through our Lord Jesus Christ, your Son, who lives and reigns	Almighty God, you chose your faithful servant Matthias to be numbered among the Twelve. Grant that your Church, being delivered from false apostles, may always be taught and guided by faithful and true pastors; through your Son, Jesus Christ our Lord, who lives and reigns with you and the Holy Spirit, one God, now and forever.	Almighty God, who in the place of Judas chose your faithful servant Matthias to be numbered among the Twelve: Grant that your Church, being delivered from false apostles, may always be guided by faithful and true pastors; through Jesus Christ our Lord, who lives and reigns with you, in the unity of the Holy Spirit, one God, now and for ever.

98

February 25

ROMAN	LUTHERAN	EPISCOPAL

ROMAN

with you and the
Holy Spirit,
one God, for ever and
ever.

*(Text from the English
translation of the Roman
Missal © 1973, Interna-
tional Committee on Eng-
lish in the Liturgy, Inc.
All rights reserved.)*

Acts 1:15-17, 20-26
Psalm 113
John 15:9-17

LUTHERAN

Isaiah 66:1-2
Psalm 56
Acts 1:15-26
Luke 6:12-16

EPISCOPAL

*(Text from the Book of
Common Prayer [Pro-
posed], copyright 1977 by
Charles Mortimer Guilbert
as Custodian of the Stan-
dard Book of Common
Prayer. All rights reserved.
Used by permission.)*
Acts 1:15-26

Psalm 15
Philippians 3:13-21
John 15:1, 6-16
Preface of the
Apostles

Hymn of the Day: "O Zion haste, your mission high fulfilling" (397)

Prayers: for those who give testimony to the resurrection
for a renewed life
for faithfulness to Christ

Preface: Apostles

Color: Red

February 25

Elizabeth Fedde, Deaconess, 1921

Elizabeth Fedde was born on Christmas Day, 1850 at Feda, near Flekkefjord, Norway. She received her deaconness training at Lovisenberg Deaconess House under the supervision of Mother Katinka Guldberg, who had been trained at Fliedner's Motherhouse at Kaiserswerth, Germany.

On her thirty-second birthday (Christmas Day, 1882), Sister Elizabeth received a letter asking her to come to New York and take up a ministry to the Norwegian seamen in port and on the ships in the harbor. The letter was written by Gabriel Fedde, then the secretary to the Norwegian seamen's pastor, Mr. Mortensen. Sister Elizabeth accepted the challenge and left Christiana on March 25, 1883, and arrived in New York on April 9.

The work of the Norwegian deaconesses was officially established in America at a meeting held at Pastor Mortensen's home on April 19, 1883, under the name of the Norwegian Relief Society. The work had its beginning in three small rooms (rented at $9 per month) at 109 Williams Street, next to the Seamen's Church and was marked by a service in that church June 11, 1883. In 1885 the Deaconess House in Brooklyn was opened. Sister Elizabeth also established the Lutheran Deaconess Home and Hospital of the Lutheran Free Church in Minneapolis in 1889.

Sister Elizabeth returned to Norway in November 1895. She died at her home, Slettebo, Egersund on February 25, 1921.

Erling Nicolai Rolfsrud. *The Borrowed Sister. The Story of Elizabeth Fedde.* Minneapolis: Augsburg, 1953.

Amalie Wilhelmina Sieveking might appropriately be remembered with Sister Elizabeth Fedde. She was born July 25, 1794 in Hamburg, Germany and was orphaned at an early age. Not long afterward, her brother, who had been her support, also died. She grew in her love of the Bible and in her desire to help the poor. At length, in 1832, she organized in Hamburg a women's society for the care of the poor and needy. This group of women volunteered their time for social welfare work. She declined repeated calls from Pastor Theodor Fliedner to come to the Deaconess Motherhouse at Kaiserswerth. Amalie Sieveking, an early and forceful worker for the emancipation of women, died April 1, 1859.

Reading

(From *Light of Christ* by Evelyn Underhill.)

The Triumphant Church is not a collection of pious people with robes washed white—it is the whole of life's energy running right, sublimated and woven into the loving self-expression of God—it is the Kingdom of Heaven. Its frontiers must stretch till they embrace the whole Universe in its power, mystery and beauty and bring it under the rule of Christ, the intellectual radiance full of love. For the work of the Incarnation, as St. Paul saw, is not finished till the whole of the created order is filled with God and, at the heart of the universe, ruling it in its most majestic sweep and its homeliest detail, we find His uttered Word, His love. . . .

And you and I are committed as baptized Christians, to what has been given His deep and touching earthly revelation, to the steady loyal effort, in our own small place and way, towards bringing that mounting vision a little nearer completeness, bringing a little more of that Kingdom in. Each faithful upward glance, each movement of trust, each act of selfless love, helps it on. A time such as we have had here is only justified if it brings that mounting vision into focus again; reminds us of what it means to be Inheritors of Heaven. The Hallowing of the whole Universe, physical, mental and spiritual in all its grades, the infinitely great and the infinitely small, giving our lives at whatever cost to the helping of the fulfillment of their sacramental promise—we must take sides in some way for that, because we are the Children of God.

Evelyn Underhill, *Light of Christ* (London: Longman's, 1945) 91-92.

Propers: Renewers of Society

Hymn of the Day: "Lord of glory, you have bought us" (424)

Prayers: for the spirit of selfless service
for the sick, the needy, the forgotten
for those who minister to those in need
for the liberation of women and men everywhere from
bondage to stereotypes

Color: White

George Herbert, Priest, 1633

George Herbert was born in Montgomery Castle April 3, 1593, the fifth son of an aristocratic and distinguished Welsh family. His father died in 1596, and the young son was raised by his mother, Magdalen Herbert, who was a friend of John Donne. Handsome, elegant, witty, Herbert excelled in classical scholarship, languages (Greek, Latin, Italian, Spanish, French), and music at Trinity College, Cambridge, and, as University Orator (1620-1627), seemed destined for high political office.

He served as member of Parliament for Montgomery, 1624-1625, but the death of his patron, James I, together with the influence of his friend Nicholas Ferrar, whose religious community called Little Gidding he frequently visited, led him to decide upon the study of divinity, to which he had long been drawn. He was made a deacon sometime between 1624 and 1626 and was assigned to Leighton Bromswold in the diocese of Lincoln. Although he was still University Orator, he devoted himself to rebuilding the ruined church. He married Jane Danvers in 1629 after a courtship of three days; the marriage was apparently a happy one.

In April 1630, Herbert was instituted as rector of St. Peter's Fugglestone and St. Andrew, Bemerton (near Salisbury). He was ordained priest September 19, 1630. He served this tiny rural parish for but three years, exercising there unusual diligence in pastoral care and taking pains to instruct his largely unlettered parishioners in the significance of every part of the liturgy and in the meaning of the church year. Isaac Walton's biography of "holy Mr. Herbert" (1670) reports that at the sound of the church bell announcing morning and evening prayer, many of the parishioners "let their plough rest" that they might join their prayers with the morning and evening prayers of their beloved pastor.

Herbert, whose health had never been strong, died of consumption March 1, 1633 at the age of forty and was buried two days later beneath the high altar of his parish church in Bemerton.

His English poems were published shortly after his death by Nicholas Ferrar, to whom they had been left with the instructions that if Ferrar thought they might do good to "any dejected poor soul" he should have them published; otherwise he should burn them. Two editions of the collection, *The Temple,* were published before the year was out; there were thirteen editions by 1679. The poems, called "the best collection of religious lyrics in English," breathe a gentle freshness and grace, not without earnest wrestling with worldly ambition and a continued struggle to submit to his vocation. Some of the poems are still sung as hymns: "Teach me my God and King," "The king of love my shepherd is," "Let all the world in every corner sing." The graceful and moving poetry is the counterpart of Jeremy Taylor's prose, and it is W. H. Auden's judgment that "together they are the

finest expressions we have of Anglican piety at its best." Herbert's
poetry is like John Bunyan's prose in that, although most carefully
done, it leaves the impression of an unsophisticated mind, drawing its
images from ordinary life.

Herbert also wrote *A Priest to the Temple; or the Country Parson*,
a simple and moving description of the clergyman as well-read, temperate, given to prayer, devoted to his people: "Now love is his business and aim." In this book, Herbert might well have been describing
himself.

Amy M. Charles. *A Life of George Herbert*. Ithaca: Cornell, 1978.
F. E. Hutchinson. *The Complete Works of George Herbert*. Oxford: Clar-
    endon, 1941.
Joseph H. Summers. *George Herbert, His Religion and His Art*. Cam-
    bridge, Mass.: Harvard, 1954.
Rosemond Tuve. *A Reading of George Herbert*. University of Chicago
    Press, 1952.
Helen Vendler. *The Poetry of George Herbert*. Cambridge, Mass.: Harvard,
    1975.

Reading

(From *A Priest in the Temple*.)

The Countrey Parson's Library is a holy life: for besides the blessing that that brings upon it, there being a promise, that if the kingdom of God be first sought, all other things shall be added, even
itself is a sermon. For the temptations with which a good man is
beset, and the ways which he used to overcome them, being told to
another, whether in private conference or in the Church, are a sermon. He that hath considered how to carry himself at table about
his appetite, if he tell this to another, preacheth; and much more
feelingly and judiciously than [if] he writes his rule of temperance
out of books. So that the Parson having studied and mastered all his
lusts and affections within, and the whole army of temptations without, hath ever so many sermons ready penned, as he hath victories.
And it fares in this as it doth in Physick: he that hath been sick of a
Consumption and knows what recovered him, is a Physician so far
as he meets with the same disease and temper; and can much better,

and particularly do it than he that is generally learned and was never sick. And if the same person had been sick of all diseases and were recovered of all by things that he knew, there were no such physician as he, both for skill and tenderness. Just so it is in Divinity, and that not without manifest reason: for though the temptations may be diverse in diverse Christians, yet the victory is alike to all, being by the self-same Spirit. Neither is this true only in the military state of a Christian life but even in the peaceable also; when the servant of God, freed for a while from temptation, in a quiet sweetness seeks how to please his God.

Thus the Parson considering that repentance is the great virtue of the Gospel, and one of the first steps of pleasing God, having for his own use experienced the nature of it, is able to explain it after to others.

. . . The like he doth in other Christian virtues, as of faith and love and the cases of conscience belonging thereto, wherein (as Saint Paul implies that he ought, Romans 2) he first preacheth to himself and then to others.

George Herbert, *A Priest to the Temple,* chapter XXXIII "The Parson's Library." *The Works of George Herbert* ed. F. E. Hutchinson (Oxford: Clarendon, 1941) 278-279.

Propers

ROMAN

LUTHERAN

Heavenly Father, shepherd of your people, we thank you for your servant George, who was faithful in the care and nurture of your flock; and we pray that, following his example, and the teaching of his holy life, we may by your grace grow into the full stature of our Lord and Savior Jesus Christ.

EPISCOPAL

(February 27)
Almighty and merciful God, who called your servant George Herbert from the pursuit of worldly honors to be a humble pastor of souls: Grant us also the grace to offer our talents, with singleness of heart, in humble obedience to your service; through Jesus Christ our Lord, who lives and reigns with

104 *March 2*

ROMAN	LUTHERAN	EPISCOPAL

you and the Holy Spirit, one God, now and for ever.

Common of Pastors:

Ezekiel 34:11-16
Psalm 84
1 Peter 5:1-4
John 21:15-17

Common of a Pastor:
Psalm 112:1-9
Ezekiel 34:11-16
Psalm 23
1 Peter 5:1-4
John 21:15-17
Preface of a Saint

Hymn of the Day: "Come, my way, my truth, my life (513) *or* "Teach me my God and King (SBH 451)

Prayers: for poets and those who make language sing
for humility
for grace to find God in everyday life
for the spirit of love

Color: White

John Wesley, 1791; Charles Wesley, 1788; Renewers of the Church

John (born June 17, 1703) was the fifteenth and his brother Charles (born December 18, 1707) the eighteenth child of Susanna Wesley and her husband Samuel, the rector of Epworth in Lincolnshire, who was descended from an old puritan family. Susanna was a demanding mother and imparted to her sons a sense of holiness and seriousness which remained with them to the end. The two brothers were both educated at Christ Church College, Oxford. John was ordained a priest in 1728, Charles in 1735. At Oxford, John became a member of the "Holy Society" founded by Charles. The group was composed of those who were dissatisfied with contemporary religious life and who sought mutual improvement in spirituality. They emphasized frequent communion and fasting twice a week, and their service extended to social work as well. Their program earned them the derogatory name "Methodists." John's powerful personality soon made him the leader of the group.

In 1735 the brothers went to Georgia. John was sent by the Society for the Propagation of the Gospel, and Charles was secretary to the governor, James Oglethorpe. John's purpose was to evangelize the colonists and Indians. His preaching against the slave trade and against gin alienated the colonists. The experience of both brothers was unhappy. John broke with the Calvinists and joined with the Moravians. They returned to London in 1738 and frequented the Moravian chapel in Fetter Lane. Both received an inner conversion, Charles on May 21, 1738 and John three days later at a meeting in Aldersgate Street with a Moravian group.

The eighteenth century evangelical revival was born, and John spent the rest of his long life in evangelistic work. He visited Count von Zinzendorf in Germany. The brothers were increasingly excluded from the established church, though they continued to respect it, and they turned more and more to preaching in the fields. It is said that John travelled nearly a quarter of a million miles on horseback all over England and preached more than forty thousand sermons, often several each day. On June 11, 1739 John wrote in his Journal, "I look upon all the world as my parish; thus far I mean, that, in whatever part of it I am, I judge it meet, right, and my bounden duty, to declare unto all that are willing to hear, the glad tidings of salvation. This is the work which I know God has called me to; and sure I am that his blessing attends it."

In 1740 the brothers ended their connection with the Moravians and opened a "Methodist" chapel in Bristol. Both brothers wished to remain in the established church but differed with each other concerning their right to ordain ministers when none were forthcoming.

Charles retired from itinerant preaching in 1756 and thereafter lived in Bristol and in London. When there was a desperate and unfulfilled need for ministers, John, against the advice of Charles, ordained a minister for America in 1784 and ministers for Scotland in 1785.

Charles was responsible for a huge output of hymns—more than six thousand of them—and he is considered the best of the hymnwriters of the time. John was perhaps the greatest single force in the eighteenth century revival. He incurred hostility and violence at times. A ruthless antagonist, he was an able organizer and produced an enormous quantity of writing—a long journal, a Christian library, hymns, and two editions of George Herbert's poems. Much of his editing seems to have been done while travelling on horseback.

Charles died March 29, 1788 and was buried in the graveyard of Old Marylebone Church. John died on March 2, 1791 and was buried in the cemetery behind his chapel and house on City Road, London.

Frank Baker. *John Wesley and the Church of England.* London: Epworth, 1970.
Albert C. Outler, ed. *John Wesley.* 2nd ed. New York; 1970.
Kenneth E. Rowe, ed. *The Place of Wesley in the Christian Tradition.* Metuchen, N. J.: Scarecrow Press, 1976.
Charles Wesley. *Journal* ed. T. Jackson. 2 vols. London, 1849.
John Wesley. *Journal 1739-1791.* 4 vols. London, 1827. 8 vols., ed. N. Curnock, 1906-1916. Abridged, Everyman, 1902.
F. L. Wiseman. *Charles Wesley. Evangelist and Poet.* New York: Abingdon, 1932.

On this day, Nicolaus Ludwig, Count of **Zinzendorf** (1700-1760), might also be remembered. He bears a relationship to the Lutheran Church not unlike the relationship of the Wesleys to the Church of England, and, moreover, contact with the Moravians contributed significantly to the profound religious experience of John Wesley.

Zinzendorf was born into a noble Austrian Lutheran family at Dresden and was trained at Halle, the center of Pietism. As he travelled, he found a deep love of Jesus in all the churches and developed a consuming ambition to bring the splinter groups back into the church and to bring the churches together. His intense piety and his work were not welcome in the Lutheran church of the time. In 1737 Zinzendorf was consecrated a bishop in the Church of the Czech Brethren, a continuation of the *Unitas Fratrum* (Unity of the Brethren) begun by followers of John Hus three centuries before, and which, because so much of its early history centered in Moravia, a province of Czechoslovakia, became known as the Moravian Church. Zinzendorf sent out more than two hundred missionaries, and their influence throughout the world was enormous. He was a hymnwriter, whose hymns are still sung in churches of many denominations. His piety was not only intensely personal; he also had a deep concern for social justice. Zinzendorf died May 9, 1760.

Arthur J. Lewis. *Zinzendorf: The Ecumenical Pioneer*. Philadelphia: Westminster, 1962.
John R. Weinlick. *Count Zinzendorf*. New York and Nashville: Abingdon, 1956.

Reading

(From the *Journal* of John Wesley, May 24, 1738.)

I think it was about five this morning that I opened my Testament on those words, "There are given unto us exceeding great and precious promises, even that ye should be partakers of the divine nature." Just as I went out, I opened it again on those words, "Thou art not far from the kingdom of God." In the afternoon I was asked to go to St. Paul's. The anthem was, "Out of the deep have I called unto thee, O Lord. O let thine ears consider well the voice of my complaint. If thou, Lord, wilt be extreme to mark what is done amiss, O Lord, who may abide it? For there is mercy with thee; therefore shalt thou be feared. O Israel, trust in the Lord; for with the Lord there is mercy, and with him is plenteous redemption. And he shall redeem Israel from all his sins."

In the evening I went very unwillingly to a society in Aldersgate Street, where one was reading Luther's preface to the Epistle to the Romans. About a quarter before nine, while he was describing the change which God works in the heart through faith in Christ, I felt my heart strangely warmed. I felt I did trust in Christ, Christ alone, for my salvation; and an assurance was given me that He had taken away my sins, even mine, and saved me from the law of sin and death.

I began to pray with all my might for those who had in a more especial manner despitefully used me and persecuted me. I then testified openly to all there what I now first felt in my heart. But it was not long before the enemy suggested, "This cannot be faith; for where is thy joy?" Then was I taught that peace and victory over sin are essential to faith in the Captain of our salvation; but that, as to the transports of joy that usually attend the beginning of it, especially in those who have mourned deeply, God sometimes giveth, sometimes withholdeth them, according to the counsels of His own will.

The Heart of John Wesley's Journal, ed. Percy Livingston Parker (London: Revell, n.d.) 28-30.

Propers

ROMAN	LUTHERAN	EPISCOPAL

LUTHERAN

Almighty God, we praise you for the men and women you have sent to call the Church to its tasks and renew its life, such as your servants John and Charles. Raise up in our own day teachers and prophets inspired by your Spirit, whose voices will give strength to your church and proclaim the reality of your kingdom; through your Son, Jesus Christ our Lord.

EPISCOPAL

(March 3)

O God of mercy, enlighten the hearts of your faithful people, and grant us, after the example of your servants John and Charles Wesley, not to mind earthly things, but to love things heavenly; through Jesus Christ our Lord, who lives and reigns with you and the Holy Spirit, one God, now and for ever.

(Text from Lesser Feasts and Fasts, Revised Edition, copyright 1973 by Charles Mortimer Guilbert as Custodian of the Standard Book of Common Prayer. All rights reserved. Used by permission.)

Common of Renewers
of the Church:
Jeremiah 1:4-10
Psalm 46
1 Corinthians 3:11-23
Mark 10:35-45

Psalm 126
Hosea 6:1-6
Psalm 119:105-112
Luke 10:1-9

Preface of Pentecost

Hymn of the Day: "Oh, for a thousand tongues to sing" (559) *or* "O for a heart to praise my God" (*SBH* 389)

Prayers: for a heart burning with love for God

for a deepened spiritual life
for a social conscience
for the reconciliation of the Methodist and Anglican
   Churches

Color: White

Perpetua and her Companions
Martyrs at Carthage, 202

No saints are more uniformly honored in all the early calendars and martyrologies than these African martyrs. In 202 the emperor Septimus Severus forbade conversions to Christianity and harsh persecution ensued. Arrested in Carthage were Vibia Perpetua, a noblewoman from Thuburbo, twenty-two years old; her infant child; Felicity, a pregnant slave; Revocatus, a slave; Saturninus; Secundulus—all catechumens. Later their catechist, Saturus, was arrested also. While under house arrest they were baptized.

Perpetua's father urged her to renounce the faith, but she refused, and was imprisoned. In prison, she had a vision of a golden ladder guarded by a dragon and sharp weapons that prevented ascent, but nonetheless she walked over the dragon and reached a beautiful place. Her father repeated his plea in vain and repeated it again before the people in the arena.

The steadfast Christians were condemned to be given to wild beasts at a celebration in honor of Caesar Geta. Perpetua had another vision, this time of her seven year old brother Dinocrates, who had died of cancer, in heaven. Felicity was not to have been executed with the others since it was illegal to execute a pregnant woman, but three days before the spectacle Felicity gave birth prematurely to a girl, who was adopted by a Christian family, and gladly joined the others in martyrdom. After scourging, they were led to the amphitheater, and according to the apparently contemporary account of the martyrdom, were mangled by the beasts, but survived to be beheaded with a sword.

The record of the *Passion of Perpetua and Felicity* is one of the most ancient reliable histories of the martyrs extant. Part of the *Passion* is said to have been written by Perpetua herself as a kind of diary record of her visions, and part by Saturus. The introduction and the conclusion are by an apparent eyewitness, said by some to have been the church father Tertullian. The *Passion*, which recalls the biblical book of Revelation, is an important document in understanding early Christian ideas of martyrdom, providing a vivid insight into the beliefs of the young and vigorous African church. It was enormously popular, and St. Augustine, who quotes it often, had to warn against it being put on the same level as Holy Scripture. Perpetua and her companions were very popular in Carthage, and a basilica was erected over their tomb.

In the *Passion*, four other martyrs of Carthage are also mentioned: Jocundus, Saturninus, and Artaxius, all of whom had been burned, and Qunitus, who died in prison.

In the Roman church, the commemoration of Perpetua and Felicity had been moved to March 6 to make room for Thomas Aquinas on March 7. The new Roman calendar restores the commemoration of Perpetua and Felicity to March 7 and moves Thomas to January 28.

The Acts of the Christian Martyrs ed. and tr. Herbert Musurillo. New York: Oxford, 1972.
E. R. Dodds. *Pagan and Christian in an Age of Anxiety*. Cambridge, 1965.
The Passion of SS. Perpetua and Felicity, MM, ed. and tr. W. Shewring. London: Sheed and Ward, 1931.

Reading

(From the *Martyrdom of Saints Perpetua and Felicitas*)

The day of their victory dawned, and they marched from the prison to the amphitheatre joyfully as though they were going to heaven, with calm faces, trembling, if at all, with joy rather than fear. Perpetua went along with shining countenance and calm step, as the beloved of God, as a wife of Christ, putting down everyone's stare by her own intense gaze. With them also was Felicitas, glad that she had safely given birth so that now she could fight the beasts, going from one blood bath to another, from the midwife to the gladiator, ready to wash after the childbirth in a second baptism.

They were then led up to the gates and the men were forced to put on the robes of priests of Saturn, the women the dress of the priestesses of Ceres. But the noble Perpetua strenuously resisted this to the end.

"We came to this of our own free will, that our freedom should not be violated. We agreed to pledge our lives provided that we would do no such thing. You agreed with us to do this."

Even injustice recognized injustice. The military tribune agreed. They were to be brought into the arena just as they were. Perpetua then began to sing a Psalm: she was already treading on the head of the Egyptian. Revocatus, Saturninus, and Saturus began to warn the onlooking mob. Then when they came within sight of Hilarianus, they suggested by their motions and gestures; "You have condemned us, but God will condemn you" was what they were saying.

At this the crowds became enraged and demanded that they be scourged before a line of gladiators. And they rejoiced at this that they had obtained a share in the Lord's sufferings.

First the heifer tossed Perpetua and she fell on her back. Then sitting up she pulled down the tunic that was ripped along the side so that it covered her thighs, thinking more of her modesty than of her pain. Next she asked for a pin to fasten her untidy hair: for it was not right that a martyr should die with her hair in disorder, lest she might seem to be mourning in her hour of triumph.

Then she got up. And seeing that Felicitas had been crushed to the ground, she went over to her, gave her her hand, and lifted her up. Then the two stood side by side.

. . . but the mob asked that their bodies be brought out into the open that their eyes might be the guilty witnesses of the sword that pierced their flesh. And so the martyrs got up and went to the spot of their own accord as the people wanted them to go, and kissing one another they sealed their martyrdom with the ritual kiss of peace. The others took the sword in silence and without moving, especially Saturus, who being the first to climb the stairway, was the first to die. For once again he was waiting for Perpetua. Perpetua, however, had yet to taste more pain. She screamed as she was struck on the bone; then she took the trembling hand of the young gladiator and guided it to her throat. It was as though so great a woman, feared as she

112 *March 7*

was by the unclean spirit, could not be dispatched unless she herself were willing.

Ah, most valiant and blessed martyrs! Truly are you called and chosen for the glory of Christ Jesus our Lord! And any man who exalts, honors, and worships his glory should read for the consolation of the Church these new deeds of heroism which are no less significant than the tales of old. For these new manifestations of virtue will bear witness to one and the same Spirit who still operates, and to God the Father almighty, to his Son Jesus Christ our Lord, to whom is splendour and immeasurable power for all the ages. Amen.

The Acts of the Christian Martyrs, ed. and tr. Herbert Musurillo, 129-131. © Oxford University Press 1972. Used by permission of Oxford University Press.

Propers

ROMAN

Father,
your love gave the Saints Perpetua and Felicity
courage to suffer a cruel martyrdom.
By their prayers, help us to grow in love of you.
We ask this through our Lord Jesus Christ, your Son, who lives and reigns with you and the Holy Spirit, one God, for ever and ever.

(Text from the English translation of the Roman Missal © 1973, International Committee on English in the Liturgy, Inc. All rights reserved.)

LUTHERAN

Gracious Lord, in every age you have sent men and women who have given their lives for the message of your love. Inspire us with the memory of those martyrs for the Gospel, like your servants Perpetua and her companions, whose faithfulness led them in the way of the cross, and give us courage to bear full witness with our lives to your Son's victory over sin and death; through Jesus Christ our Lord.

EPISCOPAL

Almighty and everlasting God, with whom your meek ones go forth as the mighty: Grant us so to cherish the memory of your blessed martyrs Perpetua and her companions, that we may share their pure and steadfast faith in you; through Jesus Christ our Lord, who lives and reigns with you and the Holy Spirit, one God, in glory everlasting.

(Text from Lesser Feasts and Fasts, Revised Edition, copyright 1973 by Charles Mortimer Guilbert as Custodian of the Standard Book of Common Prayer. All rights reserved. Used by permission.)

ROMAN	LUTHERAN	EPISCOPAL
Common of Martyrs	Common of Martyrs: Ezekiel 20:40-42 Psalm 5 Revelation 6:9-11 Mark 8:34-38	Psalm 124 Hebrews 10:32-39 Psalm 138 Matthew 24:9-14 Preface of Holy Week

Hymn of the Day: "Jerusalem the golden" (347)

Prayers: for faithfulness
for confidence in God's care
for courage to confess Christ
for strength to support those who suffer

Color: Red

Thomas Aquinas, Teacher, 1274

Surprisingly little is known with certainty about the life of this influential theologian. Thomas was born of a noble family at Roccasecca, near Aquino in southern Italy, ca. 1225. He was one of nine children. In 1231, at the age of five or six, he was given to the nearby Benedictine monastery of Monte Cassino of which an uncle had been abbot. His parents had planned that he follow in the footsteps of his successful relative. As a monk, he was sent to complete his education at the University of Naples from 1239 to 1244. While there he was introduced to the writings of Aristotle, who was just becoming known again after the "dark ages." One skill that Thomas never learned was good handwriting. His manuscripts are notorious for their near illegibility.

The young monk was drawn to the new Dominican Order of Preachers when he was 19, and toward the end of April 1244, he received the mendicant habit at the Priory of San Domenico in Naples. His family strongly opposed his entrance into this new order of begging monks and brought him home by force. They were, however, unable to change his mind, and by the summer of 1245 he returned to Naples to rejoin the monastery there. In 1245 or 1246 Thomas went to Paris, then to Cologne, where he studied under Albert the Great. (As a student, because he was large in stature and shy by nature, Thomas was dubbed by his fellow students the Dumb Ox.) At Paris a conflict between the mendicant and the secular clergy became so intense that when Thomas finally gave his inaugural lecture as a master, he and his audience had to be protected by soldiers. The university refused to recognize his status, despite papal intervention on his behalf. Thomas and Bonaventure at last were admitted to full magistral privileges August 12, 1257 with the bishop and most of the secular masters conspicuously absent. Thomas returned to Italy in 1259—his biography is unclear at this point—and in 1265 was in charge of a studium at Rome in the priory of Santa Sabina and spent much of his time writing.

According to Bartholomew of Lucca, Thomas composed the Corpus Christi office which was introduced in 1264. The feast had been celebrated for some years earlier in Belgium, however, and the hymns antedate Thomas. Perhaps Thomas, at the command of Pope Urban IV, compiled the office, editing the existing materials.

Thomas returned to Paris by 1269. The old controversy broke out again, this time concerning the traditional Augustinian theology versus the newly discovered Aristotle, as well as the old hostility against the mendicants. The hostility of the traditionalists against Aristotle led the bishop of Paris on December 10, 1270, to condemn eighteen errors in the teaching of what was an exaggerated Aristotelianism.

The atmosphere at Paris was clearly uncongenial to scholarship, so Thomas left for Florence in 1272 to attend a general meeting of the order, and then went to Naples where he taught for the remaining two years of his life. On December 6, 1273 at the conclusion of the St. Nicholas' Mass, he departed from his usual custom of spending the rest of the day after mass writing or teaching, and never again wrote or dictated anything. For whatever reason—stroke, mystical experience, mental breakdown (questioned by his companion Reginald, he is said to have replied, "I cannot go on . . . All that I have written seems to me like so much straw compared to what I have seen and what has been revealed to me")—his productive life was over.

In poor health, he was summoned to the second Council of Lyons, where reconciliation of the Eastern and Western churches was planned. He fell sick on the journey and was taken to the Cistercian

Abbey of Gossanuova near Maenza and died there March 7, 1274, not yet fifty years old. He was canonized in 1323 and since 1567 has been known as the Angelic Doctor.

Thomas' work is one of the great expressions of the relationship between the experienced facts of everyday life and the teaching of Catholic theology. His boldly innovative system attempted to make sense of life without destroying its mystery, and it saved Christian theology from the corroding effects of non-Christian Aristotelian and Arabic philosophy. Finally, Thomas, for all his intellectual gifts, was a man of humility and deep piety.

He is commemorated in the Roman Catholic and Episcopal churches on January 28, the date of the removal of his relics to Toulouse in 1369. He is commemorated then rather than on the date of his "heavenly birthday" so that his commemoration will not conflict with that of Perpetua and her companions. It is for Lutheran churches too a possible alternate date.

Angelus Walz. *Saint Thomas Aquinas: A Biographical Study*, tr. S. Bullough. Westminster, Md.: Newman, 1951.
James A. Weisheipl. *Friar Thomas D'Aquino. His Life, Thought, and Works*. Oxford: Blackwell, 1975.

Reading

(From *Summa Contra Gentiles*, by Thomas Aquinas.)

The pursuit of wisdom is more perfect than all human pursuits, more noble, more useful, more full of joy.

It is more perfect because as one gives oneself to the pursuit of wisdom one even now shares in true beatitude. Therefore a wise man has said, "Happy are those who fix their thoughts on wisdom" (Ecclesiasticus 14:20).

The pursuit of wisdom is more noble because especially through this pursuit one approaches a likeness to God, who made all things by wisdom (Psalm 104:24). And since likeness is the cause of love, the pursuit of wisdom joins humanity to God in friendship. That is why it is said of wisdom, "She is an inexhaustible treasure for humanity, and those who profit by it become God's friends" (Wisdom 7:14).

The pursuit of wisdom is more useful because through wisdom we arrive at the everlasting kingdom: "Honor wisdom so that you may reign forever" (Wisdom 6:21).

The pursuit of wisdom is more full of joy because "there is no bitterness in her company, no pain in life with her, only gladness and joy" (Wisdom 8:16).

And so, in the name of the divine Mercy, I have the confidence to embark upon the work of wisdom, even though this may surpass my powers; and I have set myself the task of making known, so far as my limited powers will permit, the truth that the Catholic faith professes, and of setting aside the errors that are opposed to it. In the words of Hilary, "I am aware that I owe this to God as the chief duty of my life, that every word and sense may speak of him."

(Translation by P.H.P. based on the translation of Anton C. Pegis. It should be understood that the meaning of "Catholic" in this passage is the same as the meaning of "Catholic" in the Apostles' and Nicene Creeds: whole, entire, complete in all its parts. The opposite of Catholic is heretic: a person, faith, or church which accepts only selected parts of the received teaching.)

Propers

ROMAN

(January 28)
God our Father, you made Thomas Aquinas known for his holiness and learning.
Help us to grow in wisdom by his teaching, and in holiness by imitating his faith.
Grant this through our Lord Jesus Christ, your Son, who lives and reigns

LUTHERAN

Almighty God, your Holy Spirit gives to one the word of wisdom, and to another the word of knowledge, and to another the word of faith. We praise you for the gifts of grace imparted to your servant Thomas, and we pray that by his teaching and holiness of life we may be led to a fuller knowledge of the truth

EPISCOPAL

(January 28)
Almighty God, who enriched your Church with the singular learning and holiness of your servant Thomas: Grant us to hold fast and conform our lives to the true doctrine of your Son our Savior Jesus Christ, to the glory of your great Name and the benefit of your holy Church; through Jesus Christ

ROMAN	LUTHERAN	EPISCOPAL
with you and the Holy Spirit, one God, for ever and ever. *(Text from the English translation of the Roman Missal © 1973, International Committee on English in the Liturgy, Inc. All rights reserved.)*	which we have seen in your Son Jesus Christ our Lord.	our Lord, who lives and reigns with you and the Holy Spirit, one God, now and for ever. *(Text from Lesser Feasts and Fasts, Revised Edition, copyright 1973 by Charles Mortimer Guilbert as Custodian of the Standard Book of Common Prayer. All rights reserved. Used by permission.)*
Common of Doctors or Pastors	Common of Theologians: Wisdom 7:7-14 *or* Proverbs 3:1-7 Psalm 119:89-104 1 Corinthians 2:6-10, 13-16 John 17:18-23	Common of a Theologian and teacher I: Psalm 119:33-40 Wisdom 7:7-14 Psalm 119:97-104 1 Corinthians 2:6-10, 13-16 John 17:18-23 Preface of a Saint

Hymn of the Day: "Thee we adore, O hidden Savior" (199)

Prayers: for the spirit of inquiry
for the gift of wisdom
for grace to perceive the mystery of God's presence
for teachers of theology

Color: White

March 12

Gregory the Great, Bishop of Rome, 604

Gregory I, called "the Great," was born in Rome ca. 540 to a distinguished Christian family of senatorial rank. His grandfather had been a pope after he had become a widower. Gregory as a young man had a palace and immense wealth. He was educated in the law and entered civil service. As Prefect of Rome—the chief administrative officer of the city—he presided over the Roman Senate, gathering knowledge of political and business affairs. Shortly after Gregory took office his father died, and not long afterward Gregory became a monk.

About 575 he turned his family home into a monastery dedicated to St. Andrew, provided for the founding of six monasteries on his father's property in Sicily, and gave the surplus of his inheritance to the poor.

He re-entered what he liked to call the turbulence of life in the world when he was ordained deacon by Benedict I. In 579 he was sent as the papal representative to the Byzantine court at Constantinople where he increased his knowledge of the political and religious problems disturbing the empire. (During his stay in Constantinople he lived with the monks who accompanied him and apparently never learned Greek.)

He was recalled to Rome ca. 586 to be a counselor to Pope Pelagius II. It was a troubled time for the city. A plague spread through Rome killing many, including the pope, and Gregory was elected his successor by popular acclaim. His consecration as Bishop of Rome was delayed until the approval of the Byzantine emperor could be secured. Meanwhile, Gregory ministered to the sick and dying in the plague-ridden city and organized penitential processions.

In 592 the Lombards invaded Rome. In the absence of secular leadership, Gregory rallied the people to defend the city and agreed to pay a yearly tribute to save Rome. The Byzantine emperor had refused aid; civil government had failed. The pope was therefore seen by the people as their protector who had assumed responsibility when they had no other helper.

Gregory showed concern for the poor and for justice, insisted upon a high standard of spirituality in church administrators, and reformed the process of raising money from the papal patrimonies so that unjust amounts of money were not collected. He put his stamp upon the liturgy by reviving the "station churches" to which the pope processed and celebrated Mass on certain days; writing some prayers of the Gregorian Sacramentary; changing the second petition in the three-fold Kyrie to "Christ have mercy"; ordering that Alleluia be sung throughout the year except on penitential days; fostering the development of music; emphasizing the importance of the sermon; and fixing the present position of the Our Father in the Mass.

Gregory struggled with the Patriarch of Constantinople who claimed to be the "ecumenical patriarch" and in opposition to him claimed universal jurisdiction for the Bishop of Rome, not as lord but as "servant of the servants of God" (a title not original with Gregory but typical of his approach).

Gregory's use of monks as missionaries to the Anglo-Saxons was his single most influential act in determining the future of Christian culture and institutions. In 597 he sent Augustine of Canterbury and forty monks to evangelize Britain. The story told by Bede is that Gregory saw some fair-haired slaves in Rome and, being told that they were Angles, is said to have replied, "Not Angles but angels" and decided that they must be Christianized.

Gregory is remembered not for the brilliance of his writing or his thought—although his *Pastoral Care* is a classic work on the ministry—but rather as an austere and masterful statesman who ably managed the church in a complex and changing world. And all this was the work of a man who described himself as sickly and who constantly yearned to return to monastic seclusion. Called by some the greatest man of the sixth century, Gregory forms a bridge between the ancient and the medieval worlds, and his episcopate was a model for his successors.

Gregory died March 12, 604. His feast day on the Roman Catholic calendar is September 3, the date of his election as Bishop of Rome. This avoids celebrating his day during Lent. The Episcopal church retains March 12 as the date of his commemoration.

Pierre Battifol. *St. Gregory the Great*, tr. J. Stoddard. New York, 1929.
Frederick Holmes Dudden. *Gregory the Great. His Place in History and Thought*. New York: Russell and Russell, 1967 [1905].
Gregory. *Pastoral Care*, tr. H. Davis. London, 1950.

Reading

(From a sermon on Ezekiel by Gregory the Great.)

Son of man, I have made you a watchman for the house of Israel. Note that a man whom the Lord sends forth as a preacher is called a watchman. A watchman always stands on a height so that he can see from afar what is coming. Anyone appointed to be a watchman for the people must stand on a height for all his life to help them by his foresight.

How hard it is for me to say this, for by these very words I denounce myself. I cannot preach with any competence, and yet insofar as I do succeed, still I myself do not live my life according to my own preaching.

I do not deny my responsibility; I recognize that I am slothful and negligent, but perhaps the acknowledgement of my fault will win me pardon from my just judge. Indeed when I was in the monastery I could curb my idle talk and usually be absorbed in my prayers. Since I assumed the burden of pastoral care, my mind can no longer be collected; it is concerned with so many matters.

I am forced to consider the affairs of the Church and of the monasteries. I must weigh the lives and acts of individuals. I am responsible for the concerns of our citizens. I must worry about the invasions of roving bands of barbarians, and beware of the wolves who lie in wait for my flock. I must become an administrator lest the religious go in want. I must put up with certain robbers without losing patience and at times I must deal with them in all charity.

With my mind divided and torn to pieces by so many problems, how can I meditate or preach wholeheartedly without neglecting the ministry of proclaiming the Gospel? Moreover, in my position I must often communicate with worldly men. At times I let my tongue run, for if I am always severe in my judgments, the worldly will avoid me, and I can never attack them as I would. As a result I often listen patiently to chatter. And because I too am weak, I find myself drawn little by little into idle conversation, and I begin to talk freely about matters which once I would have avoided. What once I found tedious I now enjoy.

So who am I to be a watchman, for I do not stand on the mountain of action but lie down in the valley of weakness? Truly the all-powerful Creator and Redeemer of mankind can give me in spite of my weaknesses a higher life and effective speech; because I love him, I do not spare myself in speaking of him.

Propers

ROMAN

(September 3)
Father,
you guide your people
with kindness
and govern us with
love.
By the prayers of
Saint Gregory
give the spirit of
wisdom
to those you have
called
to lead your Church.
May the growth of
your people in
holiness
be the eternal joy of
our shepherds.
We ask this through
our Lord Jesus
Christ, your Son,
who lives and reigns
with you and the
Holy Spirit,
one God, for ever and
ever.

(Text from the English translation of the Roman Missal © 1973, International Committee on English in the Liturgy, Inc. All rights reserved.)

Common of Pastors
(for a pope)
or Doctors:
Matthew 16:13-19
or John 21:15-17

LUTHERAN

Heavenly Father, shepherd of your people, we thank you for your servant Gregory, who was faithful in the care and nurture of your flock; and we pray that, following his example and the teaching of his holy life, we may by your grace grow into the full stature of our Lord and Savior Jesus Christ.

Common of Pastors:
Ezekiel 34:11-16
Psalm 84
1 Peter 5:1-4
John 21:15-17

EPISCOPAL

Almighty and merciful God, who raised up Gregory to be a servant of the servants of God, by whose zeal the English people were brought into the knowledge of the Catholic and Apostolic faith: Preserve in your Church a thankful remembrance of his devotion; that your people, being fruitful in every good work, may receive with him and your servants everywhere the crown of glory that never fades away; through Jesus Christ our Lord, who lives and reigns with you and the Holy Spirit, one God, now and for ever.

(Text from Lesser Feasts and Fasts, Revised Edition, copyright 1973 by Charles Mortimer Guilbert as Custodian of the Standard Book of Common Prayer. All rights reserved. Used by permission.)

Psalm 27:1-8
Ecclesiasticus 47:8-11
Psalm 43
Mark 10:42-45
Preface of Apostles

Hymn of the Day: "O Christ our king, creator, Lord" (101)

Prayers: for the poor
for social justice
for renewed appreciation of the liturgy
for a spirit of service

for harried pastors and administrators, distracted by
    many concerns
Color: White

Patrick, Bishop, Missionary to Ireland, 461

Patrick, (Patricius) the Apostle of Ireland, was born ca. 389 in
Roman Britain, the son of the alderman and later deacon Calpornius.
He was a man of action with little inclination toward learning. The
details of his biography are uncertain. At the age of sixteen, while
staying at his father's country estate, he was seized by Irish raiders
and sold as a slave in Ireland. He was a shepherd there for six years
until he managed to escape, find a ship, and eventually reach home.
His experience had been a spiritual conversion, and he now had a
certain conviction of his vocation: he was to preach the faith to the
Irish people. He studied for the priesthood on the continent. His superiors did not favor his mission to Ireland, apparently because of
his deficient education, but upon the death in 431 of Bishop Palladius
who had been sent by Pope Celestine to the Irish, Patrick was named
his successor and was consecrated bishop for Ireland.

His mission concentrated on the west and north of Ireland where
the Gospel had not been preached before. He secured the protection
of local kings and travelled extensively making many converts and
founding monasteries. The clergy for the country were first brought
from Gaul and Britain but increasingly they were drawn from the
native converts. The claim of Armagh to be Patrick's church, although
not recorded before the seventh century, seems to be genuine.

Patrick was criticized by the British when he demanded the excommunication of the British Prince Coroticus, who, in a retaliatory
raid on Ireland, killed some of Patrick's converts and sold others into
slavery. Despite physical danger and harassment, his was a vigorously heroic life. He died at Down in 461.

Ludwig Bieler. *The Life and Legend of St. Patrick*. Dublin, 1942.
————. St. Patrick and the Coming of Christianity. Dublin: M. H. Gill, 1967.
James Carney. *The Problem of St. Patrick*. Dublin: Dublin Institute, 1961.
R. P. C. Hanson. *St. Patrick: His Origins and Career*. New York: Oxford,
    1968.

Eoin MacNeill. *St. Patrick, Apostle of Ireland* 2nd ed., ed. J. Ryan. London: Burns & Oates, 1964.

Reading

(From the confession of Saint Patrick)

I give unceasing thanks to my God, who kept me faithful *in the day of my testing*. Today I can offer him sacrifice with confidence, giving myself as *a living victim* to Christ, who *kept me safe through all my trials*. I can say now: *Who am I, Lord,* and what is my calling, that you worked through me with such divine power? You did all this so that today *among the Gentiles* I might constantly *rejoice* and *glorify your name* wherever I may be, both in prosperity and in adversity. You did it so that, whatever happened to me, I might accept good and evil equally, always giving thanks to God. God showed me how to have faith in him for ever, as one who is never to be doubted. He answered my prayer in such a way that *in the last days*, ignorant though I am, I might be bold enough to take up so holy and so wonderful a task, and imitate in some degree those whom the Lord had so long ago foretold as heralds of his Gospel, *bearing witness to all nations*.

How did I get this wisdom, that was not mine before? I did not know *the number of my days,* or have knowledge of God. How did so great and salutary a gift come to me, the gift of knowing and loving God, though at the cost of homeland and family? I came to the Irish people to preach the Gospel and endure the taunts of unbelievers, putting up with reproaches about my earthly pilgrimage, suffering many persecutions, *even bondage,* and losing my birthright of freedom for the benefit of others.

If I am worthy, *I am ready* also to give up *my life,* without hesitation and most willingly, for his name. I want to *spend myself* in that country, *even in death,* if the Lord should grant me this favor. I am deeply in his debt, for he gave me the great grace that through me many people should be reborn in God, and then made perfect by confirmation and everywhere among them clergy ordained for a people so recently coming to believe, one people gathered by the Lord *from the ends of the earth.* As God had prophesied of old through the

prophets: *The nations shall come to you from the ends of the earth,
and say: How false are the idols made by our fathers: they are useless.* In another prophecy he said: *I have set you as a light among the
nations, to bring salvation to the ends of the earth.*

It is among that people that I want to *wait for the promise* made
by him, who assuredly never tells a lie. He makes this promise in his
Gospel: *They shall come from the east and west, and sit down with
Abraham, Isaac, and Jacob.* This is our faith: believers are to come
from the whole world.

From the English translation of the Office of Readings from the Liturgy
of the Hours © 1974, International Committee on English in the Liturgy,
Inc. All rights reserved. (The italicized phrases are biblical quotations and
borrowings.)

Propers

ROMAN

God our Father,
you sent Saint Patrick
to preach your glory
to the people of
Ireland.
By the help of his
prayers,
may all Christians
proclaim your love
to all men.
Grant this through our
Lord Jesus Christ,
your Son,
who lives and reigns
with you and the
Holy Spirit,
one God, for ever and
ever.

*(Text from the English
translation of the Roman
Missal © 1973, Interna-
tional Committee on Eng-
lish in the Liturgy, Inc.
All rights reserved.)*

LUTHERAN

God of grace and might,
we praise you for your servant Patrick, to whom you
gave gifts to make the good
news known to the people
of Ireland. Raise up, we
pray, in every country, heralds and evangelists of
your kingdom, so that the
world may know the im-
measurable riches of our
Savior, Jesus Christ our
Lord.

EPISCOPAL

Almighty God, who in
your providence chose
your servant Patrick to
be the apostle of the
Irish people, to bring
those who were wan-
dering in darkness and
error to the true light
and knowledge of
you: Grant us so to
walk in that light, that
we may come at last
to the light of ever-
lasting life; through
Jesus Christ your Son
our Lord, who lives
and reigns with you
and the Holy Spirit,
one God, now and for-
ever.

*(Text from Lesser Feasts
and Fasts, Revised Edi-
tion, copyright 1973 by
Charles Mortimer Guilbert
as Custodian of the Stan-
dard Book of Common
Prayer. All rights reserved.
Used by permission.)*

ROMAN	LUTHERAN	EPISCOPAL
Common of Pastors (for Missionaries) Isaiah 52:7-10 1 Corinthians 1:18-25 Matthew 28:16-20 *or* Mark 16:15-20 *or* Luke 5:1-11	Common of Missionaries: Isaiah 62:1-7 Psalm 48 Romans 10:11-17 Luke 24:44-53	Psalm 131 Revelation 22:1-5 Psalm 119:73-80 Matthew 5:43-48 Preface of Apostles

Hymn of the Day: "I bind unto myself today" (188)

Prayers: for the church and people of Ireland
        for missionaries in physical danger and harassment
        for zeal in God's service
        for renewed respect for the natural world

Preface: Epiphany

Color: White

March 19

Joseph, Guardian of Our Lord

No fully historical account of even a part of Joseph's life is possible, for he left only a faint imprint on the tradition. He is not mentioned in Mark's gospel; John mentions but his name as Jesus' father (1:45; 6:42—"Jesus son of Joseph").

Genealogies of Matthew 1:2-16 and Luke 3:23-38, although different, both trace Joseph's ancestry through David and are concerned with showing that Joseph was Jesus' legal father. While Matthew and Luke agree that Joseph's historical connections were with Bethlehem, Matthew implies that Joseph was a resident of Bethlehem who settled in Nazareth to avoid living under Archelaus in Judea (2:22-23), while Luke says that he lived in Nazareth before the birth of Jesus and went to Bethlehem according to the requirement of the enrollment (2:1ff; 39).

Joseph is an accessory figure in the infancy narratives who was present at the birth of Jesus (Luke 2:16), the circumcision (2:21), the presentation (2:22), and the search for Jesus in the temple (2:41-52). His trade was that of a carpenter (Matt. 13:55)—although the Greek term could mean simply "artisan"—as was Jesus' also (Mark

6:3). Joseph is portrayed as a "just" man (Matt. 1:19), i.e. a devout adherent to the Law; one who was kind and wise, like the patriarchs gladly responding to visionary dreams; a faithful and affectionate father to Jesus.

He was apparently alive when Jesus' ministry began (Matt. 13:55), but we do not hear of him again. Presumably he had died by the time of the crucifixion, so that Jesus commended his mother to the care of the Beloved Disciple (John 19:26-27), a gesture that would have been unnecessary if Mary's husband had been alive. Yet the usual portrayal of Joseph as an old man is not supported by the Gospels; it begins rather in the second century in a gospel attributed to James the Less. A fifth century *History of Joseph the Carpenter* says that Joseph was widowed at 89 and that Mary became his ward when he was 91.

The first known commemoration of Joseph occurs in an eighth century calendar from northern France or Belgium, which for March 20 lists Joseph and calls him "spouse of Mary." (He is still identified on the Roman Catholic calendar as "husband of Mary.") In the early ninth century calendars Joseph is commemorated on March 19; the reason for the change of date is unknown. The celebration was introduced in Rome about 1479 and, especially since the fifteenth century, its popularity has greatly increased. In 1955 the Roman Catholic Church added on May 1 the commemoration of St. Joseph the Worker as a response to the Socialist May Day in honor of labor. The Feast of the Holy Family on the Sunday with the octave of Christmas (or if there is no Sunday within the octave, on December 30) also commemorates the parents of Jesus.

In the Eastern churches, Joseph is grouped with the patriarchs of the Old Testament. He is the last of that line, which culminates in Jesus the "pioneer and perfecter of our faith" (Heb. 12:2), and when Joseph flees to Egypt with his family, he recapitulates the pilgrimage of the patriarch Joseph as a preparation for the new exodus and the Christian Passover. (Gen. 37; 50:22-26; Hos. 11:1; Matt. 2:13-23).

St. Joseph is regarded as a patron saint of Canada.

Raymond E. Brown. *The Birth of the Messiah*. Garden City, N.Y.: Doubleday, 1977.

R. Bulbeck, "The Doubt of St. Joseph," *Catholic Biblical Quarterly* X (1948) 296-309.

F. L. Filas, S. J. *The Man Nearest to Christ. The Nature and Historic Development of Devotion to St. Joseph*. Milwaukee: Bruce, 1944.

Reading

(From a sermon by Bernardine of Siena)

There is a general rule concerning all special graces granted to any human being. Whenever the divine favor chooses someone to receive a special grace, or to accept a lofty vocation, God adorns the person chosen with all the gifts of the Spirit needed to fulfill the task at hand.

This general rule is especially verified in the case of Saint Joseph, the foster-father of our Lord and the husband of the Queen of our world, enthroned above the angels. He was chosen by the eternal Father as the trustworthy guardian and protector of his greatest treasures, namely, his divine Son and Mary, Joseph's wife. He carried out this vocation with complete fidelity until at last God called him, saying, *Good and faithful servant, enter into the joy of your Lord.*

What then is Joseph's position in the whole Church of Christ? Is he not a man chosen and set apart? Through him and, yes, under him, Christ was fittingly and honorably introduced into the world. Holy Church in its entirety is indebted to the Virgin Mother because through her it was judged worthy to receive Christ. But after her we undoubtedly owe special gratitude and reverence to Saint Joseph.

In him the Old Testament finds its fitting close. He brought the noble line of patriarchs and prophets to its promised fulfillment. What the divine goodness had offered as a promise to them, he held in his arms.

From the English translation of the Office of Readings from the Liturgy of the Hours © 1974, International Committee on English in the Liturgy, Inc. All rights reserved.

Propers

ROMAN	LUTHERAN	EPISCOPAL
Father, you entrusted our Savior to the care of Saint Joseph. By the help of his prayers	Lord God, you have surrounded us with so great a cloud of witnesses. Grant that we, encouraged by the	O God, who from the family of your servant David raised up Joseph to be the guardian of your incarnate Son and the spouse of

March 22

ROMAN	LUTHERAN	EPISCOPAL
may your Church continue to serve its Lord, Jesus Christ, who lives and reigns with you and the Holy Spirit, one God, for ever and ever.	example of your servant Joseph, may persevere in the course that is set before us, to be living signs of the Gospel and at last, with all the saints, to share in your eternal joy; through your Son, Jesus Christ our Lord. common of saints or:	his virgin mother: Give us grace to imitate his uprightness of life and his obedience to your commands; through Jesus Christ our Lord, who lives and reigns with you and the Holy Spirit, one God, for ever and ever.

2 Samuel 7:4-5a, 12-14a, 16 Psalm 89:2-5, 27, 29 Romans 4:13, 16-18, 22 Matthew 1:16, 18-21, 24a *or* Luke 2:41-51a	*2 Samuel 7:4, 8-16* *Psalm 89:1-29* *Romans 4:13-18* *Luke 2:41-52*	2 Samuel 7:4, 8-16 Psalm 89:1-29 *or* 89:1-4, 26-29 Romans 4:13-18 Luke 2:41-52 Preface of the Epiphany

Hymn of the Day: "Our Father, by whose name" (357)

Prayers: for quiet confidence
for humble service
for those who work with their hands: artisans and laborers
of thanksgiving for the patriarchs and prophets

Preface: Lent

Color: White

Jonathan Edwards, Teacher, Missionary to the American Indians, 1758

Jonathan Edwards, an important thinker who influenced theology not only in America but in Britain as well, was born in East Windsor, Connecticut October 5, 1703. He was the fifth of eleven children and the only son of his father, who was the pastor of the Congregational church there. After a rigorous education at home, the son enrolled at Yale when he was thirteen and received the B.A. in 1720. He continued in the study of divinity there for a time before a short pastorate in New York, August 1722-May 1723. He returned to Yale for the M.A. which he received in 1723 and stayed on again as tutor until 1726 when he became the assistant to his grandfather Samuel Stoddard at Northampton, the most important church in Massachusetts outside Boston. He was ordained February 22, 1727. Five months later he married the seventeen-year-old Sarah Pierrepont; they were to have eleven children. In 1729 he succeeded his grandfather as pastor of the Northampton church.

As a young man he had already shown remarkable powers of observation and analysis and a wide variety of interests. At the age of fourteen—before any other American thinker—he had discovered in Locke's *Essay Concerning Human Understanding* a new theory of knowledge and a psychology that he was able later to use in support of traditional Calvinist doctrines. He had passionately worked through intellectual objections to his theological heritage and in a conversion experience early in 1721 had discovered a "delightful conviction" of divine sovereignty. He joined his profound learning with mystical experience and remarkable gifts in logic.

Edwards became convinced that the ills of the time were attributable to Arminianism, a popular theological position which minimized original sin, stressed free will, and tended to make morality the essence of religion. He preached a series of sermons on justification by faith alone in November 1734, which resulted in a revival of religion in the Connecticut valley in 1734-1735. Edwards reported the events in *A Faithful Narrative of the Surprising Work of God* (1737) in which he examined the several kinds of conversion experience.

Shortly after this revival of religion, the preaching of George Whitefield, the English Methodist evangelist, and Gilbert Tennant, a New Jersey Presbyterian preacher, led to the Great Awakening, 1740-1742. This widespread revival was defended by Edwards, notably in *A Treatise Concerning Religious Affections* (1746) in which he maintained that the essence of all religion lies in holy love which proves itself by practical results.

Despite the increasing reputation of the pastor (and in some measure perhaps because of it) Edwards' relations with his congregation had become strained. Edwards restricted admission to the Holy Communion to the converted and so opposed the more liberal policies of his grandfather who had accepted the "Halfway Covenant" which allowed those who were baptized but not clearly converted to share the Lord's Supper and have their children baptized. Edwards' position was more in keeping with the situation of the Congregational church after disestablishment and the position eventually triumphed. Edwards himself, however, was dismissed by his congregation. He preached a dignified and moving farewell sermon July 1, 1750 and went to the frontier at Stockbridge, Massachusetts to be a missionary to the Indians. Despite difficulties with the language, sickness, conflict with personal enemies, and Indian wars, he nonetheless was able to publish his *Freedom of the Will* (1754) and the *Great Christian Doctrine of Original Sin Defended* (1758).

Late in 1757 Edwards accepted the presidency of the College of New Jersey (later Princeton University) and took up his duties in January. Princeton was at the time suffering from an outbreak of smallpox. Edwards was innoculated but suffered from a secondary infection and died March 22, 1758.

A. C. Aldridge. *Jonathan Edwards.* New York: Washington Square Press, 1966.
Clarence E. Faust and Thomas H. Johnson eds. *Jonathan Edwards: Representative Selections,* rev. ed. New York: Hill and Wang, 1962.
Perry Miller. *Jonathan Edwards.* New York: Sloane, 1949.
Ola Elizabeth Winslow. *Jonathan Edwards.* New York: Macmillan, 1940.

Reading

(From Jonathan Edwards' *Personal Narrative.*)

The sense I had of divine things would often of a sudden kindle up, as it were, a sweet burning in my heart; an ardor of soul, that I know not how to express.

Not long after I began to experience these things, I gave an account to my father of some things that had passed in my mind. I was pretty much affected by the discourse we had together; and when the discourse was ended, I walked abroad alone, in a solitary place in my father's pasture for contemplation. And as I was walking there and looking up on the sky and clouds, there came into my mind so sweet a sense of the glorious *majesty* and *grace* of God, that I know not how to express. I seemed to see them both in a sweet conjunction; majesty and meekness joined together; it was a gentle, and holy majesty; and also a majestic meekness; a high, great, and holy gentleness.

After this my sense of divine things gradually increased, and became more and more lively, and had more of that inward sweetness. The appearance of everything was altered; there seemed to be, as it were, a calm, sweet cast, or appearance of divine glory, in almost every thing. God's excellency, his wisdom, his purity, and love, seemed to appear in every thing; in the sun, moon, and stars; in the clouds, and blue sky; in the grass, flowers, trees; in the water, and all nature; which used greatly to fix my mind. I often used to sit and view the moon for continuance; and in the day, spent much time in viewing the clouds and sky, to behold the sweet glory of God in these things; in the mean time, singing forth, with a low voice, my contemplations of the Creator and Redeemer. And scarce any thing, among all the works of nature, was so delightful to me as thunder and lightning; formerly, nothing had been so terrible to me. Before, I used to be uncommonly terrified with thunder, and to be struck with terror when I saw a thunder storm rising; but now, on the contrary, it rejoiced me. I felt God, so to speak, at the first appearance of a thunder storm; and used to take the opportunity, at such times, to fix myself in order to view the clouds, and see the lightnings play, and hear the majestic and awful voice of God's thunder, which oftentimes was exceedingly entertaining, leading me to sweet contemplations of my great and glorious God. While thus engaged, it always seemed natural to me to sing, or chant for my meditations; or, to speak my thoughts in soliloquies with a singing voice.

From *The Works of President Edwards* ed. S. B. Dwight, vol. I (New York: Converse, 1829) 60-62.

Propers: Theologians (or Missionaries)

Hymn of the Day: "My God, how wonderful thou art" (524)
   or "Eternal God, whose power upholds" *(SBH* 322;
   WS 748)

March 25

Prayers: for a deepened sense of the majesty of God
        for the spirit of inquiry
        for an awakened conscience

Color: White

THE ANNUNCIATION OF OUR LORD

The celebration of the angel's announcement to Mary that she was to become the mother of the Savior seems to have originated in the East in the fifth century, where it is called *evangelismos,* the good news. The festival was introduced in the West during the sixth and seventh centuries and was universally celebrated by the time of the Tenth Synod of Toledo in 656. The date of March 25 is practically universal, but some churches in Spain kept the commemoration on December 18. In the eleventh century Spain accepted the traditional date but retained the December date also, so that the Annunciation was celebrated twice. In the eighteenth century Rome made December 18 "The Expectation of the Blessed Virgin of the Birth" of Christ.

The observance of March 25, exactly nine months before Christmas, presents problems, for the day always falls in Lent, when joyful celebration seems out of place, and often in Holy Week, when the celebration must be postponed until after Easter week. Periodically therefore the suggestion is made that the day be moved to a time in Advent, closer to Christmas, when the church is anticipating the coming of Christ, but as yet the suggestion has not been accepted.

In the Middle Ages it was thought that, following a mystical conjunction of events, March 25 was the day on which creation began, the day on which the incarnation began, and the day on which Christ was crucified; so the great doctrines of creation, incarnation, and atonement were brought together. The Annunciation was therefore observed at New Year's Day for much of Christian Europe from the sixth century down even to the eighteenth century.

Although the festival is often associated with Mary (it is called "Lady Day" in England), in its origins, the day is a festival of the

Lord; the oldest titles for the day are "Annunciation of the Lord" and the "Conception of Christ."

The Moravian Church observes this date as the Festival of All the Choirs. That observance suggests the possibility of a celebration in honor of those who have served the church through music, which joins the songs of earth with the praises of the heavenly chorus.

Reading

(From Athanasius, *On the Incarnation.*)

. . . the incorporeal and incorruptible and immaterial Word of God comes to our realm, howbeit he was not far from us before. For no part of creation is left void of him: he has filled all things everywhere, remaining present with his own Father. But he comes in condecension to show loving-kindness upon us, and to visit us. And seeing the race of rational creatures in the way to perish, and death reigning over them; seeing, too, that the threat against transgression gave a firm hold to the corruption which was upon us, and that it was monstrous that before the law was fulfilled it should fall through; seeing, once more, the unseemliness of what was to come to pass: that the things whereof he himself was artificer were passing away; seeing, further, the exceeding wickedness of men, and how by little and little they had increased it to an intolerable pitch against themselves; and seeing, lastly, how all men were under penalty of death, he took pity on our race, and had mercy on our infirmity, and condescended to our corruption, and, unable to bear that death should have the mastery—lest the creature should perish, and his Father's handiwork in men be spent for nought—he takes unto himself a body, and that of no different sort than ours.

For he did not simply will to become embodied, or will merely to appear. For if he willed merely to appear, he was able to effect his divine appearance by some other and higher means as well. But he takes a body of our kind, and not merely so, but from a spotless and stainless virgin, knowing not a man, a body clean and in very truth pure from intercourse of men. For being himself mighty, and artificer of everything, he prepares the body in the virgin as a temple unto himself, and makes it his very own as an instrument, in it manifested, and in it dwelling. And thus taking from our bodies one of like nature, because all were under penalty of the corruption of death he gave it over to death in the stead of all, and offered it to the Father—doing this, moreover, of his loving-kindness, to the end that, firstly, all being held to have died in him, the law involving the ruin of men might be undone (inasmuch as its power was fully spent in the Lord's body, and had no longer holding ground against men, his peers), and that, secondly, whereas men had turned toward corruption, he might turn them again toward incorruption, and quicken them from death by the appropriation of his body and by the grace of the resurrection, banishing death from them like straw from the fire.

From *Christology of the Later Fathers*, Vol. III, The Library of Christian Classics, ed. by Edward Rochie Hardy and Cyril C. Richardson, 62-63. Published in the U.S.A. by The Westminster Press, 1954. Used by permission.

Propers

ROMAN	LUTHERAN	EPISCOPAL

ROMAN

God our Father, your Word became man and was born of the Virgin Mary. May we become more like Jesus Christ, whom we acknowledge as our redeemer, God and man. We ask this through our Lord Jesus Christ, your Son, who lives and reigns with you and the Holy Spirit, one God, for ever and ever.

LUTHERAN

Pour your grace into our hearts, O Lord, that we who have known the incarnation of your Son Jesus Christ, announced by an angel, may be his cross and passion be brought to the glory of his resurrection; through your Son, Jesus Christ our Lord, who lives and reigns with you and the Holy Spirit, one God, now and forever.

EPISCOPAL

Pour your grace into our hearts, O Lord, that we who have known the incarnation of your Son Jesus Christ, announced by an angel to the Virgin Mary, may by his cross and passion be brought to the glory of his resurrection; who lives and reigns with you, in the unity of the Holy Spirit, one God, now and for ever.

ROMAN	LUTHERAN	EPISCOPAL
Isaiah 7:10-14	Isaiah 7:10-14; 8:10c	Isaiah 7:10-14
Psalm 40:7-11	Psalm 45	Psalm 40:1-11
Hebrews 10:4-10	1 Timothy 3:16	*or* 40:5-10
Luke 1:26-38	Luke 1:26-38	*or* Magnificat
		Hebrews 10:5-10
		Luke 1:26-38
		Preface of the Epiphany

Hymn of the Day: "The advent of our God" (22)
　　　　　　or "Blest are the pure in heart" (*SBH* 394)

Prayers: for purity of heart
　　　　for obedience to the word of God
　　　　for joyful submission to the will of God

Preface: Christmas

Color: White

March 29

Hans Nielsen Hauge
Renewer of the Church, 1824

Hans Nielsen Hauge was born April 3, 1771 on a farm in Rolfsøen in southeastern Norway, about fifty miles from Oslo. His father, Niels Mikkelsen was a farmer, and the farm was known as "Hauge Gaard" from which Hans Nielsen took his surname. The family was deeply concerned with their Christian faith, having regular family prayers and daily Bible reading, and from time to time attending lay religious meetings in the village. As a young boy Hauge thought deeply about religious matters and was troubled with a fear that he would not go to heaven when he died. This fear intensified through several experiences that brought him face to face with death.

Hauge never had much formal education, but he became very skilled in practical tasks such as carpentry and the repair of mechanical things. Acting as village handyman and helping on the family farm, Hauge also became experienced in business affairs, and all of his life he not only was able to support himself while engaging in religious work but also was able to assist others in their everyday affairs.

He worked for a time in Fredrikstad where the temptations he encountered made him aware of the conflict between God and the world. As a young man his first interest was religion. He read deeply in Lutheran catechetical and devotional literature and participated in the worship of the parish church and in private prayer meetings. He spoke to others so frequently about their faith that his companions called him "holy".

His parents called him home to work on their farm, and it was while working there on April 5, 1796 that he had a mystical experience that set the course of his life. He felt suddenly at peace about his own salvation and felt sure of his call to preach to his countrymen. He launched a one-man preaching crusade, beginning in his own community and then travelling through all Norway and visiting Denmark in 1800. He also wrote about his faith, eventually producing some thirty books, of which the best known is his *Reiser og Vigtigste Haendsler* (Journeys and Important Events). The central concept of his preaching and writing was what he called "the living faith," the personal commitment to the Lord which transforms the believer's life.

He encountered stern opposition, for it was thought unprecedented that a farm boy should teach religion, an area traditionally reserved for the clergy. He was in violation of the Ordinance of 13th January 1741 which required that the local pastor be informed of the time and place of any religious meetings to be held within his parish. The pastor was obliged to attend and had authority to forbid such meetings. Only a few people were permitted to gather, the meetings had to be held during the day, men and women were to meet in separate places, and it was forbidden that laypeople travel about and preach. The church authorities were opposed to Hauge because some thought that he laid too much stress on good works; the civil authorities were opposed to him because some feared he would stir up a peasants' revolt. After repeated arrests he was taken into custody in 1804 to be held for full investigation, and his imprisonment lasted ten years. In prison, in the absence of Christian fellowship, Hauge's faith weakened. In 1809 he was released from prison to work on a project to extract salt from sea water (war with England had cut off supplies of salt by ship). He was arrested again, although he was permitted more freedom than before. In 1811 he was permitted to move to a small farm just outside Christiana called Bakkehaugen. In December 1813 he was sentenced to two years at hard labor and the costs of the trial for breaking the Ordinance of 13th January 1741 and for "invectives" against the clergy.

On January 27, 1815 Hauge married Andrea Nyhus, the house-keeper at his farm. She died leaving an infant son, Andreas. In 1817 Hauge married Ingeborg Oldsdatter who bore him three sons, all of whom died young. Hauge moved to another farm, Bredvedt where he was visited by his friends among whom by now some bishops were numbered. His health broken after his long ordeal, Hauge died at 4 a.m. on March 29, 1824. He is buried in the cemetery at Aker Church in Oslo where his grave is marked:

> He lived in the Lord,
> He died in the Lord,
> And by the grace of Christ he partakes of salvation.

Since Hauge's influence in Norway was at its peak during the period of greatest Norwegian immigration to America, the Haugean spirit was one of the mainstreams of Norwegian-American Lutheranism. It was an important force in the growth of the church and in deepening the spiritual life of the laity. The Hauge Lutheran Synod, established in 1846 merged in 1917 with other Norwegian Lutheran bodies. A few churches in North America are named for him.

Andreas Aarflot. *Hans Nielsen Hauge: His Life and Message*. Minneapolis: Augsburg, 1979.

G. Everett Arden. *Four Northern Lights. Men Who Shaped the Scandinavian Churches*. Minneapolis: Augsburg, 1964. [Ruotsalainen, Hauge, Grundtvig, Rosenius].

M. Arntzen. *The Apostle of Norway, Hans Nielsen Hauge*. Minneapolis: Lutheran Free Church Publishing Co., 1933.

Hans Nielsen Hauge. *Autobiographical Writings* tr. Joel M. Njus. Minneapolis: Augsburg, 1954.

E. C. Nelson and E. L. Fevold. *The Lutheran Church Among Norwegian-Americans*. 2 vols. Minneapolis: Augsburg, 1960.

Joseph Shaw. *Pulpit Under the Sky. A Life of Hans Nielsen Hauge*. Minneapolis: Augsburg, 1955.

Reading

(From Hauge's *Autobiography*, April 5, 1796.)

The desire to please God grew more and more. In prayer to Him, I would kneel in heartfelt unworthiness of the great goodness He had shown me, ashamed because I had not served the Lord as I ought. Sometimes I fell on my knees and prayed almighty God for the sake of His Son to establish me on the spiritual rock, Christ Jesus. For I believed that then even the gates of hell would be powerless against me. I called upon the God of my salvation to reveal His Son's love in me and grant His Holy Spirit to expose my wretchedness and impotence and teach me the way I should walk in order to follow in the footsteps of Christ.

One day while I was working outside under the open sky, I sang from memory the hymn, "Jesus, I Long for Thy Blessed Communion." I had just sung the second verse:

> Mightily strengthen my spirit within me,
> That I may learn what Thy Spirit can do;
> Oh, take Thou captive each passion and win me,
> Lead Thou and guide me my whole journey through!
> All that I am and possess I surrender,
> If Thou alone in my spirit mayest dwell,
> Everything yield Thee, O Savior most tender,
> Thou, only Thou, canst my sadness dispel.

At this point my mind became so exalted that I was not myself aware of, nor can I express, what took place in my soul. For I was beside myself. As soon as I came to my senses, I was filled with regret that I had not served this loving transcendentally good God. Now it seemed to me that nothing in this world was worthy of any regard. That my soul experienced something supernatural, divine, and blessed; that there was a glory that no tongue can utter—that I remember as clearly as if it had happened only a few days ago. And it is now nearly twenty years since the love of God visited me so abundantly.

Nor can anyone argue this away from me. For I know all the good that followed in my spirit from that hour, especially a deep, burning love to God and my neighbor. I know that I received an entirely changed mind, a sorrow for sin and a desire that other people should become partakers with me of the same grace. I know that I was given a special desire to read the holy Scriptures, especially Jesus' own teachings. At the same time I received new light to understand the Word and to bring together the teachings of all men of God to one focal point: that Christ has come for our salvation, that we should by His Spirit be born again, repent, and be sanctified more and more in accord with God's attributes to serve the triune God alone, in order that our souls may be refined and prepared for eternal blessedness.

It was as if I saw the whole world submerged in evil. I grieved much over this and prayed God that He would withhold punishment so that some might repent. Now I wanted very much to serve God. I asked Him to reveal to me what I should do. The answer echoed in my heart, "You shall confess My name before the people; exhort them to repent and seek Me while I may be found and call upon Me while I am near; and touch their hearts that they may turn from darkness to light."

From Hans Nielsen Hauge, *Autobiographical Writings* tr. Joel M. Njus (Minneapolis: Augsburg, 1954) 41-43.

Propers: Renewers of the Church

Hymn of the Day: "In heaven above, in heaven above" (330)
(The tune *I himmelen, I himmelen* is called *Hauge* in SBH.)

Prayers: for lay readers and preachers
for those persecuted for the exercise of their faith
for confidence and courage
for deepened spiritual life
for growth in grace

Color: White

John Donne, Priest, 1631

John Donne (his last name rhymes with "sun") was born in London in 1572, the son of a prosperous iron monger of an old Roman Catholic family at a time when anti-Catholic feeling was at its height. His father died in 1576. From 1584 to 1594 Donne studied at Oxford, Cambridge, and the Inns of Court where barristers got their training, and before 1596 travelled in France, Spain, and Italy. During these years his adherence to the Roman Catholic Church seems to have weakened, and he began to study the claims of the churches of the Reformation. He probably became an Anglican by the end of the century.

With Raleigh and Essex he took part in hit and run naval expeditions to Cadiz in 1596 and to the Azores in 1597. In 1598 he became secretary to Sir Thomas Egerton and seemingly was set for a career in public service. He entered Elizabeth's last Parliament in 1601. He secretly married the sixteen-year-old niece of Egerton, Anne More. Furious at this breach of convention, Anne's father had Donne dismissed and imprisoned on the charge of marrying a minor without parental consent. His career ruined and his money gone ("John Donne, Anne Donne, Undone" he wrote), they were forced to live on the generosity of friends. He studied canon and civil law and travelled on the Continent again. Although his circle of influential friends grew, he was unable to secure state employment. It was a time of debt, illness, frustration, and inner conflict.

In 1610 Donne contributed to the controversy between the Church of England and the Jesuits, urging English Roman Catholics to take the oath of allegiance to the crown. Donne still had secular hopes and won the king's favor, but after another trip to the Continent with Sir Robert and Lady Drury, his hopes of civil employment were again dashed. In 1614 Donne entered Parliament, but the king dissolved Parliament within two months. Donne made one more application for state employment, but the king refused the petition, indicating that he wanted Donne to enter the church. Donne was ordained in 1615.

He was appointed royal chaplain and was entrusted with diplomatic correspondence on a mission to Germany. His fame as a preacher grew, for the pulpit seemed to release anew the creative energies that earlier found expression in his poetry. In 1621 he was considered the most renowned preacher of the time and was appointed Dean of St. Paul's Cathedral in London.

A serious illness in 1623, from which he nearly died, was the occasion for the composition of his *Devotions*. He was able to return to a strenuous life of preaching, administration, and pastoral care. But in 1630 he was sick again, and on the first Friday in Lent, 1631, he preached what he knew was to be his last sermon, his funeral sermon. In March he had an artist sketch him in his shroud for his contemplation in his last days and for a design for his funeral monument. He died March 31, 1631, and was buried in his church with a marble monument that survived the fire of 1666 and the bombing of 1941.

His poetry is divided into the secular poems, with their passion and intellectual wit, an intensity and excitement unrivaled in English poetry; and his divine poetry, much of which was composed before he took orders. In his poetry he is constantly preoccupied with the interrelationship of spiritual and the physical, presenting amorous experience in religious terms and presenting devotional experiences in erotic terms. His religious prose, written after his ordination, showed the richness of his mind. In poetry and prose he revealed an ability forcefully to touch the truth of experience with directness and honesty and give to the dim intuition of his readers and his hearers a universal voice. He distinguished himself not so much as a theologian but as a preacher.

In 1963 Donne's name, which had not previously appeared on any calendar, was proposed for inclusion on the calendar of the Episcopal Church and is listed in the Proposed Book of Common Prayer.

R. C. Bald. *John Donne. A Life*. New York: Oxford, 1970.
John Donne. *Sermons* ed. E. M. Simpson and G. R. Potter. 10 vols. University of California, 1953-1962.
Robert S. Jackson. *John Donne's Christian Vocation*. Evanston, Ill.: Northwestern University Press, 1970.

Lancelot Andrewes, who might be remembered with Donne, was a learned preacher and patristic scholar and a translator of portions of the Old Testament in the Authorized [King James] Version. Born in 1555, he was educated at Cambridge. Ordained in 1580, he became dean of Westminster in 1601. He twice refused a bishopric but at length was persuaded by King James I to accept the see of Chichester in 1605. He was transferred to Ely in 1609 and Winchester in 1619. He died September 25, 1626 and is buried in Southwark Cathedral. He is remembered today for his devotional manual, *Private Prayers*, and for his key role in the formation of the English church.

Reading

Nunc lento sonitu dicunt,
Morieris.

Now, this bell tolling
softly for another, says
to me, Thou must die.

Perchance he for whom this bell tolls may be so ill as that he knows not it tolls for him; and perchance I may think myself so much better than I am, as that they who are about me and see my state may have caused it to toll for me, and I know not that. The Church is Catholic, Universal, so are all her actions; all that she does, belongs to all. When she baptizes a child, that action concerns me; for that child is thereby connected to that Head which is my Head too, and engrafted into that body of which I am a member. And when she buries a man, that action concerns me: all mankind is of one author and is one volume; when one man dies, one chapter is not torn out of the book but translated into a better language; and every chapter must be so translated; God employs several translators; some pieces are translated by age, some by sickness, some by war, some by justice; but God's hand is in every translation; and his hand shall bind up all our scattered leaves again, for that library where every book shall lie open to one another: as therefore the bell that rings for a sermon calls not upon the preacher only, but upon the congregation to come; so this bell calls us all: but how much more me, who am brought so near the door by this sickness.

There was a contention as far as a suit (in which both piety and dignity, religion and estimation were mingled) which of the religious orders should ring to prayers first in the morning; and it was determined that they should ring first that rose earliest. If we understand aright the dignity of this bell that tolls for our evening prayer, we would be glad to make it ours, by rising early in that application that it might be ours as well as his, whose indeed it is. The bell doth toll for him that thinks it doth; and though it intermit again, yet from that minute that that occasion wrought upon him, he is united to God. Who casts not up his eye to the sun when it rises? but who takes off his eye from a comet when that breaks out? Who bends not his ear to any bell, which upon any occasion rings? but who can remove it from that bell which is passing a piece of himself out of this world?

No man is an island, entire of itself; every man is a piece of the continent, a part of the main; if a clod be washed away by the sea, Europe is the less, as well as if a promontory were, as if a manor of thy friends or of thine own were; any man's death diminishes me, because I am involved in mankind; and therefore never send to know for whom the bell tolls; it tolls for thee. Neither can we call this a begging of misery or a borrowing of misery, as though we were not miserable enough of ourselves but must fetch in more from the next house in taking upon us the misery of our neighbors. Truly it were an excusable covetousness if we did; for affliction is a treasure and scarce any man hath enough of it.

No man hath affliction enough that is not matured and ripened by it, and made fit for God by that affliction. If a man carry treasure in bullion or in a wedge of gold and have none coined into current monies, his treasure will not defray him as he travels. Tribulation is treasure in the nature of it, but it is not current money in the use of it except we get nearer and nearer our home, heaven, by it. Another man may be sick too, and sick to death, and this affliction may lie in his bowels, as gold in a mine, and be of no use to him; but this bell that tells me of his affliction digs out and applies that gold to me; if by this consideration of another's danger I take mine own into contemplation and so secure myself by making recourse to my God, who is our only security.

John Donne, *Devotions Upon Emergent Occasions* (London, 1925) 107-109.

Propers

ROMAN	**LUTHERAN**	**EPISCOPAL**

LUTHERAN

God of grace and might, we praise you for your servant John, to whom you gave gifts to make the good news known. Raise up, we pray, in every country, heralds and evangelists of your kingdom, so that the world may know the immeasurable riches of our Savior, Jesus Christ our Lord.

Common of Missionaries (i.e. heralds of the Gospel, preachers):

EPISCOPAL

Almighty God, who in this wondrous world show forth your power and beauty: open the eyes of all men to see, with your servant John Donne, that whatever has any being is a mirror in which we may behold you, the root and fountain of all being; through your Son Jesus Christ our Lord, who lives and reigns with you and the Holy Spirit, one God, now and for ever.

(Text from Lesser Feasts and Fasts, Revised Edition, copyright 1973 by Charles Mortimer Guilbert as Custodian of the Standard Book of Common Prayer. All rights reserved. Used by permission.)

Isaiah 62:1-7
Psalm 48
Romans 10:11-17
Luke 24:44-53
or the Common of Artists

Psalm 19:1-6
Proverbs 8:1-11
Psalm 16:1-8
John 12:23-26
Preface of the Incarnation

Hymn of the Day: "O Lord, send forth your spirit (392)

Prayers: for those who preach the Gospel
for poets and writers
for an awareness of the shortness of life

Color: White

Albrecht Duerer, Artist, 1528

Albrecht Duerer, a methodical explorer of the world and of humankind's place in it, was born in Nuremberg, May 21, 1471, the son of a goldsmith. His artistic talent was recognized early, and at age sixteen he was apprenticed to a local painter. After three years he left his apprenticeship to travel in the Netherlands, Alsace, and Switzerland. By the end of May, 1494, he was back in Nuremberg. On the seventh of July he married Agnes Frey; they had no children. In the autumn Duerer went to Italy, and this visit, which lasted until the following spring, was a great influence on his work: Duerer was the first northern European artist to immerse himself in the art of the Italian Renaissance. Upon his return to Nuremberg in 1495, Duerer renewed his association with his boyhood friend Willibald Pirkheimer (1470-1530), the noted humanist. Like Leonardo, Duerer had an enormously inquisitive mind and was one of the most learned of Renaissance artists and the friend of many of the distinguished people of the time.

His painting style vacillated between Gothic and the Italian Renaissance style until the end of the century when he moved toward the Renaissance spirit. In the fall of 1505 he made his second journey to Italy and spent most of his time in Venice. The visit lasted until the winter of 1507. He returned to Nuremberg by February, 1507, and bought a house near the zoological garden. This "Duerer Haus" still stands.

For a time he worked for the Emperor Maxmillian I. In July, 1520, he went to the Netherlands again. At the coronation of Charles V, the successor of Maxmillian, at Aachen, Duerer met Matthias Gruenewald, who ranked second only to Duerer in German art of the time. In April, 1521, Luther stood before the Diet at Worms, and the Emperor Charles V had concluded that he would "proceed against him as a notorious heretic." On the seventeenth of May in Antwerp Duerer heard the news. He wrote in his diary:

O Lord, you desire before you come to judgment that as your Son Jesus Christ had to die at the hands of the priests and rise from the dead and ascend to heaven, even so should your disciple Martin Luther be made conformable to him.

Not knowing of Luther's refuge in the Wartburg, Duerer wrote again
in his diary:

I know not whether he lives or is murdered, but in any case he has suffered for the Christian truth. . . . If we lose this man, who has written
more clearly than any other in centuries, may God grant his spirit to another. . . . His books should be held in great honor, and not burned as
the emperor commands, but rather the books of his enemies. O God, if
Luther is dead, who will henceforth explain to us the gospel? What might
he not have written for us in the next ten or twenty years?

Nonetheless, despite his admiration of Luther, Duerer remained a
Catholic.

Duerer returned to Nuremberg July 12, 1521. His health declined,
and he spent his time writing letters, poems, and treatises on fortifica-
tion. He died April 6, 1528 and was buried in the churchyard of the
Johanniskirche in Nuremberg. Luther, learning of his death, wrote to
Eoban Hesse:

Affection bids us mourn for one who was the best of men, yet you may
well consider him happy that he has made so good an end, and that
Christ has taken him from the midst of this time of trouble. . . . May he
rest in peace with his fathers. Amen.

Deeply religious in spirit, Duerer was affected by the apocalyptic
spirit of the time in the face of famine, plague, and social and religious upheaval. His paintings and woodcuts are a close examination
of the splendor of creation—the human body, animals, grasses, and
flowers. He was, unfortunately, never able to fulfill his desire to paint
Luther "as a lasting memorial to the Christian man who has helped
me out of great anxiety."

John Canaday. "Albrecht Duerer," *Horizon* VI, 3 (summer 1964), 16-31.
Erwin Panofsky. *The Life and Art of Albrecht Duerer.* Princeton Univer-
    sity Press, 1955.

Lucas Cranach (d. 1553) was able to be the portraitist of the Reformers. His work is lighter and more joyful than that of Duerer. He
was a prolific conveyor of the message of the Reformation, and was
highly regarded by the humanists of his day. A court painter and
friend of Luther, he was a student of nature, morals, and eroticism.

An exhibit of his work at Basel in 1974 vindicated his reputation in the eyes of many critics. Beneath the apparent simplicity, there lies a serious and intense effort of the northern Renaissance, a search for balance between the spirit and the body, God and the flesh, good and evil, people and nature.

It would also be appropriate to remember **Matthias Gruenewald** with Duerer and Cranach. This fascinating and enigmatic painter was born, it seems, in Wuerzburg sometime between 1455 and 1480. The name by which he is known is a fabrication of a seventeenth century biographer. His real surname was Gothardt, to which he sometimes added the surname of his wife, Neithardt. He spent most of his life in the upper Rhine area under the patronage of the Archbishop of Mainz and then of Albrecht von Brandenburg. Gruenewald's limited influence and renown is in contrast to Duerer, yet his works are highly valued. He was fascinated by the Crucifixion as a subject for painting. His greatest work, inspired by the mystical *Revelations* of Birgitta of Sweden, is the Isenheim altarpiece with its combination of horror and mystical elevation. He died at Halle in August 1528, at the time secretly siding with the Reformation.

Arthur Burkhard. *Matthias Gruenewald: Personality and Accomplishment.* Cambridge, Mass.: Harvard, 1936.
Nikolaus Pevsner and Michael Meier. *Gruenewald.* London: Thames, 1958.

Reading

(From Thomas Traherne, *Centuries.*)

You never enjoy the world aright till the Sea itself floweth in your veins, till you are clothed with the heavens, and crowned with the stars: and perceive yourself to be the sole heir of the whole world, and more than so, because men are in it who are every one sole heirs as well as you. Till you can sing and rejoice and delight in God, as misers do in gold, and Kings in scepters, you never enjoy the world.

Till your spirit filleth the whole world, and the stars are your jewels; till you are as familiar with the ways of God in all Ages as with your walk and table: till you are intimately acquainted with that shady nothing out of which the world was made: till you love men so as to desire their happiness, with a thirst equal to the zeal of your own; till you delight in God for being good to all: you never enjoy the world. Till you more feel it than your private estate, and are more present in the hemisphere, considering the glories and the beauties there, than in your own house: Till you remember how lately you were made, and how wonderful it was when you came into it: and more rejoice in the palace of your glory, than if it had been made but to-day morning.

Yet further, you never enjoy the world aright, till you so love the beauty of enjoying it, that you are covetous and earnest to persuade others to enjoy it. And so perfectly hate the abominable corruption of men in despising it, that you had rather suffer the flames of Hell than willingly be guilty of their error. There is so much blindness and ingratitude and damned folly in it. The world is a mirror of infinite beauty, yet no man sees it. It is a Temple of Majesty, yet no man regards it. It is a region of Light and Peace, did not men disquiet it. It is the Paradise of God. It is more to man since he is fallen than it was before. It is the place of Angels and the Gate of Heaven. When Jacob waked out of his dream, he said *God is here, and I wist it not. How dreadful is this place! This is none other than the House of God, and the Gate of Heaven.*

Thomas Traherne, *Centuries* (1672), I: 29, 30, 31. Introduction by John Farrar. (New York: Harper and Brothers, 1960) 14-15.

Michaelangelo Buonarroti, Artist, 1564

The famed creator of gigantic sculpture was himself an awe-inspiring figure who was accorded, even in his lifetime, the high respect usually reserved for the great religious teachers.

Michaelangelo was born March 6, 1475 at Caprese, a small town near Florence. He was of aristocratic stock, his father claiming descent from the counts of Canossa, but the family fortunes had declined. Overcoming family objections to his becoming an artist, Michaelangelo at age thirteen was apprenticed briefly to Ghirlandaio, the most successful Florentine painter of the period, and then under the sculptor Bertoldo. The young artist attracted the attention of Lorenzo de Medici and lived for a time in his palace, meeting many artists and writers there. Before the expulsion of Piero de Medici in 1494, Michaelangelo went to Venice and then Bolognia and read Dante and Petrarch.

Michaelangelo arrived in Rome in the summer of 1496 and there carved the *Pieta* of St. Peter's Basilica in which the Virgin Mary holds the body of her dead Son in her lap. The work is a marvelous feat of technical skill and shows the sculptor's consummate mastery of his craft.

In 1501 Michaelangelo went back to Florence to carry out commissions which expressed the pride, vigor, and idealism of the Medicis. The *David* is the great figure of power and magnificence from this period.

In March 1505 Michaelangelo was summoned to Rome again to design the tomb of Pope Julius II. For eight months Michaelangelo was at Carrara supervising the quarrying of huge blocks of marble for what was to be the greatest tomb in Christendom. He was inaccessible in that awe-inspiring landscape, surrounded by stone. He made such sojourns in Carrara several times in his life and these times, like religious retreats, were preludes to spells of his greatest activity. When he returned to Rome in the winter of 1506-1507, he was refused immediate access to Pope Julius and in April 1506, returned to Florence. Seven months later Michaelangelo returned to Rome and the papal presence. He went to Bolognia to make a bronze statue of the pope for the door of San Petronio there; then he went to Florence, but was recalled to Rome and was given the task of painting the ceiling of the papal chapel (called the Sistine Chapel). The prodigious frescoes were unveiled October 31, 1512 and illustrated the progression from servitude of the body (The Drunkenness of Noah) to the liberation of the soul (The Creation).

From this point on, Michaelangelo's mood becomes more grave and his confidence in physical beauty diminishes. He becomes increasingly preoccupied with death. Leo X succeeded Julius, and Raphael was the favored artist. Michaelangelo returned to Florence, which underwent a revolution in 1527, and he was put in charge of the fortifications of the city against the expelled Medici.

In 1534 Paul III called Michaelangelo back to Rome to paint the

Last Judgment, which he completed in 1541. He then turned to designing the dome of St. Peter's. He spent his last years with poetry, architecture, and drawing, writing in a sonnet that "only in darkness can men fully be." He died in his 89th year.

Michaelangelo believed that classical antiquity and Christianity could be served simultaneously by a devotion to the human figure, and the greatest accomplishment of this sculptor, architect, painter, poet, draftsman was his exploration of the mystery of life locked in the human body, particularly seen in his drawings of the nude male body in action. For him the human form was the expression of God's purpose.

In commemoration of the 500th anniversary of his birth, the *New York Times* said in an editorial:

The art of Michaelangelo was fueled by a largeness of soul and a frighteningly powerful belief—a terribilita—that would not be possible today. Grandeur is a term applied to the creative spirit on rare occasions, and the world is changed by it forever.

So that great spirit and its transforming impact upon the world is celebrated.

Robert J. Clements. *The Poetry of Michaelangelo*. New York: New York
    University Press, 1965.
Howard Hibbard. *Michaelangelo*. New York: Harper and Row, 1974.
The Letters of Michaelangelo trans. and ed. by E. H. Ramsden. 2 vols.
    Stanford: Stanford University Press, 1963.
J. A. Symonds. *The Life of Michaelangelo Buonaroti.* 1892.
Herbert Von Einem. *Michaelangelo* trans. Ronald Taylor. London: Methuen, 1973.

Reading

(Michaelangelo, "On the Brink of Death")

> Now hath my life across a stormy sea
>   Like a frail bark reached that wide port where all
>   Are bidden, ere the final reckoning fall
> Of good and evil for eternity.

Now know I well how that fond phantasy
Which made my soul the worshiper and thrall
Of earthly art, is vain; how criminal
Is that which all men seek unwillingly.
Those amourous thoughts which were so lightly dressed,
What are they when the double death is nigh?
The one I know for sure, the other dread.
Painting nor sculpture now can lull to rest
My soul that turns to His great love on high,
Whose arms to clasp us on the cross were spread.
                                        trans. J. A. Symonds

Propers: Artists

Hymn of the Day: "How marvelous God's greatness" (515)

Prayers: for painters, sculptors, and architects
for a renewed appreciation of beauty as an attribute of God
for joy in the natural world
for an inquiring mind to explore the beauty of creation

Color: White

April 9

Dietrich Bonhoeffer, Theologian, Martyr, 1945

Dietrich Bonhoeffer was born in Breslau February 4, 1906 and grew up in the university circles of Berlin where his father Karl was professor of psychiatry and neurology. He studied at the universities of Berlin and Tuebingen from 1923-1927. His doctoral thesis was published in 1930 as *Communio Sanctorum*. From 1928-1929 he was the assistant pastor of a German-speaking congregation in Barcelona. He then spent a year as an exchange student at Union Seminary in New York City, and returned to Germany in 1931 to lecture in systematic theology at the University of Berlin.

From the first days of the Nazi accession to power, 1933, Bonhoeffer was involved in protests against the regime, especially its anti-Semitism. From 1933 to 1935 he was the pastor of two small German congregations in London, but nonetheless was a leading spokesman for the Confessing Church, the center of Protestant resistance to the Nazis. In 1935 Bonhoeffer was appointed to organize and head a new seminary for the Confessing Church at Finkenwald, which continued in a disguised form until 1940. He described the community in *Life Together* (1939, English translation 1954) and wrote the *Cost of Discipleship* (1948, English translation 1959) which attacked the notion of "cheap grace," an unlimited offer of forgiveness which masked moral laxity.

The Bishop of Chichester, England, G. K. A. Bell, became interested in efforts to interpret the church struggle (Kirchenkampf) and became a friend of Bonhoeffer. Bonhoeffer's own involvement became increasingly political after 1939, when he was introduced by his brother-in-law to the group seeking Hitler's overthrow. In 1939 Bonhoeffer considered refuge in the United States, but he returned to Germany where he was able to continue his resistance as an employee of the Military Intelligence Department, which was a center of resistance. In May of 1942 he flew to Sweden to meet Bishop Bell and convey through him to the British government proposals for a negotiated peace. The offer was rejected by the Allies who insisted upon unconditional surrender.

Bonhoeffer was arrested April 5, 1943, and imprisoned in Berlin. (He had just announced his engagement.) After an attempt on Hitler's life failed April 9, 1944, documents were discovered linking Bonhoeffer to the conspiracy. He was taken to Buchenwald concentration camp, then to Schoenberg Prison. On Sunday, April 8, 1945, just as he concluded a service in a school building in Schoenberg in the Bavarian forest, two men came in with the chilling summons, "Prisoner Bonhoeffer . . . come with us." As he left, he said to Payne Best, an English prisoner who described the event in *The Venlo Incident*, "This is the end. For me, the beginning of life." Bonhoeffer was hanged the next day, April 9, 1945, at Flossenbürg Prison.

On the new Lutheran calendar for North America he is not accounted a martyr since he was killed not for his adherence to the Christian faith but for his political activities against the German government. The distinction cannot be pressed, however, for his resistance was surely rooted in his Christian commitment. The German Evangelical Calendar of Names lists him as "Martyr in the Church Struggle," and there is in Bonhoeffer's life a remarkable unity of faith, prayer, writing, and action. The pacifist theologian came to accept the guilt of plotting the death of Hitler because he was convinced that not to do so would be a greater evil. Discipleship was to be had only at great cost.

In remembering key figures in important religious and social movements such as Bonhoeffer or Martin Luther King Jr., one needs to keep in mind that these people are representative figures who both clarify and have been nourished by the struggle of countless more obscure people who were no less brave in their witness.

Eberhard Bethge. *Dietrich Bonhoeffer*, tr. Eric Mesbacher et al. New York: Harper and Row, 1970.

Reading

(From a letter by Dietrich Bonhoeffer.)

I often ask myself why a "Christian instinct" often draws me more to the religionless people than to the religious, by which I don't in the least mean with any evangelizing intention, but, I might almost say, "in brotherhood". While I'm often reluctant to mention God by name to religious people—because that name somehow seems to me here not to ring true, and I feel myself to be slightly dishonest (it's particularly bad when others start to talk in religious jargon; I then dry up almost completely and feel awkward and uncomfortable)—to people with no religion I can on occasion mention him by name quite calmly and as a matter of course. Religious people speak of God when human knowledge (perhaps simply because they are too lazy to think) has come to an end, or when human resources fail—in fact it is always the *deus ex machina* that they bring on to the scene, either for the apparent solution of insoluble problems, or as strength in human failure—always, that is to say, exploiting human weakness or human boundaries. Of necessity, that can go on only till people can by their own strength push those boundaries somewhat further out, so that God becomes superfluous as a *deus ex machina*. I've come to be doubtful of talking about any human boundaries (is even death, which people now hardly fear, and is sin, which they now hardly understand, still a genuine boundary today?) It always seems to me that we are trying anxiously in this way to reserve some space for God; I should like to speak of God not on the boundaries but at the center, not in weakness but in strength; and therefore not in death and guilt but in man's life and goodness. As to the boundaries, it seems to me better to be silent and leave the insoluble unsolved. Belief in the resurrection is *not* the "solution" of the problem of death. God's "beyond" is not the beyond of our cognitive faculties. The transcendence of epistemological theory has nothing to do with the transcendence of God. God is beyond in the midst of our life. The church stands, not at the boundaries where human powers give out, but in the middle of the village. That is how it is in the Old Testament, and in this sense we still read the New Testament far too little in the light of the Old. How this religionless Christianity looks, what form it takes, is something that I'm thinking about a great deal, and I shall be writing to you again about it soon. It may be that on us in particular, midway between East and West, there will fall a heavy responsibility.

Propers: Martyrs (color: red)
    or Theologians (color: white)

Hymn of the Day: "God of grace and God of Glory" (415)

Prayers: for a deepened discipleship
    for courage to resist tyranny in all its forms
    for strength to pay the price of following Christ into
        places where we are beyond familiar rules
    for those whose names we do not remember who with
        Bonhoeffer resisted tyranny

Color: Red or white

155

April 10

Mikael Agricola, Bishop of Turku, 1557

Mikael Agricola (the accent is on the first syllable of his surname: AH-gree-co-la) was born in Uusimaa, Finland (which was then a province of Sweden) sometime between 1508 and 1512. He went to school in Viipuri and later moved to Turku, where he stayed for six or seven years. He did well in his studies, and he was one of the eight Finnish students whom the aged Martinus Skytte, Bishop of Turku (1528-1550), a former Dominican monk, sent to study under Luther and Melanchthon at the University of Wittenberg. He received his master's degree there in 1539 and, returning with Luther's special recommendation in a letter to the king, became rector of the cathedral school and, in 1548, assistant to the bishop.

In 1554, after the death of Bishop Skytte, he was consecrated Bishop of Turku by the Swedish hierarchy without submitting his name for papal approval. He carried out in Finland a thorough-going Lutheran reformation comparable to that of the Petri brothers in Sweden, retaining much of the historic doctrines and practices of the church, but eliminating unscriptural elements and encouraging greater participation of the laity.

Bishop Agricola realized the need for the Finns to read the Scripture and participate in the services of the church in their own language. He therefore devised an orthography, which is the basis for modern Finnish spelling, and prepared an ABC book; a prayer book (1544), which contained miscellaneous secular information in addition to prayers—probably his most widely read book; a translation of the New Testament (1548); and a vernacular translation of the mass (1549). He began a collection of Finnish hymns and translated others. For these and other writings he became recognized as the father of the Finnish literary language.

Bishop Agricola was one of the members of a royal mission sent to Russia to negotiate peace after the Russian-Swedish hostilities of 1555-1557, and on his return from this strenuous trip he fell ill on Palm Sunday, April 9, 1557 and died that night. He had been bishop but three years and was not yet fifty years old.

He is remembered as a learned man, interested in mysticism and the ancient religion of his homeland, moderate and conciliatory in dealings with others, but anxious for the well-being of the church and the Christian life of its members. In 1948 on the four hundredth anniversary of his death, he was widely commemorated and many new articles and books on his life and works were published. The Finnish Lutheran Church in Toronto is named for him.

With Agricola, **Paavali** (Paul) **Juusten** (1516-1576) might also be remembered. He too had been sent by Bishop Skytte to Wittenberg, 1543-1546. He was rector of the cathedral school at Turku, and in 1554 he was consecrated the first bishop of the newly-established diocese of Viipuri (Viborg), near the Russian border. He later became a successor of Agricola and served as Bishop of Turku for thirteen years. Juusten wrote a catechism and a manual for the clergy, was concerned for the spiritual and intellectual welfare of the clergy of Finland, and together with Agricola revived the spirituality of the church in Finland.

Paavo Henrik Ruotsalainen was a lay evangelist who in the eighteenth century revitalized the springs of the religious tradition. He was born July 9, 1777 and spent most of his life in Nilsia. A poor peasant, without formal education, this "prophet of the wilderness" nonetheless became the outstanding layman in the Church of Finland. He was known as a sympathetic confessor and spiritual counsellor, an effective preacher despite harassment by ecclesiastical and secular officials. He died January 27, 1852.

G. Everett Arden. *Four Northern Lights: Men Who Shaped Scandinavian Churches.* Minneapolis: Augsburg, 1964. [Ruotsalainen]
Geert Sentzke. *Finland: Its Church and Its People.* Helsinki, 1963.

Reading

(From *Orthodoxy,* by G. K. Chesterton.)

Mysticism keeps man sane. As long as you have mystery you have health; when you destroy mystery you create morbidity. The ordinary man has always been sane because the ordinary man has always been a mystic. He has permitted the twilight. He has always had one foot in earth and the other in fairy land. He has always left himself free to doubt his gods; but (unlike the agnostic of to-day) free also to believe in them. He has always cared more for truth than for consistency. If he saw two truths that seemed to contradict each other, he would take the two truths and the contradiction along with them. His spiritual sight is stereoscopic, like his physical sight: he sees two different pictures at once and yet sees all the better for that. Thus he has always believed that there is such a thing as fate, but such a thing as free will also. Thus he believed that children were indeed the kingdom of heaven, but nevertheless ought to be obedient to the kingdom of earth. He admired youth because it was young and age because it was not.

It is exactly this balance of apparent contradictions that had been the whole buoyancy of the healthy man. The whole secret of mysticism is this: that man can understand everything by the help of what he does not understand. The morbid logician seeks to make everything lucid, and succeeds in making everything mysterious. The mystic allows one thing to be mysterious, and everything else becomes lucid. The determinist makes the theory of causation quite clear, and then finds that he cannot say "if you please" to the housemaid. The Christian permits free will to remain a sacred mystery; but because of this his relations with the housemaid become of a sparkling and crystal clearness. He puts the seed of dogma in a central darkness; but it branches forth in all directions with abounding natural health. As we have taken the circle as the symbol of reason and madness, we may very well take the cross as the symbol at once of mystery and of health. Buddhism is centripetal, but Christianity is centrifugal: it breaks out. For the circle is perfect and infinite in its nature; but it is fixed for ever in its size; it can never be larger or smaller. But the cross, though it has at its heart a collision and a contradiction, can extend its four arms for ever without altering its shape. Because it has a paradox in its centre it can grow without changing. The circle returns upon itself and is bound. The cross opens its arms to the four winds; it is a signpost for free travellers.

G. K. Chesterton, *Orthodoxy* (New York and London: John Lane, 1908) 48-50.

Propers: Renewers of the Church

Hymn of the Day: "Lord, as a pilgrim through life I go" (485)

Prayers: for the Church in Finland: its archbishop, bishops, clergy,
     and people
     for increasingly intelligent participation in the worship
     of the church
     for compassion and a conciliatory spirit.
     for those who study language and culture.

Color: White

April 19

Olavus Petri, Priest, 1552;
Laurentius Petri, Archbishop of Uppsala, 1573;
Renewers of the Church

Olavus and Laurentius Petri were the two brothers who led the
Reformation in Sweden in the sixteenth century. Olavus, the elder
brother, was born in 1493, Laurentius in 1499, both in Örebro, the
chief town of Nerike (modern Närke), from which Laurentius is
sometimes called Nericius. The boys were educated in the local monastery, Uppsala, Leipzig, and then at Wittenberg, where they were
deeply influenced by Martin Luther. Olavus seems to have been in
Wittenberg at the time of the posting of the Ninety-five Theses, for
he received his bachelor's degree in 1516 and the master's degree in
1518.

When Olavus returned to Sweden he became chancellor to Bishop
Matthias of Strengnäs and a close friend of Laurentius Andreae, who
was the archdeacon. Olavus was ordained deacon and spread the
teachings of the reformers among the clergy and laity of the church.
After his coronation at Strangnäs, King Gustavus Vasa (who liberated
Sweden from Danish rule) took Laurentius Petri to Stockholm as his
chancellor and Olavus as pastor of the city church there and secretary
of the city council. Half the townspeople were German, and Olavus'
study in Germany stood him in good stead.

The character of the Reformation in Sweden was determined to a
great extent by the writings of Olavus. He understood that the reformation of the church depended upon the education of the clergy and

people, and his writing gave the intellectual and liturgical basis for such education. He prepared a Swedish version of the New Testament based on the Vulgate, but with some reference to Luther's translation from the Greek. In the same year, 1526, he published a book of catechetical instruction, *A Useful Teaching*. In 1531 he issued a Swedish version of the Latin mass, simplified along the lines of Luther's *Deutsche Messe*, and in 1530 he published a collection of hymns and canticles in Swedish. In 1540 he was condemned to death for lèse majesté because of his opposition to the king's desire for complete ecclesiastical control. Later he was pardoned and wrote his *Swedish Chronicles*. He died April 19, 1552.

Laurentius returned from Wittenberg in 1527 and, in spite of his youth (he was 28), was appointed to a professorship at the University of Uppsala. He was ordained to the priesthood and four years later was the king's choice to fill the vacant see of Uppsala. An assembly of the clergy from the whole realm was called, and they voted overwhelmingly in favor of the young priest-professor. He was consecrated on September 22, 1531 at Stockholm, the first evangelical archbishop of Sweden. Uppsala had first become the seat of an archbishop in 1164 with Stephen as its first incumbent; the nine hundredth anniversary of this event was celebrated in 1964. Laurentius succeeded (against Gustavus Vasa who thought of abolishing the episcopal office) in preserving the historic episcopate for Lutheranism.

In 1541 the complete Bible in Swedish, the joint work of the Petri brothers, appeared with full royal approval. In the same year a revised liturgy prepared by Laurentius was issued in which the reformer began the transformation of the sloemn mass in Latin without congregational communion into a service of Holy Communion sung in Swedish by the people, with a sermon required after the Gospel.

In 1561 at the coronation of King Eric XIV, Archbishop Laurentius preached a sermon setting forth the principles of the Reformation and making clear the relation between the two autonomous instruments of God's rule, the secular and the religious. Laurentius died in 1573, and twenty years later, when the Augsburg Confession was officially endorsed, the Reformation in Sweden was complete. During the lifetime of the two Petri brothers Sweden had passed from Danish rule, subject to Rome, to an independent nation with a firmly-established evangelical church.

April 19

Conrad Bergendoff. *Olavus Petri and the Ecclesiastical Transformation in Sweden.* Philadelphia: Fortress, 1965 [1928].

Reading

The chief article and foundation of the gospel is that before you take Christ as an example, you accept and recognize him as a gift, as a present that God has given you and that is your own.

Now when you have Christ as the foundation and chief blessing of your salvation, then the other part follows: that you take him as your example, giving yourself in service to your neighbor just as you see that Christ has given himself for you. See, there faith and love move forward, God's commandment is fulfilled, and a person is happy and fearless to do and to suffer all things. Therefore make note of this, that Christ as a gift nourishes your faith and makes you a Christian. But Christ as an example exercises your works. These do not make you a Christian. Actually they come forth from you because you have already been made a Christian. As widely as a gift differs from an example, so widely does faith differ from works, for faith possesses nothing of its own, only the deeds and life of Christ. Works have something of your own in them, yet they should not belong to you but to your neighbor.

So you see that the gospel is really not a book of laws and commandments which requires deeds of us, but a book of divine promises in which God promises, offers, and gives us all his possessions and benefits in Christ. . . .

When you open the book containing the gospels and read or hear how Christ comes here or there, or how someone is brought to him, you should therein perceive the sermon or the gospel through which he is coming to you, or you are being brought to him. For the preaching of the gospel is nothing else than Christ coming to us, or we being brought to him. When you see how he works, however, and how he helps everyone to whom he comes or who is brought to him, then rest assured that faith is accomplishing this in you and that he is offering your soul exactly the same sort of help and favor through the gospel. If you pause here and let him do you good, that is, if you believe that he benefits and helps you, then you really have it. Then Christ is yours, presented to you as a gift.

After that it is necessary that you turn this into an example and deal with your neighbor in the very same way, be given also to him as a gift and example.

Martin Luther, "A Brief Instruction on What to Look for in the Gospels," *Luther's Works*, vol. 35 Word and Sacrament I ed. E. Theodore Bachmann (Philadelphia: Muhlenberg, 1960) 119-121. Used by permission.

Propers: Renewers of the Church

Hymn of the Day: "Oh, sing jubilee to the Lord (256)

Prayers: for the Church in Sweden: its archbishop, bishops, clergy
and people
for the gift of wisdom and learning for the clergy
for a deepened appreciation of the tradition of the church

Color: White

April 21

Anselm, Archbishop of Canterbury, 1109

Anselm was born in 1033 of noble parents near Aosta in what is now Italy and what was then on the frontier of Lombardy and Burgundy. After the death of his mother and quarreling with his father, Anselm left home at the age of twenty-three for travel in Burgundy and France, furthering his education. He was attracted to the Benedictine monastery of Bec in Normandy which had been founded in 1040. His father died and left him all his property, and Anselm debated whether he should return to Italy or become a monk. He entered Bec as a novice in 1060, attracted by the intellectual brilliance of the prior Lanfranc, a fellow Italian. (There were a number of Italian scholars who came to Normandy in the late tenth and eleventh centuries.) After three years, when Lanfranc went to become prior of a new monastery, Anselm was elected his successor as prior of Bec. In 1078 when the founding abbot of Bec, Herluin, died, Anselm was unanimously elected abbot of the monastery. His skill as a teacher and his scholarly work made Bec an even more influential school of philosophical and theological studies than it had been under Lanfranc, and it became the foremost intellectual center of Europe.

Lanfranc had become Archbishop of Canterbury, and in 1078 Anselm visited him, making a favorable impression in England. Lanfranc died in 1089 and after a delay of four years while King William Rufus kept the see vacant to secure as much of the revenues of Canterbury as possible, Anselm was chosen successor. After extended pressure from all sides to accept the appointment, Anselm was enthroned as Archbishop of Canterbury September 25, 1093 and was consecrated archbishop December 4.

The gentle and scholarly monk now began a protracted and intense struggle with the king over ultimate authority. William Rufus refused to recognize Pope Urban IV and the bishops, fearing the king, sided with him against Anselm at the Council of Rockingham in March 1095. The intervention of the secular princes prevented his immediate removal, but the struggle continued and Anselm, realizing that the situation was hopeless, left England for Rome without the king's permission October 15, 1097, and the king took possession of the see of Canterbury.

The pope received Anselm graciously, refused to accept his resignation, and gave him the place of honor at the Council of Bari in 1098, which sought reunion with the Greek Church. Anselm there defended the teaching that the Holy Spirit proceeds from the Father and the Son and also had the council's excommunication of the English king postponed.

Anselm stayed for a time with the archbishop of Lyons and there learned of the death of William Rufus, August 2, 1100. His successor, Henry I immediately recalled Anselm to England, but the struggle over authority was renewed when Anselm in obedience to a decree of the Council of Bari refused the king's insistence upon an oath of allegiance to the crown. When no solution seemed possible, the king asked Anselm to go to Rome. At length, in 1106, a compromise was effected and Anselm returned to his see. The difficulties were not yet over, for York claimed the primacy in England that had always belonged to Canterbury.

Anselm was by this time in poor health. His biographer, Eadmer, tells of his approaching death:

Palm Sunday dawned and we were sitting beside him as usual. One of us therefore said to him: "My lord and father, we cannot help knowing that you are going to leave the world to be at the Easter court of your Lord." He replied: "And indeed if his will is set on this, I shall gladly obey his will. However, if he would prefer me to remain among you, at least until I can settle a question about the origin of the soul, which I am turning over in my mind, I should welcome this with gratitude, for I do not know whether anyone will solve it when I am dead.

Anselm died Wednesday in Holy Week, April 21, 1109.

Before Anselm, the study of theology consisted of collecting authoritative texts. Anselm strove to demonstrate the truh of faith by going beyond faith to an insight into it. He devised an ingenious and durable argument for the existence of God "than whom nothing greater can be conceived", a provocative explanation of the atonement (the "satisfaction theory," Aulen calls it), and emphasized the role of the maternal in Christianity by encouraging devotion to Mary (although he opposed the doctrine of her immaculate conception) and in a prayer addressing Jesus, "are you not a mother too? . . . Indeed you are, and the mother of all mothers, who tasted death in your longing to bring forth children to life." Above all he understood the pursuit of theology as prayer.

Joseph Clayton, *Saint Anselm*. Milwaukee: Bruce, 1933.
Richard W. Church. *Saint Anselm*. London: Macmillan, 1937.
R. W. Southern, ed. *The Life of St. Anselm by Eadmer*. London: Thomas Nelson, 1962.
———. *St. Anselm and His Biographer*. Cambridge, 1963.

Reading

(From Anselm's *Proslogion*.)

. . . I have written the little work that follows . . . in the role of one who strives to raise his mind to the contemplation of God and who seeks to understand what he believes.

I acknowledge, Lord, and I give thanks that you have created your image in me, so that I may remember you, think of you, love you. But this image is so obliterated and worn away by wickedness, it is so obscured by the smoke of sins, that it cannot do what it was created to do, unless you renew and reform it. I am not attempting, O Lord, to penetrate your loftiness, for I cannot begin to match my understanding with it, but I desire in some measure to understand your truth, which my heart believes and loves. For I do not seek to understand in order to believe, but I believe in order to understand. For this too I believe, that "unless I believe, I shall not understand" (Isa. 7:9).

St. Anselm's Proslogion. Oxford: Clarendon Press, 1965, Preface, I, Trans. P.H.P.

Propers

ROMAN

Father, you called Saint Anselm to study and teach the sublime truths you have revealed. Let your gift of faith come to the aid of our understanding and open our hearts to your truth. Grant this through our Lord Jesus Christ, your Son, who lives and reigns with you and the Holy Spirit, one God, for ever and ever.

(Text from the English translation of the Roman Missal © 1973, International Committee on English in the Liturgy, Inc. All rights reserved.)

Common of Pastors or Martyrs

LUTHERAN

Almighty God, your Holy Spirit gives to one the word of wisdom, and to another the word of knowledge, and to another the word of faith. We praise you for the gifts of grace imparted to your servant Anselm, and we pray that by his teaching we may be led to a fuller knowledge of the truth which we have seen in your Son Jesus Christ our Lord.

Common of Theologians: Wisdom 7:7-14 Psalm 119:89-104 1 Corinthians 2:6-10, 13-16 Matthew 13:47-52

EPISCOPAL

O God who enlightened your Church by the teaching of your servant Anselm: Enrich us evermore with your heavenly grace, and raise up faithful witnesses who by their life and doctrine will set forth the truth of your salvation; through Jesus Christ our Lord, who lives and reigns with you and the Holy Spirit, one God, now and for ever.

(Text from Lesser Feasts and Fasts, Revised Edition, copyright 1973 by Charles Mortimer Guilbert as Custodian of the Standard Book of Common Prayer. All rights reserved. Used by permission.)

Psalm 37:32-39 Romans 5:1-11 Psalm 119:49-56 Matthew 11:25-30

Preface of the Incarnation

Hymn of the Day: "O Love, how deep, how broad, how high" (88)

Prayers: for a sense of the majesty of God
for forgiveness for those who wrong us
for a spirit of prayer and devotion
for those who inquire into the mysteries of God and his
    relation to the world
for those who seek to be certain of the existence of God

Preface: Christmas (because Anselm taught about the Incarnation)

Color: White

Toyohiko Kagawa, Renewer of Society, 1960

Kagawa was born July 10, 1888, at Kobe, Japan, the son of a member of the Japanese Cabinet and a geisha girl. He was orphaned at the age of four and was raised by his father's wife in Awa. It was an unhappy situation. He left to live with an uncle, and enrolled in a Bible class to learn English. When in his teens he became a Christian, he was disinherited. With the help of missionaries, he studied at Presbyterian College in Tokyo 1905-1908. From 1910-1924 he spent all but two years in a six foot by six foot hut in the slums of Kobe, called Shinkawa—the worst slums anywhere in the world. In 1912 he organized the first labor union in Japan among shipyard workers. From 1914-1916 at Princeton he studied social techniques to relieve poverty and misery. In 1918 he founded the Labor Federation, in 1921 the Farmers' Union. He was arrested during the rice riots of 1919 and the shipyard strikes of 1921. He worked successfully for universal male suffrage which was achieved in 1925 and for the modification of laws against trade unions.

In 1923 he was asked to supervise relief and social work in Tokyo. He organized the Bureau of Social Welfare, and his writings drew the attention of the government to the appalling conditions in the slums. He insisted upon a reorganization of the economic structure of the world to realize the Christian ideal of social order. In 1928 he founded the Anti-War League. In 1930 he began the Kingdom of God movement to promote the conversion of Japan to Christianity. He established credit unions, schools, hospitals, churches and visited the United States five times to gain support for his projects of social reform.

In 1940 he was arrested for apologizing to China for Japan's attack upon that country. In 1941 he was one of a group that went to the United States to try to avert the coming war. He returned to Japan in September 1941. After the war, in poor health, he led in the effort to adapt democratic institutions to Japan. He died in Tokyo April 23, 1960.

William Axling. *Kagawa*. 8th rev. ed. New York: Harpers, 1946.
J. M. Trout. *Kagawa, Japanese Prophet*. New York: Association, 1959.

Reading

(From *Love: the Law of Life*.)

My soul, whither wilt thou flee, and where wilt thou find an oasis in this parched, loveless waste? Where wilt thou find a spring of healing Love? Search thou not for the springs of Love in the deep valleys, nor yet may they be found in the bosom of another being. Thou art wrong to try to quench thy thirst for Love from another. Thou must seek Love in thine own breast. The spring of Love must well up in thine own heart.

Therefore I do not lose hope, nor do I fear when I see this drought in the land. I shall dig down deeper, still deeper into my own soul. I shall dig down to the God who is within me. Then, if I strike the underground stream that murmurs softly in the depths of my heart, I will tenderly cherish this oasis of the soul; and to it will I lead a few thirsting comrades.

My real experience of religion came when I entered the Kobe slums. Everything in the slums was ugly: the people, the houses, the clothes, the streets—everything was ugly and full of disease. If I had not carried God beside me, I should not have been able to stay. But because I believed in God, and in the Holy Spirit, I had a different view of life, and I assure you that I enjoyed living in the slums. With active love and the love-motive, every moment was full of joy. Because I felt that the Holy Spirit of the Heavenly Father was living inside me, I was not afraid of anything—not of the many repeated threats from pistols, swords, ruffians, not even from the infectious diseases which infested the slums. My job was to help these people. I had free access to their homes, and so knew even more about them than did the doctors. For me prayer is very real. If you pray with selfishness it will never be answered, but prayer for the sake of God and for the love of your fellow men will surely be answered. A gambler, dying, said to me that he was going back to his Heavenly Father. Then for the first time, like a flash, I was convinced that any man, even the most depraved, is able to grasp the idea of Jesus Christ.

Toyohiko Kagawa, *Love: the Law of Life* (St. Paul, Minn.: Macalester Park Publishing Co., 1951) 25, 13-14.

Propers: Renewers of Society

Hymn of the Day: "Where restless crowds are thronging" (430)

Prayers: for a renewed spirit of love for all people
       for the poor, the outcast, the forgotten
       for peace
       for the reconciliation of peoples and nations
       for laborers
       for those who work among the poor, diseased, unemployed

Color: White

168

April 25

ST. MARK, EVANGELIST

St. Mark is usually identified with the John Mark of the book of Acts, although Marcus was a very common Roman name. His mother Mary owned the house where the infant church gathered for prayer (Acts 12:12), and some have suggested that this was also the site of the Last Supper. John Mark accompanied his cousin Barnabas and St. Paul on the first missionary journey. He had a falling out with Paul for some reason (youthful impulsiveness, jealousy over Paul's assuming the leadership over Barnabas, anger at the change of itinerary have all been suggested), and Paul refused to take him on the second journey (Acts 15:36-40). Later, however, they were reconciled.

The attribution of the Gospel which bears his name—thought to be the earliest gospel—goes back to a statement by Papias (ca. 140) that Mark was the interpreter of Peter from whom he got much of the material for the gospel.

According to an unsupported tradition, Mark was the first bishop of Alexandria and was martyred there in A.D. 64 because of his attempt during the reign of the emperor Trajan to stop the worship of Serapis. In 829 Mark's supposed remains were removed from Alexandria to Venice and the famous cathedral there.

Since the beginning of the seventh century, April 25 has in the West been kept as a rogation day marked by a procession known as the Major Litany, which replaced an old pagan procession, the *robigalia*, which took place on the same day and was designed to prevent wheat mildew (ribigo). Perhaps because of this procession, the understanding arose that April 25 was the day when Peter entered Rome for the first time. Later, in the ninth century, the commemoration of Mark was assigned to the day. The commemoration is thought to have been earlier than the eighth century in the East. The commemoration of Mark does not appear on Roman calendars until the twelfth century, doubtless because Mark was not martyred or buried there.

The celebration of the feast day of St. Mark is especially appropriate in Year B of the lectionary cycle, when the Gospel readings are drawn from St. Mark.

Paul J. Achtemeier. *Mark.* Proclamation Commentaries. Philadelphia: Fortress, 1975.

Helen Gardner. "The Poetry of St. Mark," *The Business of Criticism.* London: Oxford, 1959.

Frank Kermode. *The Genesis of Secrecy. On the Interpretation of Narrative.* Cambridge, MA: Harvard, 1979.

Reading

(From *Worship* by von Allmen.)

The mystery of writing and reading—which might almost be called paschal, a death and resurrection—is something that has become so common that we have ceased to be aware of it. . . . It is forgotten that the Gospel is enclosed in the letter of the Bible and must be freed, that to read scripture is to experience the paschal joy; the Lord reappears, He who is the Word, to tell us of His love and His will, to teach us who He is and who we are, to summon us and give us life. But he does not reappear automatically. In deciphering scripture, we can also draw from it a corpse, a dead letter. Hence, the reading of the Bible in worship is traditionally preceded by an epiklesis, an invocation of the Holy Spirit, that the Word may really come alive for us so as to accomplish its work of salvation and judgment. If reading alone had been incapable of this spiritual miracle, if preaching had been necessary to achieve it, the apostles would have written nothing and would have trusted oral tradition alone. The very fact that they buried their witness to Jesus Christ in these hieroglyphic signs that are letters proves that they believed the Spirit-inspired interpretation of these hieroglyphics would be able to resurrect their witness and enable them themselves to remain alive in the Church. "In the reading of the apostolic word, the apostle of Jesus Christ himself appears, with his witness that is basic for the Church, *hic et nunc* at the heart of the community, to feed it with that living Word" (P. Brunner).

J.-J. von Allmen, *Worship: Its Meaning and Practice* (New York: Oxford, 1965) 132-133. Used by permission of Lutterworth Press.

Propers

ROMAN	LUTHERAN	EPISCOPAL
Father, you gave Saint Mark the privilege of proclaiming your gospel. May we profit by his wisdom and follow Christ more faithfully. Grant this through our Lord Jesus Christ, your Son, who lives and reigns with you and the Holy Spirit, one God, for ever and ever.	Almighty God, you have enriched your Church with Mark's proclamation of the Gospel. Give us grace to believe firmly in the good news of salvation and to walk daily in accord with it; through your Son, Jesus Christ our Lord, who lives and reigns with you and the Holy Spirit, one God, now and forever.	Almighty God, by the hand of Mark the evangelist you have given to your Church the Gospel of Jesus Christ the Son of God: We thank you for this witness, and pray that we may be firmly grounded in its truth; through Jesus Christ our Lord, who lives and reigns with you and the Holy Spirit, one God, for ever and ever.

ROMAN	LUTHERAN	EPISCOPAL
1 Peter 5:5b-14 Psalm 89:2-3, 6-7, 16-17 Mark 16:15-20	Isaiah 52:7-10 Psalm 57 2 Timothy 4:6-11, 18 Mark 1:1-15	Isaiah 52:7-10 Psalm 2 *or* 2:7-10 Ephesians 4:7-8, 11-16 Mark 1:1-15 *or* 16:15-20 Preface of All Saints

Hymn of the Day: "O God of light, your Word, a lamp unfailing" (237)

Prayers: for a heart to hear the Gospel
for faith to acknowledge Jesus as the Son of God
for a sense of the mystery of the resurrection
for fruitful fields and good crops

Preface: All Saints

Color: Red

Catherine of Siena, Teacher, 1380

Catherine was born in Siena probably in 1347, the twenty-third and last child in the large, devout Benincasa family. At age six she began to have visions of Christ, and throughout her life she continued to have mystical experiences, including visions and prolonged trances. Near the beginning of Lent, 1367, a vision convinced her that she was to be a bride of Christ, and she accepted his command to carry her love for him to the world, subsequently receiving the stigmata:

I saw the crucified Lord coming down to me in a great light. . . . Then from the marks of his most sacred wounds I saw five blood-red rays coming down upon me, which were directed toward the hands and feet and heart of my body. Perceiving the mystery, I exclaimed, "Ah, my Lord God, do not let the marks appear outwardly on the body." While I was speaking, before the rays reached me, they changed their blood-red color to splendor and like pure light they came to the five places in my body—the hands, feet, and heart. The pain that I feel in those five places, but especially in my heart, is so great that unless the Lord works a new miracle, it does not seem possible that the life of my body can endure such agony. (E. G. Gardner, *St. Catherine of Siena* [1907], 134, quoted in Rufus M. Jones, *Studies in Mystical Religion* [London: St. Martin's, 1909] 302. Rev.)

She claimed to have encountered St. Dominic in a vision and thereafter was permitted to wear the habit of the Dominican Third Order of Penance. She stubbornly clung to the vow of celibacy she made while still a child, despite her family's persistent pleas for a suitable marriage. Eventually, at the age of sixteen, she won the reluctant permission of her parents to live in a special closed-off room in her family's house, fasting and praying, and leaving the room only to go to church.

After three years, she emerged from her seclusion to devote herself to good works, doing household chores for her family and ministering to the sick and unfortunate in hospitals and in their homes. From 1368 to 1374 she gathered about her in Siena a group of friends whom she called her "family." They were men and women, priests and laity, and all (though older than she) called her "mother." During this period she fasted almost constantly and continued the intense devotion to the Sacrament which she had begun earlier. At the same time, she is reported to have maintained her merry, unpretentious manner, and she had a powerful spiritual influence on many people. She dictated letters of spiritual instruction and dealt also with public affairs, urging a crusade against the Turks. Her outspoken advice brought her misunderstanding and opposition.

The Dominican Order, which had been guiding her spiritual life for some years, gave her official protection in late spring 1374. During the period 1374-1378 her influence in public affairs was at its height. She opposed the war of Florence and its allies against the papacy (1376-1378). She pressed for the renewal of the church, which was clearly in need of reform. Her naive but earnest holiness made an impression on Gregory XI, whom she met at Avignon in June 1376. She urged him to return from his residence in France to his see in Rome. In the following year he did return to Rome, and the "Babylonian Captivity" of the church was ended.

In November 1378 Catherine went to Rome, where she worked for the unity of the church and engaged in writing and prayer. Although she had not learned to read and write until her teens, she carried on a voluminous correspondence with leaders of the church and state. Many of her letters have been preserved. She also dictated to her secretaries a book called the *Dialogue or A Treatise on Divine Providence* in which she reported what she felt were God's words to her about the fundamentals of Christian faith and practice. The book is still read by many who find comfort and wisdom in the words of this unschooled woman.

After a period of almost complete paralysis, Catherine at the age of thirty-three died in Rome, April 29, 1380, surrounded by her "family." She was buried in the Church of the Minerva. A woman of boundless energy, singlemindedness and devotion to her ideals, she was able to deal effectively with rulers, diplomats, and leaders of all kinds, and she was also loved by the common people for her mystical Christocentric spirituality. She was a forerunner of those women of later centuries who were to find their fulfillment not in marriage or in the convent but in a professional career of service.

Catherine has been widely commemorated in Christian churches. She was canonized by the Roman Catholic Church in 1461 and her feast day set as April 30, but the new Roman calendar as well as the Episcopal calendar commemorates her on the day of her death, April 29. Her day was popular in northern Europe, and she was retained on a number of Lutheran calendars after the Reformation.

A. Curtayne. *Saint Catherine of Siena.* New York: Sheed and Ward, 1935.
Johannes Jorgensen. *St. Catherine of Siena.* New York: Longman's, Green, 1938.
Rufus M. Jones. *Studies in Mystical Religion,* London; Macmillan, 1909.
A. Levasti. *My Servant Catherine,* tr. D. M. White. Westminster, Md.; Newman, 1954.
Raymond of Capua. *Leggenda Maior,* tr. G. Lamb, *The Life of St. Catherine of Siena.* New York: Kenedy, 1960.

With Catherine, it may be useful also to remember the other influential mystics of the fourteenth century. Johannes "Meister" Eckhart, the founder of German mysticism and the father of German philosophical language, was born probably in Thuringia, Germany, about 1260. He became a member of the Dominican Order, studied at Paris, and returned to Germany as Provincial-Prior of the Dominican Order for Saxony, and then went back to Paris for further study. He then went to Strasbourg, the foremost religious center of Germany, and there became known as a great preacher.

Rufus Jones said of him (*Studies in Mystical Religion,* p. 217), "He is a remarkable example of the union of a profoundly speculative mind and a simple, childlike spirit. No mystic has ever dropped his plummet deeper into the mysteries of the Godhead, nor has there ever been a bolder interpreter of those mysteries in the language of the common people." He was allowed to teach unmolested until the end of his life although his teaching seemed to many to verge on pantheism. In 1326 the Archbishop of Cologne brought charges against him and before the matter was settled, Eckhart died in 1327. Two years later certain of his writings were declared heretical by a papal bull which concluded, "He has wished to know more than he should."

The Friends of God was a lay movement which sought to renew the languishing church. In a time of earthquake, natural disaster, and black death, the movement drew upon the strong apocalyptic strain in the German visionaries of earlier centuries St. Hildegarde (1098-1179), St. Elizabeth of Schoenau (d. 1164), and St. Matilda of Magdeburg. The movement was founded by **Rulman Merswin** (d. 1382), with whom were associated Margaret and Christina Ebner, Henry of Noerdlingen, and the unknown author of the classic *Theologica Germanica,* praised by Luther as for him next in value to the Bible and the writings of Augustine.

John Tauler, "the illuminated Doctor," and one of the noblest leaders of the Friends of God, was born in Strasbourg about 1300 and
was ordained a priest of the Dominican Order. In 1339 he settled in
Basel, returned to Strasbourg in 1352, and died there in 1361. In his
teaching he insisted on a religion of experience "entering in and
dwelling in the Inner Kingdom of God, where pure truth and the
sweetness of God are found."

Henry Suso (originally Berg) was born ca. 1300 of a noble Swabian
family. He too entered a Dominican monastery for five years of study.
At the age of eighteen he had a spiritual awakening endured extreme
ascetic penance, and at length found what he sought. He went
through Swabia as an itinerant preacher, ca. 1335-1348, and then
settled in Ulm. He died in 1366. He had all the characteristic marks
of the Friends of God: spiritual visions, spiritual crises, austerities,
ecstasies, consciousness of the immediate presence of God.

In addition to these, another pre-reformation movement toward
renewal might be remembered. **John Ruysbroek** "the Ecstatic Doctor"
who joined the Friends of God with the Brethren of the Common
Life, was born in 1293, probably of German parents in the village of
Ruysbroek between Brussels and Hal. He was illiterate yet learned
sufficient Latin to be ordained priest. After a long and diligent pastorate, he retired at the age of sixty to the Augustinian monastery at
Groenendal and gave himself to meditation and writing. He died in
1381. He had influenced Tauler and later helped found the Brethren
of the Common Life. He was beatified by the Roman Catholic Church
in 1908.

Gerard Groote, a Dutch reformer, was born at Deventer in Holland
about 1340. He excelled as a student, but after a spiritual experience
went into retirement to prepare for a different life. From 1379 he
wandered as an itinerant lay preacher noted for the simplicity both
of his dress and his message. He founded the Brethren of the Common Life which emphasized reading the Bible and included both
clerical and lay members who cultivated a biblical piety, stressing the
inner life and the practice of virtues. Their spirituality was known as
the *Devotio Moderna* and was influential in both Catholic and Protestant traditions of prayer. Erasmus was one of their pupils.

Thomas Hammerken (or Haemerlein) was born in 1379 or 1380 in
Kempen (about forty miles from Cologne)—hence his usual name
Thomas a Kempis. In 1392 he went to Deventer, Holland to receive

his education in the school of the Brethren of the Common Life. He then entered the community at Mount Saint Agnes in the Low Countries about 1400 and remained there until his death July 25, 1471. At the monastery he wrote or compiled the *Imitation of Christ,* "the most perfect flower of medieval Christianity" which continues to influence the spiritual life of Christian people of all denominations. He is commemorated on the Episcopal calendar on July 24.

Reading

(From Catherine of Siena, *A Treatise on Divine Providence,* Chap. 5)

[God is speaking.] Dearest daughter, the willing desire to bear every pain and fatigue, even unto death, for the salvation of souls is very pleasing to me. The more the soul endures, the more she shows that she loves me; loving me, she comes to know more of my truth, and the more she knows, the more pain and intolerable grief she feels at the offenses committed against me. You asked me to sustain you and to punish the faults of others in you, and you did not recognize that you were really asking for love, light, and knowledge of the truth, since I have already told you that with the increase of love, grief and pain increase; for whoever grows in love grows in grief. Therefore I say to you all, ask, and it will be given to you, for I deny nothing to anyone who asks of me in truth. Remember that the love of divine charity is in the soul so closely joined with perfect patience, that neither can leave the soul without the other. Therefore, if the soul choose to love me, she should choose to endure pains for me in whatever way or circumstance I may send them to her. Patience cannot be proved in any other way than by suffering, and patience is one with love. Therefore bear yourselves with courage, for, unless you do, you will not prove yourselves to be spouses of my truth and faithful children nor part of the company of those who relish the taste of my honor and the salvation of souls.

Translated by P.H.P. based on the translation of Algar Thorold, *The Dialogue of the Seraphic Virgin, Catherine of Siena* . . . , new and abridged from the 1896 London edition (Westminster, MD: Newman, 1944); and reprinted in the Library of Christian Classics XIII, *Late Medieval Mysticism* ed. Ray C. Petry (Philadelphia: Westminster, n.d.) 277-278.

Propers

ROMAN

Father,
in meditating on the
   sufferings of your
   Son
and in serving your
   Church,
Saint Catherine was
   filled with the
   fervor of your love.
By her prayers,
may we share in the
   mystery of Christ's
   death,
and rejoice in the
   revelation of his
   glory,
for he lives and reigns
   with you and the
   Holy Spirit,
one God, for ever and
   ever.

*(Text from the English
translation of the Roman
Missal © 1973, Interna-
tional Committee on Eng-
lish in the Liturgy, Inc.
All rights reserved.)*

Common of Virgins
   or 1 John 1:5—2:2

LUTHERAN

Lord God, you have sur-
rounded us with so great a
cloud of witnesses. Grant
that we, encouraged by the
example of your servant
Catherine, may persevere
in the course that is set
before us, to be living signs
of the Gospel and at last,
with all the saints, to share
in your eternal joy; through
your Son, Jesus Christ our
Lord.

Common of Saints:
   Micah 6:6-8
      Psalm 9:1-10
   1 Corinthians 1:26-31
   Luke 6:20-23
   or Common of
      Renewers of the Church
   or Renewers of Society

EPISCOPAL

Almighty and everlast-
ing God, who kindled
the flame of your love
in the heart of your
servant Catherine:
Grant to us, your
humble servants, a like
faith and power of
love; that, as we re-
joice in her triumph,
we may profit by her
example; through Je-
sus Christ our Lord,
who lives and reigns
with you and the
Holy Spirit, one God,
now and for ever.

*(Text from Lesser Feasts
and Fasts, Revised Edi-
tion, copyright 1973 by
Charles Mortimer Guilbert
as Custodian of the Stan-
dard Book of Common
Prayer. All rights reserved.
Used by permission.)*

Psalm 36:5-11
2 Corinthians 12:2-10
   Psalm 137:1-6
Luke 10:21-24

Preface of a Saint

Hymn of the Day: "Love divine, all loves excelling" (315)

Prayers: for a desire to imitate the love of Christ
   for a willingness to endure suffering with him
   for a spirit of prayer and meditation

Preface: All Saints

Color: White

ST. PHILIP AND ST. JAMES, APOSTLES

Philip was born in Bethsaida, the same fishing village on the shores of Galilee from which Peter and Andrew came. He was one of the first disciples to follow Jesus, and brought Nathanael (sometimes identified with Bartholomew) to the Lord (John 1:43-51). Apart from his own calling, the story of Nathanael, and mention along with the other Apostles, the only other incidents of his life recorded in the Gospels are the occasion when some Greeks came to him to ask his help in getting an interview with Jesus (John 12:20-22) and the time Jesus asked Philip how they would be able to feed the crowds (John 6:5-7).

According to tradition, after Pentecost Philip went first to Scythia to preach the Gospel, where he was remarkably successful, and then to Phrygia where he stayed until his death. He is said to have met his death in the town of Hierapolis in Phrygia (in modern Turkey), according to some accounts by crucifixion and stoning. Traditions also tell of Philip's two unmarried daughters who survived him, lived to an old age, and were also buried in Hierapolis.

James the son of Alphaeus is usually called James the Less (meaning either "short" or "younger") to distinguish him from James the Elder, the brother of John, and from James of Jerusalem, the brother of the Lord. The only mention of James in the Scriptures, apart from his name in the apostolic lists, is the statement that his mother Mary was one of those present at the crucifixion (Matt. 27:55 and Mark 15:40), which also tells us that he had a brother named Joseph or the Greek form of the name, Joses.

May 1 has been kept as the feast day of St. Philip and St. James since 561 when on that date the supposed remains of the two saints were interred in the Church of the Apostles in Rome. To counteract the effects of the twentieth-century dedication of May 1 to the working classes and socialism, Pope Pius XII made May 1 the Feast of St. Joseph the Worker, and shifted the feast of Philip and James to May 11. The new Roman calendar commemorates the two apostles on May 3. Lutherans and Anglicans have retained the traditional date. In the Eastern churches, St. Philip's Day is November 14 and St. James the son of Alphaeus is remembered on October 9.

Reading

(From *The Saints in Daily Life* by Romano Guardini.)

If we were to probe a little further . . . we would be able to recognize the outlines of the figure of a new type of saint. It is no longer a matter of a man or woman who does exceptional things, but simply one who does what every man and woman who wishes to act well in a given situation will do. No more. No less.

To desire these things: that is true love. And in that love, let us repeat, there are limitless possibilities: that of a truth which is always to be more complete, of good always to be made more pure, of action always to be more resolute. To see in these beginnings the all of which our Lord speaks: all of the heart, all of the soul, all of the strength; to be able to see all in these humble beginnings: it is that in which sanctity consists. And this sanctity grows in the continuing struggles against oneself: in the necessary renunciations, in the challenging effort toward an ever purer sincerity of spirit and intention.

Sanctity nurtured in this way is less and less an obvious thing. One could almost say that this is a deliberately hidden sanctity: one that hides its greatness, one that does things of lesser and lesser importance *rightly;* but by that fact they become of greater and greater significance.

The saint will no longer be characterized by extraordinary behavior (as the historian, say, understands it); he will no longer appear to the world as separated from his fellow men or above them. On the contrary, he will be doing the same thing as everyone else: what needs to be done, what is right and just. But he will join to his behavior a purity of intention more and more deeply united to a great love of God; more and more detached from selfishness and self-satisfaction.

Romano Guardini, *The Saints in Daily Christian Life* (Philadelphia and New York: Chilton, 1966) 56-58, 61, 67-68. Used by permission of the publisher, Dimension Books, Inc.

Propers

ROMAN	LUTHERAN	EPISCOPAL
(May 3) God our Father, every year you give us joy on the festival of the apostles Philip and James. By the help of their prayers may we share in the suffering, death, and resurrection of your only Son and come to the eternal vision of your glory. We ask this through our Lord Jesus Christ, your Son, who lives and reigns with you and the Holy Spirit, one God, for ever and ever.	Almighty God, to know you is to have eternal life. Grant us to know your Son as the way, the truth, and the life, and guide our footsteps along the way of Jesus Christ our Lord, who lives and reigns with you and the Holy Spirit, one God now and forever.	Almighty God, who gave to your apostles Philip and James grace and strength to bear witness to the truth: Grant that we, being mindful of their victory of faith, may glorify in life and death the Name of our Lord Jesus Christ; who lives and reigns with you and the Holy Spirit, one God, now and for ever.

ROMAN	LUTHERAN	EPISCOPAL
1 Corinthians 15:1-8 Psalm 19:2-5 John 14:6-14	Isaiah 30:18-21 Psalm 44:1-3, 20-26 2 Corinthians 4:1-6 John 14:8-14	Isaiah 30:18-21 Psalm 119:33-40 2 Corinthians 4:1-6 John 14:6-14 Preface of Apostles

Hymn of the Day: "You are the way; through you alone" (464)

Prayers: for strength to follow Christ the way
        for grace to know the truth in Christ
        for courage to live the life of Christ

Preface: Apostles

Color: Red

Athanasius, Bishop of Alexandria, 373

Athanasius was one of the champions of Christian orthodoxy against the Arians, who denied that Christ was "one in Being with the Father" and claimed that "there was a time when the Son was not." Athanasius was born in Alexandria about 295. Nothing is known of his family. His parents probably were Egyptians, and more than one commentator remarks about the unusual darkness of Athanasius' skin. He received a good education in the classics and in the Christian Scriptures and theology. For a time he seems to have served Antony (Ca. 251-356; see July 11), the father of Christian monasticism, who had sought increasingly barren and remote places for his spiritual struggle.

About the year 312, Athanasius entered the Alexandrian clergy and was ordained a deacon about 318 by Bishop Alexander, whose successor he was. Athanasius accompanied his bishop to the Council of Nicaea in 325 where Arius' views were condemned and the Nicene Creed was written. Alexander, before his death in 328, designated Athanasius his successor and the choice was confirmed by the Egyptian bishops. The new bishop made extensive pastoral visits to the entire Egyptian province, but he faced vicious attacks by the Meletians and the Arians who had opposed his selection as bishop.

Athanasius was summoned to the Council of Tyre in 335, but since it was composed almost entirely of his enemies, appealed directly to the emperor Constantine who had him exiled to northern Gaul. When Constantine died in 337, his son allowed Athanasius to resume his episcopal duties, but at the Synod of Antioch in 337 or 338 he was deposed. This time Athanasius appealed to Rome with the support of other victims of anti-Nicene reaction. Pope Julius I convened a synod which declared Athanasius innocent of the charges against him. Since the Eastern bishops refused to accept the verdict, Athanasius remained in the West, travelling through Italy and Gaul.

Eventually Athanasius was allowed to return to Alexandria. He arrived in October 346, welcomed by the ninety-year-old Antony, and enjoyed a decade of relative peace, writing and promoting monasticism. Upon the death of the emperor Constans in 350, however, the enemies of Athanasius renewed their attack upon him, concentrating this time on the West. They got the Council of Arles in 353 and the

Council of Milan in 355 to condemn him. In February 356 a detachment of soldiers interrupted a vigil service with the intention of arresting Athanasius, but he managed to escape and for six years went into hiding in the Libyan desert, moving secretly from place to place, supported by loyal monks and clergy who enabled him to make several secret visits to Alexandria. He spent his time keeping in touch with developments in the world and writing.

In 361 a new emperor, Julian the Apostate, set the exiled bishops free. Athanasius returned to Alexandria in February 362 and convened a synod which anathematized Arianism, supported the Nicene Creed, and made room for reconciliation with his opponents. Julian, however, promoted a revival of paganism, and, not interested in a strong Christianity, had Athanasius exiled yet again in October 362. The emperor died the following June, and Athanasius returned to his see. In February 364, the co-emperor Valens resumed the persecution of those who opposed the Arian creed, and yet again Athanasius went into hiding for four months before he was permitted to return to Alexandria where he remained until his death May 2, 373. During his forty-five year episcopate he had been exiled five times and had spent altogether seventeen years away from his see.

The writings of this small but dauntless man are mainly polemical but are nonetheless of considerable importance. His *Defense against the Arians* and the *History of the Arians* are the best sources of knowledge about Christianity in the period 300-350. His brilliant pamphlet *On the Incarnation,* written in his youth, and his most famous work, *Discourse against the Arians,* remain among the clearest and most forceful explanations of the unity of the triune God and of the Incarnation of Christ. His *Life of St. Antony* was immensely popular and had a wide influence in spreading monastic ideals. In an Easter Letter he sent in 367, Athanasius produced our *oldest* surviving list of the twenty-seven books now in the New Testament (although in a different order than in modern Bibles) and declared them to be the New Covenant.

In some Lutheran churches, following older Roman Catholic practice, the creed named after him, the Athanasian Creed (*Quicunque vult*), is used at Matins on Trinity Sunday. The text of the creed, one of the ecumenical creeds of Christianity, is in the *Lutheran Book of Worship* and had appeared before that in *The Lutheran Hymnal.*

By his tireless defense of the faith, Athanasius earned the title

"Father of Orthodoxy" and became recognized as one of the four great Greek teachers of the church.

Hans von Campenhausen. *The Fathers of the Greek Church* tr. Stanley
    Godman (New York: Pantheon, 1959) 67-79.
Frank L. Cross. *The Study of St. Athanasius.* Oxford, 1945.
J. N. D. Kelly. *Early Christian Creeds.* 3rd ed., London: Longmans, 1972.
———. *The Athanasian Creed.* New York: Harper and Row, 1964.
Jaroslav Pelikan. *The Light of the World.* New York: Harper and Row,
    1962.

With Athanasius might also be remembered the principal Western defender of the Nicene faith, **Hilary,** Bishop of Poitiers. He was born in southwest Gaul and became bishop about the middle of the fourth century. As a consequence of his refusal to accede to the Emperor Constantinus' attempt to make all western bishops adhere to a credal formula which compromised the Nicene faith, Hilary was exiled to the East for four years, 356-360. His *On the Trinity* and *On the Synods* were the earliest Latin defences of Nicene theology. Among his disciples was Martin of Tours. Hilary died January 13, 367 and is commemorated on that date by the Episcopal and Roman Catholic churches.

Reading

(From Athanasius *On the Incarnation* 6, 8, 54)

. . . death having gained upon us and corruption abiding upon us, the human race was perishing; the rational creature made in God's image was disappearing, and the handiwork of God was in process of dissolution. . . . So, since the rational creatures were wasting into ruin, what was God in his goodness to do? Allow corruption to prevail against them and let death hold them fast? What then would be the point of making them in the first place? It would be far better had they not been made than, once made, be left to neglect and ruin. For neglect reveals weakness and not goodness on God's part should he allow his own work to be ruined—more so than if he had never made human beings at all. For had he not made them, no one could attribute weakness to him, but once he had made them, creating them out of nothing, it would be monstrous for that work to be ruined, especially before the eyes of the creator. It was then out of the question to abandon mortals to the current of corruption because this would be unseemly and unworthy of God's goodness.

Therefore the incorporeal and incorruptible and immaterial Word of God comes to our realm, even though he was not far from us before. For no part of creation is without him; he has filled everything everywhere, yet remains present with his Father. Nonetheless, in condescension he comes to show mercy to us and to visit us. And seeing the race of rational creatures on their way to perish and death reigning over them by corruption . . . he took pity on our race, had mercy on our weakness, condescended to our corruption, and . . . takes for himself a body—a body no different from ours. . . . And . . . he handed it over in death in the stead of all and in mercy offered it to the Father.

If one should wish to see God, who by his nature is invisible, one may know and apprehend him in his works. Likewise, those who fail to see Christ with their understanding can at least apprehend him by the works of his body and test whether they are human works or divine. If they are human, let them scoff; but if they are not human but divine, let them recognize it and not laugh at what is no scoffing matter but rather let them marvel that by so ordinary a means things divine have been manifested to us and that by death immortality has reached us all, and that by the Word becoming flesh the universal providence has been known and its giver and maker the very Word of God. For he was made human that we might be made God; and he manifested himself by a body that we might receive the idea of the unseen Father; and he endured the insolence of mortals that we might inherit immortality. . . . And wherever one turns one's glance, one may behold the divinity of the Word and be struck with exceedingly great awe.

Translated by P.H.P. based on the translation of Archibald Robertson in the Library of Christian Classics III, *Christology of the Later Fathers* ed. Edward Rochie Hardy (Philadelphia: Westminster, n.d.) 60-62, 107-108.

Propers

ROMAN	LUTHERAN	EPISCOPAL
Father, you raised up Saint Athanasius to be an outstanding defender of the truth of Christ's divinity. By his teaching and protection may we grow in your knowledge and love. Grant this through our Lord Jesus Christ, your Son, who lives and reigns with you and the Holy Spirit, one God, for ever and ever.	Almighty God, your Holy Spirit gives to one the word of wisdom, and to another the word of knowledge, and to another the word of faith. We praise you for the gifts of grace imparted to your servant Athanasius, and we pray that by his teaching we may be led to a fuller knowledge of the truth which we have seen in your Son Jesus Christ our Lord.	Almighty and eternal God, our Father, whose servant Athanasius testified that you are truly with us in the Word made flesh: Grant us so to see the glory of your Word and to grow into his likeness, that we may be fulfilled in knowledge of you, the only God; through Jesus Christ our Lord, to whom with you and the Holy Spirit be honor and glory, one God, forever and ever.

ROMAN	LUTHERAN	EPISCOPAL
Common of Pastors or Doctors or 1 John 5:1-5 or Matthew 10:22-25a	Common of Theologians or *Acts 20:19-35* *Psalm 71:1-8* *2 Corinthians 4:5-14* *Matthew 10:23-32* or Common of Pastors	Psalm 125 2 Corinthians 4:5-14 Psalm 71:1-8 Matthew 10:23-32 Preface of the Incarnation

Hymn of the Day: "Father most holy, merciful and tender" (169)
   or "Holy, holy, holy Lord God of Hosts" (*SBH* 135)
   to the tune of *St. Athanasius*

Prayers: for a deeper knowledge of Jesus Christ the Son of God
   for tireless pursuit of truth
   for singleminded devotion
   for reconciliation between quarreling parties in the church

Preface: Christmas (because Athanasius taught of the Incarnation)

Color: White

Monica, Mother of Augustine, 387

The mother of Augustine was born of Christian parents in North Africa, probably at Tagaste in Numidia, about 322. She married a pagan official Patricius who treated her respectfully and who was converted by her to Christianity just before he died in 371. After she bore Augustine, Monica seems to have had two other children, a son Navigius, and a daughter Perpetua.

She followed her eldest son's career with pride and attention, had him enrolled as a catechumen without his being baptized (a common custom at the time). Apprehensive at her son's waywardness, she prayed for his conversion and in 383 followed him to Rome and then to Milan where he came under the influence of Bishop Ambrose. She tried to arrange a marriage for her son, but this hope was frustrated although her prayers were answered when her son was baptized and converted to a celibate life.

Following her son's baptism, the two planned to return to North Africa in the fall of 387. But at Ostia, Monica fell sick and, after sharing a beautifully mystical experience with her son, died and was buried there.

In 1162 her bones were removed to an Augustinian monastery near Arras, France and her cult spread throughout the Western church. Other relics of her were brought to the Church of St. Augustine in Rome in 1430. Recently a fragment of her actual tombstone was discovered at Ostia, on which her name was spelled Monnica as it is the new Episcopal calendar.

The Roman Catholic Church now commemorates her on August 27, the day before her son's feast day. The Episcopal and Lutheran calendars retain the May 4 date, making Monica available as a model for Mother's Day in places where that observance is expected.

Reading

(From St. Augustine's *Confessions*, Book IX, 10-11)

The day was now approaching when my mother Monica would depart from this life; you knew that day, Lord, though we did not.

She and I happened to be standing by ourselves at a window that overlooked the garden in the courtyard of the house. At the time we were in Ostia on the Tiber. We had gone there after a long and wearisome journey to get away from the noisy crowd, and to rest and prepare for our sea voyage. I believe that you, Lord, caused all this to happen in your own mysterious ways. And so the two of us, all alone, were enjoying a very pleasant conversation, *forgetting the past and pushing on to what is ahead.* We were asking one another in the presence of the Truth—for you are the Truth—what it would be like to share the eternal life enjoyed by the saints, which *eye has not seen, nor ear heard, which has not entered into the heart of man.* We desired with all our hearts to drink from the streams of your heavenly fountain, the fountain of life.

That was the substance of our talk, though not the exact words. But you know, O Lord, that in the course of our conversation that day, the world and its pleasures lost all their attraction for us. My mother said, "Son, as far as I am concerned, nothing in this life now gives me any pleasure. I do not know why I am still here, since I have no further hopes in this world. I did have one reason for wanting to live a little longer: to see you become a Catholic Christian before I died. God has lavished his gifts on me in that respect, for I know that you have even renounced earthly happiness to be his servant. So what am I doing here?"

I do not really remember how I answered her. Shortly, within five days or thereabouts, she fell sick with a fever. Then one day during the course of her illness she became unconscious and for a while she was unaware of her surroundings. My brother and I rushed to her side but she regained consciousness quickly. She looked at us as we stood there and asked in a puzzled voice, "Where was I?"

We were overwhelmed with grief, but she held her gaze steadily upon us and spoke further, "Here you shall bury your mother." I remained silent as I held back my tears. However, my brother haltingly expressed his hope that she might not die in a strange country but in her own land, since her end would be happier there. When she heard this, her face was filled with anxiety, and she reproached him with a glance because he had entertained such earthly thoughts. Then she looked at me and spoke, "Look what he is saying." Thereupon she said to both of us, "Bury my body wherever you will; let not care of it cause you any concern. One thing only I ask you, that you remember me at the altar of the Lord wherever you may be." Once our mother had expressed this desire as best she could, she fell silent as the pain of her illness increased.

Then on the ninth day of her sickness, the fifty-sixth year of her age and the thirty-third of mine, that religious and holy soul was freed from the body.

Text from the English translation of the Office of Readings from the Liturgy of the Hours © 1974, International Committee on English in the Liturgy, Inc. All rights reserved. The last paragraph, added to the text of the Office of Readings, was translated by P.H.P.

Propers

ROMAN

(August 27)
God of mercy,
comfort of those in
sorrow,
the tears of Saint
Monica moved you
to convert her son
Saint Augustine to
the faith of Christ.
By their prayers, help
us to turn from our
sins
and to find your loving
forgiveness.
Grant this through our
Lord Jesus Christ,
your Son,
who lives and reigns
with you and the
Holy Spirit,
one God, for ever and
ever.

*(Text from the English
translation of the Roman
Missal © 1973, Interna-
tional Committee on Eng-
lish in the Liturgy, Inc.
All rights reserved.)*

Common of Saints
especially Ecclesiasti-
cus 26:1-4, 16-21
or Luke 7:11-17

LUTHERAN

Lord God, you have surrounded us with so great a cloud of witnesses. Grant that we, encouraged by the example of your servant Monica, may persevere in the course that is set before us, to be living signs of the Gospel and at last, with all the saints, to share in your eternal joy; through your Son, Jesus Christ our Lord.

Common of Saints
Micah 6:6-8
Psalm 9:1-10
1 Corinthians 1:26-31
Luke 6:20-23

EPISCOPAL

O God, who gave to blessed Monnica the grace of fervent and effective prayer for the conversion of her family to the true knowledge and love of you: Give us a like zeal and love for all spiritual discipline, that we may show forth in our lives what we believe and pray in our hearts; through Jesus Christ our Lord, who lives and reigns with you and the Holy Spirit, one God, now and ever.

*(Text from Lesser Feasts
and Fasts, Revised Edi-
tion, copyright 1973 by
Charles Mortimer Guilbert
as Custodian of the Stan-
dard Book of Common
Prayer. All rights reserved.
Used by permission.)*

Psalm 115:12-18
Proverbs 31:10-12,
26-31
Psalm 116:10-17
John 16:20-24

Preface of a Saint

Hymn of the Day: "O what their joy and their glory must be" (337)

Prayers: for mothers
      for the spirit of unceasing prayer
      for the unity of families in Christ

Preface: All Saints

Color: White

May 18

Erik, King of Sweden, Martyr, 1160

Erik was a twelfth-century king known for his crusades to spread Christianity in Scandinavia. As Erik IX Jedvardsson, he ruled over a considerable part of Sweden from about 1150 until his death a decade later. According to the *Legend of St. Erik* (dating from ca. 1270), Erik made an expedition to conquer and Christianize Finland, probably in 1155, accompanied by Henry of Uppsala (later St. Henry), who founded the church in Finland. Erik was a man of great personal goodness, who instituted salutary laws and helped the poor, and showed concern for the sick and infirm.

There are many stories of his crusades and of his murder in the church of Old-Uppsala on May 18, 1160 or 1161 at the hands of a Danish pagan prince, reinforced by rebels against Erik's rule. It was the day after Ascension Day. During Mass Erik was told that a Danish army was close by. He is said to have replied, "Let us at least finish the sacrifice; the rest of the feast I shall keep elsewhere." The conspirators rushed upon him as he left the church and beheaded him.

As early as the end of the twelfth century a calendar from the diocese of Uppsala mentions Erik as a saint (there was no formal canonization.) National pride and independence mingled with religious memories. Erik's son Cnut encouraged the honor of his father to help strengthen his position. At the same time Sweden was struggling to establish a separate archbishopric, and in 1164 a Swedish archbishop had been installed at Old-Uppsala. Soon afterward, Sweden, not to be outdone by Norway and St. Olaf, had its own patron saint. His body was placed in the cathedral at Uppsala, and, during the turmoil of the Reformation, his relics were not disturbed. The silver reliquary in which his remains still rest dates from the 1570s. Erik was honored as the ancestor of a line of Swedish kings and came to be recognized as the principal patron of Sweden. He is honored not only in Sweden (where his image appears on coins) but in Finland, Denmark, and Norway as well.

Steward Oakley. *A Short History of Sweden.* New York: Praeger, 1966.

Reading

(From *Imitation of Christ.*)

Jesus has many who love his Kingdom in Heaven, but few who bear his Cross. He has many who desire comfort, but few who desire suffering. He finds many to share his feast, but few his fasting. All desire to rejoice with him, but few are willing to suffer for his sake. Many follow Jesus to the Breaking of Bread, but few to the drinking of the Cup of his Passion. Many admire his miracles, but few follow him in the humiliation of his Cross. Many love Jesus as long as no hardship touches them. Many praise and bless him, as long as they are receiving any comfort from him. But if Jesus withdraw himself, they fall to complaining and utter dejection.

They who love Jesus for his own sake, and not for the sake of comfort for themselves, bless him in every trial and anguish of heart, no less than in the greatest joy. And were he never willing to bestow comfort on them, they would still always praise him and give him thanks.

Thomas a Kempis, *Imitation of Christ*, II, 11 trans. Leo Sherley-Price (Baltimore: Penguin, 1952) 83. Copyright © Leo Sherley-Price 1952. Reprinted by permission of Penguin Books, Ltd.

Propers: Martyrs (red) or Saints (white) since Erik's death may
        have been the result of political rather than religious
        controversy

Hymn of the Day: "At the Name of Jesus" (179)
                (sung to the tune *St. Erik, SBH* 430)

Prayers: for the land and government and people of Sweden
        for all who govern
        for a spirit of self-sacrificing service
        for a right relationship between church and state
        for those who struggle with national pride and religious
           loyalty

Color: Red or white

Dunstan, Archbishop of Canterbury, 988

Dunstan was born of a noble family at Baltonborough, Somerset, near Glastonbury in 909. He was educated by Irish clerics and joined the household of his uncle Athelm, the Archbishop of Canterbury, and the court of King Athelstan. In 936 he made a private monastic profession to Alphege, the Bishop of Winchester, and was ordained. He lived as a hermit near Glastonbury, supporting himself by working as a scribe, embroiderer, and silversmith. In 940, King Edmund, after a narrow escape from death while on a stag hunt, installed Dunstan as abbot of Glastonbury and provided financial support for the abbey. Dunstan introduced the Benedictine Rule, enlarged the buildings, and added to the library.

In 956, having criticized King Edwig's conduct, Dunstan was exiled to Mont Blandin in Ghent (Belgium) where he became acquainted with continental monasticism. He was recalled to England by King Edgar in 957, and was made Bishop of Worcester to which was added the diocese of London in 959 and in the following year Dunstan was made Archbishop of Canterbury. The collaboration between the king and the archbishop was regarded by later writers as a golden age.

Under the aegis of King Edgar, Dunstan, together with Aethelwold (d. 984), Abbot of Abingdon before he became Bishop of Winchester, and Oswald, (d. 992) Bishop of Worcester and then Archbishop of York, reestablished monasticism in England along Benedictine lines.

The three great leaders of the renewal were deeply influenced by continental reforms which sought independence from lay founders and landlords and a strict adherence to the Rule of St. Benedict. During this flowering of monasticism, monks occupied several important sees and the monasteries enjoyed royal protection. In the south and the midlands Dunstan himself seems to have reformed or refounded Malmesbury, Bath, Westminster, and perhaps introduced monks at Canterbury Cathedral. In addition, he built churches, corrected abuses such as the neglect of celibacy by the clergy, encouraged laypeople in their devotions, and deepened the concern for justice. He is said also to have cast bells and made organs. He was a man of wide-ranging interests from books to affairs of court, but his chief fame is the reform of the monasteries which became centers of religion and culture and provided bishops for England and missionaries for Scandinavia.

He sang his last service on Ascension Day 988 and died two days later, May 19. He is buried near the high altar of his cathedral.

In art, Dunstan is often represented with a pair of tongs. There is a legend that one day, while working in metal, the devil came to torment him. Dunstan turned, tweaked the devil's nose with his tongs hot from the fire, and returned to his work.

Eleanor S. Duckett. *Saint Dunstan of Canterbury.* New York: Macmillan, 1955.
David Knowles. *The Monastic Order in England.* 2d ed. Cambridge University Press, 1963.
J. A. Robinson. *The Times of Saint Dunstan.* Oxford, 1923.

Reading

(From *The Silent Life* by Thomas Merton.)

Let us face the fact that the monastic vocation tends to present itself to the modern world as a problem and as a scandal.

In a basically religious culture, like that of India, or of Japan, the monk is more or less taken for granted. When all society is oriented beyond mere transient quest of business and pleasure, no one is surprised that men should devote their lives to an invisible God. In a materialistic culture which is fundamentally irreligious the monk is incomprehensible because he "produces nothing." His life appears to be completely useless. Not even Christians have been exempt from anxiety over this apparent "uselessness" of the monk, and we are familiar with the argument that the monastery is a kind of dynamo which, though it does not "produce" grace, procures this infinitely precious spiritual commodity for the world.

The first Fathers of monasticism were concerned with no such arguments, valid though they may be in their proper context. The Fathers did not feel that the search for God was something that needed to be defended. Or rather, they saw that if men did not realize in the first place that God was to be sought, no other defence of monasticism would avail with them.

Is God then to be sought?

The deepest law in man's being is his need for God, for life. God is Life. "In Him was life, and the life was the light of men, and the light shineth in the darkness and the darkness comprehendeth it not" (John 1:5). The deepest need of our darkness is to comprehend the light which shines in the midst of it. Therefore God has given us, as His first commandment: "Thou shalt love the Lord thy God with thy whole heart, and with thy whole soul and with all thy strength." The monastic life is nothing but the life of those who have taken the first commandment in deadly earnest, and have, in the words of St. Benedict, "preferred nothing to the love of Christ."

But Who is God? Where is He? Is Christian monasticism a search for some pure intuition of the Absolute? A cult of the supreme Good? A worship of perfect and changeless Beauty? The very emptiness of such abstractions strikes the heart cold. The Holy One, the Invisible, the Almighty is infinitely greater and more real than any abstraction of man's devising. But He has said: "No one shall see me and live" (Exodus 33:20). Yet the monk persists in crying out with Moses: "Show me Thy face" (Exodus 33:13).

The monk, then, is one who is so intent upon the search for God that he is ready to die in order to see Him. That is why the monastic life is a "martyrdom" as well as a "paradise," a life that is at once "angelic" and "crucified."

St. Paul resolves the problem: "God who commanded the light to shine out of darkness, hath shined in our hearts to give the light of the knowledge of the glory of God, in the face of Christ Jesus" (2 Corinthians 4:6).

The monastic life is the rejection of all that obstructs the spiritual rays of this mysterious light. The monk is one who leaves behind the fictions and illusions of a merely human spirituality in order to plunge himself in the faith of Christ. Faith is the light which illumines him in mystery. Faith is the power which seizes upon the inner depths of his soul and delivers him up to the action of the divine Spirit, the Spirit of liberty, the Spirit of love. Faith takes him, as the power of God took the ancient prophets, and "stands him upon his feet" (Ezekiel 2:2) before the Lord. The monastic life is life in the Spirit of Christ, a life in which the Christian gives himself entirely to the love of God which transforms him in the light of Christ.

Thomas Merton, *The Silent Life* (1957), viii-ix. Copyright © by the Abbey of Our Lady of Gethsemani. Reprinted by permission of Farrar, Straus and Giroux, Inc.

Propers

ROMAN

LUTHERAN

Lord God, you have surrounded us with so great a cloud of witnesses. Grant that we, encouraged by the example of your servant Dunstan, may persevere in the course that is set before us, to be living signs of the gospel and at last, with all the saints, to share in your eternal joy; through your Son, Jesus Christ our Lord.

EPISCOPAL

O God, by whose grace your blessed servant Dunstan, kindled with the fire of your love, became a burning and a shining light in your Church: Grant that we also may be inflamed with the spirit of discipline and love, and ever walk before you as children of light; through Jesus Christ our Lord, who lives and reigns with you and the Holy Spirit, one God now and for ever.

ROMAN	LUTHERAN	EPISCOPAL
	Common of Saints:	Psalm 92:1-4
	Micah 6:6-8	Ecclesiasticus 44:1-7
	Psalm 9:1-10	Psalm 92:11-14
	1 Corinthians 1:26-31	Matthew 24:42-47
	Luke 6:20-23	Preface of a Saint

Hymn of the Day: "Let the whole creation cry" (242)
or "All who would valiant be" (498): the tune is
St. Dunstan's
or "From thee all skill and science flow" (*SBH* 216)

Prayers: for deepened commitment to the Christian life
for monasteries and those who seek to serve God there
for those who seek to join religion and culture
for musicians and artists

Preface: All Saints

Color: White

May 21

John Eliot,
Missionary to the American Indians, 1690

John Eliot, the Apostle to the Indians and one of the most remarkable men of seventeenth-century New England, was born in England July 31, 1604 and baptized in the parish of St. John the Baptist in Widford, Hertfordshire, August 5, the third of seven children. His father owned considerable property. He entered Jesus College, Cambridge, in 1619 and received the B.A. in 1622. He excelled as a student, especially of the classics. He taught for a time at the grammar school at Little Baddow in Essex, where he came under the influence of Thomas Hooker. His religious life began, and he determined to become a clergyman.

He left England aboard the *Lyon* with some Puritan friends and the Winthrop family whom he served as minister. They reached Boston November 3, 1631. A year later (October 1632), Eliot married

Ann (or Hannah) Mumford and was ordained as a "teacher" of the church at Roxbury. Friends from Essex came to Massachusetts and settled at Roxbury, and for sixty years Eliot served as their minister— for forty years their only pastor.

From a captured Long Island native Eliot learned of Indian customs and language. In 1646 he first preached to the Indians (in English) at Dorchester Mills and Newton (Noantun). He began regular bi-weekly preaching and catechization, using the native language by the summer of 1647. In 1649, inspired by Eliot's work, the first genuine missionary society, "The Company for Propagating the Gospel in New England and Parts Adjacent in North America," was incorporated in England and was a source of financial support. Eliot published *A Primer or Catechism* in 1654 and by 1658 translated the Bible into Algonkian, the dialect of the Massachusetts Indians. The New Testament was printed at Cambridge in 1661 and the Old Testament in 1663—the first Bible to be printed in North America. A revised edition was published in 1685.

Eliot established a small Indian college at Cambridge and had hopes of Christianizing all the Native Americans in New England; but recognizing their dislike of being too close to the whites, he planned an Indian town in the wilderness at Natick. In 1651 the town was laid out and several families of "praying Indians" settled there as a self-governing community, free to manage their own affairs under the general laws of Massachusetts. By 1674 there were fourteen such towns with several thousand inhabitants. Each village had a school where the Indians learned English and handicrafts to support themselves. Eliot carefully trained Native Americans to be missionaries to their own people, and himself travelled all over New England, encountering some opposition. The first Indian minister, Daniel Takawambpait, was ordained at Natick in 1681.

The outbreak of King Philip's War in 1675 scattered the praying communities. Ten were never restored, and the remaining four dwindled away.

In the summer of 1680, Jasper Danckaerts, a visiting Dutch Reformed minister, reported in his diary of a visit to Boston.

July 7th. Sunday. We heard preaching in three churches, by persons who seemed to possess zeal, but no just knowledge of Christianity. The auditors were very worldly and inattentive. The best of the ministers whom we have yet heard is a very old man, named Mr. John Eliot, who has charge of the instruction of the Indians in the Christian religion. He has translated the Bible into their language. After we had already made inquiries of the booksellers for this Bible, and there was none to be obtained in Boston, and they told us if one was to be had, it would be from Mr. Eliot, we determined to go on Monday to the village where he resided, and was the minister, called Rocsberry. . . .

July 8th. Monday. We went accordingly, about six o'clock in the morning, to Rocsberry, which is three-quarters of an hour from the city, in order that we might get home early . . . and in order that Mr. Eliot might not be gone from home. On arriving at his house, he was not there, and we therefore went to look around the village and the vicinity. We found it justly called Rocsberry, for it was very rocky, and had hills entirely of rocks. Returning to his house, we spoke to him, and he received us politely. As he could speak neither Dutch nor French, and we spoke but little English, we were unable to converse very well; however, partly in Latin, partly in English, we managed to understand each other. He was seventy-seven years old, and had been forty-eight years in these parts. He had learned very well the language of the Indians, who lived about there.

. . . We enquired how it stood with the Indians, and whether any good fruit had followed his work. Yes, much, he said, if we meant true conversion of the heart; for they had in various countries, instances of conversion, as they called it, and had seen it amount to nothing at all. . . . He could thank God, he continued, and God be praised for it, there were Indians whom he knew, who were truly converted of heart, and whose profession, he believed, was sincere. (*Journal of Jasper Danckaerts* 1679-1689, ed. Bartlett Burleigh James and J. Franklin Jameson New York: Scribner's, 1913. Trans. Henry C. Murphy 1867).

Eliot, who, Perry Miller says, "incarnated the Puritan ideal of saintly piety," wrote prolifically. Among his works were *The Christian Commonwealth* (1659), *Up-Bookum Psalmes* (1663), *The Communion of Churches* (1665), *The Indian Primer* (1669), *The Harmony of the Gospels* (1678). He joined with Richard Mather and Thomas Wilder in the production of the *Bay Psalm Book*, which was in use for a century.

John Eliot died May 21, 1690, at Roxbury, survived by two of his six children.

Also on this day, **Daniel Takawambpait** might be remembered. He was the first Indian minister and was ordained at Natick, Massachusetts, in 1681.

Carleton Beals. *John Eliot.* New York: Messner, 1957. (Beals gives the date of Eliot's death as May 20.)

Perry Miller and Thomas H. Johnson, eds. *The Puritans,* rev. ed. Vol. II. (New York: Harper, 1963), 404-408; 496-511.

Francis Russell, "Apostle to the Indians," *American Heritage* IX, 1 (December 1957), 4-9, 117-119.

Ola E. Winslow. *John Eliot. "Apostle to the Indians."* Boston: Houghton Mifflin, 1968.

Reading

(From *Magnalia Christi Americana* by Cotton Mather.)

It has been observed, that they who have spoke many considerable things in their lives usually speak few at their deaths. But it was otherwise with our Eliot, who after much speech of and for God in his lifetime, uttered some things little short of oracles on his deathbed, which, 'tis a thousand pities, they were not more exactly regarded and recorded. . . .

This was the peace in the end of this perfect and upright man; thus was there another star fetched away to be placed among the rest that the third heaven is now enriched with. He had once, I think, a pleasant fear, that the old saints of his acquaintance, especially those two dearest neighbors of his, Cotton of Boston and Mather of Dorchester, which were got safe to heaven before him, would suspect him to be gone the wrong way, because he staid so long behind them. But they are now together with a blessed Jesus, beholding his glory and celebrating the high praises of him that has called them into his marvelous light. Whether heaven was any more heaven to him because of his finding there so many saints, with whom he once had his desirable intimacies, yea, and so many saints which had been the seals of his own ministry in this lower world, I cannot say; but it would be heaven enough unto him, to go unto that Jesus, whom he had loved, preached, served, and in whom he had been long assured, there does all fullness dwell. In that heaven I now leave him. . . . Blessed will be the day, O blessed the day of our arrival to the glorious assembly of spirits, which this great saint is now rejoicing with!

. . . If the dust of dead saints could give us any protection, we are not without it; here is a spot of American soil that will afford a rich crop of it at the resurrection of the just. Poor New England has been as Glastonbury of Old was called, A Burying Place of Saints. But we cannot see a more terrible Prognostic, than tombs filling space with such bones as those of the renowned Eliot's; the whole building of this country trembles at the fall of such a pillar.

Cotton Mather, *Magnalia Christi Americana.* (London, 1702), Book III.

Propers: Missionaries

Hymn of the Day: "The God of Abraham praise" (544)

Prayers: for justice for the American Indians
for respect for the Native American traditions
for concern for their welfare
for the spirit of prayer
for those who teach the church to sing

Preface: Epiphany

Color: White

Ludwig Nommensen, Missionary to Sumatra, 1918

Ludwig Ingwer Nommensen, the Apostle to the Bataks, was born February 6, 1834 on the island of Nordstrand in Schleswig-Holstein, which was at that time under the Danish crown. He was a man of deep faith, courage, prophetic vision, and indomitable resolution. He worked for a time as a hired hand and then as an assistant teacher. In 1857 he enrolled in the Barmen missionary school of the Rhenish Missionary Society. On December 14, 1861 the course of his life was set, and after a brief period of training in Holland, he left on the 24th for Sumatra to join two German missionaries who had begun work there that year. On June 25, 1862 Nommensen landed at Barus, on the northwest coast and spent the rest of his life on the island. He moved inland, where he labored among the Bataks, a large tribal group then untouched either by Islam or Christianity.

In 1866 he was joined by P. H. Johannsen, a teacher, writer, and linguist. After initial troubles stemming partly from the difficulty of reconciling clan responsibilities and Christian faith, the mission began to succeed, first with the conversion of a number of chiefs and then thousands of their followers. By 1876 the membership reached two thousand. In 1885, to counter the advance of Islam, Nommensen moved northward to the Lake Toba plain and then further north in 1903. His wife and four children died. In 1892 he married again, but his second wife died in 1909, leaving three children.

Almost from the beginning the church in Sumatra had a thoroughly Batak flavor. The New Testament had been translated into Batak by 1878. Nommensen sought to preserve the social structure of the village community, and many features of the local customary law were maintained. He introduced a teacher-preacher office to aid in the growth and support of the local churches and their schools and sought missionaries "who take God at his word, who count with God as they count with numbers, and who joining in battle look forward to victory." An indigenous church order was drafted by Nommensen and was in use until 1930.

The Batak Christian community prospered and grew under the benevolent leadership of Nommensen until his death on May 23, 1918. It continued in much the same form until 1940 when the missionaries were interned and the Batak people took over full management of their own church, adopting a church constitution in 1950 and joining the Lutheran World Federation in 1952. The Batak church, which now numbers more than half a million, presided over by the Ephorus, a bishop of set term, is a living memorial to the vision of Nommensen. In 1952 a monument to Nommensen was erected in the Silindung valley where he had labored; it now includes a bust of the missionary sculpted by an artist from Dusseldorf. In 1954 Nommensen University was founded by the Batak church to serve the educational needs of the area, and in 1961 Christians in Europe and Indonesia celebrated the one hundredth anniversary of the establishment of the church and published a volume of studies in his honor.

N. de Waard. *Pioneer in Sumatra*. London, 1962.

Reading

(From *The Company of the Committed* by Elton Trueblood.)

There is no better way, in contemporary thought, of approaching the meaning of commitment than by reference to Marcel's distinction between "believing that" and "believing in." To be committed is to believe *in*. Commitment, which includes belief but far transcends it, is determination of the total self to act upon conviction. Always and everywhere, as Blaise Pascal and many other thinkers have taught us, it includes an element of wager. This is why in great religious literature, including the New Testament, the best light that can be thrown upon commitment is that provided by marriage. For everyone recognizes the degree to which marriage is a bold venture, undertaken without benefit of escape clauses. The essence of all religious marriage vows is their *unconditional* quality. A man takes a woman not, as in a contract, under certain specified conditions, but "for better, for worse; for richer, for poorer; in sickness and in health." Always, the commitment is unconditional and for life. The fact that some persons fail in this regard does not change the meaning of that glorious undertaking.

One way of stating the crucial difference between belief and commitment is to say that when commitment occurs there is attached to belief an "existential index" which changes its entire character. Belief *in* differs from belief *that*, in the way in which the entire self is involved. "If I believe in something," says Marcel, "it means that I place myself at the disposal of something, or again that I pledge myself fundamentally, and this pledge affects not only *what I have* but also *what I am.*"

. . . A Christian is a person who confesses that, amidst the manifold and confusing voices heard in the world, there is one Voice which supremely wins his full assent, uniting all his powers, intellectual and emotional, into a single pattern of self-giving. That Voice is Jesus Christ. A Christian not only believes *that* He was; he believes *in Him* with all his heart and strength and mind. Christ appears to the Christian as the one stable point or fulcrum in all the relativities of history. Once the Christian has made this primary commitment he still has perplexities, but he begins to know the joy of being used for a mighty purpose, by which his little life is dignified.

Elton Trueblood, *The Company of the Committed* (New York: Harper and Row, 1961) 22-23. Copyright © 1961 by David Elton Trueblood. Reprinted by permission of Harper and Row, Publishers, Inc.

Propers: Missionaries

Hymn of the Day: "Jesus shall reign where'er the sun" (530)

Prayers: for the Batak church
   for respect for the indigenous customs and traditions in
    missionary churches
   for faithfulness to God rather than human demands
   for native scholars and teachers

Preface: Epiphany

Color: White

May 24

Nicolaus Copernicus, Teacher, 1543

Copernicus (Mikolaj Kopernik) was born February 19, 1473 at the port city of Torun in Eastern Poland, the son of a socially prominent copper merchant. His parents died before he was twelve and he was entrusted to a maternal uncle. In 1491 he entered the University of Cracow where he became interested in astronomy. He returned to his uncle's home about 1494, and his uncle, the newly-elected bishop of Ermland, wanted him to become a canon of Frauenburg Cathedral in Polish Prussia in order that he might have a life of financial security. While he waited for a vacancy, he was sent by his uncle to the University of Bologna where he associated with the German students and spent three and a half years in the study of Greek, mathematics, and Plato. In 1497 he was elected canon. He went to Rome in 1500, returned briefly to his cathedral, and left again for Italy to continue his study at the University of Padua in law and medicine. In 1503 he was granted the degree of Doctor of Canon Law by the University of Ferrara and returned to Poland, acting as his uncle's advisor until the uncle's death in 1512. He then settled per-

manently in Frauenburg, making use of his medical knowledge in
helping the poor. In 1520 he was made commander of the defences
of Ermland in a war with the Teutonic knights.

Copernicus' interests were wide-ranging: mathematics, astronomy,
medicine, theology, poetry. His fame as an astronomer increased, but
he was increasingly dissatisfied with the Ptolemaic geocentric system,
as were many others of his time. Although the Greek astronomer
Aristarchus of Samos as far back as the third century B.C. had suggested that the sun was the center of the universe, the geocentric
theory had become firmly entrenched in astronomical and theological
thought. It had, however, become an unwieldily and enormously
complex system of circles upon circles that tried to account for the
observed variations in the movement of the heavens. Copernicus
searched for a simpler description, and he renewed interest in the
old heliocentric theory. With meager instruments he eventually verified the heliocentric system to his own satisfaction and cautiously
announced his theory in a manuscript first circulated in 1530 privately
among friends, who urged its publication. After decades of hesitation,
Copernicus sent his pupil Georg Joachim Rhaeticus with the manuscript to Nurenberg for printing. Rhaeticus, appointed professor at
Leipzig, went to that city with the manuscript where it was published
(with a preface inserted by the Lutheran pastor Andreas Osiander
emphasizing that the hypothesis of a stationary sun was only a convenient way of simplifying the model of the universe). A copy of the
printed book, *De Revolutionibus Orbium Caelestium* (*The Revolu-
tions of the Heavenly Bodies*), was brought to Copernicus a few
hours before his death May 24, 1543 at Frauenburg.

Copernicus' revolutionary rejection of the prevailing model of the
solar system displaced the earth from the center of the universe. The
earth was no longer seen as the epitome of creation, and Copernicus'
theory implied a much larger universe than had previously been
imagined. His writing was on the Index of Prohibited Books from
1616 to 1758.

Angus Armitage. *Copernicus: The Founder of Modern Astronomy*. London:
    W. H. Allen, 1957. (New York: Norton, 1938).
———. *Sun, Stand Thou Still*. Toronto: Oxford, 1947.
Maria Bogucka. *Nicholas Copernicus: The Country and Times* tr. Leon
    Szwajcer. Warsaw: Ossolinski State Publishing House, 1973.

"The Copernican Revolution," *Horizon IX*, 1 (Winter 1972), 39-45.
Thomas S. Kuhn. *The Copernican Revolution.* Toronto: Random House,
1959.

Reading

There have always been two ways of looking for truth. One is to
find concepts which are beyond challenge, because they are held by
faith or by authority or the conviction that they are self-evident. This
is the mystic submission to truth which the East has chosen, and
which dominated the axiomatic thought of the scholars of the Middle
Ages. So St. Thomas Aquinas holds that faith is a higher guide to
truth than knowledge is: the master of medieval science puts science
firmly into second place.

But long before Aquinas wrote, Peter Abelard had already challenged the whole notion that there are concepts which can only be
felt by faith or authority. All truth, even the highest, is accessible to
test, said Abelard: "By doubting we are led to inquire, and by inquiry
we perceive the truth." The words might have been written five
hundred years later by Descartes, and could have been a recipe for
the Scientific Revolution; for in effect what Luther said in 1517 was
that we may appeal to a demonstrable work of God, the Bible, to
override any established authority. The Scientific Revolution begins
when Copernicus implied the bolder proposition that there is another
work of God to which we may appeal even beyond this: the great
work of nature. No absolute statement is allowed to be out of reach
of the test, that its consequence must conform to the facts of nature.

This habit of testing and correcting the concept by its consequences
in experience has been the spring within the movement of our civilization ever since. In science and in art and in self-knowledge we
explore and move constantly by turning to the world of sense to ask,
Is this so? This is the habit of truth, always minute yet always urgent,
which for four hundred years has entered every action of ours; and
has made our society and the value it sets on man, as surely as it has
made the linotype machine and the scout knife, and *King Lear* and
the *Origin of Species* and Leonardo's *Lady with a Stoat.*

204   *May 24*

Jacob Bronowski, *Science and Human Values* (New York: Harper & Row, 1975) 45-46. Copyright © 1956, 1965 by J. Bronowski. Reprinted by permission of Julian Messner, a Simon and Schuster division of Gulf and Western Corporation.

May 24

Leonhard Euler, Scientist, 1783

Leonhard Euler, one of the most prolific mathematicians of all time, was born in Basel April 15, 1707, the son of a Calvinist pastor who himself had an interest in mathematics. Euler, at his father's insistence, pursued the study of theology but then was permitted to turn his attention to mathematics and earned his master's degree at the age of 17. It was not a promising profession; there were few jobs for mathematicians in Switzerland at the time.

In 1727 he became an associate of the St. Petersburg Academy of Sciences and in 1730 was appointed to the chair of mathematics. In 1738 he lost the sight of his right eye through disease.

In 1741 he was invited to Berlin by Frederick the Great. Euler remained there for twenty-five years and kept up a steady stream of publications in geometry, calculus, mechanics, number theory, and astronomy. He was also responsible for numerous administrative duties and was also a consultant to the government.

When Frederick became less cordial, Euler returned to Russia in 1766. A cataract formed in his good eye. Surgery helped only temporarily, and in 1771 he went totally blind. His work was nonetheless not interrupted, for he had a remarkable facility at mental computations. He continued his scholarly studies until the day of his death, September 18, 1783. He was buried in the Lutheran Smolenskoye cemetery in St. Petersburg.

A. P. Youschkevitch, "Leonard Euler," *Dictionary of Scientific Biography* IV (New York: Scribner's, 1971) 467-484.

Reading

(From John Calvin's *Institutes.*)

Since the perfection of blessedness consists in the knowledge of God, he has been pleased, in order that none might be excluded from the means of obtaining felicity, not only to deposit in our minds that seed of religion of which we have already spoken, but so to manifest his perfections in the whole structure of the universe, and daily place himself in our view that we cannot open our eyes without being compelled to behold him. His essence, indeed, is incomprehensible, utterly transcending all human thought; but on each of his works his glory is engraven in characters so bright, so distinct, and so illustrious, that none, however dull and illiterate, can plead ignorance as their excuse. Hence, with perfect truth, the Psalmist exclaims, "He covers himself with light as with a garment" (Psalm 104:2); as if he had said, that God for the first time was arrayed in visible attire when, in the creation of the world, he displayed those glorious banners, on which, to whatever side we turn, we behold his perfections visibly portrayed. In the same place, the Psalmist aptly compares the expanded heavens to his royal tent, and says, "He lays the beams of his chambers upon the waters, makes the clouds his chariot, and walks upon the wings of the wind," sending forth the winds and lightnings as his swift messengers. And because the glory of his power and wisdom is more refulgent in the firmament, it is frequently designated as his palace. And, first, wherever you turn your eyes, there is no portion of the world, however minute, that does not exhibit at least some sparks of beauty; while it is impossible to contemplate the vast and beautiful fabric as it extends around, without being overwhelmed by the immense weight of glory.

John Calvin, *Institutes of the Christian Religion* trans. Henry Beveridge (Grand Rapids, MI: Eerdmans, 1957 [1845]), vol. I, p. 51.

Propers: Artists and Scientists

Hymn of the Day: "Eternal ruler of the ceaseless round" (373)

Prayers: for astronomers and watchers of the skies
        for mathematicians and all scientists

for courage to pursue truth
for humility and awe in the face of mystery
for a new vision of the beauty of creation

Color: White

John Calvin, Renewer of the Church, 1564

John Calvin, who gave Protestant doctrine its most systematic formulation, was born at Noyon, France, July 10, 1509, the second son
of Gerard Cauvin (Calvin is a Latinized form), a secretary to the
bishop. The son was a serious and able student, and at fourteen he
was sent to Paris to continue his studies in grammar, rhetoric, and
theology. He took particular interest in the Fathers, especially Augustine. He received the M.A. in 1528 at the age of nineteen.

His father, thinking law a more lucrative profession (and because
of his own excommunication over a dispute concerning the closing
of an estate) had his son change his course of study. He went to the
University of Orleans, then to Bourges to study law and humanism.
Calvin's father died in May, 1531, and Calvin left the study of law
and turned to literary scholarship at the new College de France in
Paris, studying both Greek and Hebrew.

Late in 1533 or 1534, he underwent a "sudden conversion" as he
called it, and embraced the doctrines of the Protestant reformers. He
broke with the Roman Church and devoted himself to the cause of
Protestant reformation. He left France for Protestant Basel. There he
began the formulation of new theological ideas and published the
first edition of the *Institutes of the Christian Religion* in 1536. In
that year Calvin returned briefly to Paris to settle some family business. He left Paris, intending to go to Strassburg, but he was forced
to detour through Geneva where his friend Guillaume Farel persuaded him to remain. The neighboring city of Berne had been
Protestant since 1528 and supplied Geneva with Protestant preachers
from 1532. Farel was one of these.

Calvin undertook the task of establishing and organizing the new church in Geneva under rigidly uniform, theocratic discipline. In 1538 the government of Geneva passed to those hostile to Calvin, and Farel and Calvin were banished. From April 1538 to September 1541 they were in Strassburg upon the invitation of Martin Bucer. In 1540 Calvin married the widow of one of his converts. She bore him a son who died shortly after birth; she died in 1549. Calvin agreed to return to Geneva in September 1541 after the town had returned to the rule of the pro-Calvin faction. The new constitution provided for four kinds of ministers—pastors, teachers, elders, deacons—and a consistory of elders and pastors to maintain discipline.

Struggle and conflict over doctrinal points led to the beheading of Jacques Gruet for blasphemy and the burning of Michael Servetus, an anti-Trinitarian Spanish physician. Although the dispute continued, Calvin's rule was secure. Despite ill health in his last years, he kept up preaching, teaching, and writing. He died at Geneva May 27, 1564.

John Calvin. Autobiographical Preface to *Commentary on Psalms.* 1557.
Georgia E. Harkness. *John Calvin: The Man and His Ethics.* New York; Abingdon, 1958.
T. H. L. Parker. *John Calvin: A Biography,* Philadelphia: Westminster, 1976.
Francois Wendel. Calvin. *Origins and Development of His Religious Thought.* trans. Philip Mairet. New York: Harper, 1964.

John Knox, the Scottish reformer, is appropriately remembered with Calvin. Knox was born ca. 1505 at Haddington, Scotland. He was ordained in minor orders, but gave up the ministry to become a private tutor. Soon afterward, he embraced the Reformation, and in 1547 he became a preacher at St. Andrew's. He was taken prisoner by the French, released in 1549, and went to England, where he was made chaplain to Edward VI. Upon Mary's accession to the throne, he fled to the continent where he met Calvin.

In 1555 the French-born queen regent of Scotland attempted to end the expansion of Protestantism in her realm, and the Protestants recalled Knox for their defence. England and Scotland stood together against France, which had designs on all three countries. Knox's preaching and writing met with success, but continuing persecution led him to move to the English Church at Geneva in 1556. Even there, he was in constant conflict with the crown, but in the grim winter of

1559, Knox's resolution kept the British cause alive until their victory the following spring.

Knox then turned to the organization of the Scottish church. In a democratic fashion, he gave a large role to the laity in the government of the church. Deep, personal, and vindictive hatred grew between Knox and Queen Mary until her abdication in 1567. After suffering a paralytic stroke, Knox died November 24, 1572 at Edinburgh.

A balanced assessment of Knox is difficult. He was a controversial leader—intolerant (as were many in his time), yet occasionally tender, and single-minded in his devotion to his religious creed.

Jasper G. Ridley. *John Knox*. New York: Oxford, 1968.
W. Stanford Reid. *Trumpeter of God: A Biography of John Knox*. New York: Scribner's, 1974.

Reading

(From John Calvin's *Institutes*.)

First of all, the pious mind does not devise for itself any kind of God, but looks alone to the one true God; nor does it feign for him any character it pleases, but is contented to have him in the character in which he manifests himself, always guarding, with the utmost diligence, against transgressing his will and wandering with a daring presumption from the right path. He by whom God is thus known, perceiving how he governs all things, confides in him as his guardian and protector, and casts himself entirely upon his faithfulness—perceiving him to be the source of every blessing, if he is in any strait or feels any want, he instantly recurs to his protection and trusts to his aid—persuaded that he is good and merciful, he reclines upon him with sure confidence and doubts not that in the divine clemency a remedy will be provided for his every time of need—acknowledging him as his Father and his Lord, he considers himself bound to have respect to his authority in all things, to reverence him majesty, aim at the advancement of his glory, and obey his commands—regarding him as a just judge, armed with severity to punish crimes, he keeps the judgment-seat always in his view. Standing in awe of it, he curbs himself and fears to provoke his anger. Nevertheless, he is not so terrified by an apprehension of judgment as to wish he could withdraw himself, even if the means of escape lay before him; nay, he embraces him not the less as the avenger of wickedness than as the rewarder of the righteous; because he perceives that it equally appertains to his glory to store up punishment for the one and eternal life for the other. Besides, it is not the mere fear of punishment that restrains him from sin. Loving and revering God as his father, honoring and obeying him as his master, although there were no hell, he would revolt at the very idea of offending him.

Such is pure and genuine religion, namely, confidence in God coupled with serious fear—fear, which both includes in it willing reverence and brings along with it such legitimate worship as is prescribed by the law. And it ought to be more carefully considered that all men promiscuously do homage to God, but very few truly reverence him. On all hands there is abundant evidence of ostentatious ceremonies, but sincerity of heart is rare.

John Calvin, *Institutes of the Christian Religion*, trans. Henry Beveridge (Grand Rapids, MI: Eerdmans, 1957 [1845]), vol. I, 41-42.

Propers: Renewers of the church

Hymn of the Day: "Before Jehovah's awesome throne" (531)

Prayers: for a sense of the majesty and sovereignty of God
for earnestness in God's presence
for excellence in preaching
for the Reformed Churches

Color: White

May 29

Juraj Tranovsky, Hymnwriter, 1637

Juraj (George) Tranovsky (or Trzanowski), sometimes called "the Luther of the Slavs" and the father of Slovak hymnody, was born April 9, 1591 in Tesin in Silesia, the son of a blacksmith. His first name also appears as Jiri or in the non-Slavic form George; his family name often appears in the Latinized form Tranoscius. He studied at

Guben and Kolberg and in 1607 entered the University of Wittenberg. After about 1612 he travelled through Bohemia and Silesia and eventually taught in the Gymnasium of St. Nicholas in Prague and then became rector of a school in Holesov in Moravia. He next moved to Medzirieci where he taught and in 1616 was ordained and was pastor from 1616 to 1620. Tranovsky was forced to flee to Tesin during the persecution of the Lutherans under Ferdinand II of Bohemia. He was imprisoned in 1623 and in the following year lost two of his children in the plague.

In 1625 Tranovsky was called to be pastor in Bilska, Silesia, and in 1627 he became chaplain to Count Kaspar Illehazy. In 1629 (1620?) he issued a translation of the Augsburg Confession which has gone through many editions; in 1930 on the four hundredth anniversary of the Augsburg Confession a jubilee edition of the Tranovsky translation with historical notes was issued. From 1631 until his death at 46 years of age Tranovsky was pastor in Liptov Svaty Mikulas in Slovakia. He died after a long illness May 29, 1637 and was buried in an unmarked grave in his church.

Tranovsky was a lover of poetry and compiler and author of hymns. In 1629 he issued a collection of hymns (*Odarum Sacrarum sive Hymnorum Libri III*) and his famous hymnal *Cithara Sanctorum*, "Lyre of the Saints," which appeared in 1636 has remained the basis of Slovak Lutheran hymnody to the present day. The *Cithara Sanctorum* and the Kralice Bible translation are the two great monuments of the Reformation among the Slavs.

The *Cithara Sanctorum*, which is often referred to by the compiler's name as Tranoscius, is a collection of originally some four hundred hymns and spiritual songs. Some are translations of old Latin hymns or German Reformation chorales, and the majority are adaptations of hymns used by the Hussites or the Czech Brethren. About 150 of them, however, were by Tranovsky himself and some were by his contemporaries. The *Tranoscius* has gone through over a hundred editions and is a proud possession of many Slovak Lutheran households, often being beautifully printed and bound and placed in a position of honor.

In 1935-1936 the three hundredth anniversary of the appearance of the *Cithara Sanctorum* was widely celebrated in Czechoslovakia and elsewhere, and the pastor and hymnodist of the Reformation among the Slavs was commemorated.

Juraj Tranovsky 211

Peter Brock. *The Slovak National Awakening.* Toronto: University of Toronto Press, 1976.
A. A. Skodacek. *Slovak Lutheran Liturgy Past and Present.* n.p., 1968.
Jaroslav Vajda. *A History of the Cithara Sanctorum (Tranoscius).* B.D. Thesis. Concordia Seminary, St. Louis, 1944.

Reading

(From Martin Luther, "Preface to Georg Rhau's *Symphoniae Iucundae*")

. . . next to the Word of God, music deserves the highest praise. She is a mistress and governess of those human emotions—to pass over the animals—which as masters govern men or more often overwhelm them. No greater commendation than this can be found—at least not by us. For whether you wish to comfort the sad, to terrify the happy, to encourage the despairing, to humble the proud, to calm the passionate, or to appease those full of hate—and who could number all these masters of the human heart, namely, the emotions, inclinations, and affections that impel men to evil or good?—what more effective means than music could you find? The Holy Ghost himself honors her as an instrument for his proper work when in his Holy Scriptures he asserts that through her his gifts were instilled in the prophets, namely, the inclination to all virtues, as can be seen in Elisha. On the other hand, she serves to cast out Satan, the instigator of all sins, as is shown in Saul, the king of Israel.

Thus it was not without reason that the fathers and prophets wanted nothing else to be associated as closely with the Word of God as music. Therefore, we have so many hymns and Psalms where message and music join to move the listener's soul, while in other living beings and [sounding] bodies music remains a language without words. After all, the gift of language combined with the gift of song was only given to man to let him know that he should praise God with both word and music, namely, by proclaiming [the Word of God] through music and by providing sweet melodies with words. For even a comparison between different men will show how rich and manifold our glorious Creator proves himself in distributing the gifts of music, how much men differ from each other in voice and manner of speaking so that one amazingly excels the other. No two men can be found with exactly the same voice and manner of speaking, although they often seem to imitate each other, the one as it were being the ape of the other.

But when [musical] learning is added to all this and artistic music which corrects, develops, and refines the natural music, then at last it is possible to taste with wonder (yet not to comprehend) God's absolute and perfect wisdom in his wondrous work of music.

Luther's Works, vol. 53, Liturgy and Hymns ed. Ulrich S. Leupold. (Philadelphia: Fortress Press, 1965), 323-324. Used by permission.

Propers: Artists

Hymn of the Day: "Make songs of joy to Christ our head" (150)

Prayers: for the Slovak churches
for those who teach congregations to sing
for faithful pastors
that song might lift the hearts of the depressed

Color: White

THE VISITATION

The feast of the visitation of Elizabeth by her cousin Mary was first observed by Franciscans in the thirteenth century. It was added to the Roman calendar by Pope Urban IV in 1389 and was extended to the whole Western church at the Council of Basel in 1441. In the Eastern church the festival is unknown (except for a few Uniate churches which have taken it from the Roman Church). Although the Visitation is a minor festival and one that was added to the calendar at a late date, Lutheran calendars generally retained it because of its scriptural basis. The Church of England, however, dropped it from the calendar, but beginning with the 1662 calendar of the Church of England all churches of the Anglican Communion, except the Irish and the American, made it a "black letter day"—a day listed on the calendar but without official provision for liturgical observance. In the 1979 Book of Common Prayer propers are provided.

The Visitation is basically a festival of Christ, celebrating a stage in his incarnation. On earlier Roman Catholic and Lutheran calendars the day was observed on July 2, but following the lead of the Roman church, the Lutheran and the Episcopal churches have moved the observance to May 31 so that the day would make better chronological sense by coming before the birthday of John the Baptist, June 24. In the Roman church, during the Marian year 1954, May 31 was made the feast of the Queenship of Mary to crown the close of May, the month of Mary. On the new Roman calendar that feast has now been moved to August 22, the octave of the Assumption.

Reading

(From *Holy Living* by Jeremy Taylor.)

God is present everywhere by his power. He rolls the orbs of heaven with his hand; he fixes the earth with his foot; he guides all the creatures with his eye, and refreshes them with his influence; he makes the powers of hell to shake with his terrors, and binds the devils with his word, and throws them out with his command; and sends the angels on embassies with his decrees; he hardens the joints of infants, and confirms the bones, when they are fashioned beneath secretly in the earth. He it is that assists at the numerous productions of fishes; and there is not one hollowness at the bottom of the sea, but he shows himself to be Lord of it by sustaining there the creatures that come to dwell in it; and in the wilderness, the bittern and the stork, the dragon and the satyr, the unicorn and the elk, live upon his provisions, and revere his power, and feel the force of his almightiness.

God is especially present in the hearts of his people, by his Holy Spirit: and indeed the hearts of holy men are temples in the truth of things, and, in type and shadow, they are heaven itself. For God reigns in the hearts of his servants: there is his kingdom. The power of grace hath subdued all his enemies: there is his power. They serve him night and day, and give him thanks and praise: that is his glory. This is the religion and worship of God in the temple. The temple itself is the heart of man; Christ is the High Priest, who from thence sends up the incense of prayers, and joins them to his own intercession, and presents all together to his Father; and the Holy Ghost, by his dwelling there, hath also consecrated it into a temple; and God dwells in our hearts by faith, and Christ by his Spirit, and the Spirit by his purities, so that we are also cabinets of the mysterious Trinity; and what is this short of heaven itself, but as infancy is short of manhood, and letters of words? The same state of life it is, but is not the same age. It is heaven in a looking glass, dark, but yet true, representing the beauties of the soul, and the graces of God, and the images of his eternal glory, by the reality of a special presence.

Jeremy Taylor, *Holy Living* rev. and ed. by Thomas Smith (London: Henry G. Bohn, 1851) 20-23.

Propers

ROMAN

Eternal Father, you inspired the Virgin Mary, mother of your Son, to visit Elizabeth and assist her in her need. Keep us open to the working of your Spirit, and with Mary may we praise you for ever. We ask this through our Lord Jesus Christ, your Son, who lives and reigns with you and the Holy Spirit, one God, for ever and ever.

(Text from the English translation of the Roman Missal © 1973, International Committee on English in the Liturgy, Inc. All rights reserved.)

LUTHERAN

Almighty God, in choosing the Virgin Mary to be the mother of your Son, you made known your gracious regard for the poor and the lowly and the despised. Grant us grace to receive your Word in humility, and so to be made one with your Son, Jesus Christ our Lord, who lives and reigns with you and the Holy Spirit, one God, now and forever.

EPISCOPAL

Father in heaven, by your grace the virgin mother of your incarnate Son was blessed in bearing him, but still more blessed in keeping your word: Grant us who honor the exaltation of her lowliness to follow the example of her devotion to your will; through Jesus Christ our Lord, who lives and reigns with you and the Holy Spirit, one God, for ever and ever.

(Text from the Book of Common Prayer [Proposed], copyright 1977 by Charles Mortimer Guilbert as Custodian of the Standard Book of Common Prayer. All rights reserved. Used by permission.)

ROMAN	**LUTHERAN**	EPISCOPAL
Zephaniah 3:14-18a or Romans 12:9-16b Psalm: Isaiah 12:2-6 Luke 1:39-56	Isaiah 11:1-5 Psalm 113 Romans 12:9-16 Luke 1:39-47	Zephaniah 3:14-18a Psalm 113 or Isaiah 12:2-6 Colossians 3:12-17 Luke 1:39-49 Preface of the Epiphany

Hymn of the Day: "Hark, the glad sound! the Savior comes" (35)
or "Blest are the pure in heart" (*SBH* 394)

Prayers: for the poor, the forgotten, the despised
for grace to acknowledge Christ and to perceive his coming
for a deepening sense of Emmanuel—God with us

Preface: Christmas (Advent is also appropriate)

Color: White

June 1

Justin, Martyr at Rome, ca. 165

Justin, known as one of the foremost of early Christian apologists and perhaps the greatest figure between the Apostles and Irenaeus, was born of pagan Greek parents at Flavia Neapolis in Samaritan territory (ancient Shechem, modern Nablus) about the year 100. Early in his life he began an intense search for a satisfying philosophy and religious truth. To this end, he studied philosophy at Ephesus. Justin was impressed with the Christian martyrs, and after all his study, an old Christian by the seashore, whom he met by chance, told him of the Old Testament prophets, and Justin became a Christian. He taught Christian philosophy for a time at Ephesus but soon after 135 appears in Rome. There he addressed two famous defences of Christianity to the emperor Antoninus Pius and the Roman Senate—a precious testimony to primitive Christian liturgy and belief. He became involved in a bitter debate with the Cynic philosopher Crescens. About 165, perhaps as a result of this controversy, Justin and some of his students, refusing to make a pagan sacrifice, were scourged and beheaded. A Greek account of his martyrdom survives in three forms and seems to rest on a contemporary record.

Many writings have been attributed to him, but only his *Dialogue with Trypho* and the two *Apologies* seem authentically his. Justin is an important witness to the emerging New Testament corpus, and, while possessing no great philosophical or literary skill, he was the first Christian thinker to seek to reconcile the claims of faith and reason. He saw no sharp discontinuity between Platonism and Christianity: Christianity fulfills the highest aspirations of Platonism, and the pagan thinkers found the truth by studying the Old Testament, he suggested, as well as by independent revelation.

L. W. Barnard. *Justin Martyr. His Life and Thought.* Cambridge University Press, 1967.
Hans von Campenhausen. *The Fathers of the Greek Church* tr. Stanley Godman. New York: Pantheon, 1959.
H. Chadwick, "Justin Martyr's Defense of Christianity," *Bulletin of the John Rylands Library* XLVII (1965), 275-297.
Justin Martyr. *The Dialogue with Trypho* tr. A. L. Williams. New York: Macmillan, 1931.

Reading

(From the Acts of the martyrdom of Saint Justin and his companion saints)

The saints were seized and brought before the prefect of Rome, whose name was Rusticus. As they stood before the judgment seat, Rusticus the prefect said to Justin: "Above all, have faith in the gods and obey the emperors." Justin said: "We cannot be accused or condemned for obeying the commands of our Savior, Jesus Christ."

Rusticus said: "What system of teaching do you profess?" Justin said: "I have tried to learn about every system, but I have accepted the true doctrines of the Christians, though these are not approved by those who are held fast in error."

The prefect Rusticus said: "Are those doctrines approved by you, wretch that you are?" Justin said: "Yes, for I follow them with their correct teaching."

The prefect Rusticus said: "What sort of teaching is that?" Justin said: "Worship the God of the Christians. We hold him to be from the beginning the one creator and maker of the whole creation, of things seen and things unseen. We worship also the Lord Jesus Christ, the Son of God. He was foretold by the prophets as the future herald of salvation for the human race, and the teacher of distinguished disciples. For myself, since I am a human being, I consider that what I say is insignificant in comparison with his infinite godhead. I acknowledge the existence of a prophetic power, for the one I have just spoken of as the Son of God was the subject of prophecy. I know that the prophets were inspired from above when they spoke of his coming among men."

Rusticus said: "You are a Christian, then?" Justin said: "Yes, I am a Christian."

The prefect said to Justin: "You are called a learned man and think you know what is true teaching. Listen: if you were scourged and beheaded, are you convinced that you would go up to heaven?" Justin said: "I hope that I shall enter God's house if I suffer in that way. For I know that God's favor is stored up until the end of the whole world for all who have lived good lives."

The prefect Rusticus said: "Do you have an idea that you will go up to heaven to receive some suitable rewards?" Justin said: "It is not an idea that I have; it is something I know well and hold to be most certain."

The prefect Rusticus said: "Now let us come to the point at issue, which is necessary and urgent. Gather round then and with one accord offer sacrifice to the gods." Justin said: "No one who is right-thinking stoops from true worship to false worship."

The prefect Rusticus said: "If you do not do as you are commanded you will be tortured without mercy." Justin said: "We hope to suffer torment for the sake of our Lord Jesus Christ, and so be saved. For this will bring us salvation and confidence as we stand before the more terrible and universal judgment-seat of our Lord and Savior."

In the same way the other martyrs also said: "Do what you will. We are Christians; we do not offer sacrifice to idols."

The prefect Rusticus pronounced sentence, saying: "Let those who have refused to sacrifice to the gods and to obey the command of the emperor be scourged and led away to suffer capital punishment according to the ruling of the laws." Glorifying God, the holy martyrs went out to the accustomed place. They were beheaded, and so fulfilled their witness of martyrdom in confessing their faith in their Savior.

Propers

ROMAN	LUTHERAN	EPISCOPAL
Father, through the folly of the cross you taught Saint Justin the sublime wisdom of Jesus Christ. May we too reject falsehood and remain loyal to the faith. We ask this through our Lord Jesus Christ, your Son, who lives and reigns with you and the Holy Spirit, one God, for ever and ever.	Gracious Lord, in every age you have sent men and women who have given their lives for the message of your love. Inspire us with the memory of those martyrs for the Gospel like your servant Justin, whose faithfulness led them in the way of the cross, and give us courage to bear full witness with our lives to your Son's victory over sin and death; through Jesus Christ our Lord.	Almighty God, who gave your servant Justin boldness to confess the Name of our Savior Jesus Christ before the rulers of this world, and courage to die for this faith: Grant that we may also be ever ready to give a reason for the hope that is in us, and to suffer gladly for the sake of our Lord Jesus Christ, who lives and reigns with you and the Holy Spirit, one God, now and for ever.
(Text from the English translation of the Roman Missal © 1973, International Committee on English in the Liturgy, Inc. All rights reserved.)		*(Text from Lesser Feasts and Fasts, Revised Edition, copyright 1973 by Charles Mortimer Guilbert as Custodian of the Standard Book of Common Prayer. All rights reserved. Used by permission.)*
Common of Martyrs or 1 Corinthians 1:18-25	Common of Martyrs: Ezekiel 20:40-42 Psalm 5 Revelation 6:9-11 Mark 8:34-38	Psalm 31:1-5 1 Peter 3:14-18, 22 Psalm 16:5-11 John 12:44-50 Preface of Holy Week

Hymn of the Day: "Thine is the glory" (145)
       or "Let us now our voices raise" (*SBH* 546)

Prayers: for those who search for truth, especially philosophers
       and theologians
       for those who defend the faith against the doubts of those
       who cannot believe
       for those who preserve and interpret the liturgical
       traditions of the church

Preface: All Saints

Color: Red

John XXIII, Bishop of Rome, 1963

Angelo Roncalli, the third of thirteen children, was born to a family of farmers November 25, 1881 at Sotto il Monte in northern Italy. At the age of twelve he entered the diocesan seminary at Bergamo and came under the influence of progressive leaders of the Italian social movement. He then went to the seminary in Rome on a scholarship, interrupted his education there to serve for a year as a volunteer in the Italian army, and returned to the seminary to take a doctorate in theology. He was ordained August 10, 1904.

He was appointed the secretary to the new bishop of Bergamo and with him learned forms of social action and gained an understanding of the problems of the working classes. Meanwhile he taught at the diocesan seminary.

In 1915 he was recalled to the army in World War I and served in the medical and chaplaincy corps. After the war he was made the spiritual director of the seminary. In 1921 he was called to Rome by the pope and made director of the Society for the Propagation of the Faith in Italy.

He was consecrated archbishop in 1925 and made apostolic representative to Bulgaria. At Sofia the capital he dealt with the problem of Eastern Rite Catholics in a troubled oriental land.

In 1934 he was named apostolic delegate to Turkey and Greece. There he fostered harmony among various national groups in Istanbul in a time of anti-religious fervor under Kemal Ataturk. Archbishop Roncalli introduced the use of the Turkish language in worship and in the official documents of the church and eventually won the esteem of some high Turkish statesmen. He made a series of conciliatory gestures toward the Orthodox and met with the Ecumenical Patriarch Benjamin in 1939. During World War II Istanbul was a center of intrigue and espionage, and the archbishop gathered information useful to Rome and helped Jews flee persecution. His work in Greece, which was occupied by the Nazis, was less successful.

When he was sixty-four years old (1944), an age when most men are thinking of retirement, Roncalli was chosen by Pius XII for the difficult post of nuncio to Paris where he worked to heal the divisions caused by the war. He travelled widely.

At age seventy-two he was made cardinal and Patriarch of Venice and he had charge of a large diocese for the first time in his life. He quickly won the affection of his people, visiting parishes, caring for the working classes, establishing new parishes, and developing forms of social action.

In 1958, nearly seventy-seven years old, he was elected pope upon the death of Pius XII. He was expected by many to be a caretaker and transitional pope, but he astonished the church and the world with his energy and reforming spirit. He expanded and international-ized the college of cardinals, called the first diocesan synod of Rome in history, revised the code of canon law, and called the Second Vati-can Council to revitalize the church. This council was the major achievement of his life to renew the life of the church and its teach-ing, with the ultimate goal of the unification of Christianity. More-over, as Bishop of Rome, he was unremitting in his care of his diocese, visiting hospitals, prisons, and schools. When he died June 3, 1963, he had won the widespread affection of Christian and non-Christian alike.

Lawrence Elliott. *I Will Be Called John. A Biography of Pope John XXIII.* London: Collins, 1974.
John XXIII. *Journal of a Soul* tr. Dorothy White. New York: McGraw-Hill, 1965.
Paul Johnson. *Pope John XXIII.* Boston: Little Brown, 1974.

Reading

(From John XXIII, *Journal of a Soul.*)

[1959] Since the Lord chose me, unworthy as I am, for this great service, I feel I have no longer any special ties in this life, no family, no earthly country or nation, nor any particular preferences with re-gard to studies or projects, even good ones. Now, more than ever, I see myself only as the humble and unworthy "servant of God and servant of the servants of God" (Gregory the Great, Epistolarum XIII, 1). The whole world is my family. This sense of belonging to everyone must give character and vigor to my mind, my heart, and my actions.

The welcome immediately accorded to my unworthy person and the affection still shown by all who approach me are always a source of surprise to me. The maxim "Know thyself" suffices for my spiritual serenity and keeps me on the alert. The secret of my success must lie there: in not "searching into things which are above my ability" (Ecclesiasticus 3:22) and in being content to be "meek and humble of heart." Meekness and humbleness of heart give graciousness in receiving, speaking, and dealing with people, and the patience to hear, to pity, to keep silent and to encourage. Above all, one must always be ready for the Lord's surprise moves, for although he treats his loved ones well, he generally likes to test them with all sorts of trials such as bodily infirmities, bitterness of soul, and sometimes opposition so powerful as to transform and wear out the life of the servant of God, the life of the servant of the servants of God, making it a real martyrdom.

John XXIII, *Journal of a Soul* trans. Dorothy White (New York: McGraw-Hill, 1965) 298-299. Used by permission of Geoffrey Chapman, a division of Cassell Ltd.

Hymn of the Day: "Thee will I love, my strength, my tower" (502) or "Sometimes a light surprises" (*SBH* 495)

Prayers: for the renewal of the church
for the unity of Christ's church
for humility and humor
for the spirit of love and service
for openness to the surprises of God

Propers: Pastors

Color: White

June 5

Boniface, Archbishop of Mainz, Missionary to Germany, Martyr, 754

Boniface, the Apostle of Germany, whose original name was Wynfrid (or Wynfrith), was born in Crediton, Wessex, England sometime between 672 and 675. When his father became seriously ill, the son was sent to the Benedictine school at Exeter and then to the Bencdictine monastery at Nursling, between Winchester and Southampton, a place of learning and concern for missionary activity. Wynfrid was ordained there, and he became director of the monastic school and wrote a Latin grammar and several poems.

When he was about forty years old (ca. 716), he received permission from his abbot to begin missionary activity in Frisia (Holland), a part of the kingdom of the Franks and the scene of widespread rejection of Christianity. Willibrord, the Apostle of Frisia (died November 7, 739), had prepared the way from his base at Utrecht by establishing relations with the Frankish rulers and gaining papal support for missionary work there. After exploring the possibility of a mission, Wynfrid recognized that the time was not ripe and within a year returned to his monastery. His abbot died in 717, and Wynfrid was elected his successor, but in 718 he resigned in order to go to Rome to ask permission from the pope for a missionary assignment. On May 15, 719, Gregory II gave him broad missionary jurisdiction, urged him to consult with Rome whenever difficulties arose, and gave Wynfrid the name of Boniface.

The newly-commissioned missionary went to Thuringia, preaching to secular leaders and attempting to reform the partly pagan clergy. In 719 he went again to Frisia, after the hostile Duke Radbod had died, to study Willibrord's missionary methods. In 721 he went on his own to Hesse, established a monastery there and baptized many (thousands, his biographer says) converts on the Day of Pentecost, 722. The pope, learning of his success, invited Boniface to Rome and consecrated him bishop for the German frontier without a fixed diocese, November 30, 722. He provided him with a collection of rules and letters of recommendation to important persons whose protection was essential to Boniface's success. He returned to the mission field, and one of his first acts, it is said, was to fell the sacred oak tree of Thor at Geisman in Hesse. When he was not harmed, many of the people were converted, and Boniface built a chapel in honor of St. Peter with the wood of the tree.

Bishop Boniface stayed two years in Hesse and then for ten years (725-735) worked again in Thuringia, where Frankish and Irish missionaries had made a start. Despite struggles with pagan corruption of Christian clergy and ceremonies, Boniface enjoyed a fruitful mission, supported by gifts from the Benedictines in England.

Pope Gregory III elevated Boniface to the rank of archbishop in

732 and asked him to consecrate missionary bishops. In 737 Boniface made his final visit to Rome, spent a year there, and was asked by the pope to organize the German church. In 738 he returned to Germany as papal legate and established new bishoprics and abbeys. In 744 he established the most famous of his monasteries at Fulda, which became the center of German spiritual and intellectual life. Boniface assisted in reforming the Frankish Church (742-747), and upon the deposition of Gewiliob, the bishop of Mainz, who had killed his father's murderer, Boniface was made archbishop of Mainz; for although he had been archbishop since 742, he had never been assigned a see. For about a year Boniface was successful in one last mission to the Frisians. But at sunrise on June 5, 754 at Dokkum, Boniface, while reading the Gospel to a group of neophytes on Pentecost, was attacked by a band of pagan Frisians and all were massacred. At Fulda, along with the remains of Boniface, is preserved a gospel book, which has been slashed in several places and which is purported to have been held by Boniface when he was killed.

Clinton Albertson, S. J. *Anglo-Saxon Saints and Heroes.* New York: Fordham, 1967.
Eleanor Shipley Duckett. *Anglo-Saxon Saints and Scholars.* New York: Macmillan, 1947. Chapter IV, "Boniface of Devon."
Ephraim Emerton. *The Letters of St. Boniface.* New York: Columbia, 1940.
The English Correspondence of St. Boniface ed. and tr. Edward Kylie. London, 1911, 1924. Reprinted 1966.
G. W. Greenaway. *Saint Boniface.* London: A. & C. Black, 1955.
J. M. Williamson. *The Life and Times of St. Boniface.* London, 1904.
Willibald. *The Life of St. Boniface* tr. G. W. Robinson. Cambridge, Mass.: Harvard, 1916.

Willibrord, the Apostle to Frisia (Holland), with Boniface laid the foundations of Christianity in Western Europe. He was born in England ca. 658 and was raised and educated in a monastery at Ripton. While studying in Ireland he gained an interest in missionary work. In 690 he set out for Holland, established a base at Utrecht, and in 695 was made bishop and given the name Clement. His work was frequently disturbed by the conflict between the pagan Frisians and the Christian Franks, and for a time he left to work among the Danes. Willibrord died at Echternach November 7, 739, and this is his feast day in the Episcopal Church.

Reading

(From the Letters of St. Boniface. Letter 78)

In her voyage across the ocean of this world, the Church is like a great ship being pounded by the waves of life's different stresses. Our duty is not to abandon ship but to keep her on her course.

The ancient fathers showed us how we should carry out this duty: Clement, Cornelius, and many others in the city of Rome, Cyprian at Carthage, Athanasius at Alexandria. They all lived under emperors who were pagans; they all steered Christ's ship—or rather his most dear spouse, the Church. This they did by teaching and defending her, by their labors and sufferings, even to the shedding of blood.

I am terrified when I think of all this. *Fear and trembling came upon me and the darkness* of my sins *almost covered me.* I would gladly give up the task of guiding the Church which I have accepted if I could find such an action warranted by the example of the fathers or by Holy Scripture.

Since this is the case, and since the truth can be assaulted but never defeated or falsified, with our tired mind let us turn to the words of Solomon: *Trust in the Lord with all your heart and do not rely on your own prudence. Think on him in all your ways, and he will guide your steps.* In another place he says: *The name of the Lord is an impregnable tower. The just man seeks refuge in it and he will be saved.*

Let us stand fast in what is right and prepare our souls for trial. Let us wait upon God's strengthening aid and say to him: *O Lord, you have been our refuge in all generations.*

Let us trust in him who has placed this burden upon us. What we ourselves cannot bear let us bear with the help of Christ. For he is all-powerful and he tells us: *My yoke is easy and my burden is light.*

Let us continue the fight on the day of the Lord. *The days of anguish and of tribulation* have overtaken us; if God so wills, *let us die for the holy laws of our fathers,* so that we may enter into the eternal inheritance with them.

Let us be neither dogs that do not bark nor silent onlookers nor paid servants who run away before the wolf. Instead let us be careful shepherds watching over Christ's flock. Let us preach the whole of God's plan to the powerful and to the humble, to rich and to poor, to men of every rank and age, as far as God gives us the strength, in season and out of season. . . .

Propers

ROMAN	LUTHERAN	EPISCOPAL
Lord, your martyr Boniface spread the faith by his teaching and witnessed to it with his blood. By the help of his prayers keep us loyal to our faith and give us the courage to profess it in our lives. Grant this through our Lord Jesus Christ, your Son, who lives and reigns with you and the Holy Spirit, one God, for ever and ever.	God of grace and might, we praise you for your servant Boniface to whom you gave gifts to make the good news known to the German people. Raise up, we pray, in every country, heralds and evangelists of your kingdom, so that the world may know the immeasurable riches of our Savior, Jesus Christ our Lord.	Almighty God, who called your faithful servant Boniface to be a witness and martyr in Germany, and by his labor and suffering raised up a people for your own possession: Pour forth your Holy Spirit upon your Church in every land, that by the service and sacrifice of many, your holy Name may be glorified and your kingdom enlarged; through Jesus Christ our Lord, who lives and reigns with you and the Holy Spirit, one God, now and ever.

Common of Martyrs or Pastors (for Missionaries)	Common of Missionaries Isaiah 62:1-7 Psalm 48 Romans 10:11-17 Luke 24:44-53 or Common of Martyrs	Acts 20:17-28 Psalm 94:12-19 97 Matthew 28:16-20 Preface of Holy Week

Hymn of the Day: "Lord of our life and God of our salvation" (366)

Prayers: for the church in Germany and the Netherlands

for the government and people of Germany and the
  Netherlands
for those who teach the faith
for courage in the face of disappointments

Preface: All Saints

Color: Red

Seattle,
Chief of the Duwamish Confederacy, 1866

Noah Seattle (his name is sometimes transliterated Sealth) was born ca. 1790 in the Puget Sound area of Washington State. He was chief of the Suquamish Tribe and became chief of the Allied Tribes, the Duwamish Confederacy. Unlike many of his time, he rejected war and chose the path of peace.

In the 1830s he became a Roman Catholic and from that time on lived in such a way that he earned the respect of both Native Americans and whites. He began the custom, which survived his death, of holding morning and evening prayer in the tribe. He befriended new settlers. On January 22, 1855 he signed the treaty at Point Elliot in the heart of modern Seattle, which ceded to the whites his ancestral land, and by which the Duwamish accepted a small reservation north of Seattle. At a ceremony marking that occasion, Governor Isaac Stevens of the newly-formed Washington Territory addressed the residents, and Seattle responded in a rich and poignant oration. The exact words of the speech are uncertain—as is the case with the transcription and translation of many great Native American speakers—but beneath what may be the fustian oratorical style of the translator, there lies an undeniable base of graceful and moving poetry that characterized the Indian speeches of the time. In his day Seattle was regarded as extraordinarily eloquent, and on the occasion of this treaty he refused to speak the pidgin English or Chinook preferred by Governor Stevens and used instead his native Duwamish tongue.

Seattle died June 7, 1866, and on the centennial of his birth the city of Seattle, Washington—named for him against his wishes—erected a monument over his grave.

C. B. Bagley. "Chief Seattle and Angeline," *Washington Historical Quarterly*, October 1931.
Frank Carlson. *Chief Sealth.* 1903.
T. W. Prosch. "Seattle and the Indians of Puget Sound," *Washington Historical Quarterly*, July 1908.
Luke Starnes, "The Saga of Seattle," *Golden West Magazine* 4:2. January, 1968.
Uncommon Controversy. A Report Prepared by the American Friends Service Committee. University of Washington Press, 1970.
Roberta Frye Watt. *The Story of Seattle.* Seattle: Lowman and Hanford, 1931.

Reading

(From Seattle's speech at the ceding of his land.)

It matters little where we pass the remnant of our days. They will not be many. The Indian's night promises to be dark. Not a single star of hope hovers above the horizon. Sad-voiced winds moan in the distance. Grim fate seems to be on the Red Man's trail, and wherever he goes he will hear the approaching footsteps of his fell destroyer and prepare stolidly to meet his doom, as does the wounded doe that hears the approaching footsteps of the hunter.

A few more moons. A few more winters—and not one of the descendents of the mighty hosts that once moved over this broad land or lived in happy homes, protected by the Great Spirit, will remain to mourn over the graves of a people—once more powerful and hopeful than yours. But why should I mourn at the untimely fate of my people? Tribe follows tribe, and nation follows nation, like the waves of the sea. It is the order of nature, and regret is useless. Your time of decay may be distant, but it will surely come, for even the White Man whose God walked and talked with him as friend with friend, cannot be exempt from the common destiny. We may be brothers after all. We will see.

We will ponder your proposition and when we decide we will let you know. But should we accept it, I here and now make this condition that we will not be denied the privilege without molestation of visiting at any time the tombs of our ancestors, friends, and children. Every part of this soil is sacred in the estimation of my people. Every hillside, every valley, every plain and grove, has been hallowed by some sad or happy event in days long vanished. Even the rocks, which seem to be dumb and dead as they swelter in the sun along the silent shore, thrill with memories of stirring events connected with the lives of my people, and the very dust upon which you now stand responds more lovingly to their footsteps than to yours, because it is rich with the blood of our ancestors, and our bare feet are conscious of the sympathetic touch. Our departed braves, fond mothers, glad, happy-hearted maidens, and even our little children who lived here and rejoiced here for a brief season, will love these somber solitudes and at eventide they greet the shadowy returning spirits.

And when the last Red Man shall have perished, and the memory of my tribe shall have become a myth among the White Men, these shores will swarm with the invisible dead of my tribe, and when your children's children think themselves alone in the field, the store, the shop, upon the highway, or in the silence of the pathless woods, they will not be alone. In all the earth there is no place dedicated to solitude. At night when the streets of your villages are silent and you think them deserted, they will throng with the returning hosts that once filled them and still love this beautiful land. The White Man will never be alone.

Let them be just and deal kindly with my people, for the dead are not powerless. Dead, did I say? There is no death, only a change of worlds.

Louis Thomas Jones. *Aboriginal American Oratory*. Los Angeles: Southwest Museum, 1965.

Propers: Saints

Hymn of the Day: "Jesus, still lead on" (341)

Prayers: for faithfulness in daily prayer
　　　　　for hospitality to strangers and newcomers
　　　　　for Native Americans
　　　　　for understanding of the traditions of the Native Americans
　　　　　　　who came to this land first

Color: White

Columba, Abbot of Iona, 597

Three confessors from the British Isles who kept alive the light of learning and devotion during the dark ages are commemorated together on this day by the new Lutheran calendar. They are commemorated separately on the Episcopal calendar; only Bede is on the general Roman calendar. June 9 is the traditional date for the commemoration of St. Columba.

From the first, the Irish church was organized on a different basis than the church of Rome. It had a primitive and tribal organization, suited to a rural and rather rude society, was monastic rather than episcopal in administration, and emphasized right living rather than elaborate theology. The Irish monasteries were Christian colonies in a pagan land, "holy experiments" for the practice of Christian living and virtue.

Columba, abbot and missionary (his name is said to have been originally Cremthann), was born at Gartan, Donegal of the royal Niall (O'Neill) dynasty about 521. He was educated and ordained deacon at the monastery of Moville; he studied at Clonard and was ordained priest in 551 at Glasnevin, near Dublin. He established several churches and monasteries in Ireland.

About 563 he left Ireland with twelve companions and established a community on the island of Hy (later called Iona), off the west coast of Scotland. This monastery served as a center for missions to the Irish who had settled in Scotland and also to the Picts (the original inhabitants of Scotland), and the Northumbrians. Columba lived at Iona some thirty-four years (Bede says thirty-two), evangelizing the mainland and establishing monasteries in the islands nearby.

There is a legend that in 565 he rebuked the Loch Ness monster and commanded it to cease its vicious ways after it had killed one man and was about to attack another. A powerful personality, a great open-air preacher, an able organizer, and something of a poet, Columba has been described (Hodgkin, *Political History of England,* 150) as a kind of sixth-century John Wesley. Bede calls him "a true monk in life no less than habit," who turned the Picts to the "faith of Christ by his words and example and so received the island of

Iona from them in order to establish a monastery there." Columba
died on Sunday, June 9, 597 at Iona, according to Bede, aged seventy-
seven years. He was buried on his island, but his remains were moved
to Kells in Ireland in 849 for safekeeping in a time of turmoil.

Viking raiders in the eighth and ninth centuries ravaged the island,
and it underwent periodic destruction. But throughout unsettled centuries of invasion and warfare, the reputation of Iona as a holy place
flourished, and it became the burial place of Scottish, Irish, and Norwegian kings. The monastery was suppressed at the time of the
Reformation. The Norman church, built in the thirteenth century,
was abandoned in the time of Cromwell and fell into decay. In 1899
the ruined abbey became the property of the Church of Scotland. It
was gradually rebuilt and opened again for worship in 1912. In 1938
George MacLeod, a Glasgow minister of the Church of Scotland,
founded the Iona Community to restore both the church and the
spiritual life of the island. Evelyn Underhill in her *Collected Papers*
(1945) tells of a woman who had spoken to a gardener on Iona of
the beauties of the island. "Yes, mum," he said, Iona's a very thin
place." Asked what he meant by that, he explained, "Well, on Iona,
mum, there's very little between you and God."

Reading

(From Adomnan's *Life of Columba*.)

. . . the saint entered the church for the vesper office of the Lord's-
night. As soon as that was finished, he returned to his lodging, and
reclined on his sleeping-place, where during the night he used to
have for a bed, the bare rock; and for pillow, a stone, which even today stands beside his grave as a kind of epitaph. So while reclining
there, he gave his last commands to the brothers, in the hearing of
his attendant alone, and said: "I commend to you, my children, these
latest words, that you shall have among yourselves mutual and un-
feigned charity, with peace. If you follow this course after the examples of the holy fathers, God, who gives strength to the good, will
help you; and I, abiding with him, shall intercede for you. And not
only will the necessities of this life be sufficiently provided by him,

but also the rewards of eternal good things will be bestowed, that are prepared for those who follow the divine commandments."

We have carried down to this point, briefly told, the last words of the venerable patron, when he was, as it were, crossing over to the heavenly country from this weary pilgrimage.

After them the saint was silent for a little, as the happy latest hour drew near. Then, when the beaten bell resounded at midnight, he rose in haste and went to the church and, running, entered in advance of the others, alone; and bowing his knees in prayer he sank down beside the altar. In that moment Diormit, the attendant, following later, saw from a distance the whole church filled inside with angelic light about the saint. As Diormit approached the doorway, that light that he had seen quickly faded. A few more of the brothers also had seen it, when they too were a little way off.

So Diormit entering the church cried with a tearful voice: "Where are you, where are you, father?" And groping in the darkness, since the lamps of the brothers had not yet been brought, he found the saint lying before the altar. Raising him a little, and sitting down beside him, he placed the holy head upon his lap. Meanwhile the company of monks ran up with lights; and when they saw that their father was dying they began to lament. And as we have learned from some men who were present there, the saint, whose soul had not yet departed, opened his eyes, and looked around on either side, with wonderful joy and gladness of countenance; for he was gazing upon the holy angels that had come to meet him. Then Diormit raised the holy right hand, to bless the saint's company of monks. And the venerable father himself at the same time moved his hand, as much as he was able, in order that he might be seen to bless the brothers even by the movement of his hand, a thing that in the departure of his soul he could not do by voice. And after the holy benediction thus expressed, he presently breathed out his spirit.

When that had left the tabernacle of the body, his face continued to be ruddy, and in a wonderful degree gladdened by the vision of angels, so much that it seemed like the face not of a dead man, but of a living sleeper. Meanwhile the whole church resounded with sorrowful lamentations.

Adomnan's *Life of Columba* ed. and trans. Alan Orr Anderson and Marjorie Ogilvie Anderson (London and New York: Thomas Nelson, 1961)

525-531. Used by permission of Thomas Nelson and Sons Limited. [Adomnan (or Adamnan) was the ninth abbot of Iona and wrote the account between 679 and 704.]

Propers

ROMAN	LUTHERAN	EPISCOPAL
		O God, who by the preaching of your blessed servant Columba caused the light of the gospel to shine in Scotland: Grant, we pray, that having his life and labors in remembrance, we may show forth our thankfulness to you by following the example of his zeal and patience; through Jesus Christ our Lord, who lives and reigns with you and the Holy Spirit, one God, now and for ever.
		(Text from Lesser Feasts and Fasts, Revised Edition, copyright 1973 by Charles Mortimer Guilbert as Custodian of the Standard Book of Common Prayer. All rights reserved. Used by permission.)
	Common of Missionaries	Psalm 139:1-9 Isaiah 41:1-5 Psalm 89:20-28 Luke 10:17-20
		Preface of Apostles

Aidan, Bishop of Lindisfarne, 651

Aidan, a monk of Iona and of Irish descent, was invited by King Oswald (who himself had lived at Iona, where he was converted and baptized) to revive missionary work in England and reconvert the lapsed Northumbrians. Aidan was consecrated bishop in 635 and established his headquarters on the island of Lindisfarne, off the northeast coast of England. From there he made long journeys to the mainland as far south as London, strengthening Christian communities and founding new missionary outposts, and teaching the practice of the Celtic church. He adhered to the Celtic method of dating Easter, which depended upon an eighty-four year cycle, rather than the Roman nineteen-year cycle.

Aidan was admired both for his asceticism and his gentleness. He died August 31, 651, at Bamborough; the cause of his death was said to have been his grief at the murder of King Oswald who had been a companion in his missionary travels. Aidan's traditional feast day is August 31.

L. Gougaud. *Christianity in Celtic Lands.* tr. M. Joynt. London: Sheed and Ward, 1932.

Reading

(From Bede, *Ideals of the Priesthood*)

5. From this island [Iona], then, from the company of these monks, Aidan, having received episcopal rank, was sent to the province of the Angles to instruct it in Christ. Among other teachings of how life ought to be lived, he left to his clergy a most wholesome example in his abstinence and chastity. His doctrine was particularly recommended to all by the fact that he himself taught nothing different from the way he lived with his monks. He desired to seek nothing of this world, to love nothing. Everything given him by the kings or the wealthy of this world he was soon glad to give to the poor who came to beg from him. He used to journey about through all the cities and countryside, not on horseback but on foot, unless greater necessity compelled him to ride. Whenever he saw, as he walked, either rich or

poor, turning at once to them, he would summon those not of the faith to the sacrament of receiving faith; or if he saw the faithful, he would strengthen them in that faith itself and would arouse them by word and deed to perform acts of charity and good works.

Early Medieval Theology, Vol. IX, The Library of Christian Classics, tr. and ed. by George E. McCracken, 406-407. Published simultaneously in Great Britain and the U.S.A. by the SCM Press, Ltd., London, and The Westminster Press, Philadelphia, 1957. Used by permission.

Propers

ROMAN	LUTHERAN	EPISCOPAL

EPISCOPAL

(August 31)
Almighty God, who in your providence chose your servant Aidan to be an apostle to the English people, that he might bring those who were wandering in darkness and error to the true light and knowledge of you: Grant us so to walk in that light, that we may come at last to the light of everlasting life; through the merits of Jesus Christ your Son our Lord, who lives and reigns with you and the Holy Spirit, one God, now and for ever.

(Text from Lesser Feasts and Fasts, Revised Edition, copyright 1973 by Charles Mortimer Guilbert as Custodian of the Standard Book of Common Prayer. All rights reserved. Used by permission.)

LUTHERAN

Common of Missionaries

EPISCOPAL

Psalm 15
1 Corinthians 9:16-23
Psalm 85:7-13
Matthew 19:27-30

Preface of Apostles

Bede the Venerable
Priest and Monk of Jarrow, 735

Bede was a biblical scholar and "the father of English history." Born in 672 or 673 near Durham in northeast England, when he was seven years old he was sent to the new monastery of Wearmouth and from there went to the monastery of Jarrow when it was founded ca. 681. The two places were considered one monastery. He was made a deacon at the early age of nineteen (the canonical age was twenty-five) and was ordained priest when he was thirty (703).

The rest of his life was that of a typical scholarly monk, remarkably uneventful. He travelled little and devoted himself to study, teaching, and writing, making considerable use of the monastic library. He was the greatest scholar of his time, the most learned man in Western Europe. He had a wide-ranging interest in history, grammar, metrics, chronology (he introduced the dating of years by the birth of Christ), and Scripture. He wrote of himself:

I have spent all my life in this monstery, applying myself entirely to the study of the Scriptures; and, amid the observance of the discipline of the Rule and the daily task of singing in the church, it has always been my delight to learn or to teach or to write.

His traditional title "the Venerable" was applied from the fourth century to people of notable sanctity and learning.

Bede died on the eve of Ascension Day, May 25, 735, while dictating an English translation of St. John's Gospel. Since the eleventh century his remains have been in Durham Cathedral. For many centuries his feast day was May 27, for he was considered to have died on Ascension Day, May 26 that year (the feast begins with its vigil) and since the 26th was the day of St. Augustine of Canterbury, the commemoration of St. Bede the Venerable was moved to May 27. In the new Roman Catholic and Episcopal calendars, however, he is remembered on the actual date of his death, May 25.

Peter Hunter Blair. *The World of Bede.* New York: St. Martins, 1971.
Eleanor Shipley Duckett. *Anglo-Saxon Saints and Scholars.* New York: Macmillan, 1947.
A. Hamilton Thompson, ed. *Bede: His Life, Times, and Writings.* Oxford: Clarendon, 1935.

Reading

(From a letter on the death of the Venerable Bede by Cuthbert)

When it came to the Tuesday before Ascension Day, his breathing became very much worse, and a slight swelling had appeared in his feet; but all the same he taught us the whole of that day, and dictated cheerfully, and among other things said several times: "Learn your lesson quickly now; for I know not how long I may be with you, nor whether after a short time my Maker may not take me from you." But it seemed to us that he knew very well when his end should be. So he spent all that night in thanksgiving, without sleep; and when day broke, which was the Wednesday, he gave instructions for the writing, which we had begun, to be finished without delay. We were at it until nine o'clock; at nine o'clock we went in procession with the relics, as the custom of that day required. One of us stayed with him, and said to him: "There is still one chapter short of that book you were dictating, but I think it will be hard on you to ask any more questions." But he replied: "It is not hard. Take your pen and mend it, and then write fast." And so he did. At three o'clock he said to me: "I have a few treasures in my box, some pepper, and napkins, and some incense. Run quickly and fetch the priests of our monastery, and I will share among them such little presents as God has given me." I did so, in great agitation; and when they came, he spoke to them and to each one singly, urging and begging them to offer masses and prayers regularly on his behalf, and they promised with a will. But they were very sad, and they all wept, especially because he had said that he thought they would not see his face much longer in this world. Yet they rejoiced at one thing that he said: "It is time, if it so please my Maker, that I should be released from the body, and return to Him who formed me out of nothing, when as yet I was not. I have lived a long time, and the righteous Judge has well provided for me all my life long. The time of my departure is at hand, and my soul longs to see Christ my King in all His beauty."

This he said, and other things, to our great profit, and so spent his last day in gladness until the evening. Then the boy of whom I spoke, whose name was Wilberht, said once again: "There is still one sentence, dear master, that we have not written down." And he said:

Bede 237

"Write it." After a little the boy said: "There! Now it is written." And he replied: "Good! It is finished; you have spoken the truth. Hold my head in your hands, for it is a great delight to me to sit over against my holy place in which I used to pray, that as I sit there I may call upon my Father." And so upon the floor of his cell, singing "Glory be to the Father and to the Son and to the Holy Spirit" and the rest, he breathed his last. And well may we believe without hesitation that, inasmuch as he had laboured here always in the praise of God, so his soul was carried by angels to the joys of Heaven which he longed for. So all who heard or saw the death of our saintly father Bede declared that they had never seen a man end his days in such great holiness and peace; for, as I have said, as long as his soul remained in the body, he chanted the "Gloria Patri" and other songs to the glory of God, and spreading out his hands ceased not to give God thanks.

Bede's Ecclesiastical History of the English People ed. Bertram Colgrave and R. A. B. Mynors, © Oxford University Press 1961, 581-587. Used by permission of Oxford University Press.

Propers

ROMAN

(May 25)
Lord,
you have enlightened
your Church
with the learning of
Saint Bede.
In your love
may your people learn
from his wisdom
and benefit from his
prayers.
Grant this through our
Lord Jesus Christ,
your Son,
who lives and reigns
with you and the
Holy Spirit,
one God, for ever and
ever.

LUTHERAN

Lord God, you have surrounded us with so great a cloud of witnesses. Grant that we, encouraged by the examples of your servants Columba, Aidan, and Bede, may persevere in the course that is set before us, to be living signs of the Gospel and at last, with all your saints, to share in your eternal joy; through your Son, Jesus Christ our Lord.

EPISCOPAL

Almighty God, who enriched your Church with the learning and holiness of your servant Bede: Grant us to hold fast the true doctrine of your Son our Savior Jesus Christ, and to show forth his teaching in our lives, to the glory of your great Name and the benefit of your holy Church; through Jesus Christ our Lord, who lives and reigns with you and the Holy Spirit, one God, now and for ever.

238   June 11

ROMAN	LUTHERAN	EPISCOPAL

Common of Pastors or Doctors

Common of Saints
Micah 6:6-8
Psalm 9:1-10
1 Corinthians 1:26-31
Luke 6:20-23

Malachi 3:16-18
Psalm 78:1-7
19:7-14
Matthew 13:47-52

Preface of a Saint

Preface: Apostles

Hymn of the Day: "The king of love my shepherd is" (456) (tune: *St. Columba*)

Prayers: for all those who through the darkness keep alive the light of learning
for those who persevere in prayer
for a spirit of gentleness and self-denial
for students and teachers of history
for the Iona Community of the Church of Scotland

Preface: All Saints

Color: White

June 11

ST. BARNABAS, APOSTLE

Barnabas, a Jew of the tribe of Levi, was born on the island of Cyprus (Acts 4:36) about the beginning of the Christian era. He was therefore, like Paul, a Jew of the Diaspora in contrast to Palestinian Jews, like Peter. A man of means, he gave the young church the proceeds from the sale of a piece of land. His name was originally Joseph but was changed by the apostles to Barnabas, meaning "son of encouragement," probably because of his ability as a preacher. He is mentioned repeatedly in the Acts of the Apostles and several places in Paul's letters, and everything that is known with certainty about him is found in these New Testament passages. Although he was not one of the original twelve, he was—like St. Paul—called an apostle.

The book of Acts lists Barnabas among the early believers in Jerusalem. He is traditionally regarded as one of the seventy disciples commissioned by Jesus, and he is commemorated as such by the Eastern churches. It was Barnabas at Jerusalem who was convinced of the genuineness of St. Paul's conversion and vouched for him to the community. Somewhat later the church at Jerusalem sent Barnabas to Antioch to the growing group of Gentile Christians there, and he in turn brought Paul from Tarsus to assist him (Acts 11:19-22).

After the church at Antioch reached a flourishing state with its own leaders, the two apostles, after fasting and prayer and the laying-on of hands by the faithful, set off on missionary travels, taking young John Mark with them. They preached the gospel in Cyprus and Pamphylia, where Mark left them, and they continued in the cities of Asia Minor, preaching to Jews and Gentiles but winning converts chiefly from the latter. On the island of Cyprus, it seems, Paul took over the leadership, and when they moved on to the mainland the group was known as "Paul and his company."

In the disagreement over the responsibilities of Jewish and of Gentile Christians, Barnabas tended to side with his fellow worker Paul, although on one occasion he followed Peter in refraining from eating with Gentiles. Somewhat later Barnabas and Paul disagreed on whether to take John Mark with them again, and they finally split up, with Barnabas taking Mark to Cyprus with him, while Paul went with Silas. Nothing is known of the life of Barnabas after this (as far as the record goes, the rift was final, although in 1 Cor. 9:6 Paul praises Barnabas as a working apostle). Legend has it that St. Barnabas was stoned to death in the city of Salamis on Cyprus, probably about the year 60.

Several writings bearing the name of Barnabas have circulated at various times; one of them, the *Epistle of Barnabas,* was widely read in the early church and was held by many to be genuine and worthy of inclusion in the New Testament. Modern scholarship attributes it to the second century, but it is acknowledged to be a valuable early Christian document. Tertullian proposed Barnabas as the author of Hebrews.

St. Barnabas' Day was observed in the Eastern churches at least as early as the fifth century; they also commemorate St. Bartholomew on the same day. The observance in the West began in the ninth century, and the Anglican reformers kept his feast day on the Prayer Book calendar as did many Lutheran churches.

Reading

(From *Worship* by von Allmen.)

The Church . . . appears as . . . an apostolic or missionary community.

First of all, why does the Church, in and through its cult, emerge as an apostolic community? Because by its worship—to quote the words of K. Barth—"it issues, without pretension, but firmly, from the profanity of the milieu in which it is normally immersed," i.e., by its worship it is differentiated from the world. And this is in two ways. Firstly, it does not yet embrace all men, but only the baptized. From this fact there emerges a special attitude towards those who are not yet members of the Church. Her very existence is, for those who do not belong to her, at once a challenge and a promise. Secondly, it does not include all men, but also it is not always gathered together but has a day of its own, a day of worship, Sunday. The fact that one day is singled out for divine worship teaches the Church that it is still in the world, that the hour of the great Sabbath has not yet struck. If the comparison were not too bold, I would say that the Church emerges, week by week, rather as a cetaceous animal, at regular times, comes up for air. But this very intermission, the fact that the cult is not continuous but sporadic, emphasizes the Church's otherness in relation to the world, and thus confronts the Church with the question of its justification for existing in the world and for the world.

And how does the Church, in and through its worship become aware of itself as an apostolic community? . . . it does so precisely through the realization that it is only as yet . . . the firstfruits of the creatures (Jas. 1:18), and not the totality, and that as yet it is gathered together only on the first day of the week (cf. Acts 20:7, etc.) and not every day of the week. In other words, the cult is an epiphany of the Church as a missionary community in the sense that it obliges the Church to send forth, into the world throughout the rest of the week, those whom it has assembled out of the world on the first day. This gives us an opportunity of introducing a brief aside on the term "Mass" which, from the fourth century, gradually supplanted in the West all other terms denoting the cult and which, among the Lutherans, even survived the Reformation. The origin of the word has given rise to some doubt. It now seems established, in spite of some risky hypotheses, that the term "Mass" comes from the Low Latin *Missa—missio—*i.e. *dismissal:* in other words it is the last note of the cult, the solemn act of dismissal which sends the faithful forth into the world (cf. Luke 24:46-53), which has been used to denote the cult as a whole as though to emphasize the justification of the Christian cult in the world which is not yet the Kingdom. "The cult," affirms A. D. Mueller who insists on the term, "must be understood as the Mass, *missio,* dismissal. In it is kindled the light which is to illuminate the world."

J.-J. von Allmen, *Worship: Its Theology and Practice* (New York: Oxford, 1965) 51-52. Used by permission of Lutterworth Press.

Propers

ROMAN	LUTHERAN	EPISCOPAL
God our Father, you filled Saint Barnabas with faith and the Holy Spirit and sent him to convert the nations. Help us to proclaim the gospel by word and deed. We ask this through our Lord Jesus Christ, your Son, who lives and reigns with you and the Holy Spirit, one God, for ever and ever.	Grant, Almighty God, that we may follow the example of your faithful servant Barnabas, who, seeking not his own renown but the well-being of your Church, gave generously of his life and substance for the relief of the poor and the spread of the Gospel; through Jesus Christ our Lord, who lives and reigns with you and the Holy Spirit, one God, now and forever.	Grant, O God, that we may follow the example of your faithful servant Barnabas, who, seeking not his own renown but the well-being of your Church, gave generously of his life and substance for the relief of the poor and the spread of the Gospel; through Jesus Christ our Lord, who lives and reigns with you and the Holy Spirit, one God, for ever and ever.
(Text from the English translation of the Roman Missal © 1973, Interna-		*(Text from the Book of Common Prayer [Pro-*

242   June 14

ROMAN	LUTHERAN	EPISCOPAL

ROMAN	LUTHERAN	EPISCOPAL
Acts 11:21b-26; 13:1-3	Isaiah 42:5-12	Isaiah 42:5-12
Psalm 98:1-6	Psalm 112	Psalm 112
Matthew 10:7-13	Acts 11:19-30; 13:1-3	Acts 11:19-30; 13:1-3
	Matthew 10:7-16	Matthew 10:7-16
		Preface of Apostles

Hymn of the Day: "Lift high the cross, the love of Christ proclaim" (377)

Prayers: for preachers of the Gospel
for reconciliation of those at variance with one another
for Cyprus and Turkey

Preface: Apostles

Color: Red

Basil the Great, Bishop of Caesarea, 379

Theologians of the Eastern church have sometimes been commemorated in groups. In the East, "Three Holy Hierarchs" are remembered together—Basil, Gregory of Nazianzus, and John Chrysostom. In the West, Basil, Gregory of Nazianzus, John Chrysostom, and Athanasius are considered the four Greek Doctors (i.e. teachers) of the church. In the *Lutheran Book of Worship,* the three Cappadocian Fathers are commemorated jointly—Basil, Gregory of Nazianzus, and Gregory of Nyssa.

Basil, known as the Administrator and the Patriarch of Eastern monks, was born in a Christian family of aristocratic landowners in Pontus in Asia Minor, ca. 329. His was a saintly family; his parents and grandparents were all canonized. Basil was trained in rhetoric and the best of pagan and Christian culture at Constantinople and Athens. He became a close friend of Gregory of Nazianzus. They were baptized together, ca. 358, and Basil gave up what promised to be a brilliant administrative career for the then unpopular life of asceticism that his family was leading at Annesi in Pontus. His brother Peter and other followers soon joined him.

Basil established a common life for the service of society, discouraging extreme asceticism. After a brief period in Syria and Egypt, Basil settled as a hermit by the river Iris in Caesarea. He joined the clergy there and was ordained ca. 365. In the famine of 367-368, he sold his extensive property for the benefit of the starving, raised other money, and organized relief work, forbidding any distinction between Christian and Jew.

In the spring of 370 he was elected bishop of Caesarea, a post which had jurisdiction over the dioceses of nearly all Asia Minor and Armenia, and was consecrated June 14 (his traditional feast day in the West). He struggled against the Arianism of the civil administration and also against the party that denied the divinity of the Holy Spirit. He organized missionary activity in Armenia. He sought to reunite all the Orthodox churches divided by the schism of Antioch. He was eloquent, statesmanlike, and of surpassing holiness. He died January 1, 379 and was mourned by the entire city, Jews and pagans as well as Christians. He was immediately eulogized by his brother Gregory of Nyssa and his friend Gregory of Nazianzus, but none of his contemporaries wrote his biography. Basil's feast days in the East are January 1 and 30. On the new Roman Calendar he is commemorated with Gregory of Nazianzus on January 2.

Basil's ascetic training convinced him that only the purified spirit could know the divine incomprehensibility. He is sometimes known as the Doctor of the Holy Spirit, and his treatise *On the Holy Spirit* was a major contribution to the doctrine of the Trinity. He is the father of Eastern communal monasticism, and monastic life in the Orthodox church is still based on principles which he laid down.

Donald Attwater. *The Golden Book of Eastern Saints.* Milwaukee: Bruce, 1938.
Hans von Campenhausen. *The Fathers of the Greek Church* tr. Stanley Godman (New York: Pantheon) 80-94.
W. K. Lowther Clarke, ed. *The Ascetic Works of St. Basil.* London: SPCK, 1925.

Margaret Mary Fox. *The Life and Times of St. Basil the Great.* Washington: Catholic University Press, 1939.
Jaroslav Pelikan. *The Christian Tradition. I. The Emergence of the Catholic Tradition (100-600).* University of Chicago Press, 1971.

Reading

(From a letter of St. Basil.)

The Christian should not be envious of another's good reputation, nor rejoice over his faults. Through love for Christ he should be grieved and distressed at his brother's faults and rejoice over his successes. He should not be indifferent to sinners or silent before them. He who reproves another should do so with all tenderness, in fear of God and with a view to reforming the sinner. He who is reproved or reprimanded should endure it willingly, recognizing the benefit received in being set aright. When a person is being accused, the Christian should not, before him or other persons, contradict the accuser. But if the accusation should ever seem unjust, the Christian should arrange a private conversation with the accuser, and either give or receive full information.

Each one should, according to his power, entertain a kindly feeling for everyone who has a grievance against him. He should not hold past wrongs against the repentant sinner, but should grant forgiveness from the bottom of his heart. He who says that he repents of a sin should not only feel remorse for his sin, but should also produce fruits worthy of repentance. And he who has been corrected for his first faults and has been thought worthy of forgiveness, if he sins again, prepares for himself a judgment of anger worse than the first. And he who, after the first and second admonition, abides by his shortcoming, should be disclosed to the one in authority, if perchance he may repent when admonished by more. If even so he is not set aright, he should be cut off from the rest as a cause for scandal, and should be regarded as a heathen and publican, for the sake of the safety of those zealous in obedience, according to the saying, "When the impious fall, the righteous tremble." Yet all should mourn for him, as though a member has been cut off from the body.

The sun should never set on a brother's wrath, lest sometime night stand between both and leave an inevitable charge for the day of judgment. The Christian should not await an opportunity for his own reform, because the morrow is not secure, since many who have made many plans have not reached the morrow. He should not be deceived by the filling of his belly, for nightmares come from this. He should not busy himself with excessive work, and thus overstep the bounds of sufficiency, as the apostle says, "Having food and wherewith to be covered, with this we are content;" because an abundance which goes beyond necessity gives appearance of avarice, and avarice has the condemnation of idolatry. He should not be desirous of money, nor treasure up unnecessary things to no avail. He who approaches God ought to embrace poverty in all things, and be pierced with the fear of God, according to him who said, "Pierce thou my flesh with thy fear, for I am afraid of thy judgments."

The Lord grant that you may receive all these admonitions with all assurance, and that you may exhibit fruits worthy of the Holy Spirit to the glory of God, with God's approval and the assistance of our Lord Jesus Christ. Amen.

Saint Basil, the Letters trans. Roy J. Deferrari, vol. I (Cambridge, MA: Harvard University Press, 1926) 137-141. Loeb Classical Library. Used by permission.

June 14

Gregory of Nazianzus, Bishop of Constantinople, 389

Gregory, called "the Theologian" by the Eastern church because of his profound influence and eloquence, was born at Arianzus near Nazianzus in Cappadocia ca. 330 of well-to-do parents. His father was a bishop. (Celibacy had not yet become universal.) Gregory was educated at Caesarea, where he met Basil, and then in Palestine, Alexandria, and Athens. On the way to Athens, he was shipwrecked (although he was a catechumen, he was not yet baptized), and he dedicated the remainder of his life to God in thanksgiving for his deliverance. Throughout his career he was torn between his desire to live a life of solitary contemplation and the church's summons to involvement in its conflicts and controversy. At Athens he again met

Basil. After eight years of study, in 367 or 368, he left for Nazianzus.
There he was baptized, probably by his father. He taught rhetoric
briefly, but soon joined Basil in his monastery on the river Iris. Together they wrote monastic rules, edited the sayings of Origen, and
enlisted Gregory of Nyssa for the monastery.

Gregory's father, in poor health, brought his son back to Nazianzus
for ordination at Christmas in 362. Gregory assisted his father and
helped elect Basil to the see of Caesarea.

The Emperor Valens in 372 divided the province of Cappadocia in
half. Basil persuaded Gregory to accept election as bishop of Sasima,
the new diocese, but under threats of violence from the bishop of the
new capital city of Tyana he never took possession of it. A rift between Basil and Gregory resulted that was never fully healed.

Gregory continued to assist his father until his father died in 374.
Gregory then withdrew to Isauria until 378 and then accepted a call
to be bishop of the Nicene community in the capital city of Constantinople. The hostility of the Arian majority became violent. At the
Council of Constantinople in 381 Gregory resigned the see to prevent
further division in the church and retired to his estate at Arianzus,
where he spent the last years of his life writing. He died there in
390. His feast day in the West has traditionally been May 9; in the
East it is January 25, and he is also commemorated with John Chrysostom and Basil on January 30, the Feast of Greek Letters. On the
new Roman calendar he is commemorated with Basil on January 2.
His relics are in St. Peter's Basilica in Rome.

Hans von Campenhausen. *The Fathers of the Greek Church* tr. Stanley
Godman (New York: Pantheon, 1959) 95-106.
Rosemary R. Reuther. *Gregory of Nazianzus. Rhetor and Philosopher.* New
York: Oxford, 1969.

Reading

(From Gregory's *Theological Ovations.*)

What is this that has happened to me, O friends, and initiates, and
fellow lovers of the truth? I was running to lay hold on God, and
thus I went up into the Mount, and drew aside the curtain of the
cloud, and entered away from matter and material things, and as far

as I could I withdrew within myself. And then when I looked up, I scarce saw the back parts of God; although I was sheltered by the rock, the Word that was made flesh for us. And when I looked a little closer, I saw, not the first and unmingled nature, known to itself—to the Trinity, I mean; not that which abides within the first veil, and is hidden by the cherubim; but only that nature, which at last even reaches to us. And that is, as far as I can learn, the majesty, or, as holy David calls it, the glory which is manifested among the creatures, which it has produced and governs. For these are the back parts of God, which he leaves behind him, as tokens of himself, like the shadows and reflection of the sun in the water, which show the sun to our weak eyes, because we cannot look at the sun himself, for by his unmixed light he is too strong for our power of perception. In this way then you shall discourse of God; even were you a Moses and a god to Pharaoh; even were you caught up like Paul to the third heaven, and had heard unspeakable words; even were you raised above them both, and exalted to angelic or archangelic place and dignity. For though a thing be all heavenly, or above heaven, and far higher in nature and nearer to God than we, yet it is farther distant from God, and from the complete comprehension of his nature, than it is lifted above our complex and lowly and earthward-sinking composition.

Therefore we must begin again thus: It is difficult to conceive God, but to define him in words is an impossibility. . . . But in my opinion it is impossible to express him, and yet more impossible to conceive him. For that which may be conceived may perhaps be made clear by language, if not fairly well, at any rate imperfectly, to anyone who is not quite deprived of his hearing, or slothful of understanding. But to comprehend the whole of so great a subject as this is quite impossible and impracticable, not merely to the utterly careless and ignorant, but even to those who are highly exalted, and who love God, and in like manner to every created nature; seeing that the darkness of this world and the thick covering of the flesh is an obstacle to the full understanding of the truth.

From *Christology of the Later Fathers*, Vol. III, The Library of Christian Classics, ed. by Edward Rochie Hardy and Cyril C. Richardson, 137-139. Published in the U.S.A. by The Westminster Press, 1954. Used by permission.

248

Gregory, Bishop of Nyssa, ca. 385

Gregory of Nyssa, known as "the Philosopher and Mystic," was born at Caesarea ca. 335 of a famous Christian family; he was Basil's brother. He was ordained a lector but seems to have abandoned his vocation to follow the profession of his father, a rhetorician. He married, but after the death of his wife Gregory was persuaded to enter the monastery founded by his brother on the river Iris. At Basil's insistence, he was consecrated bishop of Nyssa, a suffragan see of Cappadocia, in 371. He lacked his brother's administrative talent and was accused of negligence in financial matters and deposed by an Arian-dominated synod in 376. After the death of the Arian emperor Valens in 378, Gregory returned to Nyssa. When Basil died in the following year, Gregory continued his brother's work and became one of the leaders of the church. He took part in the Council of Antioch in 379, and at the Council of Constantinople in 381 he was acknowledged to be a pillar of orthodoxy. When he went to Constantinople he remarked on the people's zeal for theology as well as the pervasiveness of Arianism:

If you ask someone how many obols a certain thing costs, he replies by dogmatizing on the born and unborn. If you ask the price of bread, they answer you, "The Father is greater than the Son and the Son is subordinate to him." If you ask "Is my bath ready?" they answer you, "The Son has been made out of nothing."

In his last years Gregory was involved in a bitter controversy over Apollinarianism, the first great Christian heresy which claimed that Christ lacked perfect manhood. Gregory died after attending the Council of Constantinople in 394. His traditional feast day is March 9.

His is a long and impressive list of writings, refuting heresies and clarifying the corresponding Orthodox position, especially regarding the Holy Trinity. In his exposition of Scripture he attempted to explain Genesis in light of the philosophical and scientific accounts of the formation of the world. Gregory is the most speculative of the Greek fathers, with a strong interest in philosophy. In him three strains come together: Scripture, philosophy, and mysticism.

Hans von Campenhausen. *The Fathers of the Greek Church* tr. Stanley Godman (New York: Pantheon, 1959) 107-116.
J. Danielou, comp. *From Glory to Glory: Texts from Gregory of Nyssa's Mystical Writings* ed. and tr. H. Musurillo. New York: Scribners, 1961.
E. C. Messenger. *Evolution and Theology.* New York: Macmillan, 1931.

Reading

(From *Address on Religious Instruction* by Gregory of Nyssa.)

God's goodness, wisdom, justice, power, and incorruptible nature are all to be seen in his plan for us. His goodness and justice are to be seen in the way he saved us. His power is clear in this: that he came in the likeness of man and in the lowly form of our nature, inspiring the hope that, like man, he could be overcome by death; and yet, having come, he acted entirely in accordance with his nature. Now it belongs to light to dispel darkness, and to life to destroy death. Seeing, then, we have been led astray from the right path, with the result we were diverted from the life we once had and were involved in death, what is there improbable in what we learn from the gospel revelation? Purity lays hold of those stained with sin, life lays hold of the dead, and guidance is given to those astray, so that the stain may be cleansed, the error corrected, and the dead may return to life.

There is no good reason for those who do not take too narrow a view of things to find anything strange in the fact that God assumed our nature. For when he considers the universe, can anyone be so simple-minded as not to believe that the Divine is present in everything, pervading, embracing, and penetrating it? For all things depend on Him who is, and nothing can exist which does not have its being in Him who is. If, then, all things exist in him and he exists in all things, why are they shocked at a scheme of revelation which teaches that God became man, when we believe that even now he is not external to man? For, granted that God is not present in us in the same way as he was in the incarnation, it is at any rate admitted he is equally present in us in both instances. In the one case he is united to us in so far as he sustains existing things. In the the other case he united himself with our nature, in order that by its union with the Divine it might become divine, being rescued from death and freed

250 June 14

from the tyranny of the adversary. For with *his* return from death, our mortal race begins *its* return to immortal life.

From *Christology of the Later Fathers*, Vol. III, The Library of Christian Classics, ed. by Edward Rochie Hardy and Cyril C. Richardson, 301-302. Published in the U.S.A. by The Westminster Press, 1954. Used by permission.

Propers

ROMAN

St. Basil the Great and St. Gregory Nazianzen
(January 2)

God our Father, you inspired the Church with the example and teaching of your saints Basil and Gregory. In humility may we come to know your truth and put it into action with faith and love. Grant this through our Lord Jesus Christ, your Son, who lives and reigns with you and the Holy Spirit, one God, for ever and ever.

(Text from the English translation of the Roman Missal © 1973, International Committee on English in the Liturgy, Inc. All rights reserved.)

Common of Pastors or Doctors

LUTHERAN

Almighty God, your Holy Spirit gives to one the word of wisdom, and to another the word of knowledge, and to another the word of faith. We praise you for the gifts of grace imparted to your servants Basil and Gregory of Nazianzus and Gregory of Nyssa, and we pray that by their teaching we may be led to a fuller knowledge of the truth which we have in your Son Jesus Christ our Lord.

Common of Theologians
Proverbs 3:1-7
Psalm 119:89-104
1 Corinthians 2:6-10, 13-16
John 17:18-23

EPISCOPAL

Basil the Great
(June 14)
Almighty, everlasting God, whose servant Basil steadfastly confessed your Son Jesus Christ to be true God and true Man: Grant that we may hold fast to this faith, and magnify the holy Name of your Son, our Lord and Savior Jesus Christ, who lives and reigns with you and the Holy Spirit, one God, now and for ever.

(Text from Lesser Feasts and Fasts, Revised Edition, copyright 1973 by Charles Mortimer Guilbert as Custodian of the Standard Book of Common Prayer. All rights reserved. Used by permission.)

Psalm 135:1-5
1 Corinthians 2:6-13
Psalm 119:33-40
Luke 10:21-24

Preface of Trinity Sunday

Gregory of Nazianzus
(May 9)
Psalm 33:13-22
Wisdom 7:7-14
Psalm 71:15-22
John 8:25-32

ROMAN **LUTHERAN** EPISCOPAL

Collect and Preface as
above for Basil
Gregory of Nyssa
(March 9)
Almighty God, whose
eternal Being of glori-
ous majesty and per-
fect love has been re-
vealed to your Church
as one God in Trinity
of Persons: Give us
grace, after the exam-
ple of your servant
Gregory, to abide
steadfast in the con-
fession of this faith
and constant in our
worship of you, in
spirit and in truth,
who live and reign,
one God, Father, Son,
and Holy Spirit, now
and for ever.

*(Text from Lesser Feasts
and Fasts, Revised Edi-
tion, copyright 1973 by
Charles Mortimer Guilbert
as Custodian of the Stan-
dard Book of Common
Prayer. All rights reserved.
Used by permission.)*

Psalm 33:3-11
Wisdom 7:24-28
Psalm 37:32-39
John 5:19-24

Preface of Trinity
Sunday

Hymn of the Day: "Come, Holy Ghost, our souls inspire" (472, 473)

Prayers: for the relief of the poor
for zeal for the truth
for teachers of the catholic faith
for pastors who long for time for prayer and contemplation

Preface: Trinity Sunday (because the Cappadocian fathers explored
the mystery of the Triune God)

Color: White

Onesimos Nesib, Translator, Evangelist, 1931

Onesimos, born in 1855, was captured by slave traders and taken from his Galla homeland in western Ethiopia to Eritrea, where he was bought and freed by Swedish missionaries. They educated, baptized, and shared with him their concern for the evangelizing of the Galla, the largest ethnic group in Ethiopia. Onesimos became an evangelist, translated the entire Bible into Galla, and, in spite of difficulties, returned to preach the gospel in his homeland. He died at Naqamte, Wollega Province, Ethiopia, according to the Ethiopian calendar on Sunday Sene 25, 1923. The Gregorian date is June 21, 1931. According to the diary of Olle Eriksson, a missionary who conducted the funeral service, Onesimos fell ill just before he reached the present Mekane Yesus Church at Naqamte where he was to preach. He died peacefully in the evening. On his tombstone is the inscription from Jeremiah 22:29, "O Land, O Land, hear the word of the Lord."

Nils Dahlberg. *Onesimos. Fran slav till bibel översättare* (From slave to Bible translator). Stockholm, 1932.

With Onesimos, **Frumentius** might also be remembered. He was a fourth century Syrian who converted Ethiopia to Christianity. His dates are uncertain (ca. 300-380). He was consecrated bishop for the region of his apostolate by Athanasius, linking the Ethiopian church and the see of Alexandria. Frumentius' feast day is October 27 in the west, August 1 in the Ethiopian church, November 30 for the Greeks, and December 18 for the Copts.

Reading

(From Martin Luther, *Lectures on Galatians*, 1519)

Behold, this is what Christ has gained for us, namely, that the name of the Lord (that is, the mercy and truth of God) is preached to us and that whoever believes in this name will be saved. Therefore if your conscience troubles you and you are a sinner and are seeking to become righteous, what will you do? Will you look around to see what works you may do or where you may go? No. On the contrary, see to it that you hear or recall the name of the Lord, that is, that God is righteous, good, and holy; and then cling to this, firmly believing that he is such a One for you. Now you are at once such a one, like him. But you will never see the name of the Lord more clearly than you do in Christ. There you will see how good, pleasant, faithful, righteous, and true God is, since he did not spare his own Son (Rom. 8:32). Through Christ he will draw you to himself.

And so you must not imagine that the Christian's life is a standing still and a state of rest. No, it is a passing over and a progress from vices to virtue, from clarity to clarity, from virtue to virtue. And those who have not been enroute you should not consider Christians either. On the contrary, you must regard them as people of inactivity and peace, upon whom the prophet calls down their enemies. . . . Love is not idle, but it continually crucifies the flesh and is unable to rest content at its own level; it expands itself to purge a man throughout his being.

Therefore . . . the servitude of the spirit and freedom from sin, or from the Law, are identical, just as the servitude of sin and of the Law are identical with freedom from righteousness, or from righteousness and the Spirit. A person goes from servitude to servitude, from freedom to freedom, that is, from sin to grace, from fear of punishment to love of righteousness, from the Law to fulfillment of the Law, from the word to reality, from a figure to truth, from a sign to substance, from Moses to Christ, from the flesh to the spirit, from the world to the Father. All this takes place at the same time.

Luther's Works. Vol. 27, pp. 221, 289-290, 349. © 1964 Concordia Publishing House. Used by permission.

Propers: Missionaries

Hymn of the Day: "How blest are they who hear God's word" (227)

Prayers: for the church in Ethiopia
        for social justice

for courage to press on in the Christian pilgrimage
for deepened understanding of political and spiritual freedom
Color: White

THE NATIVITY OF ST. JOHN THE BAPTIST

John the Baptist was born in a priestly family of the Jews at about the same time as Jesus. Events of his life and teaching are known from accounts in all four gospels and in the writings of Flavius Josephus, the Jewish historian of the first century. According to the gospels, the birth of John was predicted miraculously to Zacharias and Elizabeth. At his birth his aged father sang the hymn of praise called the Benedictus, which is the traditional Gospel Canticle at the church's Morning Prayer.

John lived "in the desert" where he apparently came in contact with the beliefs and practices of the Jewish sect called the Essenes, or as they called themselves, the Sons of Zadok. Some think that John may have been a novice in this community and that his own teachings represent an adaptation for ordinary Jewish people of the exclusive ethic of the Essenes with its requirements of celibacy, common property, and pacificism. In any case, about the year 29 in the wilderness of Judaea, near the Jordan River, John began to preach a call to repentance and a baptismal washing. He gathered a group of disciples; Andrew and probably Peter and John the apostle were among them.

In the course of his preaching, John the Baptist denounced the immoral life of the Herodian rulers, and Herod Antipas, the tetrarch of Galilee, had him arrested and imprisoned in the huge fortress of Machaerus, which Herod the Great had built in the wilderness east of the Dead Sea. It was there that Herod Antipas had John beheaded. The story of his death has been told again and again in music and in art as well as in the lessons and devotions of the church.

St. John the Baptist was highly regarded by the early Christians, and the Eastern churches especially have always accorded him an important place in their prayers and worship. The Eastern Orthodox churches observe days of commemoration of the Old Testament prophets, the "Holy Forefathers," of whom John was the last and greatest. The birthday of John the Baptizer was one of the earliest festivals in the calendar of the church, an exception to the general principle that the church remembers martyrs on the day of their death. There is an observance of the Beheading or "Decollation" of St. John the Baptist on August 29, which has been kept in both East and West; the Orthodox churches also remember him on the day after the Epiphany and on September 23, and commemorate his parents on September 5. A Feast of St. Zacharias and of St. Elizabeth is kept in Palestine and elsewhere on November 5. At the time of the Reformation, the Feast of the Nativity of St. John the Baptist was retained on Lutheran and Anglican calendars, and a few also kept the day of his beheading.

St. John the Baptist is the patron saint of Quebec, and his birthday is celebrated as an important holiday in French Canada.

Charles H. H. Scobie. *John the Baptist.* Philadelphia: Fortress, 1964.

Reading

(From *A Search for God in Time and Memory* by John S. Dunne.)

The turning points in Jesus' life, according to our hypothesis, were the points where his life intersected with that of John the Baptist. At each of these junctures he went over from an ignorance to a knowledge. The first was in his baptism at the hands of John. That he presented himself for a baptism of repentance suggests that he was uncertain of his standing with God. His uncertainty, however, was changed into assurance as he underwent the baptism and experienced himself as beloved and well-pleasing to God. This left him still uncertain, nevertheless, as to whether the boundless acceptance he was receiving from God was for him alone or whether it was for others too. This uncertainty was removed at the second turning point, the imprisonment of John, when he saw John silenced and felt himself called upon to step into John's place and proclaim the kingdom of God. At this point the uncertainty remained as to how the kingdom would come about, whether it would come through a conversion of Israel to God by his preaching. The third turning point, the execution of John the Baptist, seems to have been the beginning for Jesus of the realization that the kingdom would not come in this way, that instead his preaching would fail, and he himself would be put to death.

John S. Dunne, *A Search for God in Time and Memory* (New York: Macmillan, 1970) 212-213. Copyright © 1967, 1969 by John S. Dunne, C.S.C. Used by permission of the Macmillan Publishing Co.

Propers

ROMAN

God our Father,
you raised up John the
   Baptist
to prepare a perfect
   people for Christ
   the Lord.
Give your Church joy
   in spirit
and guide those who
   believe in you
into the way of
   salvation and peace.
We ask this through
   our Lord Jesus
   Christ, your Son,
who lives and reigns
   with you and the
   Holy Spirit,
one God, for ever and
   ever.

(Text from the English translation of the Roman Missal © 1973, International Committee on English in the Liturgy, Inc. All rights reserved.)

Isaiah 49:1-6
   Psalm 139:1-3,
      13-15
Acts 13:22-26
Luke 1:57-66, 80

LUTHERAN

Almighty God, you called John the Baptist to give witness to the coming of your Son and to prepare the way. Grant to your people the wisdom to see your purpose and the openness to hear your will, that we too may witness to Christ's coming and so prepare his way; through your Son, Jesus Christ our Lord, who lives and reigns with you and the Holy Spirit, one God, now and forever.

Malachi 3:1-4
Psalm 141
Acts 13:13-26
Luke 1:57-67 (68-80)

EPISCOPAL

Almighty God, by whose providence your servant John the Baptist was wonderfully born, and sent to prepare the way of your Son our Savior by preaching repentance: Make us so to follow his teaching and holy life, that we may truly repent according to his preaching; and, following his example, constantly speak the truth, boldly rebuke vice, and patiently suffer for the truth's sake; through Jesus Christ your Son our Lord, who lives and reigns with you and the Holy Spirit, one God, for ever and ever.

(Text from the Book of Common Prayer [Proposed], copyright 1977 by Charles Mortimer Guilbert as Custodian of the Standard Book of Common Prayer. All rights reserved. Used by permission.)

Isaiah 40:1-11
   Psalm 85
   or 85:7-13
Acts 13:14b-26
Luke 1:57-80

Preface of Advent

Hymn of the Day: "The Lord will come and not be slow" (318)

Prayers: for justice
       for a zeal for the truth
       for renewal of life
       for an earnest expectation of the coming of Christ

Preface: Advent

Color: White

June 25

The Presentation of the Augsburg Confession, 1530
Philipp Melanchthon, Renewer of the Church, 1560

Just as all Christians can look to the Day of Pentecost as the birthday of the whole Christian Church, many Lutheran Christians regard June 25 as the anniversary of the beginning of the Church of the Reformation. On that day in 1530 the statement of faith called the Augsburg Confession, which had been drafted by Philipp Melanchthon and endorsed by Luther, was read aloud to the emperor of the Holy Roman Empire, Charles V, and his Diet (assembly) of Princes at Augsburg.

Philipp Schwarzerd, better known by the Greek form of his name, Melanchthon ("black earth"), was born February 16, 1497 at Bretten in Baden. After attending Latin school in Pforzheim he attended the University of Heidelberg (1509-1512) and then the University of Tuebingen (1512-1518), where he received his master's degree in 1516. He was a brilliant student of the classics and soon became known as one of the outstanding young scholars of the humanist movement. In 1518 he was called to the new University of Wittenberg. At Luther's urging Melanchthon undertook the teaching of theology and Scripture in addition to his work on Aristotle and classical studies. He was a popular teacher, lecturing often to hundreds of students, and the combination of Luther and Melanchthon made Wittenberg one of the leading universities of Europe during much of the sixteenth century.

In the fall of 1520 Melanchthon married the daughter of the mayor of Wittenberg and the Melanchthons had four children. Although his salary was small, both husband and wife were extremely generous to others and their family life was happy. Melanchthon remained a professor at Wittenberg until his death on April 19, 1560, and he frequently travelled to meetings and disputations, and he was often called upon to draft statements of positions, refutations, and bases for reconciliation between differing groups.

In 1521 Melanchthon published his *Loci Communes,* the first compendium of Lutheran doctrine, which finally appeared in an annotated English edition in 1944. Beginning in the year 1525 Melanchthon turned his attention to the question of general education. With Luther he reorganized the schools in Eisleben and Magdeburg, and he established the gymnasium (secondary school) in Nuremburg. In 1527 Melanchthon took part in the visitation of schools in Saxony, and in 1528 he made a similar tour through parts of Thuringia. Melanchthon thus played a leading role in the development of elementary and secondary education in Germany, making the study of the classics the basis of Christian education in a system that lasted for centuries. He came to be called *Praeceptor Germaniae,* the Teacher of Germany.

In April 1530, the Emperor Charles V summoned a Diet to settle the religious controversies of his realm and so present a united front in his military ventures against the Turks. Since Luther himself was under papal excommunication and imperial ban, it was Melanchthon who had the duty of being the chief representative of the Lutheran cause. He drafted a confession in early May which he twice revised, sending it each time to Luther for approval. On June 25 it was presented to the Emperor and his Diet in Latin and German by Christian Bayer, the Chancellor of Saxony; it was signed by seven German princes and the representatives of two free cities.

Their statement of faith attempts to make clear that the Lutherans were not to be lumped together with other opponents of the Roman Catholic Church, and it emphasizes not the differences from Rome. but the agreements with Rome. As the Preface says,

. . . we are prepared, in obedience to your Imperial Majesty, our most gracious Lord, to discuss . . . such practical and equitable ways as may restore unity. Thus . . . our differences may be reconciled, and we may be united in one, true religion, even as we are all under one Christ and should confess and contend for Christ. . . . that it may be done according to divine truth we invoke Almighty God in deepest humility and implore Him to bestow his grace to this end. Amen.

Luther saw in the presentation of the Confession a fulfillment of Psalm 119:46, which has ever since been carried as the motto in editions of the Augustana: "I will tell of your decrees before kings and will not be ashamed."

The Augsburg Confession spread rapidly among the churches, and within fifteen years almost all of evangelical Germany subscribed to it. After 1535, assent to the doctrines of the Confession was required for the ordination of evangelical pastors at Wittenberg. During the sixteenth century many copies of the Confession circulated, some with expansions and changes of wording. The best known of these is the so-called *Variata* ("altered") edition of 1540, which contained a number of changes made by Melanchthon. Almost all Lutheran church bodies today specify the Unaltered (*Invariata*) of 1530 in their official statements of confessional subscription.

From the day of its delivery translations were made into other languages. Three years after its presentation to the Emperor a Danish translation was published, and in 1536 an English edition. A version in classical Greek was prepared by the Reformers and used in discussions with the Orthodox churches. In some areas of Europe the Augsburg Confession was among the first documents to be published in a newly-established literary language; such was the case with the translation of the Slovenian reformer Primoz Trubar. In later centuries, as Lutheran missionaries on other continents translated the Bible and Luther's *Small Catechism* into local languages and the younger churches came into being, the Augsburg Confession began to appear in languages of Asia and Africa, such as Chinese, Japanese, Hindi, Tamil, Swahili, Zulu, and Malagasy.

The four hundredth anniversary of the Augsburg Confession was celebrated in 1930 by Lutherans in many countries, and the numerous jubilee editions of the Confession and volumes of historical and theological studies which came out at that time testify to the vitality of this symbol of the Christian faith, which for Lutherans takes its place after the great creeds of Christendom as a "pure exposition of the word of God."

Eric W. Gritsch and Robert W. Jenson. *Lutheranism. The Theological Movement and Its Confessional Writings.* Philadelphia: Fortress, 1976.
Clyde L. Manschreck. *Melanchthon, the Quiet Reformer.* New York: Abingdon, 1958.

Robert Stupperich. *Melanchthon* tr. Robert H. Fischer. London: Lutterworth, 1966.
Vilmos Vajta, ed. *Luther and Melanchthon in the History and Theology of the Reformation.* Philadelphia: Fortress, 1961.

Reading

(From Philipp Melanchthon, *Loci Communes Theologicae* [1521])

The Lord God Almighty clothed his Son with flesh that he might draw us from contemplating his own majesty to a consideration of the flesh, and especially of our weakness. Paul writes in 1 Corinthians 1:21 that God wishes to be known in a new way, i.e., through the foolishness of preaching, since in his wisdom he could not be known through wisdom. Therefore, there is no reason why we should labor so much on those exalted topics such as "God," "The Unity of the Trinity of God," "The Mystery of Creation," and "The Manner of the Incarnation." What, I ask you, did the Scholastics accomplish during the many ages they were examining only those points? Have they not, as Paul says, become vain in their disputations (Romans 11:21), always trifling about universals, formalities, connotations, and various other foolish words? Their stupidity could be left unnoticed if those stupid discussions had not in the meantime covered up for us the gospel and the benefits of Christ.

Now, if I wanted to be clever in an unnecessary pursuit, I could easily overthrow all their arguments for the doctrines of the faith. Actually, they seem to argue more accurately for certain heresies than they do for the Catholic doctrines.

But as for the one who is ignorant of the other fundamentals, namely, "The Power of Sin," "The Law," "Grace," I do not see how I can call him a Christian. For from these things Christ is known, since to know Christ means to know his benefits and not as *they* teach, to reflect upon his natures and the modes of his incarnation. For unless you know why Christ put on flesh and was nailed to the cross, what good will it do you to know merely the history about him? Would you say that it is enough for a physician to know the shapes, colors, and contours of plants, and that it makes no difference whether he knows their innate power? Christ was given us as a remedy and, to use the language of Scripture, a saving remedy (Luke 2:30; 3;6; Acts

28:28). It is therefore proper that we know Christ in another way than that which the Scholastics have set forth.

This, then, is Christian knowledge: to know what the law demands, where you may seek power for doing the law and grace to cover sin, how you may strengthen a quaking spirit against the devil, the flesh, and the world, and how you may console an afflicted conscience.

Melanchthon and Bucer, Vol. XIX, Library of Christian Classics XIX, ed by Wilhelm Pauck, 21-22. Copyright © MCMLXIX, The Westminster Press. Used by permission.

Propers: Reformation Day

Hymn of the Day: "O God, O Lord of heaven and earth" (396)

Prayers: for the unity of the church
for the preaching and teaching of pure doctrine
for a deeper knowledge of Christ and his benefits

Color: White

June 28

Irenaeus, Bishop of Lyons, ca. 202

A disciple of Polycarp of Smyrna (see February 23), Irenaeus was born in Asia Minor between 140 and 160. Little is known of his life. For reasons that are not known, he migrated to Gaul (perhaps stopping at Rome for study) and there became a presbyter of the church in Lyons during the reign of Marcus Aurelius. Lyons in the second century was an important commercial city, the seat of a garrison and headquarters for three provinces, a gateway between the Mediterranean world and the provinces north of the Alps. Like Rome, Lyons had a large Greek-speaking element in its population, and it was among this group that Christianity was first established.

During the Montanist controversy (the Montanists were an apocalyptic party which expected the immediate outpouring of the Holy Spirit), Irenaeus was sent as an envoy to Rome by the Christians at Lyons. Upon his return, he was elected bishop of that city to succeed

Pothinus, who had died in prison during the persecution of 177. Irenaeus perhaps introduced Christianity into parts of Eastern Gaul. He strenuously opposed Gnostic dualism in his major writing, *Against Heresies.*

Nothing is known of the last years of his life. He died perhaps ca. 202. In the late sixth century Gregory of Tours refers to Irenaeus as a martyr, but the tradition seems not to be older than that.

Eusebius says that Irenaeus, as his name implies, was a promoter of peace in the church and firmly protested Pope Victor's threatened excommunication of the Eastern churches which observed Easter on the Jewish date, the fourteenth of Nisan, rather than on the following Sunday. Irenaeus is important as a witness to the apostolic tradition (he knew Polycarp and Polycarp knew the Apostles) and as a champion of the inspiration of both the Old and the New Testaments.

It is also fitting to remember on this day the **Martyrs of Lyons** who died in the persecution of 177. Eusebius includes in the fifth book of his *Church History* a letter sent by the Christians in the Rhone valley to the churches of Asia Minor narrating the martyrdom. The letter is one of the most precious documents of Christian antiquity. While the governor of the province was absent mobs began to attack the Christians in Lyons and the neighboring city of Vienne, seeking them out, beating and torturing them, and throwing them into prison. Among the Christians thus persecuted was the aged Bishop Pothinus, who was more than ninety years old and who died in prison from his beating. The governor returned and Emperor Marcus Aurelius confirmed the death penalty for those Christians who refused to renounce their faith. At a pagan festival the Christians who were Roman citizens were beheaded, and the others, many of whom were natives of provinces of Asia Minor as was Irenaeus, were killed by wild beasts in the amphitheater. The names of forty-eight of these martyrs are recorded, among whom were a slave girl Blandina and her mistress, Bishop Pothinus, a deacon Sanctus, the newly-baptized Maturus, Attalus "a man of repute," and Ponticus, a fifteen year old boy. The bodies of the victims were burned and their remains thrown into the Rhone. The letter says, "We cannot describe in writing the greatness of the tribulation here or the heathens' fury against the saints or all that the blessed martyrs suffered." The traditional feast day of the Martyrs of Lyons is June 2.

Hans von Campenhausen. *The Fathers of the Greek Church.* tr., Stanley Godman (New York: Pantheon, 1959) 21-28.
Gustav Wingren. *Man and the Incarnation. A Study in the Biblical Theology of Irenaeus.* Philadelphia: Muhlenberg, 1959. [1947]

Reading

(From Irenaeus *Against Heresies,* I:10.1-2)

Now the Church, although scattered over the whole civilized world to the end of the earth, received from the apostles and their disciples its faith in one God, the Father Almighty, who made the heaven, and the earth, and the seas, and all that is in them, and in one Christ Jesus, the Son of God, who was made flesh for our salvation, and in the Holy Spirit, who through the prophets proclaimed the dispensations of God—the comings, the birth of a virgin, the suffering, the resurrection from the dead, and the bodily reception into the heavens of the beloved, Christ Jesus our Lord, and his coming from the heavens in the glory of the Father to restore all things, and to raise up all flesh, that is, the whole human race, so that every knee may bow, of things in heaven and on earth and under the earth, to Christ Jesus our Lord and God and Savior and King, according to the pleasure of the invisible Father, and every tongue may confess him, and that he may execute righteous judgment on all. The spiritual powers of wickedness, and the angels who transgressed and fell into apostasy, and the godless and wicked and lawless and blasphemers among men he will send into the eternal fire. But to the righteous and holy, and those who have kept his commandments and have remained in his love, some from the beginning [of life] and some since their repentance, he will by his grace give life incorrupt, and will clothe them with eternal glory.

Having received this preaching and this faith, as I have said, the Church, although scattered in the whole world, carefully preserves it, as if living in one house. She believes these things everywhere alike, as if she had but one heart and one soul, and preaches them harmoniously, teaches them, and hands them down, as if she had but one mouth. For the languages of the world are different, but the meaning of the Christian tradition is one and the same. Neither do the churches that have been established in Germany believe otherwise, or hand down any other tradition, nor those among the Iberians, nor those among the Celts, nor in Egypt, nor in Libya, nor those established in the middle parts of the world. But as God's creature, the sun, is one and the same in the whole world, so also the preaching of the truth shines everywhere, and illumines all men who wish to come to the knowledge of the truth. Neither will one of those who preside in the churches who is very powerful in speech say anything different from these things, for no one is above his teacher, nor will one who is weak in speech diminish the tradition. For since the faith is one and the same, he who can say much about it does not add to it, nor does he who can say little diminish it.

Early Christian Fathers, Vol. I, Library of Christian Classics, tr. and ed. by Cyril C. Richardson, 360-361. Published in the U.S.A. by The Westminster Press, 1953. Used by permission.

Propers

ROMAN	LUTHERAN	EPISCOPAL

Father, you called Saint Irenaeus to uphold your truth and bring peace to your Church. By his prayers renew us in faith and love that we may always be intent on fostering unity and peace. Grant this through our Lord Jesus Christ, your Son, who lives and reigns with you and the Holy Spirit, one God, for ever and ever.

(Text from the English translation of the Roman Missal © 1973, International Committee on Eng-

Almighty God, you have raised up faithful bishops and leaders of your Church. May the memory of your servant Irenaeus be a source of joy for us and a bulwark of our faith, so that we may serve you and confess your name before the world; through your Son, Jesus Christ our Lord.

Almighty God, who upheld your servant Irenaeus with strength to maintain the truth against every wind of vain doctrine: Keep us, we pray, steadfast in your true religion, that in constancy and peace we may walk the way that leads to life eternal; through Jesus Christ our Lord, who now lives and reigns with you and the Holy Spirit, one God, for ever and ever.

(Text from Lesser Feasts and Fasts, Revised Edition, copyright 1973 by Charles Mortimer Guilbert as Custodian of the Standard Book of Common Prayer. All rights reserved. Used by permission.)

ROMAN **LUTHERAN** **EPISCOPAL**

Common of Martyrs or Doctors or 2 Timothy 2:22b-26	Common of Pastors Ezekiel 34:11-16 Psalm 84 Ephesians 3:14-21 John 21:15-17 or Common of Theologians	Malachi 2:5-7 Psalm 145:1-13 145:14-22 Luke 11:33-36 Preface of the Incarnation

Hymn of the Day: "Holy Spirit, ever dwelling (523)

Prayers: for peace in the world
for peace in the Church
for a renewed appreciation of the apostolic tradition

Preface: Christmas (Irenaeus championed the Incarnation against
the Gnostics)

Color: White

June 29

ST. PETER AND ST. PAUL, APOSTLES

The two great apostles whose ministry embraced the whole Jewish
and Gentile world have been associated in Christian devotion since
earliest times. The Feast of SS. Peter and Paul is one of the oldest
of the saints' days, having been observed at least since 258, and it
was of such importance in the Middle Ages that it (together with
the days of Lawrence and Michael) marked a turning point in the
Pentecost season.

Simon, the son of Jonah, later called Cephas or Peter (Aramic and
Greek for "rock"), was probably born in Bethsaida of Galilee. He was
a fisherman, working in partnership with the sons of Zebedee. He was
married, and his mother-in-law, whom Jesus cured of a fever, lived
with them; later he took his wife on his missionary travels. It is likely
that he and his brother Andrew as well as the Apostle John were
among the followers of John the Baptist before they joined Jesus.

Peter has a special place among the apostles. He was not only one of the inner circle with James and John, but he was often the speaker for the Twelve as a whole, and his name was invariably put at the head of the lists of the Apostles. After the resurrection, Peter was the first of the Twelve to see the risen Lord, and he clearly acted as the leader, taking the initiative in the selection of Matthias, explaining the events of Pentecost to the assembled crowd, performing miracles, and making decisions.

Peter turned increasingly to missionary work, chiefly among the Jews, and the leadership of the church in Jerusalem passed to James the brother of Jesus. Peter was active in Samaria and in the towns of Lydda, Joppa, and Caesarea in Palestine. Of his later missionary travels little is known in detail, but tradition has connected his name with Antioch, Corinth, and Rome, and his stay at least in the first of these is confirmed by the New Testament. Although the Scriptures are silent about the latter part of his life, the weight of tradition makes it probable that Peter left Antioch about the year 55 and later went to Rome and suffered martyrdom there ca. 64.

Saul, later to be known by the Greek form of his name, Paul, the Apostle to the Gentiles, was born in the city of Tarsus in Cilicia, a Jew of the tribe of Benjamin. He probably attended a local synagogue school, and he studied with the rabbi Galaliel in Jerusalem. He learned the trade of the tentmaker, and apparently at times supported himself by it. He was a Roman citizen and was "Hellenized" and cosmopolitan in outlook, but he was also a Pharisee and an ardent supporter of the Jewish law and way of life. He persecuted the new, disruptive sect of Christians, and he was present at the stoning of St. Stephen.

After his conversion, perhaps about the year 34 or 35, he became a vigorous evangelist of the new faith. Because of the wealth of material in his preserved letters and in the Acts of the Apostles, probably more is known about the life of Paul than of any other leader of the church in the apostolic period.

Paul began his missionary work in Syria and continued it in Asia Minor, Cyprus, Greece, and Macedonia. In some places he stayed only a short time; in others much longer. Ephesus was his home for two and a half years. On several occasions in his travels he visited Jerusalem, and on his final visit there, perhaps about the year 55, he was arrested, tried before Felix the governor on the charge of provoking riots, and kept in prison for two years. He appealed his case to the emperor and the account in Acts ends with Paul in the capital city of the empire.

According to tradition, Paul made Rome his headquarters, traveled east again and possibly also to Spain, and was killed in the persecution under Nero.

From the earliest days it has been believed that Peter and Paul suffered martyrdom on the same day, June 29 in the year 67, although some accounts give the year as 68 or the date as February 22. Traditions assert that Peter was crucified upside down on Vatican Hill and that Paul was beheaded near the Via Ostia, south of Rome. St. Peter's Basilica and St. Paul's outside-the-walls are said to contain the tombs of the two apostles.

See The Confession of St. Peter, January 18 and The Conversion of St. Paul, January 25.

Reading

(From Irenaeus *Against Heresies* III.1.1-2)

We learned the plan of our salvation from no others than from those through whom the gospel came to us. They first preached it abroad, and then later by the will of God handed it down to us in writings, to be the foundation and pillar of our faith. For it is not right to say that they preached before they had come to perfect knowledge, as some dare to say, boasting that they are the correctors of the apostles. For after our Lord had risen from the dead, and they were clothed with power from on high when the Holy Spirit came upon them, they were filled with all things and had perfect knowledge. They went out to the ends of the earth, preaching the good things that come to us from God, and proclaiming peace from heaven to men, all and each of them equally being in possession of the gospel of God. So Matthew among the Hebrews issued a writing of the gospel in their own tongue, while Peter and Paul were preaching the gospel at Rome and founding the Church. After their decease, Mark, the disciple and interpreter of Peter, also handed down to us in writing what Peter had preached. Then Luke, the follower of Paul, recorded in a book the gospel as it was preached by him. Finally

John, the disciple of the Lord, who had also lain on his breast, himself published the gospel, while he was residing at Ephesus in Asia. All of these handed down to us that there is one God, maker of heaven and earth, proclaimed by the law and the prophets, and one Christ the Son of God.

Early Christian Fathers, Vol. I, Library of Christian Classics, ed and trans. by Cyril C. Richardson, 370. Published in the U.S.A. by The Westminster Press, 1953. Used by permission.

Propers

ROMAN	LUTHERAN	EPISCOPAL
God our Father, today you give us the joy of celebrating the feast of the apostles Peter and Paul. Through them your Church first received the faith. Keep us true to their teaching. Grant this through our Lord Jesus Christ, your Son, who lives and reigns with you and the Holy Spirit, one God, for ever and ever.	Almighty God, whose blessed apostles Peter and Paul glorified you by their martyrdom: Grant that your Church, instructed by their teaching and example, and knit together in unity by your Spirit, may ever stand firm upon the one foundation, which is Jesus Christ our Lord; who lives and reigns with you and the Holy Spirit, one God, now and forever.	Almighty God, whose blessed apostles Peter and Paul glorified you by their martyrdom: Grant that your Church, instructed by their teaching and example, and knit together in unity by your Spirit, may ever stand firm upon the one foundation, which is Jesus Christ our Lord; who lives and reigns with you, in the unity of the Holy Spirit, one God, now and for ever.
(Text from the English translation of the Roman Missal © 1973, International Committee on English in the Liturgy, Inc. All rights reserved.)		*(Text from the Book of Common Prayer [Proposed], copyright 1977 by Charles Mortimer Guilbert as Custodian of the Standard Book of Common Prayer. All rights reserved. Used by permission.)*
Acts 12:1-11 Psalm 34:2-9 2 Timothy 4:6-8, 17-18 Matthew 16:13-19	Ezekiel 34:11-16 Psalm 87:1-2, 4-6 1 Corinthians 3:16-23 Mark 8:27-35	Ezekiel 34:11-16 Psalm 87 2 Timothy 4:1-8 John 21:15-19 Preface of Apostles

Hymn of the Day: "God has spoken by his prophets" (238) or "O where are kings and empires now" (*SBH* 154)

Prayers: for the church of the West
  for the nations of the world
  for the continuation of the apostolic spirit
Preface: Apostles
Color: Red

Johan Olof Wallin
Archbishop of Uppsala, Hymnwriter, 1839

Wallin was born at Stora Tuna, Delarne, October 15, 1779, the son of a non-commissioned officer. Despite poverty and ill health, he graduated from the University of Uppsala in 1799 and received the M.A. in 1803 and his doctorate in theology in 1809. He became pastor at Solna in that year and in 1810 married Anna Maria Dimander. In 1812 Wallin was called to Adolf Frederick Church in Stockholm. Four years later in 1816 he was made Dean of Vasteras and in 1837 (two years before his death) was consecrated archbishop of Uppsala and primate of the Church of Sweden.

He was the leading churchman of his day in Sweden, yet his lasting fame rests upon his poetry and his hymns. In 1805 and 1809 he was awarded the highest prize for poetry by the Swedish Academy. As early as 1807 he began to publish collections of old and new hymns. He led the commission set up in 1811 to edit a new Swedish hymnbook, and when the committee's first draft failed to meet with general approval, the entire task of revising and completing the work was given to Wallin. He completed his work November 28, 1816, and after a few minor modifications, the new hymnbook was authorized by King Karl XIV on January 29, 1819. In this book of five hundred hymns, some one hundred thirty were written by Wallin and nearly two hundred more were revised or translated by him. For more than a century the Church of Sweden made no change in the 1819 hymnbook.

Henry Wadsworth Longfellow in "The Children of the Lord's Supper" praises the hymns of Wallin:

Like as Elias in heaven, when he cast from off him his mantle,
So cast off the soul its garments of earth; and with one voice
Chimed in the congregation, and sang an anthem immortal
Of the sublime Wallin, of David's harp in the North-land
Tuned to the choral of Luther; the song on its mighty pinions
Took every living soul, and lifted it gently to heaven,
And each face did shine like the Holy One's face upon Tabor.

Wallin has been praised as the unsurpassed interpreter of collective feeling in Swedish literature. In 1839 he published an epic poem of melancholy inner restlessness, *The Angel of Death*, which he had begun during a cholera epidemic in Stockholm in 1834 and which he had completed but a few weeks before he died at Uppsala, June 30, 1839.

Magnus Brostrup Landstad, the dominant figure in Norwegian hymnody, is fillingly commemorated on this day also. He was born in 1802 at Maaso, Finnmarken, was ordained and served several parishes, finally serving in Oslo. He is best remembered for his collections of folk literature and for his work on the Norwegian hymn commission. He introduced popular language into the hymns he wrote to make them contemporary expressions of faith. He died October 8, 1880.

Reading

Are not praises the very end for which the world was created? Do they not consist as it were of knowledge, complacency, and thanksgiving? Are they not better than all the fowls and beasts and fishes in the world? What are the cattle upon a thousand hills but carcasses, without creatures that can rejoice in God and enjoy them? It is evident that praises are infinitely more excellent than all the creatures because they proceed from men and angels. For as streams do, they derive an excellency from their fountains, and are the last tribute that can possibly be paid to the Creator. Praises are the breathings of interior love, the marks and symptoms of a happy life, overflowing gratitude, returning benefits, an oblation of the soul, and the heart ascending upon the wings of divine affection to the Throne of God. God is a Spirit and cannot feed on carcasses: but he can be delighted with thanksgivings, and is infinitely pleased with the emanations of our joy, because his works are esteemed and Himself is admired.

What can be more acceptable to love than that it should be prized and magnified? Because therefore God is love, and His measure infinite, He infinitely desires to be admired and beloved, and so our praises enter into the very secret of His Eternal Bosom, and mingle with Him who dwelleth in that light which is inaccessible. What strengths are there even in flattery to please a great affection? Are not your bowels moved, and your affections melted with delight and pleasure, when your soul is precious in the eye of those you love? When your affection is pleased, your love prized, and they satisfied? To prize love is the highest service in the whole world that can to be done unto it. But there are a thousand causes moving God to esteem our praises, more than we can well apprehend. However, let these inflame you, and move you to praise Him night and day forever.

Thomas Traherne, *Centuries* intro. John Farrar (New York: Harper, 1960) 155.

Propers: Pastors or Artists

Hymn of the Day: "We worship you, O God of might" (432)

Prayers: for an increased love of congregational singing
        for the bishops and leaders of the church that they may
          by their example strengthen and renew the church's
          worship
        for all interpreters of the feelings of their people

Color: White

July 1

John Mason Neale, Priest, Hymnwriter, 1866

Two translators of hymns are remembered together today. Catherine Winkworth made the riches of German hymnody available to English Christians, and John Mason Neale made available the wealth of the ancient Greek and Latin hymns.

Neale was born in London on January 24, 1818, the son of a clergyman. His father died in 1823, and the son's education was largely at the hands of his mother. He won a scholarship to Trinity College, Cambridge, where he excelled in study, and there in 1838 with B. Webb he founded the Cambridge Camden Society for the study of ecclesiastical art, architecture, and ritual.

Neale was ordained in 1842 and given the living of Crawley, Sussex, but ill health, from which he had long suffered, prevented him from taking up his duties. He went to Madeira until the summer of 1844. In 1846 he was made warden of Sackville College, East Grinstead, an institution for the poor. It was not considered a position of distinction in the church, for both his predecessor and his successor were laymen. Neale remained at this post for the rest of his short life.

In 1854 with Miss S. A. Gream, the daughter of a nearby rector, Neale founded the Sisterhood of St. Margaret for the care of the sick, with rules based on those of St. Vincent de Paul's Sisters of Charity. Opposition to Neale's churchmanship and to the society was strong and sometimes violent. He was once attacked and mauled at a funeral of a member of the sisterhood. His opponents threatened to burn his house and at another time threatened to stone him. He was prevented from exercising his priestly duties from 1847 to 1863 by the Bishop of Chichester because of his allegedly Romish leanings. He was denied preferment by his own church, and even his doctorate was given to him by an American college, Trinity College, Hartford, Connecticut. Nonetheless, his gentleness eventually won the respect even of his ecclesiastical superiors, and the sisterhood which he founded developed into one of the leading communities of the Church of England.

Neale was a student of the liturgy and church history. He translated the Eastern liturgies into English, wrote a monumental mystical commentary on the Psalms, and wrote children's liturgies, novels, and an excellent guidebook to Portugal. His most enduring accomplishment, however, was his translations of the great hymns of the church from the Greek and Latin. He had spent his career in an obscure almshouse, but he had acquired a world-wide reputation as a writer of prose and verse, and that reputation has endured. He died on the Feast of the Transfiguration, August 6, 1866, and is commemorated in the Episcopal Church on the following day.

For a suggestion concerning the commemoration of the ancient hymnwriters whose work was translated by Neale, see the commemoration of Isaac Watts (November 25).

Arthur Lough. *The Influence of John Mason Neale.* London: SPCK, 1962.
———. *John Mason Neale—Priest Extraordinary.* Newton Abbot, Devon, 1975.
Selections from the Writings of John Mason Neale. London, 1884.

July 1

Catherine Winkworth, Hymnwriter, 1878

Catherine Winkworth was born in London, September 13, 1827. In 1829 her family moved to Manchester, where she spent most of her life. Her mother died in 1841, and in the spring of 1845, the year in which her father remarried, Miss Winkworth went to Dresden to stay with an aunt for a year.

In 1853 her *Lyra Germanica* was published, and this book of translations of German hymns met with extraordinary success. By 1857 it was in its fifth edition. Winkworth had a remarkable ability to preserve the spirit of the great German hymns while rendering them in English, and she has remained the foremost translator of German hymns into English. She is also the translator of *The Life of Pastor Fliedner* (1861) and *The Life of Amelia Sieveking* (1863).

She supported the efforts of the time toward a recognition of women's rights. In 1862 she and her family moved to Clifton, England, where she became secretary of the Clifton Association for Higher Education for Women, a supporter of the Clifton High School for girls, and a member of the Cheltenham Ladies' College.

Her father died in 1869, and in the same year Catherine and her sister Susanna went to Darmstadt, Germany, as delegates to the German Conference on women's work, presided over by Princess Anne. Catherine Winkworth died suddenly of heart disease at Monnetier, near Geneva, in Savoy July 1, 1878 at the age of 51 and is buried there. A monument to her memory has been erected in Bristol Cathedral.

Catherine Winkworth was one of a notable number of nineteenth century translators of German hymns. Others were Jane Borthwick and her sister Sarah Borthwick Findlater, Frances Elizabeth Cox, and Elizabeth Rundle Charles.

Dictionary of National Biography
Robin A. Leaver. *Catherine Winkworth: The Influence of Her Translations on English Hymnody.* St. Louis: Concordia, 1978.

Reading

(From *Worship* by von Allmen.)

If we love the Kingdom which will both restore and complete the mystery of the first creation, we cannot refuse it—where its self-expression is most appropriate, i.e. in the cult of the Church—some means of expression, even if that means is ambiguous and unsatisfactory. The Church's worship . . . is the most splendid proof of love for the world. Those who do not love the cult, do not know how to love the world. [*Cult* here means the liturgy.]

But to say that the cult is the heart of the Christian community is not merely to remind them that the cult is the criterion of the real life to which they are called; it is also to remind them that if the cult ceases the community dies. It is by its worship that the Church lives, it is there that its heart beats. And in fact the life of the Church pulsates like the heart by systole and diastole. As the heart is for the animal body, so the cult is for church life a pump which sends into circulation and draws in again, it claims and it sanctifies. It is from the life of worship—from the Mass—that the Church spreads itself abroad into the world to mingle with it like leaven in the dough, to give it savor like salt, to irradiate it like light, and it is towards the cult—towards the Eucharist—that the Church returns from the world, like a fisherman gathering up his nets or a farmer harvesting his grain. The only parochial activities which have any real justification are those which spring from worship and in their turn nourish it.

J.-J. von Allmen, *Worship: Its Theology and Practice* (New York: Oxford, 1965) 37, 55-56. Used by permission of Lutterworth Press.

Propers

ROMAN	LUTHERAN	EPISCOPAL
	Common of Artists:	(August 7)

LUTHERAN

Common of Artists:
God our Father, beautiful in majesty, majestic in holiness, you have shown us the splendor of creation in the work of your servants John and Catherine. Teach us to drive from the world the ugliness of chaos and disorder that our eyes may not be blind to your glory, and that at length everyone may know the inexhaustible richness of your new creation in Jesus Christ our Lord.

EPISCOPAL

(August 7)
Grant us, O God, that in all time of our testing, we may know your presence and obey your will; that, after the example of your servant John Mason Neale, we may with integrity and courage accomplish what you give us to do, and endure that you give us to bear; through Jesus Christ our Lord, who lives and reigns with you and the Holy Spirit, one God, now and for ever.

(Text from Lesser Feasts and Fasts, Revised Edition, copyright 1973 by Charles Mortimer Guilbert as Custodian of the Standard Book of Common Prayer. All rights reserved. Used by permission.)

LUTHERAN

2 Chronicles 20:20-21
Psalm 96
Ephesians 5:19-20
Matthew 13:44-52

EPISCOPAL

Psalm 1
1 Peter 2:19-25
Psalm 3:1-5
Matthew 13:44-52

Preface of a Saint

Hymn of the Day: "Christ is made the sure foundation" (367—Neale) "If you but trust in God to guide you" (453—Winkworth)

Prayers: for students of the worship of the church
for those who revise and translate hymns that new ages might sing old songs
for the gift of gentleness and patience
for those who work for women's rights

Color: White

276

John Hus, Martyr, 1415

John Hus was born of peasant parents in Husinec in southwest Bohemia ca. 1369-1373. He was educated at Charles University in Prague, where he took his master's degree in 1396. Two years later the penniless student who had been making a living as a choirboy became a professor of theology. In 1400 he was ordained to the priesthood, and in 1402 he served a six-month term as rector of the university, a position he held again in 1409. Also in 1402 he was named preacher in the Chapel of the Holy Innocents, a large church founded in 1391 in which the preaching was in the Czech language rather than Latin and which was the center of the growing national reform movement. He became a bachelor of theology in 1404 and taught theology and philosophy.

It was a time of schism in the papacy, (at the time of the Council of Pisa in 1409 there were three claiming to be pope) and a time of the erosion of authority caused by general corruption and disillusionment. Hus, deeply influenced by the writings of the English reformer Wycliff, began to include condemnations of church abuses in his sermons and writings. As his strictures became more severe, the local archbishop and hierarchy turned against him, and after Pope Alexander V in 1409 issued a bull condemning the teachings of Wyclif, the archbishop excommunicated Hus in 1412, not for heresy but for failing to answer a summons to Rome.

Hus's doctrinal statements were largely on questions of church discipline and practice rather than on basic theological issues; there he generally followed the orthodox teachings of the church of his day. He believed in the administration of the Holy Communion in both kinds to the laity, he opposed the secular power of the church, and he denied that St. Peter was the head of the church. Later some of his followers recognized only two sacraments, Baptism and Holy Communion, and rejected much of the ceremonial of the Roman church.

By his attitude Hus alienated most of his early friends and having also offended the prelates who were guilty of the avaricious life he preached against, he was summoned to the Council of Constance in 1414 with an imperial safe-conduct for his return to Bohemia even if adjudged guilty. He came in November, and after being confined for some months in the dungeon of the Dominican monastery he eventually faced the council on June 7 and the days following. The Council lost its legal standing when Pope John XXIII fled from Constance, hoping to make the council illegitimate; Gregory XII had abdicated; Benedict XIII had refused to attend. The panel of judges consisted of enemies of Hus. After refusing to recant articles falsely ascribed to him, Hus was on July 6, 1415 sentenced to death and on the same day on the outskirts of the city he was burned at the stake, audibly praying the *Kyrie eleison* as he died. The university at Prague set aside this day for annual commemoration of this hero of the faith, and the day is on the calendar of the Moravian church.

Jerome of Prague, a disciple of Hus, supported him when other friends did not dare to do so. He intended to come to the Council of Constance but was imprisoned, condemned, and burned at the stake a year after Hus.

After Hus's death his followers continued his teaching and repeatedly won victories of arms over the forces sent to subdue them. Hus was the hero of the Bohemian common people, who fought against the power of their landlords, the ethnic discrimination of their German rulers, and against the corruption and secular power of the church. Finally in 1436 a pact was signed by the king, the Hussites, and the Roman church, which stabilized the situation, allowing the national church of Bohemia to administer the sacrament in both kinds, not just the bread only—a practice which lasted in Bohemia for centuries.

The followers of Hus and his friend Jerome of Prague continued as the Czech Brethren and eventually as the Moravian Church of the present day. Luther admired the life and teachings of "St. John Hus" as he called him, and he approved the Moravian Confession of 1535. There are several Lutheran churches in North America named for Hus, such as the one in New Kensington, Pennsylvania or the John Hus Evangelical Lutheran Church of Youngstown, Ohio; there are also Presbyterian churches named for him, such as the one in New York City which was the center of extensive observances of the 500th anniversary of his death (1915).

Matthew Spinka. *John Hus and the Czech Reform*. University of Chicago Press, 1941. Reprinted 1966.
———. *John Hus: A Biography*. Princeton University Press, 1968.
———. *John Hus at the Council of Constance*. New York: Columbia University Press, 1965.

Reading

(From John Hus, *On Simony*)

. . . I have found that ordinary poor priests and poor laymen—even women—defend the truth more zealously than the doctors or the Holy Scriptures, who out of fear run away from the truth and have not courage to defend it. I myself—alas—had been one of them, for I did not dare to preach the truth plainly and openly. And why are we like that? Solely because some of us are timid, fearing to lose worldly favor and praise, and others of us fear to lose benefices; for we fear to be held in contempt by the people for the truth's sake, and to suffer bodily pain. We are like the . . . rulers of whom Saint John says in his Gospel that "many rulers believed on him; but because of the lawyers did not confess it, lest they should be cast out of the congregation. For they loved the praise of men more than the praise of God." . . . O how many there are—princes, masters, priests, and others —who, being afraid of excommunication, have not courage to confess the truth of Christ, and thus also Christ himself; and how many there are who fear to confess the truth lest they lose their miserable goods, or, above all, who, lacking the courage to risk their earthly life, abandon the truth!

Those three fears—of losing the praise and favor of men, of losing goods, and of losing earthly life—cause timid men to abandon the truth of confessing the Saviour Jesus Christ, who promised honor, goods, and life. Honor, in saying: "Whosoever shall confess me and my words before this adulterous and sinful generation, the Son of Man also shall confess when he comes in the glory of his Father with his angels." The goods he promised under an oath, saying, "Verily I say unto you, that no one has left house, or brethren, or sisters, or mother, or father, or children, or lands, for my sake and the gospel's, but shall receive hundredfold." And he promises life, saying, "And in the age to come eternal life." And elsewhere he says, "Whosoever shall lose his life for my sake and the gospel's shall save it." . . . O woe unto us, miserable men, that we do not value the everlasting glory more than the temporal, lean, and transient, and that we do not esteem the eternal goods more than the temporal! For concerning this the Saviour says, "What does it profit a man to gain the whole world, and harm his soul?" Woe unto us that we dare not risk this miserable, sorrowful, and painful life, which is ever dying, for the eternal life—glorious, joyous, and free from pain! . . .

From *Advocates of Reform: From Wyclif to Erasmus,* Vol. XIV, The Library of Christian Classics, ed. by Matthew Spinka, 263-264. Published simultaneously in Great Britain and the U.S.A. by the SCM Press, Ltd., London, and The Westminster Press, Philadelphia, MCMLIII. Used by permission.

Propers: Martyrs or Renewers of the Church
    Gospel—Matthew 23:34-37

Hymn of the Day: "Once he came in blessing" (312)
    or "Jesus Christ our blessed Savior" (*TLH* 311)

Prayers: for fearless and faithful preachers
    for the renewal of the Christian life
    for the church in Czechoslovakia
    for the Moravian Church

Preface: All Saints

Color: Red (or white, for Renewers of the Church)

July 11

Benedict of Nursia
Abbot of Monte Cassino, ca. 540

Benedict, the father of Western monasticism, was born to a distinguished family at Norcia (Nursia) in central Italy ca. 480. Little is known of his life apart from what Gregory the Great reports in his *Dialogues* (593-594), especially Book II, which is apparently based on eyewitnesses and disciples of Benedict.

He studied in Rome where he was influenced by the Byzantine monastic centers. He was offended by the licentiousness of society and withdrew to become a hermit in a grotto thought to have been near Subiaco, forty miles west of Rome. Disciples soon came to him, among whom were Maurus and Placidus of a senatorial family, and Benedict, turning from solitary life to the communal, created twelve monasteries of twelve monks each. He was apparently not ordained and did not contemplate an order for the clergy.

Local jealousy forced him to leave Subiaco, and he took his community to Monte Cassino, a fortified hill midway between Rome and Naples, where he destroyed a sacred wood and transformed the groves into places of Christian prayer consecrated to John the Baptist and St. Martin. Monte Cassino remained the principal monastery, although another was founded in Terracina. Benedict kept in careful touch with other monastic leaders and composed his famous *Rule*, which is in part an adaptation of an earlier rule, the *Rule of the Master*, an Italian work of the early sixth century. Benedict's *Rule* is relatively short and is marked by a spirit of "prudent leniency" compared to other rules from which it is descended and fixes a daily routine of common worship, labor, and rest.

Benedict's sister Scholastica became a nun and is buried at Monte Cassino with her brother. Her feast day on the Roman calendar is February 10.

In ca. 577 the Lombards destroyed Monte Cassino. When it was restored a century and a half later, a cult developed around the tomb of Benedict. Eventually March 21 was observed as the day of his death and July 11 as the festival of the Patronage of St. Benedict. It was on July 11 that his supposed relics were transferred to a monastery at Fleury near Orleans, although Monte Cassino still claimed to have the true remains. The new Roman and Episcopal calendars both set the commemoration of St. Benedict on July 11.

In 1944 the monastery at Monte Cassino was again destroyed in an Allied attack on a Nazi stronghold, but it has since been restored.

E. C. Butler. *Benedictine Monachism*. 2nd ed. New York: Barnes and Noble, 1961.
David Knowles. *Christian Monasticism*. London: Weidenfeld, 1969.
Thomas F. Lindsay. *St. Benedict: His Life and Work*. London, 1959.
I. Schuster. *Saint Benedict and His Times*. tr. G. J. Roettiger. St. Louis: Herder, 1951.

Antony (ca. 251-356) might also be remembered with Benedict on this day. He was a hermit, the classic representative of the "Desert Fathers," who is regarded as the founder of monasticism because he gathered hermits into communities. Antony was highly regarded for his wisdom and integrity. He died in 356, more than a hundred years old, at his retreat on the Inner Mountain, twenty miles west of the Red Sea. Athanasius, who knew him and who was supported by him, wrote his biography. Antony's traditional feast day is January 17.

David Knowles. *Christian Monasticism.* London: Weidenfeld, 1969.

Reading

(From the *Rule of St. Benedict,* Prologue, 19, 20.)

. . . I am to erect a school for beginners in the service of the Lord: which I hope to establish on laws not too difficult or grievous. But if, for reasonable cause, for the retrenchment of vice or preservation of charity, I require some things which may seem too austere, you are not thereupon to be frightened from the ways of salvation. Those ways are always strait and narrow at the beginning. But as we advance in the practices of religion and in faith, the heart insensibly opens and enlarges through the wonderful sweetness of his love, and we run in the way of God's commandments. If then we keep close to our school and the doctrine we learn in it, and persevere in the monastery till death, we shall here share by patience in the passion of Christ and hereafter deserve to be united with him in his kingdom. Amen.

We believe God is everywhere, and his eye beholds the good and wicked wherever they are: so we ought to be particularly assured of his special presence when we assist at the divine office. Therefore we must always remember the advice of the prophet, "To serve God in fear": "to sing wisely": and that "the angels are witnesses of what we sing." Let us then reflect what behavior is proper for appearing in the presence of God and the angels, and so sing our psalms that the mind may echo in harmony with the voice.

If we want to ask a favor of any person of power, we presume not to approach but with humility and respect. How much more ought we to address ourselves to the Lord and God of all things with a humble and entire devotion? We are not to imagine that our prayers shall be heard because we use many words, but because the heart is pure and the spirit penitent. Therefore prayer must be short and pure, unless it be prolonged by a feeling of divine inspiration. Prayer in common ought always to be short. . . .

Library of Christian Classics XII. *Western Asceticism* tr. Owen Chadwick (Philadelphia: Westminster, 1958) 291, 293, 309-310.

Propers

ROMAN	LUTHERAN	EPISCOPAL
God our Father, you made Saint Benedict an outstanding guide to teach men how to live in your service. Grant that by preferring your love to everything else, we may walk in the way of your commandments. We ask this through our Lord Jesus Christ, your Son, who lives and reigns with you and the Holy Spirit, one God, for ever and ever.	Lord God, you have surrounded us with so great a cloud of witnesses. Grant that we, encouraged by the example of your servant Benedict, may persevere in the course that is set before us, to be living signs of the Gospel and at last, with all the saints, to share in your eternal joy; through your Son, Jesus Christ our Lord.	Almighty and everlasting God, we give you thanks for the humility and strength with which you endowed your servant Benedict; and we pray that by your grace we may conform our lives to the purpose of your most holy will; through Jesus Christ our Lord, who lives and reigns with you and the Holy Spirit, one God, now and ever.

ROMAN	LUTHERAN	EPISCOPAL
Common of Saints (for religious) or Proverbs 2:1-9	Common of Saints Micah 6:6-8 Psalm 9:1-10 1 Corinthians 1:26-31 Luke 6:20-23	Psalm 134 Acts 2:42-47 Psalm 119:161-168 Luke 14:27-33 Preface of a Saint

Hymn of the Day: "Jesus, priceless treasure" (457, 458)

Prayers: for courage to put Christ before everything else

for the gift of obedience to God's commandments
for all who seek purity of life
for those who live among us as signs of the kingdom of
heaven

Preface: All Saints

Color: White

Nathan Soderblom, Archbishop of Uppsala, 1931

This theologian and ecumenist was born in Trönö, Sweden on January 15, 1866, the son of a pietist pastor. He studied at the University of Uppsala and was ordained a priest of the Church of Sweden in 1893. He served as chaplain to the Swedish legation in Paris from 1894-1901, and while he was there studied comparative religion and received his doctorate from the Sorbonne in 1901. From 1901 to 1914 he was professor of the history of religion at Uppsala and also lectured at Leipzig, 1912-1914. In 1914 he was elected Archbishop of Uppsala and Primate of the Church of Sweden.

Söderblom was attracted to the liturgy and piety of the Roman Catholic Church but at the same time was influenced by liberal Protestant scholars. He sought to achieve an "evangelical catholicity" among Christian communions through practical cooperation on social issues. During World War I he intervened on behalf of war prisoners and displaced persons. This and his advocacy of peace through church unity earned him the Nobel prize for peace in 1930.

His interest in Christian unity began during his student years and increased following a visit to America in 1890. As a result of his efforts the Universal Christian Council on Life and Work was formed at a meeting in Stockholm in August 1925. This body, together with the predominantly Anglican Conference on Faith and Order, merged in 1948 to form the World Council of Churches.

As archbishop, his remarkable zeal and energy were directed largely toward counteracting the growing alienation from the church of both intellectuals and labor. His concern was for a greater involvement in social and ethical issues as well as for a deepened devotional life. He died July 12, 1931.

C. J. Curtis. *Söderblom: Ecumenical Pioneer*. Minneapolis: Augsburg, 1967.
Peter Katz. *Nathan Söderblom: A Prophet of Christian Unity*. London: J. Clarke, 1949.
R. Rouse and Stephen Neill, eds. *A History of the Ecumenical Movement, 1517-1948*. London: SPCK, 1954.

Reading

(From *The Living God* by Nathan Söderblom.)

God's revelation is not finished—it continues. Here a most essential distinction must be made. Heaven was not shut up after the manifestation of God recorded in the Bible. We see it open over the Bible and in the Bible as nowhere else, and go to it in order to see the Eternal Light shine through the grey mist of existence. God is ever revealing himself. God's continued revelation is history. Of course, I hold that the Church is God's work and God's instrument. The religious value of the Church is sometimes overrated, but often also underrated. God has entrusted the Church with the divine privilege and the tremendous duty of giving to the world in word and deed and sacrament the Grace of God. Our belief in God's continued revelation in history makes us consider, more diligently and more reverently than before, the value of men, means, and institutions, which God has given to the Church in the course of history. But God's revelation is not confined to the Church, although the Church has, in the Scripture and in its experience, the means of interpreting God's continued revelation. The Church ought to open its eyes, more than it does, to see how God is perpetually revealing himself. The Evangelic statement that God has revealed himself once for all in the Bible is true and must be maintained in its true sense about divine action recorded in the Scriptures. But we often fail to learn the lesson of the Bible, that our God is a living, a still living God, who has not become older and less active than in earlier days.

Nathan Söderblom, *The Living God. Basal Forms of Personal Religion.* The Gifford Lectures (London: Oxford, 1933) 378-379.

Propers: Pastors

Hymn of the Day: "In Adam we have all been one" (372)

Prayers: for the unity of the church
for the understanding and growth of evangelical catholicity
for the peace of the world
for a new respect for the insight of religions other than
our own.

Color: White

Olga, Princess of Kiev, Confessor, 969

Olga (Helga) the grandmother of Vladimir, the first Christian ruler of Russia, was born at Pskov, Russia ca. 890. She married Prince Igor, and after his death in 945 she acted as regent for their son. She has been praised for her courage and ability as a ruler, instituting salutary reforms of administration and finance. In 957 she visited Constantinople and, according to some accounts, was baptized there, although other accounts indicate that she had been a Christian for some years before her visit to the principal city of the East. In any case, her baptism did not signal the conversion of her country, for the pagans rallied around her son, who resisted her efforts to instruct him in Christianity. Olga died in 969, and her traditional feast day is July 11. She is honored especially in the Russian and Ukrainian Churches.

The Russian Primary Chronicle ed. and tr. S. H. Cross and O. P. Sherbo-witz-Wetzor (Cambridge, Mass.: Harvard, 1953) 64-87, 111.
G. Vernadsky. *Kievan Russia.* New Haven: Yale, 1948.

Vladimir, First Christian Ruler of Russia, 1015

Vladimir and Olga are honored together as the first-born of the new Christian people of Russia and its borders. Vladimir was born in 956, the youngest son of Sviatoslav of Kiev and a great grandson of Rurik, the traditional founder of the Rurkid dynasty and of the Russian state. Vladimir was made Prince of Novgorod in 970. Two years later, when his father died, a fierce struggle broke out among the three sons. Oled was killed and Vladimir was forced to flee to Scandinavia. He then returned in 980 with Scandinavian support, killed his brother Yaropolk, and made himself master of Russia. A successful military leader, he expanded Russian control from southeast Poland to the Volga valley.

By the late tenth century the influence of neighboring Christian states had become strong, and Vladimir, having consolidated all the eastern Slavs under his dynasty in Kiev, decided to make his nation Christian. In 988 he sent military aid to the Byzantine emperor Basil II, asking the hand of Basil's sister Anna in return. The emperor agreed, provided that Vladimir become a Christian. Vladimir was baptized that same year. The emperor was then reluctant to fulfill his part of the agreement; Vladimir attacked the Crimea, and Princess Anna became his wife. Christianity was then officially introduced and established in Russia.

Despite the circumstances surrounding his conversion, Vladimir was wholehearted in his adherence to the new faith. He put away his former wives and mistresses, amended his life, and publicly destroyed idols. He became an ardent promoter of Christianity and built many churches and monasteries, expanded educational and judicial institutions, aided the poor and supported Greek missionaries. The Christianization of Kievan Russian proceeded rapidly, for despite his personal sincerity, Vladimir relied largely on physical compulsion and heavily punished those who refused baptism. The emerging Russian church was under the jurisdiction of Constantinople, but it remained friendly toward the West.

Vladimir's last years were troubled by the insurrection of his sons and by his former pagan wives, and he died on an expedition against one of them at Berestova, near Kiev, July 15, 1015.

Donald Attwater. *The Golden Book of Eastern Saints.* Freeport, N.Y.: Books for Libraries Press, 1971. [1938] 81-83.

S. H. Cross. *Harvard Studies and Notes in Philology and Literature* XII (1930), 77-309.

S. H. Cross and O. P. Sherbowitz-Wetzor. *The Russian Primary Chronicle.* Cambridge, Mass.: Harvard, 1953.

F. Dvornik. *The Slavs: Their Early History and Civilization.* Boston: American Academy of Arts and Sciences, 1956.

Constantin de Grunwald. *Saints of Russia* tr. Roger Capel (New York: Macmillan, 1960) 17-30.

Reading

(From *Unseen Warfare*, A Classic of Eastern Spirituality)

So this spiritual warfare of ours must be constant and never ceasing, and should be conducted with alertness and courage in the soul; they can easily be attained, if you seek these gifts from God. So advance into battle without hesitation. Should you be visited by the troubling thought of the hatred and undying malice, which the enemies harbour against you, and of the innumerable hosts of demons, think on the other hand of the infinitely greater power of God and of His love for you, as well as of the incomparably greater hosts of heavenly angels and the prayers of saints. They all fight secretly for us and with us against our enemies, as it is written: "The Lord will have war with Amalek from generation to generation" (Exodus 17:16). How many weak women and small children were incited to fight by the thought of this powerful and ever ready help! And they got the upper hand and gained victory over all the wisdom of the world, all the wiles of the devil and all the malice of hell.

So you must never be afraid, if you are troubled by a flood of thoughts, that the enemy is too strong against you, that his attacks are never-ending, that the war will last for your lifetime, and that you cannot avoid incessant downfalls of all kinds. Know that our enemies, with all their wiles, are in the hands of our divine Commander, our Lord Jesus Christ, for Whose honour and glory you are waging war. Since He Himself leads you into battle, He will certainly not suffer your enemies to use violence against you and overcome you, if you do not yourself cross over to their side with your will. He will Himself fight for you and will deliver your enemies into your hands, when He wills and as He wills, as it is written: "The Lord thy God walketh in the midst of thy camp, to deliver thee, and to give up thine enemies before thee" (Deuteronomy 23:14).

If the Lord delays granting you full victory over your enemies and puts it off to the last day of your life, you must know that He does this for your own good; so long as you do not retreat or cease to struggle wholeheartedly. Even if you are wounded in battle do not lay down your arms and turn to flight. Keep only one thing in your mind and intention—to fight with all courage and ardour, since it is unavoidable. No man can escape this warfare, either in life or in death. And he who does not fight to overcome his passions and his enemies will inevitably be taken prisoner, either here or yonder, and be delivered to death.

Unseen Warfare being the *Spiritual Combat* and *Path to Paradise* of Lorenzo Scupoli as edited by Nicodemus of the Holy Mountain and revised by Theophan the Recluse, trans. E. Kadloubovsky and G. E. H. Palmer (London: Faber and Faber, 1963) 54-55. Used by permission.

Propers: Saints

Hymn of the Day: "God the omnipotent!" (462)

Prayers: for the Christian people of Russia
for the government of the Soviet Union
for the growth in grace of all new converts to Christianity
for Christian families

Color: White

Bartolome de Las Casas, Missionary to the Indies, 1566

Las Casas, the Apostle to the Indians, was the first to expose the oppression of the Indians by the Europeans. He was born in Seville, Spain, in August 1474, the son of a merchant. He went to America in 1502 with Governor Nicolas de Ovando, and for his participation in the expedition he was given an *encomienda*, a royal land grant in Cuba which included the Indians who lived on the land. He soon gave up colonizing to undertake the reform of a system which he came to see was inhumane. He was ordained priest in Hispaniola in 1512 or 1513, perhaps the first person to be ordained in the New World. In 1514 he experienced a kind of conversion, and in a sermon on August 15, 1514 he announced that he was returning all his Indian serfs to the governor. From 1515 to 1522 he travelled between Spain and America in a continued attempt to win approval for a series of projects that he was convinced would make for peaceful colonization and the Christianization of the Indians in new towns where Spanish and Indians together would create a new civilization in America. His experiment collapsed in 1522.

Frustrated in this attempt, Las Casas took refuge in the religious life and entered the Dominican Order in 1523. After an extended retreat, he resumed his plans for peaceful evangelization in Hispaniola, Nicaragua, and Guatemala. In 1540 he returned to Spain from Santo Domingo and worked for the "New Laws" of 1542-1543, which prohibited slavery and made colonization more humane. The laws were widely ignored.

Las Casas was made Bishop of Chiapas in Guatemala and returned to America in 1544 with forty-four Dominicans to implement the New Laws himself, but his efforts met with only limited success. Having alienated his colleagues with his uncompromising position on behalf of the Indians, he returned to Spain in 1547 and there entered upon the most fruitful period of his life. About 1550 he engaged in a bitter controversy with the theologian Gines Sepulveda of Cordova, who held that war against the Indians was justified because they were plainly inferior to the Spanish and were among the races which Aristotle had declared to be by nature destined to slavery.

Las Casas became influential at court and composed three major works: *De unico vocationis modo* (1537) on the theory of evangelical conquest; *Historia apologetica,* a detailed description of Indian abilities, which was an introduction to *Historia de Las Indias,* a condemnation of the thirty years of Spanish colonial policy and a prophetic interpretation of the events. In addition, he wrote doctrinal treatises, letters, and pamphlets. His most famous work is his *Brief Report on the Destruction of the Indians* (or *Tears of the Indians*), 1542, a sensationalist account of Spanish atrocities attributed to their greed for gold. The little book was translated into many languages and was used by the English as a weapon against Spain and the Spanish empire in the New World.

Las Casas died July 17, 1566 in the Dominican convent of Nuestra Senora de Atocha de Madrid. (Older sources give July 31 as the day.) In 1976 the Dominican Order introduced in Rome the cause of his beatification. Postage stamps commemorating Las Casas have been issued in Mexico, Cuba, and Nicaragua; and there is a statue of Las Casas in the New York Public Library.

Bartolome de Las Casas in History, ed. Juan Friede and Bryan Keen. De Kalb, Ill.: Northern Illinois University Press, 1976.

Lewis Hanke. *All Mankind Is One.* DeKalb, Ill.: Northern Illinois University Press, 1975.

———. *Aristotle and the American Indians.* Chicago: Regery, 1959.

———. *Bartolome de Las Casas: An Interpretation of His Life and Writings.* The Hague, 1951.

———. *Bartolome de Las Casas: Bookman, Scholar, and Propagandist.* Philadelphia: University of Pennsylvania Press, 1952.

———. *Bartolome de Las Casas: Historian.* Gainesville: University of Florida Press, 1952.

———. *The Spanish Struggle for Justice in the Conquest of America.* Philadelphia: University of Pennsylvania Press, 1950. Reprinted, Boston: Little Brown, 1965.

Arthur Helps. *The Life of Las Casas.* London, 1868.

Bartolome de Las Casas. *In Defense of the Indians* ed. Stafford Poole. De Kalb, Ill.: Northern Illinois University Press, 1973.

Francis Macnutt. *Bartholomew de Las Casas.* New York, 1909.

Henry Raup Wagner and H. R. Parish. *The Life and Writings of Bartolome de Las Casas.* Albuquerque: University of New Mexico Press, 1967.

Reading

(Las Casas, *In Defense of the Indians*)

. . . what man of sound mind will approve a war against men who are harmless, ignorant, gentle, temperate, unarmed, and destitute of every human defense? For the results of such a war are very surely the loss of the souls of that people who perish without knowing God and without the support of the sacraments, and, for the survivors, hatred and loathing of the Christian religion.

. . . among our Indians of the western and southern shores . . . there are important kingdoms, large numbers of people who live settled lives in a society, great cities, kings, judges and laws, persons who engage in commerce, buying, selling, lending, and the other contracts of the law of nations. . . . From the fact that the Indians are barbarians it does not necessarily follow that they are incapable of government and have to be ruled by others, except to be taught about the Catholic faith and to be admitted to the holy sacraments. They are not ignorant, inhuman, or bestial. Rather, long before they had heard the word Spaniard they had properly organized states, wisely ordered by excellent laws, religion, and custom. They cultivated friendship and, bound together in common fellowship, lived in populous cities in which they wisely administered the affairs of both peace and war justly and equitably, truly governed by laws that at very many points surpass ours, and could have won the admiration of the sages of Athens. . . .

Now Christ wanted his gospel to be preached with enticements, gentleness, and all meekness and pagans to be led to the truth not by armed forces but by holy examples, Christian conduct, and the word of God, so that no opportunity would be offered for blaspheming his sacred name or hating the true religion because of the conduct of the preachers. For this is nothing else than making the coming and passion of Christ useless, as long as the truth of the gospel is hated before it is either understood or heard or as long as innumerable human beings are slaughtered in a war waged on the grounds of preaching the gospel and spreading religion.

The Indians are our brothers, and Christ has given his life for them. Why, then, do we persecute them with such inhuman savagery when they do not deserve such treatment? The past, because it cannot be undone, must be attributed to our weakness, provided that what has been taken unjustly is restored.

The Tears of the Indians: being An Historical and true Account of the cruel Massacres and Slaughters of above Twenty Millions of innocent People; Committed by the Spaniards In the Islands of Hispaniola, Cuba, Jamaica, etc. As also in the Continent of Mexico, Peru, & other Places of the West-Indies, To the total destruction of those Countries trans. John Phillips (London, 1656) 26, 42-43, 350, 362.

Propers: Missionaries
              or Renewers of Society

Hymn of the Day: "Lord of all nations, grant me grace" (419)

Prayers: for the Indians of Central and South America
              for those who fight against slavery and inhumanity
              for increased sensitivity to human rights
              for justice and reconciliation among all peoples

Color: White

July 22

ST. MARY MAGDALENE

Mary Magdalene, called "the apostle to the Apostles" by Bernard of Clairvaux, carried the news of the resurrection to the Twelve. Whenever the gospels list the women who were with Jesus, Mary Magdalene is listed first (John 19:25 is the sole exception), perhaps because she was the first to see the risen Jesus. Luke 8:2 reports that Jesus had cured her of possession by seven demons. She has often been identified with the repentant "woman of the city" who anointed Jesus' feet as he sat at the table in the Pharisee's home (Luke 7:36-50), and her title on the calendar has been "Penitent." (There has been no one else with this title.) There is, however, no biblical basis for this identification of Mary with the penitent prostitute. Nor is she to be identified with Mary of Bethany, an identification common in the Western church since the sixth century, although it is rejected in the East.

According to the gospels, Mary of Magdala is the primary witness to the fundamental facts of the Christian proclamation: she saw the death of Jesus, she saw his burial, she saw his first resurrection appearance. Her commemoration on July 22 is observed in both the Eastern and the Western churches, and, especially since the twelfth century, she has become one of the most widely commemorated women in Christendom.

James T. Baker. "The Red-Haired Saint," *Christian Century* XCIV, 12 (April 6, 1977), 328-332.

Reading

(From a sermon on the Gospels by Gregory the Great)

When Mary Magdalene came to the tomb and did not find the Lord's body, she thought it had been taken away and so informed the disciples. After they came and saw the tomb, they too believed what Mary had told them. The text then says: *The disciples went back home,* and it adds; *but Mary wept and remained standing outside the tomb.*

We should reflect on Mary's attitude and the great love she felt for Christ; for though the disciples had left the tomb, she remained. She was still seeking the one she had not found, and while she sought she wept; burning with the fire of love, she longed for him who she thought had been taken away. And so it happened that the woman who stayed behind to seek Christ was the only one to see him. For perseverance is essential to any good deed, as the voice of truth tells us: *Whoever perseveres to the end will be saved.*

At first she sought but did not find, but when she persevered it happened that she found what she was looking for. When our desires are not satisfied, they grow stronger, and becoming stronger they take hold of their object. Holy desires likewise grow with anticipation, and if they do not grow they are not really desires. Anyone who succeeds in attaining the truth has burned with such a love. As David says:

My soul has thirsted for the living God; when shall I come and appear before the face of God? And so also in the Song of Songs the Church says: *I was wounded by love;* and again: *My soul is melted with love.*

Woman, why are you weeping? Whom do you seek? She is asked why she is sorrowing so that her desire might be strengthened; for when she mentions whom she is seeking, her love is kindled all the more ardently.

Jesus says to her: Mary. Jesus is not recognized when he calls her "woman"; so he calls her by name, as though he were saying: Recognize me as I recognize you; for I do not know you as I know others; I know you as yourself. And so Mary, once addressed by name, recognizes who is speaking. She immediately calls him *rabboni,* that is to say, *teacher,* because the one whom she sought outwardly was the one who inwardly taught her to keep on searching.

From the English translation of the Office of Readings from the Liturgy of the Hours © 1974, the International Committee on English in the Liturgy, Inc. All rights reserved.

Propers

ROMAN	LUTHERAN	EPISCOPAL

ROMAN

Father,
your Son first
    entrusted to Mary
    Magdalene
the joyful news of his
    resurrection.
By her prayers and
    example
may we proclaim
    Christ as our living
    Lord
and one day see him
    in glory,
for he lives and reigns
    with you and the
    Holy Spirit,
one God, for ever and
    ever.

(Text from the English translation of the Roman

LUTHERAN

Almighty God, your Son Jesus Christ restored Mary Magdalene to health of body and mind, and called her to be a witness of his resurrection. Heal us now in body and mind, and call us to serve you in the power of the resurrection of Jesus Christ, who lives and reigns with you and the Holy Spirit, one God, now and forever.

EPISCOPAL

Almighty God, whose blessed Son restored Mary Magdalene to health of body and mind, and called her to be a witness of his resurrection: Mercifully grant that by your g r a c e w e m a y b e healed from all our infirmities and know you in the power of his unending life; who with you and the Holy Spirit lives and reigns, one God, now and for ever.

(Text from the Book of Common Prayer [Proposed], copyright 1977 by Charles Mortimer Guilbert

ROMAN	LUTHERAN	EPISCOPAL
Song of Songs 3:1-4a or 2 Corinthians 5:14-17 Psalm 63:2-6, 8-9 John 20:1-2, 11-18	Ruth 1:6-18 or Exodus 2:1-10 Psalm 73:23-29 Acts 13:26-33a John 20:1-2, 11-18	Judith 9:1, 11-14 Psalm 42:1-7 2 Corinthians 5:14-18 John 20:11-18 Preface of All Saints

Hymn of the Day: "Now all the vault of heaven resounds" (143)

Prayers: for those in mental darkness
    for grace to perceive signs of new life around us
    for insight to find in each act of worship the coming
      of the risen Christ
    for love to lay hold of salvation and to share it with
      others

Preface: Easter (because this Preface mentions Mary Magdalene
    in her role as a principal witness to the resurrection)
    or All Saints

Color: White

July 23

Birgitta of Sweden, 1373

Bridget, or as she is called in Swedish, Birgitta, was born about 1303, the daughter of Birger Persson, the "lawman" or governor of the province of Upland in Sweden, one of the most important men in the country. On several occasions in her childhood she had dreams of Christ crucified and of Mary his mother. Her own mother died when Birgitta was twelve, and the next year Birgitta was married to Ulf Gundarsson, the young son of the lawman of West Gothland. The marriage was happy, and they had four sons and daughters, one of whom, Catherine, later accompanied her mother to Rome and who has been canonized by the Roman Catholic Church.

About 1335 Birgitta, who by virtue of her father's and her husband's positions moved in the highest circles of the realm, was called to be the principal lady-in-waiting to the newly-married queen of King Magnus. At the court, Lady Birgitta became known for her remarkable dreams and her strong denunciation of wickedness in court life. This was typical of Birgitta's actions throughout her life in dealing with high officials of church and state.

In 1340, after the death of her youngest son, Birgitta made a pilgrimage to the shrine of St. Olav in Trondheim, Norway, thus beginning the extensive pilgrimages of her life. In 1341-1342 Birgitta took her husband with her on a pilgrimage to Santiago of Compostela in Spain, one of the most popular pilgrim centers in the Middle Ages. (See the Feast of St. James, July 25.) On the return trip Ulf was taken ill, and, although he recovered, his health was broken and in 1344 he died in the monastery of Alvastra.

After her husband's death, Birgitta began to live a more ascetic life, her visions became stronger and more dominant in her life, and she devoted more of her time and efforts to helping the needy of Sweden and later of Rome. She continued in her criticisms and warnings to kings and popes, and tried to make peace among warring rulers. Like St. Catherine of Siena (see April 29) she repeatedly urged the popes to return from Avignon to Rome. In 1349 she left for Rome herself with a number of companions to observe the holy year of 1350 and to obtain papal approval of the monastic order she wanted to establish.

Birgitta founded the Order of the Holy Savior, commonly called the Brigittines, centered on the monastery she started at Vadstena in Sweden in accordance with the instructions she had received in a vision. The order consisted of both monks and nuns, governed by an abbess, and after St. Birgitta's death it spread widely in Europe. The cloister at Vadstena was one of the most important cultural and religious centers of Sweden during the Middle Ages, and at the time of the Reformation when the monastic orders were abolished, it was the last to go.

St. Birgitta is best known for her *Revelations*, which are still read throughout Western Christendom. They come down to us in a Latin version and an Old Swedish version, and modern translations and editions exist in a number of languages. The *Revelations* concern chiefly the sufferings of the Savior and judgments on persons and events.

In May 1371 Birgitta felt that God commanded her to make pilgrimage to the Holy Land, and she set out with three of her children and a number of other companions. A few months after her return she died in Rome on July 23, 1373. Her body was temporarily buried in a church there, but a little later was removed to the abbey at Vadstena. St. Birgitta was soon recognized as a patron of Sweden, and interest in her life and work has continued to the present. The Society of St. Birgitta in Sweden now is a kind of laypersons' religious association inspired by her life and *Revelations*. St. Birgitta is generally commemorated on October 8, the date of her canonization in 1391, but the date of her death, her "heavenly birthday," has also been observed in Sweden. She is remembered on the new Roman calendar on July 23.

Ingvar Andersson. A *History of Sweden* tr. Carolyn Hannay (Westport, Conn.: Greenwood Press, 1975) 54-62. [1968]
Johannes Jorgensen. St. *Bridget of Sweden* 2 vols. New York: Longman's, Green, 1954.

Reading

(From the prayers attributed to St. Birgitta)

Blessed are you, my Lord Jesus Christ. You foretold your death and at the Last Supper you marvelously consecrated bread which became your precious body. And then you gave it to your apostles out of love as a memorial of your most holy passion. By washing their feet with your holy hands, you gave them a supreme example of your deep humility.

Honor be to you, my Lord Jesus Christ. Fearing your passion and death, you poured forth blood from your innocent body like sweat, and still you accomplished our redemption as you desired and gave us the clearest proof of your love for all men.

Blessed may you be, my Lord Jesus Christ. After you had been led to Caiaphas, you, the judge of all men, humbly allowed yourself to be handed over to the judgment of Pilate.

Glory be to you, my Lord Jesus Christ, for the mockery you endured when you stood clothed in purple and wearing a crown of sharp thorns. With utmost endurance you allowed vicious men to spit upon your glorious face, blindfold you and beat your cheek and neck with cruelest blows.

Praise be to you, my Lord Jesus Christ. For with the greatest patience you allowed yourself like an innocent lamb to be bound to a pillar and mercilessly scourged, and then to be brought, covered with blood, before the judgment seat of Pilate to be gazed upon by all.

Honor be to you, my Lord Jesus Christ. For after your glorious body was covered with blood, you were condemned to death on the cross, you endured the pain of carrying the cross on your sacred shoulders, and you were led with curses to the place where you were to suffer. Then stripped of your garments, you allowed yourself to be nailed to the wood of the cross.

Everlasting honor be to you, Lord Jesus Christ. You allowed your most holy mother to suffer so much, even though she had never sinned nor even consented to the smallest sin. Humbly you looked down upon her with your gentle loving eyes, and to comfort her you entrusted her to the faithful care of your disciple.

Eternal blessing be yours, my Lord Jesus Christ, because in your last agony you held out to all sinners the hope of pardon, when in your mercy you promised the glory of paradise to the penitent thief.

Eternal praise be to you, my Lord Jesus Christ, for the time you endured on the cross the greatest torments and sufferings for us sinners. The sharp pain of your wounds fiercely penetrated even to your blessed soul and cruelly pierced your most sacred heart till finally you sent forth your spirit in peace, bowed your head, and humbly commended yourself into the hands of God your Father, and your whole body remained cold in death.

Blessed may you be, my Lord Jesus Christ. You redeemed our souls with your precious blood and most holy death, and in your mercy you led them from exile back to eternal life.

Blessed may you be, my Lord Jesus Christ. For our salvation you allowed your side and heart to be pierced with a lance; and from that side water and your precious blood flowed out abundantly for our redemption.

Glory be to you, my Lord Jesus Christ. You allowed your blessed body to be taken down from the cross by your friends and laid in the arms of your most sorrowing mother, and you let her wrap your body in a shroud and bury it in a tomb to be guarded by soldiers.

Unending honor be to you, my Lord Jesus Christ. On the third day you rose from the dead and appeared to those you had chosen. And after forty days you ascended into heaven before the eyes of many witnesses, and there in heaven you gathered together in glory those you love, whom you had freed from hell.

Rejoicing and eternal praise be to you, my Lord Jesus Christ, who sent the Holy Spirit into the hearts of your disciples and increased the boundless love of God in their spirits.

Blessed are you and praiseworthy and glorious for ever, my Lord Jesus. You sit upon your throne in your kingdom of heaven, in the glory of your divinity, living in the most holy body you took from a virgin's flesh. So will you appear on that last day to judge the souls of all the living and the dead; you who live and reign with the Father and the Holy Spirit for ever and ever. Amen.

Propers

ROMAN	LUTHERAN	EPISCOPAL
Lord our God, you revealed the secrets of heaven to Saint Bridget as she meditated on the suffering and death of your Son. May your people rejoice in the revelation of your glory. Grant this through our Lord Jesus Christ, your Son, who lives and reigns with you and the Holy Spirit, one God, for ever and ever.	Lord God, you have surrounded us with so great a cloud of witnesses. Grant that we, encouraged by the example of your servant Birgitta, may persevere in the course that is set before us, to be living signs of the Gospel and at last, with all your saints, to share in your eternal joy; through your Son, Jesus Christ our Lord.	

Common of Saints
(for religous)

or the Prayer for Wednesday in Holy Week

Common of Saints:
Micah 6:6-8
    Psalm 9:1-10
1 Corinthians 1:26-31
Luke 6:20-23

Hymn of the Day: "Jesus, refuge of the weary" (93)

Prayers: for growth in the spiritual life
　　for zeal to oppose corruption and vice
　　for the religious orders for women and men in the Lutheran
　　　church and throughout Christianity
　　for peace

Preface: Passion

Color: White

ST. JAMES THE ELDER, APOSTLE

James the Son of Zebedee was born in Galilee and, like his brother John and the apostles Peter and Andrew, was a fisherman. He is believed to have been older than his brother because his name is almost always put before John's in the biblical lists. Shortly after calling Andrew and Peter from their fishing to be his disciples, Jesus saw the sons of Zebedee in a boat with their father, mending nets. He called them, and they left their father and followed him. James and his brother were called by Jesus *Boanerges* ("sons of thunder"), presumably because of their impetuous spirit and flashing temper.

Incidents in St. James' life are recorded in all four gospels and in the book of Acts, and he was one of the "inner circle" with Peter and John. These three witnessed the cure of Peter's mother-in-law and the raising of the daughter of Jairus, and they were the ones with Jesus at the Transfiguration and at his suffering in Gethsemane on the night of his arrest.

James was apparently an active leader in the early church, although there is no reliable information on where he preached or what he did. He was put to death by Herod Agrippa I (Acts 12:2) and is said to have been buried in Jerusalem. He was the first of the apostles to die a martyr's death and the only one whose death is recorded in the Bible. The date of his death was around Easter in the year 43 or 44, and this is reflected in the date of his commemoration in the East (Orthodox churches April 30; Copts April 12). The reason for the

Western date of July 25 is not known, but it may well be connected with the transfer of his remains. His name appears on Western calendars only from the ninth century, and the supposed site of his relics in Santiago de Campostela in Spain was one of the great pilgrimage centers during the Middle Ages. (St. Birgitta of Sweden visited it with her husband in 1341-1342.)

St. James is a popular name for Lutheran churches in America—one of the five saints' names (next after St. John and St. Paul) which are most often used.

St. James the Elder is not to be confused with St. James the Less (the younger), the son of Alphaeus, who is commemorated on May 1, or with James the Just, called the brother of the Lord, who was the leader of the church in Jerusalem, who is commemorated on October 23.

Reading

(From *The Ladder of Perfection* by Walter Hilton.)

A real pilgrim going to Jerusalem leaves his house and land, wife and children; he divests himself of all that he possesses in order to travel light and without encumbrances. Similarly, if you wish to be a spiritual pilgrim you must divest yourself of all that you possess; that is, both of good deeds and bad, and leave them all behind you. Recognize your own property, so that you will not place any confidence in your own work; instead, be always desiring the grace of deeper love, and seeking the spiritual presence of Jesus. If you do this, you will be setting your heart wholly on obtaining the love of Jesus and whatever spiritual vision of Himself that He is willing to grant, for it is to this end alone that you have been created and redeemed; this is your beginning and your end, your joy and your bliss. Therefore, whatever you may possess, and however fruitful your activities, regard them all as worthless without the inward certainty and experience of this love. Keep this intention constantly in mind and hold on to it firmly; it will sustain you among all the perils of your pilgrimage.

You are now on the road, and you know how to proceed. But beware of enemies who will set themselves to obstruct you if they can.

Nothing distresses them more than your desire and longing for the love of Jesus, and their whole purpose is to uproot this from your heart, and turn you back again to the love of earthly things. Your chief enemies are the bodily desires and foolish fears which the corruption of human nature stirs up in your heart, and which would stifle your desire for the love of God and take full possession of your heart. These are your deadliest enemies. There are also others, for evil spirits employ all their tricks to deceive you. But you have one remedy, as I told you before. Whatever they say, do not believe them; keep on your way, and desire nothing but the love of Jesus. Let your answer always be, "I am nothing, I have nothing, I desire nothing but the love of Jesus."

Your enemies may begin by troubling your mind with doubts, hinting that your confessions have been invalid; that some old sin lies unremembered and unconfessed in your heart; that you must give up your desire, go back to the beginning, and make a full confession. But do not believe their lies, for you have received full absolution. Rest assured that you are on the right road, and there is no need for you to ransack your conscience about the past: keep your eye on the road and your mind on Jerusalem. And if they tell you, "You are not worthy to enjoy the love of God, so why hanker after what you cannot have and do not deserve?" carry on and take no notice of them. Reply, "I desire the love of God not because I am worthy, but because I am unworthy; for if I had it, it would make me worthy. And since I was created to this end, although I may never enjoy it, I will still desire it, pray for it, and hope to attain it." If your enemies see that your courage and determination to succeed is growing, they will begin to fear you.

However, so long as you are on the road they will not cease to harass you; at one time they will intimidate and threaten you, at another they will try to flatter you and seduce you, to make you abandon your purpose and turn back. If you persist in this desire for Jesus and continue in your first fervour, you will ruin your health or suffer from delusions and fits, as some do. Or you will beggar yourself, or suffer some injury, and no one will be willing to help you. Or the devil may put such subtle temptations in your way that you cannot resist them. For it is a dangerous course for anyone to forsake the world completely, and give himself entirely to the love of God, seeking nothing but His love, because he will encounter many perils of which he knows nothing. So turn back and forget this desire which you can never fulfill, and behave like other people in this world.

Such are the arguments of your enemies, but do not believe them. Hold firmly to your desire and reply that you desire to have Jesus and to be at Jerusalem.

Walter Hilton, *The Ladder of Perfection* trans. Leo Sherley-Price (Baltimore: Penguin, 1957) 157, 159-160. Copyright © Leo Sherley-Price, 1957. Reprinted by permission of Penguin Books Ltd.

Propers

ROMAN

Almighty Father, by the martyrdom of Saint James you blessed the work of the early Church. May his profession of faith give us courage and his prayers bring us strength. We ask this through our Lord Jesus Christ, your Son, who lives and reigns with you and the Holy Spirit, one God, for ever and ever.

(Text from the English translation of the Roman Missal © 1973, International Committee on English in the Liturgy, Inc. All rights reserved.)

2 Corinthians 4:7-15
Psalm 126:1-6
Matthew 20:20-28

LUTHERAN

O gracious God, we remember before you today your servant and apostle James, first among the Twelve to suffer martyrdom for the name of Jesus Christ; pour out upon the leaders of your Church that spirit of self-denying service which is the true mark of authority among your people; through Jesus Christ our Lord, who lives and reigns with you and the Holy Spirit, one God, now and forever.

1 Kings 19:9-18
Psalm 7:1-11
Acts 11:27-12:3a
Mark 10:33-45

EPISCOPAL

O gracious God, we remember before you today your servant and apostle James, first among the Twelve to suffer martyrdom for the Name of Jesus Christ; and we pray that you will pour out upon the leaders of your Church that spirit of self-denying service by which alone they may have true authority among your people; through Jesus Christ our Lord, who lives and reigns with you and the Holy Spirit, one God, now and for ever.

(Text from the Book of Common Prayer [Proposed], copyright 1977 by Charles Mortimer Guilbert as Custodian of the Standard Book of Common Prayer. All rights reserved. Used by permission.)

Jeremiah 45:1-5
Psalm 7:1-10
Acts 11:27-12:3
Matthew 20:20-28

Preface of Apostles

Hymn of the Day: "They cast their nets in Galilee" (449)

Prayers: for the gift of generosity and self-sacrifice
for courage and faith gladly to follow Christ
for the spirit of service

Preface: Apostles

Color: Red

July 28

Johann Sebastian Bach, Musician, 1750

Johann Sebastian Bach, the most illustrious member of a family of successful musicians, was born in Eisenach in Thuringia, March 21, 1685. His father and brother were musicians, and from an early age he learned about the violin and organ and later served as a choirboy. By the age of eighteen he already had a considerable reputation as a composer, organist, and violinist. He served a while as organist in the New Church at Arnstadt, 1703-1707 and St. Blasius in Muhlhausen, where he married his cousin, Maria Barbara Bach. In 1708 he accepted an important post as court organist to the Duke of Weimar, where he became acknowledged as an outstanding organist and where he wrote his chief works for the organ. In 1714 he was promoted to concertmaster. In 1717 he became Kapellmeister (director of music) to Prince Leopold of Cöthen. His wife died in 1720, and the following year he married Anna Magdalena Wülcken. From 1723 until his death he was at Leipzig where he was cantor at the famous St. Thomas school and music director of both St. Thomas and St. Nicholas churches, as well as the Pauliner-Kirche at the University. It was in these churches that his compositions were first performed.

Bach was a deeply religious, introspective man, who was consciously serving God in his composing and playing of music. He wrote nearly two hundred cantatas, including sets which provide a cantata for each Sunday and holy day of the Lutheran church year. But he is better known for his great works such as the *B Minor Mass* and the *St. Matthew Passion,* which was first performed in St. Thomas Church on Good Friday, 1729.

Bach had twenty children by his two wives; nine of the children survived him. Four of his sons also possessed outstanding musical ability: Wilhelm Friedemann, Carl Philipp Emanuel, Johann Christoph Friedrich, and Johann Christian. Bach died July 28, 1750, one of the greatest figures in all Western music and an ornament of the Church of the Reformation. Archbishop Nathan Söderblom called him "the fifth evangelist." Bach's body was buried without ceremony in St. John's churchyard and only on the one hundredth anniversary of his death was a tablet to his memory placed in the church. Finally, on the two hundredth anniversary in 1950, Bach's remains were moved to a resting place within St. Thomas' Church in Leipzig.

Friedrich Blume. *Protestant Church Music.* London: Gollancz, 1976.
Karl and I. Geiringer. *Music of the Bach Family.* Cambridge, Mass: Harvard, 1955.
Werner Neumann. *Bach and His World* tr. Stefan de Haan. rev. ed. London: Thames and Hudson, 1970.
Albert Schweitzer. *J. S. Bach.* tr. Ernest Newman. London, 1911. Reissued 1923.
P. Spitta. *Johann Sebastian Bach* tr. C. Bell and J. A. Fuller-Maitland 3 vols. London, 1884. 2nd ed. New York, 1951.
C. S. Terry. *Bach.* 2nd ed. London, 1933.

July 28

Heinrich Schuetz, Musician, 1672

Schuetz, the greatest German composer before Bach, was born in Koestritz, Saxony (now Bad Kosteritz, East Germany), October 8 (or 14th), 1585, one hundred years before Bach. As a boy he sang in the chapel choir of Landgrave Moritz of Hesse-Kassel, who provided him with a wide general education. In 1608 Schuetz entered Marburg University to study law, but in the following year Landgrave Moritz sent him to Venice to study music with Giovanni Gabrielli, who had a powerful influence on the young student.

After the death of Gabrielli in 1612, Schuetz returned to Germany and went to Leipzig to resume his study of the law. Shortly afterward he became the second organist at the court of Kassel. In 1614 he entered the service of the Elector of Saxony at Dresden and there introduced the Italian style that he had learned in Venice. Schuetz returned to Venice in 1628 and perhaps studied with Monteverdi, then the chief musical figure of the city. By 1630 Schuetz was back in Dresden, but three years later he left the court which was afflicted with the plague and suffering from the disorders of the Thirty Years' War. From 1633 to 1635 Schuetz was Kapellmeister at the royal court of Copenhagen. He spent time in Brunswick and Lueneberg and then returned to the elector's court in 1645 when the Dresden chapel was reestablished, and, except for visits to the Danish court, he remained in the Elector's service until his death at Dresden November 6, 1672.

He was a man of noble character and a real father to his chapel. His special achievement was the introduction into German music of the new style of the Italian modalists (typified by Monteverdi) without creating an unsatisfying hybrid; the music of Schuetz remains individual and German in feeling. Most of all, his choral settings of biblical texts show unsurpassed mastery.

Hans Joachim Moser. *Heinrich Schütz* trans. Carl F. Pfatteicher. St. Louis: Concordia, 1959.

July 28

George Frederick Handel, Musician, 1759

Handel (the German form of his name is Georg Friedrich Händel) was born at Halle, February 23, 1685, the son of a surgeon and a pastor's daughter. His father died when Handel was eleven. He was educated at Halle, originally for the law. He became the organist at the Reformed cathedral there 1702-1703. He then left the university and went to Hamburg to work on operas from 1703-1706. For the next four years he was in Italy. He then went to England and in 1726 became a British subject. He enjoyed court appointments and worked for private patrons, but chiefly he was engaged in the production of Italian operas and English oratorios. In 1729, while on a visit to the continent, Bach tried to arrange a meeting with the man whose work he admired, but the two never met.

The opera began to decline in popularity and Handel turned to the oratorio, a large-scale work developed around a religious theme, written not to be staged but sung by soloists and a chorus. In 1741-1742 at Neal's Musick Hall in Dublin his most popular work, *Messiah*, was performed. In his last years, like Bach, Handel had eye trouble. He died April 14, 1759 and was buried in the Poets' Corner of Westminster Abbey on April 20, mourned by a congregation of three thousand. His strong sense of charity and concern for others won for him the affection of the English people. He involved himself in public affairs by his generous gifts and sent bequests to the relatives in Germany.

Handel's church music is relatively unimportant. He was primarily a dramatic composer, and even his oratorios were written for the theater, not the church. Nonetheless they have been memorable proclamations and interpretations of the Scripture.

G. E. H. Abraham. *Handel. A Symposium.* New York: Oxford, 1954.
O. E. Deutsch. *Handel: A Documentary Biography.* New York: Norton, 1955.
Paul H. Lang. *George Frederic Handel.* New York: Norton, 1966.

Reading

(From *Behold the Spirit* by Alan Watts.)

Music at its highest, as in Bach or Mozart, is pure play. The preludes and fugues of Bach are simply a complex arrangement of glorious sounds, entirely sufficient in themselves. They need no programme notes to explain a moral or sociological message, or to call our attention to effects imitating natural noises or conveying emotional qualities. The intricate melodies flow on and on, and there never seems any necessity for them to stop. He composed them in tremendous quantities, with the same Godlike extravagance to be found in the unnecessary vastness of nature. Inferior music, however, needs props and commentaries, since it proceeds from human purpose rather than that playfulness of divine perfection which we find not only in Bach and Mozart, but also in the long Alleluias of Gregorian chant, the arabesques of Persian miniatures, the illuminated margins of medieval manuscripts, the wind-swept bamboos of Chinese painting, and the entirely self-satisfying and purposeless figures of the dance as it may sometimes be seen in Russian ballet. Such playfulness is the very nature of the divine Wisdom.

Alan Watts, *Behold the Spirit. A Study in the Necessity of Mystical Religion* (New York: Random House, 1947) 178. Used by permission of Pantheon Books, a Division of Random House, Inc.

Propers: Artists
       Second Lesson   Ephesians 5:15-20
       Gospel   Luke 19:37-40

Hymn of the Day: "When in our music God is glorified" (555)

Prayers: for all who make music
       for a renewed appreciation of music as a gift of God
       for God to raise up new musicians for the church and his
          people

Color: White

July 29

Mary, Martha, and Lazarus of Bethany

This little family of Bethany were Jesus' friends who shared their home with him, and it was at their house that he found refreshment, especially before the passion. Their names, on various dates, appear on lists of martyrs from the seventh and eighth centuries.

Mary (a form of Miriam) is portrayed in Luke 10:38-42 and John 11:1-12:8. She appears to be a contemplative person with single-minded absorption in the kingdom of God. In John's account, at dinner six days before the passion, Mary anointed Jesus, perhaps as a sign of his royal dignity which he took to be a consecration of himself for his approaching sacrifice.

Martha (the name means "lady" or "mistress") has come rather unfairly to represent the unrecollected activist. She was of a practical bent, to be sure, but she enjoyed the friendship and esteem of Jesus nonetheless, and it was she who made the confession of faith when Jesus came to raise Lazarus, "If you had been here my brother would not have died. Even now I know that whatever you ask of God, God will grant you" (John 11:21-22).

In Luke 10:38 the house where the three lived is called Martha's. In John 12:1-3 the supper at Bethany at which Lazarus was present and at which Martha again served, is held at the house of Simon the Leper (Matt. 26:6; Mark 14:3). This had led some to suggest that Mary may have therefore been the widow of Simon.

Lazarus, who was raised from the dead by Jesus, is in the Fourth Gospel a sign of the eternal life possessed by those who believe. Curiously, this most striking resurrection story is not found in the synoptics. His high character is evidenced by the love Mary, Martha, and Jesus all had for him.

Devotion to Lazarus was apparently widespread in the early church. He is commemorated in the Eastern church on the Saturday before Palm Sunday, called "Lazarus Saturday," which foreshadows the resurrection of Jesus the following week. According to a curious legend, Lazarus, his sisters, and some friends were put in a leaky boat by their enemies and miraculously made their way to Cyprus where Lazarus was made a bishop. In 890 what were thought to be his relics were taken to Constantinople and a church was built there in his honor. In an eleventh century legend Lazarus had been bishop of Marseilles and was martyred under Domitian. (He was perhaps confused with a fifth century Bishop Lazarus of Aix.)

In the Western church the traditional feast day of Lazarus has been December 17. The Roman Catholic calendar commemorates Martha alone on July 29 and Mary, together with Mary the wife of Cleopas, and Mary the mother of James ("The Three Marys") on May 25. The Episcopal Church commemorates Mary and Martha together on July 29. The Lutheran calendar has extended the commemoration to include their brother as well.

Reading

(From *Mixed Pasture* by Evelyn Underhill.)

St. Theresa said that to give our Lord a perfect service, Mary and Martha must combine. The modern tendency is to turn from that attitude and work of Mary; and even call it—as I have heard it called by busy social Christians—a form of spiritual selfishness. Thousands of devoted men and women today believe that the really good part is to keep busy, and give themselves no time to take what is offered to those who abide quietly with Christ; because there seem such a lot of urgent jobs for Martha to do. The result of this can only be a maiming of their human nature, exhaustion, loss of depth and of vision; and it is seen in the vagueness and ineffectuality of a great deal of the work that is done for God. It means a total surrender of the busy click-click of the life of succession; nowhere, in the end, more deadly than in the religious sphere. I insist on this because I feel, more and more, the danger in which we stand of developing a lopsided Christianity; so concentrated on service, and on this world's obligations, as to forget the needs of constant willed and quiet contact with that other world, wherefrom the sanctions of service and the power in which to do it proceed.

Evelyn Underhill, *Mixed Pasture* (London: Methuen, 1933) 74-75.

Propers

ROMAN	LUTHERAN	EPISCOPAL

(Martha)
Father,
your Son honored
  Saint Martha
by coming to her
  home as a guest.
By her prayers
may we serve Christ
  in our brothers and
  sisters
and be welcomed by
  you into heaven,
  our true home.
	Lord God you have surrounded us with so great a cloud of witnesses. Grant that we, encouraged by the examples of your servants Mary, Martha, and Lazarus, may persevere in the course that is set before us, to be living signs of the Gospel and at last,	(Mary and Martha)
		O God, by whose Spirit various gifts and graces are bestowed upon your saints: We give you humble thanks for your servants Mary and Martha, the friends of our Savior Jesus Christ; and we pray you to give us grace to love and serve you and

ROMAN	LUTHERAN	EPISCOPAL
We ask this through our Lord Jesus Christ, your Son, who lives and reigns with you and the Holy Spirit, one God, for ever and ever.	with all the saints to share in your eternal joy; through your Son, Jesus Christ our Lord.	others for his sake, our Lord Jesus Christ, who lives and reigns with you and the Holy Spirit, one God, now and ever.

ROMAN	LUTHERAN	EPISCOPAL
Common of Saints, except John 11:19-27 or Luke 10:38-42	Micah 6:6-8 Psalm 9:1-10 Romans 12:9-13 John 11:17-44	Romans 12:9-13 Psalm 121, 131 Luke 10:38-42 Preface of a Saint

Hymn of the Day: "O Jesus, king most wonderful" (537)

Prayers: for those who serve that others may be quiet for prayer and study

for those who live contemplative lives

for a certain hope of the resurrection

Preface: All Saints

Color: White

Olaf, King of Norway, Martyr, 1030

Olav Haraldsson was born in Oplandet in 995, the son of a minor king and his queen Asta. His father died before he was born, and Asta married King Sigurd Syr of Ringerike, a fertile inland district near the centers of trade in southern Norway, where Olaf was raised. Many details of his life are known and these comprise what is probably the earliest Norwegian historical work extant. As soon as fifty years after his death, however, the stories of his life were elaborated with moralizing elements.

When Olaf was still young he went on Viking expeditions with his foster father, and then with Thorkel the Tall he fought in Friesland, Holland, and England. The next year on an expedition to France and Spain the legend has it that he dreamed of a strange, powerful figure telling him to go back to his family lands, "for you shall be the eternal king of Norway." After his baptism, or more probably his confirmation, in Rouen, France in 1014, Olaf sailed for Norway in 1015 with the intention of establishing Christianity firmly there, which Olav Tryggvason (Olaf I) had failed to do, and unifying the nation under his own rule.

Olaf succeeded in rallying many to his cause, and after several battles was recognized by all as the King of Norway in 1019. In the years that followed, St. Olaf, an ardent Christian, sought to uproot the last traces of paganism in Norway and spread Christianity throughout his kingdom, and with the help of Bishop Grimkel and others he had brought with him from England and Normandy he gave the church a code of laws written in the Norwegian language. He also completely revised the civil laws of the nation, and the code, known as the "Laws of St. Olaf," became the basis of all later Norwegian jurisprudence.

King Olaf enforced his laws with strict impartiality, a practice not always welcome to the aristocracy, whose power was diminishing. When the powerful King Knut (Canute), who at that time ruled Denmark and all of Britain, joined forces with the king in Sweden in 1028 to attack King Olaf, many of the Norwegian nobles deserted their king, who was defeated and fled to Russia, taking refuge at the court of his brother-in-law Duke Jaroslav. In 1030 Olaf returned from exile and attempted to regain his kingdom, but on July 29 at the battle of Stiklestad he was slain, and Knut added Norway to his domain.

Soon after the battle the people began to talk of the dead king as a holy man, and a little over a year later his body was removed from its temporary burial place to the town of Nidaros, later called Trondheim, which Olaf I had founded in 997. The hero-king was recognized by the church and the nation as patron saint and "eternal king of Norway" and the date of his death was set for annual commemoration. From his time on Christianity was the dominant religion in Norway.

At the beginning of the thirteenth century, the Icelandic historian

Snorri Sturlusson wrote in his *Heimkringla* a full biography, the "Saga of Olaf the Saint," and Olaf the king and saint has repeatedly been the subject of literary works, painting, and sculpture ever since. The commemoration of St. Olaf spread to other countries, and churches have been named for him not only in Norway but elsewhere in Scandinavia, in Great Britain, the Baltic countries, and Russia. In the United States, Lutherans of Norwegian origin especially remember him, and there are more than thirty-five churches named for him. St. Olaf College in Minnesota and its choir are well known.

Already in the eleventh century a church was built over the burial place of St. Olaf in Trondheim, and in the twelfth and thirteenth centuries it was rebuilt as a Gothic cathedral, the most beautiful in northern Europe and long a center of pilgrimage and a place of celebration on his feast day. During the late Middle Ages this was the seat of the archbishop, and was the religious and cultural center of Norway and an important pilgrimage center for all of northern Europe. In the course of the years the cathedral was severely damaged by fires and other accidents until its restoration was begun in 1869. The present building of marble and native blue soapstone is perhaps the finest Gothic cathedral in Scandinavia.

G. Turville-Petre. *The Heroic Age of Scandinavia.* New York: Longmans, 1951.

Reading

(From *Heimskringla: History of the Kings of Norway*)

As he grew up, Olaf Haraldsson was not of tall stature, but of middle height and of stout frame and great strength. His hair was of light chestnut color and his face, broad, of light complexion, and ruddy. His eyes were unusually fine, bright and piercing, so that it inspired terror to look into them when he was furious. Olaf was a man of many accomplishments. He was a good shot, and second to none in hurling spears. He was skilled and had a sure eye for all kinds of handicraft work, whether the things were made for himself or others. He was nicknamed Olaf the Stout. He was bold and ready in speech, mature early in all ways, both in bodily strength and shrewdness; and he endeared himself to all his kinsfolk and acquaintances. He vied with all in games and always wanted to be the first in everything, as was proper, befitting his rank and birth.

It was the habit of the king [Olaf] to rise betimes in the morning, to put on his clothes and wash his hands, then go to church and listen to matins and morning mass, then to go to meetings and reconcile people, or else to deal with other matters such as seemed needful to him. He gathered at his court men both of high and low degree, and all who were of keen understanding. He had often recited in his presence the laws of Hakon, the foster son of Aethelstan, had given to the Trondheim district. He changed laws with the advice of the wisest men, taking away or adding as seemed best to him. The Christian code of laws he gave in accordance with the advice of Bishop Grimkel and other priests, laying great stress on abolishing heathendom and ancient practices such as seemed to him contrary to the spirit of Christianity. In the end the farmers agreed to the laws the king gave. As says Sigvat:

> Do thou, liege-lord, lay down
> laws for all the land that
> may prevail among all
> men and stand forever!

King Olaf was well-mannered, of an agreeable disposition, a man of rather few words, open-handed, [yet also] eager to have possessions.

Thorir struck at the king, and then they exchanged some blows; and the king's sword took no effect where Thorir's reindeer skin protected him, yet he received a wound on his hand. . . .

The king said to Bjorn, his marshall, "Strike down the dog on whom steel takes no effect!"

Bjorn turned his battle-axe and hit him with the hammer of it. The blow fell on Thorir's shoulder. It was a mighty one, and Thorir tottered. At the same moment the king turned on Kalf and his kinsmen and dealt Olaf, Kalf's kinsman, his deathblow. Then Thorir the Hound thrust with his spear at Bjorn the Marshall and pierced him in the middle and that was his death.

Then Thorir said, "Thus beat we the bears!" [The Old Norse *Bjorn* means "bear".]

Thorstein Shipbuilder hewed at King Olaf with his battleaxe, and the blow struck his left leg above the knee. Finn Arnason instantly killed Thorstein. Receiving that wound the king leaned against a boulder. He threw down his sword and prayed God to help him. Then Thorir the Hound thrust at him with his spear. It pierced him from below his coat of mail and through the belly. Then Kalf slashed at the king, and the blow struck his neck on the left side. Men disagree as to which Kalf wounded the king. These three wounds caused King Olaf's death. After his fall most of the company which had advanced with him fell too.

On the sand flat where the body of King Olaf had been interred, a fine spring arose, and people obtained relief from their ailments by drinking its water. It was walled in, and its water has been safeguarded ever since. First a chapel was built there and an altar erected where the burial place of the king had been; but now Christ Church stands on that spot. When Archbishop Eystein built the large minster which stands there now he had its high altar erected on the very spot where the king's grave had been. And on that spot stood the high altar in the old Christ Church. It is said that Saint Olaf's Church now stands where the shed in which the body of King Olaf reposed during the night. The rise up which the holy remains of the king were borne from the boat is now called Olaf's Slope, and that is now in the middle of the town.

Men who have kept close account say the Holy King Olaf was king of Norway for fifteen years after Earl Svein left the country, but that he assumed the royal title the winter before. . . . According to Priest Ari the Learned, Holy King Olaf was thirty-five years old when he fell. He had fought twenty large battles.

Snorri Sturluson, *Heimskringla* tr. Lee M. Hollander (Austin: Univ. of Texas Press, 1964), 245-246, 289, 514-515, 530, 533. Used by permission.

Propers: Saints (or Martyrs)

A model for an appropriate collection for Christian rulers is provided by the Episcopal church for St. Louis, King of France (August 25). This collect is also used, with appropriate changes in name and pronouns, for St. Margaret, Queen of Scotland (November 16): O God who called your servant Louis to an earthly throne that he might advance your heavenly kingdom, and gave him zeal for your Church and love for your people: Mercifully grant that we who commemorate his example may be fruitful in good works, and attain to the glorious crown of your saints; through Jesus Christ our Lord, who lives and reigns with you and the Holy Spirit, one God, now and for ever.

Hymn of the Day: "Who is this host arrayed in white" (314)
　　　　　　　　or "The head that once was crowned with
　　　　　　　　thorns" (173)
　　　　　　　　(tune: *St. Magnus,* son of St. Olaf)

Prayers: for the Church and people of Norway
　　　　　for the king and the government of Norway
　　　　　for those who administer justice
　　　　　for the Church and people of Iceland

Color: White or red

Lawrence, Deacon, Martyr, 258

Lawrence (whose name is also spelled Laurence) was born, perhaps of Spanish parents, in the early part of the third century. While still a young man he came to Rome where Bishop Sixtus (Xystus) II ordained him a deacon, and he was made the chief of the seven deacons of Rome, responsible for the distribution of the charities of the church and the care of its properties.

In 257 the Roman emperor Valerian began a vigorous persecution of the church, aimed primarily at the clergy and laity of the upper classes. All of the properties of the church were confiscated and assemblies for worship were forbidden. On August 4, 258 the Bishop of Rome, Sixtus II who had just become bishop the year before, and his deacons were apprehended at the cemetery of Callistus where they were celebrating the liturgy, and all except Lawrence were summarily executed and buried in the same cemetery. The Roman calendar commemorated them on August 7. Lawrence, who knew of the location of the church's treasure, was tortured and then executed on August 10.

The traditions that have come down to us concerning the martyrdom are unreliable, but they are nonetheless amusing and pleasant. It is said that the behavior of Lawrence in jail was such as to have led to the conversion and baptism of his jailer Hippolytus and his family. When the governor demanded the treasures, Lawrence is said to have gathered together a great number of the blind, the lame, the maimed, lepers, orphans, and widows of Rome and brought them to the governor's palace, saying, "Here is the treasure of the church." He was, tradition says, condemned to die slowly and painfully by roasting on an iron grill. Even there Lawrence's courage and humor were apparent, for he is reported to have said at one point to his executioners, "I am done on this side. Turn me over." (More probably Lawrence was beheaded, as was Sixtus.)

St. Lawrence met death on August 10, 258, and his feast is listed in the martyrologies as early as the fourth century. During the reign of the Emperor Constantine a church was built over his tomb in the catacomb on the Via Tiburtina. It was enlarged by Pelagius II (579-590) into the basilica now known as St. Lawrence outside the Walls (San Lorenzo fuori de Mura) and became one of the seven principal churches of Rome and a favorite place for Roman pilgrimages.

The torture and execution of a Roman citizen by Roman authorities made a deep impression on the young church, stunned by such hostility, and his martyrdom was one of the first to be commemorated by the church. He is commemorated universally but especially in the West where hundreds of churches and many cities have him as their patron. St. Lawrence's Day, the feast of SS. Peter and Paul, and the feast of St. Michael, became the feasts that divided the Pentecost season into quarters.

V. L. Kennedy. *The Saints of the Canon of the Mass.* Vatican City, 1938.

Reading

(From a sermon by St. Augustine)

The Church at Rome commends to us today the anniversary of the triumph of Saint Lawrence. For on this day he trod the furious pagan world underfoot and flung aside its allurements, and so gained victory over Satan's attack on his faith.

As you have often heard, Lawrence was a deacon of the Church at Rome. There he ministered the sacred blood of Christ; there for the sake of Christ's name he poured out his own blood. Saint John the apostle was evidently teaching us about the mystery of the Lord's supper when he wrote: *Just as Christ laid down his life for us, so we ought to lay down our lives for the brethren.* My brethren, Lawrence understood this and, understanding, he acted on it. Just as he had partaken of a gift of self at the table of the Lord, so he prepared to offer such a gift. In his life he loved Christ; in his death he followed in his footsteps.

Brethren, we too must imitate Christ if we truly love him. We shall not be able to render a better return on that love than by modelling our lives on his. *Christ suffered for us, leaving us an example, that we should follow in his steps.* In saying this, the apostle Peter seems to have understood that Christ's passion is of no avail to those who do not. The holy martyrs followed Christ even to shedding their life's blood, even to reproducing the very likeness of his passion. They followed him, but not they alone. It is not true that the bridge was broken after the martyrs crossed; nor is it true that after they had drunk from it, the fountain of eternal life dried up.

I tell you again and again my brethren, . . . that in the Lord's garden are to be found not only the roses of his martyrs. In it there are also the lilies of the virgins, the ivy of wedded couples, and the violets of widows. On no account may any class of people despair, thinking that God has not called them. Christ suffered for all. What the Scriptures say of him is true: *He desires all men to be saved and to come to knowledge of the truth.*

Let us understand, then, how a Christian must follow Christ even though he does not shed his blood for him, and his faith is not called upon to undergo the great test of the martyr's sufferings. The apostle Paul says of Christ our Lord, *Though he was in the form of God he did not consider equality with God a prize to be clung to.* How unrivaled his majesty! *But he emptied himself, taking on the form of a slave, made in human likeness and presenting himself in human form.* How deep his humility!

Christ humbled himself. Christian, that is what you must make your own. *Christ became obedient.* How is it that you are proud?

When this humbling experience was completed and death itself lay conquered, Christ ascended into heaven. Let us follow him there, for we hear Paul saying, *If you have been raised with Christ, you must lift your thoughts on high, where Christ now sits at the right hand of God.*

From the English translation of the Office of Readings for the Liturgy of the Hours © 1974, International Committee on English in the Liturgy, Inc. All rights reserved.

Propers

ROMAN	LUTHERAN	EPISCOPAL
Father, you called Saint Lawrence to serve you by love and crowned his life with glorious martyrdom. Help us to be like him in loving you and doing your work. Grant this through our Lord Jesus Christ, your Son, who lives and reigns with you and the Holy Spirit, one God, for ever and ever.	Gracious Lord, in every age you have sent men and women who have given their lives for the message of your love. Inspire us with the memory of those martyrs for the Gospel, like your servant Lawrence, whose faithfulness led them in the way of the cross, and give us courage to bear full witness with our lives to your Son's victory over sin and death; through Jesus Christ our Lord.	Almighty God, by whose grace and power your holy Deacon and martyr Laurence triumphed over suffering and despised death: Grant, we pray, that enduring hardship and waxing valiant in fight, we may with the noble army of martyrs receive the crown of everlasting life; through Jesus Christ our Lord, who lives and reigns with you and the Holy Spirit, one God, now and for ever.
(Text from the English translation of the Roman Missal © 1973, International Committee on English in the Liturgy, Inc. All rights reserved.)		*(Text from Lesser Feasts and Fasts, Revised Edition, copyright 1973 by Charles Mortimer Guilbert as Custodian of the Standard Book of Common Prayer. All rights reserved. Used by permission.)*

2 Corinthians 9:6-10
  Psalm 112:1-2, 5-9
John 12:24-26
	Common of Martyrs
	Ezekiel 20:40-42
	    Psalm 5
	Revelation 6:9-11
	Mark 8:34-38
		Common of a Martyr
		III
		  Psalm 69:18-22
		Jeremiah 15:15-21
		  Psalm 69:31-36
		1 Peter 4:12-19
		Mark 8:34-38
		
		Preface of Holy Week

Hymn of the Day: "How firm a foundation, O Saints of the Lord"
    (507)

Prayers: for those who maintain and care for the property of the
    church
    for those who serve the poor and needy
    for a recognition of the true treasure of the church

Preface: All Saints:

Color: Red

Florence Nightingale
Renewer of Society, 1910

Florence Nightingale was born May 12, 1820 at Florence, Italy.
(She was named for the city.) Her parents were well-to-do, and she
grew up in the family's homes in Derbyshire, Hampshire, and London. She received a large measure of her education from her father
and became very adept at languages.

She found social life unsatisfying, and February 7, 1837 she heard
what she described as the voice of God telling her that she had a
mission, although it was not yet specified. Study made her an acknowledged expert on public health and hospitals.

In 1846 a friend sent her the Yearbook of the Kaiserwerth Motherhouse of Deaconnesses. Her interest in the institution was aroused and
in 1850 she entered the school for training as a nurse. In 1853 she
became the superintendent of the Institution for the Care of Sick
Gentlewomen in London, but she was dissatisfied with the hospital.

The Crimean War broke out in March 1854, and reports of the
conditions of the sick and wounded shocked Britain. Women were
urged to serve as nurses like the French Sisters of Charity. Miss
Nightingale with a party of nurses left for Turkey and arrived at
Scutari, Turkey, November 5, 1854. They found conditions intolerable
and the doctors hostile. A huge influx of wounded forced the officials

to ask her help, however, and she worked hard and long, late into the night, and the picture was created of the "lady with a lamp." By May 1855 her concern shifted to the welfare of the British army. After sickness and struggle her position as general superintendent of the Female Nursing Establishment of the Military Hospitals of the Army was confirmed March 16, 1856. Not until the last patient had left Barrack Hospital did Miss Nightingale leave for England, where she had become a national hero. There she worked against considerable opposition for improvement in health and living conditions of the British soldiers. A Royal Commission on the Health of the Army was appointed in May 1857, and a similar commission for the army in India was authorized in 1859.

From 1857 Miss Nightingale was an invalid, but continued to work untiringly to keep up her enormous correspondence, and to give advice from her bed to countless visitors. In 1860 she established, with funds subscribed in commemoration of her work in the Crimea, the Nightingale School for Nurses at St. Thomas Hospital. She pressed for the reform of workhouses. In 1901 she became blind but managed to continue her work. In 1907 she was awarded the Order of Merit—the first woman to receive it. She died August 13, 1910 and in accordance with her wishes was buried in her family's grave in the churchyard of East Wellow, Hampshire where her tombstone reads simply, "F. N. Born 1820. Died 1910."

Sir Edward Cook. *The Life of Florence Nightingale.* 2 vols. 1913.
Cecil Woodham-Smith. *Florence Nightingale.* 1820-1910. New York: McGraw-Hill, 1951. Reprinted 1964.
Phyllis McGinley. *Saint Watching.* New York Viking, 1969.

August 13

Clara Maass, Renewer of Society, 1901

Clara Maass was born in 1876, the first of nine children of German immigrant parents, who lived in East Orange, New Jersey. She became one of the first five graduates of the nursing school at Newark German Hospital.

Before the Army Nurse Corps had been established, she served in the army on a contract basis during the Spanish-American War, 1898-1899. At a camp in Santiago, Cuba, she was introduced to the horrors of yellow fever, one of the scourges of the world. Her next tour of duty during 1900-01 took her to the Philippines, where again she nursed the victims of yellow fever. There she contracted another fever herself—breakbone—and was sent home.

Meanwhile, a United States-Cuba research project, in Havana had singled out the mosquito as the probable transmitter of yellow fever. Clara Maass was one of twenty people who responded to the call for subjects in experimentation. Her first mosquito bite led to a slight case of yellow fever from which she soon recovered, but ten days after she was bitten a second time she died. She was the only woman and the only American to give her life in the research which demonstrated the manner of the propagation of yellow fever. Yellow fever is now preventable.

In 1952 the name of the Newark German Hospital was changed to the Clara Maass Memorial Hospital. A United States postage stamp was issued in her honor in 1976.

Reading

(From *Notes on Nursing* by Florence Nightingale.)

It seems a commonly received idea among men and even among women themselves that it requires nothing but a disappointment in love, the want of an object, a general disgust, or incapacity for other things, to turn a woman into a good nurse.

This reminds one of the parish where a stupid old man was set to be schoolmaster because he was "past keeping the pigs."

What cruel mistakes are sometimes made by benevolent men and women in matters of business about which they know nothing and think they know a great deal.

The everyday management of a large ward, let alone of a hospital—the knowing what are the laws of life and death for men, and what the laws of health for wards—(and wards are healthy or unhealthy, mainly according to the knowledge or ignorance of the nurse)—are not these matters of sufficient importance and difficulty to require learning by experience and careful inquiry, just as much as any other art? They do not come by inspiration to the lady disappointed in love, nor to the poor workhouse drudge hard up for a livelihood.

And terrible is the injury which has followed to the sick from such wild notions!

In this respect (and why is it so?), in Roman Catholic countries, both writers and workers are, in theory at least, far before ours. They would never think of such a beginning for a good working Superior or Sister of Charity. And many a Superior has refused to admit a *Postulant* who appeared to have no better "vocation" or reasons for offering herself than these.

It is true *we* make "no vows." But is a "vow" necessary to convince us that the true spirit for learning any art, most especially an art of charity, aright, is not a disgust to everything or something else? Do we really place the love of our kind (and of nursing, as one branch of it) so low as this?

I would earnestly ask my sisters to keep clear of both the jargons now current everywhere (for they *are* equally jargons); of the jargon, namely, about the "rights" of women, which urges women to do all that men do, including the medical and other professions, merely because men do it, and without regard to whether this *is* the best that women can do; and of the jargon which urges women to do nothing that men do, merely because they are women, and should be "recalled to a sense of their duty as women," and because "this is women's work," and "that is men's," and "these are things which women should not do," which is all assertion, and nothing more. Surely woman should bring the best she has, *whatever* that is, to the work of God's world, without attending to either of these cries. For what are they, both of them, the one *just* as much as the other, but listening to the "what people will say," to opinion, to the "voices from without"? And as a wise man has said, no one has ever done anything great or useful by listening to the voices from without.

You do not want the effect of your good things to be, "How wonderful for a *woman!*" nor would you be deterred from good things by hearing it said, "Yes, but she ought not to have done this, because it is not suitable for a woman." But you want to do the thing that is good, whether it is "suitable for a woman" or not.

It does not make a thing good, that it is remarkable that a woman should have been able to do it. Neither does it make a thing bad, which would have been good had a man done it, that it has been done by a woman.

Oh, leave these jargons, and go your way straight to God's work, in simplicity and singleness of heart.

Florence Nightingale, *Notes on Nursing* (New York: Dover, 1969), 133-136. [1859, 1860.]

Propers: Renewers of Society

Hymn of the Day: "The Son of God goes forth to war" (183)
(Florence Nightingale's favorite, which she loved
to quote: "who follows in his train?")

Prayers: for nurses and all in the medical profession
for compassion, gentleness, and dedication
for courage to pursue new ways of service
for invalids that they might continue to find ways of service

Color: White

MARY, MOTHER OF OUR LORD

Mary the mother of Jesus is mentioned in a number of places in the gospels and the book of Acts, and a dozen incidents of her life are recorded: her betrothal to Joseph; the Annunciation by the angel that she was to bear the Messiah; her Visitation to Elizabeth, the mother of St. John the Baptist; the Nativity of our Lord; the visits of the shepherds and the Magi; presenting the infant Jesus in the temple in accordance with the Law; the flight into Egypt; the Passover visit to Jerusalem when Jesus was twelve; the wedding at Cana in Galilee; her presence at the crucifixion when her Son commended her to St. John; and meeting with the apostles in the upper room after the Ascension, waiting for the promised Spirit. She is thus pictured as being present at all of the important events of her Son's life.

The other books of the New Testament are silent about Mary, and little is known about the rest of her life, which traditions say she spent in Jerusalem (the tomb of the Virgin is shown in the Kidron valley) or Ephesus. The second century Protevangelium of James, which identifies her parents as Joachim and Anna, perhaps reflects a reliable tradition built on the narratives of the birth of Isaac and Samuel (Anna or Anne is a form of the name Hannah, Samuel's mother) and John the Baptist. The new Roman and Episcopal calendars commemorate Joachim and Anne on July 26.

The angel's words in Luke 1:32 imply that Mary was descended from David (or that the early church believed that she was descended from David). She is a model of bold but tender love: she stood at the cross to watch her son die as an enemy of the state. Jesus' brothers are not reported to have been present. The early Christians respected the mother of Jesus and honored her memory, and soon a special day was set aside for her commemoration. By the sixth century the date of August 15 was widespread in the East, and the feast day gradually became known as the Feast of the Dormition (the "falling asleep" or the passing from this life) of the Virgin Mary. In the seventh century this feast day spread to Rome and from there throughout the West, where by the ninth century it had come to be called the Feast of the Assumption (referring to the reception of Mary's body and soul into heaven in anticipation of the general resurrection of the bodies of all the dead at the last day). In 1950 Pope Pius XII proclaimed that the teaching of the Assumption was elevated to the status of a dogma in the Roman Catholic Church.

The feast day of the Virgin Mary remained on some Lutheran calendars well beyond the Reformation. Nonetheless, in reaction to what was seen as the excessive attention of the Roman church, the remembrance of Mary disappeared in Lutheran churches. The other days on the calendar associated with Mary—the Presentation, the Annunciation, and the Visitation—are all in reality festivals of Jesus Christ; and surely Mary, of whom more is known than is known about most of the apostles, deserves a day of her own. She represents the finest ideals of womanhood of her day—spiritual sensitivity, purity, obedience to the divine will, careful attention to the religious instruction of her Son, loyalty to him even when she did not fully understand him, faithful to the last and beyond. She has been important to Christian devotion through the centuries because in her, the God-bearer, is seen a representation of the church itself.

Mary in the New Testament ed. Raymond E. Brown, Karl P. Donfried, Joseph A. Fitzmyer, John Reumann. Philadelphia: Fortress, 1978.

Reading

(From "The Magnificat" by Martin Luther)

For he who is mighty has done great things for me,
and holy is his name.

The "great things" are nothing less than that she became the Mother of God, in which work so many and such great good things are bestowed on her as pass man's understanding. For on this there follows all honor, all blessedness, and her unique place in the whole of mankind, among which she has no equal, namely, that she had a child by the Father in heaven, and such a Child. She herself is unable to find a name for this work, it is too exceedingly great; all she can do is break out in the fervent cry: "They are great things," impossible to describe or define. Hence men have crowded all her glory into a single word, calling her the Mother of God. [The "single word" is the Greek *Theotokos*, God-bearer, a favorite title for Mary in the Eastern Church.] No one can say anything greater of her or to her, though he had as many tongues as there are leaves on the trees, or grass in the fields, or stars in the sky, or sand by the sea. It needs to be pondered in the heart what it means to be the Mother of God.

Propers

ROMAN	LUTHERAN	EPISCOPAL
All-powerful and ever-living God, you raised the sinless Virgin Mary, mother of your Son, body and soul to the glory of heaven. May we see heaven as our final goal and come to share her glory. We ask this through our Lord Jesus Christ, your Son, who lives and reigns with you and the Holy Spirit, one God, for ever and ever.	Almighty God, you chose the Virgin Mary to be the mother of your only Son. Grant that we, who have been redeemed by his blood, may share with her in the glory of your eternal kingdom; through your Son Jesus Christ our Lord, who lives and reigns with you and the Holy Spirit, one God, now and forever.	O God, you have taken to yourself the blessed Virgin Mary, mother of your incarnate Son: Grant that we, who have been redeemed by his blood, may share with her the glory of your eternal kingdom; through Jesus Christ our Lord, who lives and reigns with you, in the unity of the Holy Spirit, one God, now and for ever.
(Text from the English translation of the Roman Missal © 1973, International Committee on English in the Liturgy, Inc. All rights reserved.)		*(Text from the Book of Common Prayer [Proposed], copyright 1977 by Charles Mortimer Guilbert as Custodian of the Standard Book of Common Prayer. All rights reserved. Used by permission.)*
Revelation 11:19a; 12:1-6a, 10ab Psalm 45:10-12b, 16 1 Corinthians 15:20-26 Luke 1:39-56	Isaiah 61:7-11 Psalm 45:11-16 Galatians 4:4-7 Luke 1:46-55	Isaiah 61:10-11 Psalm 34 or 34:1-9 Galatians 4:4-7 Luke 1:46-55 Preface of the Incarnation

Hymn of the Day: "Ye watchers and ye holy ones" (175) or "Blest are the pure in heart" (*SBH* 394)

Prayers: for the poor and the forgotten
for a deeper understanding of the mystery of the Incarnation
for the gift of glad obedience to the word of God
for faithfulness to Christ

Preface: All Saints

Color: White

328

Bernard, Abbot of Clairvaux, 1153

Bernard, the third of seven children, was born of noble lineage at Fontaines-les-Dijon, a village near Dijon, France, in 1090. He studied at a monastic school. His mother died when he was seventeen, and he was deeply affected. In the year 1111 Bernard withdrew from the world and was soon joined by four of his five brothers and other relatives. At Citeaux, a recently founded Benedictine monastery and motherhouse of the Cistercian Order, they followed the strict rule of the Cistercians with excessive asceticism. After three years Bernard was chosen abbot of a new monstery. With twelve companions he chose the valley near the Aube, called Clara Vallisor Clairvaux. There he was ordained priest. He carefully organized and strengthened the new monastery as a model of strict observance and established sixty-eight other houses. From a debate with the great Benedictine monastery at Cluny grew his friendship with its abbot, Peter the Venerable.

In 1130 the Western church split when two rival popes were elected, representing two factions in the College of Cardinals. Bernard sought tirelessly to secure the recognition of Innocent II and eventually of one of his own monks and pupils Eugenius III in 1145 and so to heal the schism.

Skilled in controversy and convinced of the correctness of his views, Bernard led the opposition to those he perceived as heretics, notably the popular teacher Abelard. In 1146-1147 he led the preaching of the second Crusade and was sharply disappointed by its failure.

Yet, despite his authoritarianism, Bernard was a man of spiritual attractiveness, powerful eloquence, zealous in defence of the faith. His theology is characterized by a desire to deepen the inner experience of prayer and contemplation, and he enriched the devotion of the church by his mystical writings and by the hymns he either wrote or inspired, such as "Jesus, the very thought of you," "Light of the anxious heart," "O Sacred Head, now wounded." In his zeal he attacked the luxury of the clergy, the persecution of the Jews, and the abuses of the Roman curia. Renowned as a great preacher, he brought to an end the pre-scholastic era, and he is therefore sometimes called "the Last of the Fathers."

Bernard died at his monastery August 20, 1153. He was canonized in 1174, proclaimed a Doctor of the Church in 1830, and given the title "Doctor Mellifluous" in 1953, the 800th anniversary of his death.

Henri Daniel-Rops. *Bernard of Clairvaux.* New York: Hawthorne, 1964.
———. *Bernard of Clairvaux and the Cistercian Spirit* tr. Claire Lavoie. Kalamazoo, Mich.: Cistercian Publications, 1976.
Jean LeClercq. *The Love of Learning and the Desire for God: A Study of Monastic Culture* tr. Catherine Misrah. New York: Fordham, 1961.
Bruno Scott-James. *Saint Bernard of Clairvaux.* London, 1957.
W. W. Williams. *Saint Bernard of Clairvaux.* Westminster, Md.: Newman, 1952.

Reading

(From *On the Love of God,* VII, by St. Bernard)

The cause of our loving God is God, for he is both origin of our love and its final goal. He is himself the occasion of human love; he also gives the power to love and brings desire to its consummation. In his essential being he is himself the Lovable One, and he provides himself as the object of our love. He desires that our love for him result in our happiness, not that it be empty and void. His love both opens up the way for our love and is our love's reward. How kindly does he lead us in love's way, how generously he returns the love we give, how sweet is he to those who wait for him! He is rich to all who call upon him, for he can give them nothing better than himself. He gave himself to be our Righteousness, and he keeps himself to be our great Reward. He sets himself to the refreshment of our souls and spends himself to free the prisoners. You are good, Lord, to the soul that seeks you. What, then, are you to the soul that finds you? The marvel is, no one can seek you who has not found you already. You desire us to find so that we may seek, to seek so that we may find. We can both seek you and find you, but we can never anticipate you, for though we say, "Early shall my prayer come before you," (Psalm 88:13) a chilly, loveless thing that prayer would be, were it not warmed by your own breath and born of your own Spirit.

Trans. P.H.P., based on a translation by "A Religious of C.S.M.V." (1950) included in the Library of Christian Classics XIII, *Late Medieval Mysticism* ed. Ray C. Petry (Philadelphia: Westminster, n.d.) 59-60.

Propers

ROMAN	LUTHERAN	EPISCOPAL
Heavenly Father, Saint Bernard was filled with zeal for your house and was a radiant light in your Church. By his prayers may we be filled with this spirit of zeal and walk always as children of light. We ask this through our Lord Jesus Christ, your Son, who lives and reigns with you and the Holy Spirit, one God, for ever and ever.	Almighty God, your Holy Spirit gives to one the word of wisdom and to another the word of knowledge, and to another the word of faith. We praise you for the gifts of grace imparted to your servant Bernard, and we pray that by his teaching we may be led to a fuller knowledge of the truth which we have seen in your Son, Jesus Christ our Lord.	Almighty and everlasting God, who kindled the flame of your love in the heart of your servant Bernard: Grant to us, your humble servants, a like faith and power of love; that, as we rejoice in his triumph, we may profit by his example; through Jesus Christ our Lord, who lives and reigns with you and the Holy Spirit, one God, now and for ever.
(Text from the English translation of the Roman Missal © 1973, International Committee on English in the Liturgy, Inc. All rights reserved.)		*(Text from Lesser Feasts and Fasts, Revised Edition, copyright 1973 by Charles Mortimer Guilbert as Custodian of the Standard Book of Common Prayer. All rights reserved. Used by permission.)*
Common of Doctors or Saints (for Religious)	Common of Theologians: Proverbs 3:1-7 Psalm 119:89-104 1 Corinthians 2:6-10, 13-16 Matthew 13:47-52 or common of saints	Psalm 139:1-11 Ecclesiasticus 39:1-10 Psalm 51:11-18 John 15:7-11 Preface of a Saint

Hymn of the Day: "Jesus, the very thought of you" (316)

Prayers: for a deepened life of prayer
       for grace to contemplate the life of Christ
       for wisdom to discern the paths to truth
       for zeal for the Lord's house

Preface: All Saints

Color: White

ST. BARTHOLOMEW, APOSTLE

Bartholomew is listed as one of the twelve apostles in the gospels of Matthew, Mark, and Luke and again in Acts. In these synoptic lists his name immediately follows that of Philip. The list of the Twelve in the Fourth Gospel has the name Nathaniel rather than Bartholomew, and it is sometimes assumed that the apostle's given name was Nathaniel and that Bartholomew was a patronymic, representing the Aramaic for "son of Tolmai" (cf. "Simon Bar-Jonah" in Matthew 16:17). Nathaniel was from the town of Cana in Galilee where Jesus performed his first miracle. He was invited to discipleship by Philip, who told him that he and Andrew and Peter had found the Messiah in the person of Jesus of Nazareth. At first Nathaniel was doubtful, but after a word from Jesus, he followed.

The story of his call (John 1:45-51) is all that is recorded in the New Testament of the life of St. Bartholomew, but there are several traditions about his later labors. He is variously reported to have preached in Asia Minor, Mesopotamia, Persia, and India; in connection with India Eusebius says that Bartholomew left a copy of the Gospel of Matthew in Hebrew which Pantaenus, a missionary of the third century, found there in the hands of the local people. Most of these stories agree that St. Bartholomew spent his last years preaching in Armenia and was flayed and beheaded in Albanus (modern Derbend) on the Caspian coast. (The flayed Bartholomew is portrayed in a prominent place in the Sistine Chapel in Michaelangelo's fresco of the Last Judgment.) The Armenian Church believes that the apostles Bartholomew and Thaddeus were the first to bring the gospel to the Armenians, and that Bartholomew spent a number of years there before his death. The Armenian Church commemorates him on two days in the year: once together with St. Thaddeus and again together with an Armenian martyr.

A very different story of St. Bartholomew's mission appears in the traditions of the Coptic and Ethiopian churches, which also revere him highly, observing his day on August 29. Their accounts tell of his preaching at an oasis in Upper Egypt (there is a special commemoration of this event on November 15), then going among the Berbers where he was rescued from wild beasts by a cannibal, and finally preaching along the coast of North Africa where a local king, Agrippa, had him sewn into a leather bag and dropped into the sea. August 24 has been St. Bartholomew's day on calendars of the Western church since the eighth century, but no reason for the date is known. The Eastern Orthodox churches commemorate him with St. Barnabas on June 11. In European history St. Bartholomew's Day is remembered for the massacre of Protestants which took place on that day in Paris in 1572.

D. Browne, "Who Was Nathaniel?" *Expository Times* XXXVIII (1927), 286.

R. B. Y. Scott, "Who Was Nathaniel?" *Expository Times*, XXXVIII (1927), 93-94.

E. J. Goodspeed. *The Twelve. The Story of the Apostles.* New York: Holt, Rinehart, Winston, 1963 [1957].

Reading

(From *The Living God* by Nathan Söderblom.)

Great men of genius when serving God consciously and with all their hearts belong to the saints. The doctrine of saints lost its importance in Evangelic theology when the cult of the saints was abolished in the name of the Gospel. In this matter I agree with the Roman Church and its theology in so far as the saints are Christian men and women who specially reveal the power of God. But divine power ought not to be assigned in a primitive way to extraordinary cases of suggestion. It ought not to be defined as a miracle, but be regarded in accordance with a Christian conception of God.

A place of honor is due to those saints of religion who have put their whole soul into seeing and apprehending God's will in *history*. It is on that purpose that I put "serving" first and then "apprehending." For in God's kingdom and in the realm of the Spirit and of moral truth, man can see nothing, so long as he is standing as a mere spectator; only those who serve God fully and self-sacrificingly can perceive God's will. In other things one usually wants to look ahead and to understand before undertaking anything. But in God's kingdom it is the reverse.

Where God's rule has penetrated man's heart and life, so that the divine love and righteousness become the main factor, we speak of a saint. . . . Here I give only my definition: a saint is he who reveals God's might. Saints are such as show clearly and plainly in their lives and deeds and in their very being that God lives.

Nathan Söderblom. *The Living God. Basal Forms of Personal Religion.* The Gifford Lectures 1931 (London; Oxford, 1933) 367, 386.

Propers

ROMAN	LUTHERAN	EPISCOPAL
Lord, sustain within us the faith which made Saint Bartholomew ever loyal to Christ. Let your Church be the sign of salvation for all the nations of the world. We ask this through our Lord Jesus Christ, your Son, who lives and reigns with you and the Holy Spirit, one God, for ever and ever.	Almighty and everlasting God, who gave to your apostle Bartholomew grace truly to believe and to preach your Word: Grant that your Church may love what he believed and preach what he taught; through your Son Jesus Christ our Lord, who lives and reigns with you and the Holy Spirit, one God, now and forever.	Almighty and everlasting God, who gave to your apostle Bartholomew grace truly to believe and to preach your Word: Grant that your Church may love what he believed and preach what he taught; through Jesus Christ our Lord, who lives and reigns with you and the Holy Spirit, one God for ever and ever.
(Text from the English translation of the Roman Missal © 1973, International Committee on English in the Liturgy, Inc. All rights reserved.)		*(Text from the Book of Common Prayer [Proposed], copyright 1977 by Charles Mortimer Guilbert as Custodian of the Standard Book of Common Prayer. All rights reserved. Used by permission.)*
Revelation 21:9b-14 Psalm 145:10-13, 17-18 John 1:45-51	Exodus 19:1-6 Psalm 12 1 Corinthians 12:27-31a John 1:43-51	Deuteronomy 18:15-18 Psalm 91 or 91:1-4 1 Corinthians 4:9-15 Luke 22:24-30
		Preface of Apostles

Hymn of the Day: "You servants of God, your Master proclaim" (252)

Prayers: for the Church in Armenia

for grace to recognize the Son of God
for strength and guidance to find ways of serving him

Preface: Apostles

Color: Red

Augustine, Bishop of Hippo, 430

Aurelius Augustinus, generally known as St. Augustine, was born in the town of Tagaste, modern Souk Arrhas in Algeria, November 13, 354. His mother Monica was a Christian, and she attempted to raise him as a Christian but without success. He attended school in Carthage, where he was a serious student but was converted to Manichaeism, a dualistic religion of Persian origin that was popular at the time. He had a son by a concubine, whom he named Adeodatus ("Gift of God").

Sometime after 383 Augustine went to Rome, where he taught rhetoric and continued his studies. In 384 he went to Milan to teach, and there he was drawn by stages to the Catholic faith. First he renounced Manichaeism for a study of Neoplatonism and then came under the influence of St. Ambrose, the Bishop of Milan. After a great struggle his doubts were dispelled, and Ambrose baptized him at the Easter Vigil, 387. His mother died as she and her son were on their way back to North Africa. There Augustine lived a kind of monastic life for several years with a group of his friends. In 391, on a visit to the city of Hippo, he was against his will chosen by the Christians there to be their pastor. From that time until his death Hippo was his residence. He was ordained to the priesthood, four years later consecrated a bishop, and shortly afterwards became the Bishop of Hippo, the city which was second in ecclesiastical importance in Africa. It no longer exists. Augustine served for thirty-five years. He made many time-consuming journeys and yet was responsible for an enormous literary production.

St. Augustine was one of the great teachers of the church, and Christian thinkers, Catholic and Protestant, acknowledge his importance as a theologian and defender of the Christian faith. Of his many writings the most famous are his *Confessions* (ca. 400) and the *City of God* (after 412). The *Confessions* tell of his life and conversion; the *City of God* contains his social and political views, occasioned by the collapse of Rome; a defense of Christianity; and a vision of the ideal Christian society. He also wrote a number of more purely theological works, among them attacks on Manichaeism and polemics against various heresies such as Donatism and Pelagianism. Some of his treatises were commentaries on parts of the Scriptures. His books, sermons, and letters have been published in many languages and many editions, and there is a vast literature about him.

He established the monastic rule of St. Augustine, and more than a millenium later Martin Luther became a monk of the Augustinian Order.

St. Augustine's last years were full of turmoil from the ravages of the Vandal tribes in North Africa. City after city was destroyed, and churches were burned and the clergy scattered. During the Vandals' siege of Hippo in 430, St. Augustine was seized with a fever and died on August 28, 430, the date on which he is now commemorated. His body was later taken to Sardinia, and then in the middle of the eighth century it was moved again to the capital of Lombardy, Pavia, where it now rests in a splendid marble monument in the Church of San Pietro in Ciel d'Oro.

Gerald Bonner. *St. Augustine of Hippo: Life and Controversies*. Philadelphia: Westminster, 1963.
Peter R. L. Brown. *Augustine of Hippo*. Berkeley: University of California, 1967.
J. Burnaby. *Amor Dei: A Study of the Religion of St. Augustine*. London: Hodder and Stoughton, 1938. Reprinted 1960.
Hans von Campenhausen. *The Fathers of the Latin Church* tr. Manfred Hoffmann. Stanford, Cal.: Stanford University Press, 1964.
F. van der Meer. *Augustine the Bishop*. tr. B. Battershaw and G. R. Lamb. New York: Sheed and Ward, 1962.

Reading

(From Augustine's *Confessions*.)

I probed the hidden depth of my soul and drew together and heaped up all my misery in the sight of my heart; there arose a mighty storm, bringing a great deluge of tears. In order that I might freely pour forth those tears, I left Alypius. Solitude was more suitable for weeping, so I moved far enough away that even his presence could not embarrass me. He perceived something of what I was feeling, for I suppose that I had said something and my voice was choked with weeping. I arose, and he remained where we had been sitting, utterly bewildered. I threw myself down under a fig tree, giving full vent to my tears; and the floods of my eyes gushed out the sacrifice that you will not despise. And, not indeed in exactly these words, yet after this manner I spoke to you: "How long, O Lord, how long?" "How long, Lord, will you be angry? Remember not our past sins," for I felt that I was bound fast by them. I sent up these sorrowful words, "How long, how long? Tomorrow and tomorrow? Why not now? Why is there not this moment an end to my wickedness?"

So I was speaking and weeping in the bitter contrition of my heart, when suddenly I heard from a neighboring house a voice, of boy or girl I know not, chanting and often repeating, "Take up and read; take up and read." Instantly my countenance changed. I began to think most intently whether children in any kind of play sing such words, for I could not remember ever having heard them. So, checking the torrent of my tears, I arose, interpreting it to be nothing else but a command from God to open the book and read the first chapter I should find. (I had heard of Antony, who, coming in to church during the reading of the Gospel, received its admonition as if what was being read was spoken to him: "Go, sell all that you have and give to the poor, and you shall have treasure in heaven; and come and follow me." By such a command he was at once converted to you.) Eagerly then I returned to the place where Alypius was sitting, for when I had left there I had laid down a book of the Apostle's writings. I took it, opened it, and in silence read that passage on which my eyes first fell: "Not in reveling and drunkenness, not in debauchery and licentiousness, not in quarreling and jealousy; but put on the Lord Jesus Christ, and make no provision for the flesh to gratify its desires." I did not desire to read further, nor did I need to. Instantly, at the end of this sentence, a light of serenity flooded my heart and all the darkness of doubt vanished away.

Augustine, *Confessions* VIII, 12. trans. P.H.P. based on the translation of Edward B. Pusey. The quotations in the first paragraph are from Psalm 51:17; 6:3; 79:5, 8. The passage from the Apostle is Romans 13:13-14.

Propers

ROMAN	LUTHERAN	EPISCOPAL
Lord, renew in your Church the spirit you gave Saint Augustine. Filled with this spirit, may we thirst for you alone as the fountain of wisdom and seek you as the source of eternal love. We ask this through our Lord Jesus Christ, your Son, who lives and reigns with you and the Holy Spirit, one God, for ever and ever.	Almighty God, your Holy Spirit gives to one the word of wisdom, and to another the word of knowledge, and to another the word of faith. We praise you for the gifts of grace imparted to your servant Augustine, and we pray that by his teaching we may be led to a fuller knowledge of the truth which we have seen in your Son Jesus Christ our Lord.	O Lord our God, the light of minds that know you, the life of the souls that love you, and the strength of the hearts that serve you: Help us, after the example of your servant Saint Augustine, so to know you that we may truly love you, so to love you that we may fully serve you, whom to serve is perfect freedom; through Jesus Christ our Lord, who lives and reigns with you and the Holy Spirit, one God, now and for ever.

ROMAN	LUTHERAN	EPISCOPAL
1 John 4:7-16 Matthew 23:8-12 or Common of Pastors or Doctors	Common of Theologians: Proverbs 3:1-7 Psalm 119:89-104 1 Corinthians 2:6-10, 13-16 John 17:18-23	Psalm 65:1-5 Hebrews 12:22-24, 28-29 Psalm 87 John 17:1-8 Preface of Trinity Sunday

Hymn of the Day: "Jerusalem, my happy home" (331)

Prayers: for the churches in North Africa
for those who search for the truth
for teachers
for those who defend the faith
for a deeper love of the Scriptures

Preface: The Holy Trinity

Color: White

338

John Bunyan, Teacher, 1688

Bunyan was born in Elstow, near Bedford, England, in the heart of the agricultural midlands, November 1628. He was the son of a tinker (a maker and mender of metal pots). He had little schooling and learned his father's trade (although his own description in his autobiography of his humble origins may be something of an exaggeration). His mother died in 1644, and shortly afterward Bunyan's younger sister died. He served in the Parliamentary army 1644-1646 during the Civil War and married a woman, whose name he does not tell us, whose only dowry consisted of two popular Puritan religious books: Arthur Dent's *The Plaine Man's Pathway to Heaven* and Bayly's *The Practice of Piety.*

Bunyan endured a time of intense spiritual torment, turned to the study of the Bible after what he describes as a "dissolute" life. In 1656 his wife died. At last he found peace in a Baptist congregation in Bedford. He became a "mechanic preacher" and worked as a tinker. He remarried. He refused to attend Anglican church services.

At the Restoration in 1660 Bunyan was arrested for preaching without a license, and since he refused to desist, spent twelve years in Bedford jail preaching to his fellow prisoners and studying. Upon his release, he was named pastor of the Bedford Baptist congregation. His first substantial work was a spiritual autobiography, *Grace Abounding to the Chief of Sinners* (1666). It followed a conventional formula for books of its kind, but it was given unusual power through Bunyan's psychological insight and his superb narrative gifts. In 1675 he was again jailed for six months and wrote *The Pilgrim's Progress from This World to That Which Is to Come* (1678, 1684), the most successful allegory in the English language. It attained an enormous popularity, and together with the Authorized Version of the Bible was almost the sole reading matter for many for centuries. In 1680 Bunyan wrote *The Life and Death of Mr. Badman*, a series of narrative episodes using the popular fiction of the time; in 1682 he published *The Holy War*, an allegory of salvation, more complicated than *Pilgrim's Progress*, with social and political overtones.

On August 31, 1688 after riding through heavy rain to settle a quarrel between a father and a son, Bunyan contracted a fever (probably pneumonia) and died. He is buried in Bunhill Fields, the Non-conformists' traditional burying ground. Despite his suffering, he was a warm, sympathetic, large-hearted and lovable man who by his writing increased the pleasure and enriched the devotion of countless readers through three centuries.

Roland M. Frye. *God, Man, and Satan.* Princeton University Press, 1960.
Monica Furlong. *Puritan's Progress. A Study of John Bunyan.* London: Hodder and Stoughton, 1975.
Roger Sharrock. *John Bunyan.* London: Longmans, 1954. Rev. ed., 1968.
Ola E. Winslow. *John Bunyan.* New York: Macmillan 1961.

Reading

(From *Pilgrim's Progress.*)

Now when he [Christian] was got up to the top of the Hill, there came two men running against him amain; the name of the one was Timorous, and the name of the other Mistrust. To whom Christian said, "Sirs, what's the matter you run the wrong way?" Timorous answered that they were going to the City of Sion, and had got up that difficult place; "But," said he, "the further we go, the more danger we meet with, wherefore we turned, and are going back again."

"Yes," said Mistrust, "for just before us lie a couple of lions in the way, whether sleeping or waking we know not and we could not think, if we came within reach, but they would presently pull us in pieces."

Christian. Then said Christian, "You make me afraid, but whither shall I fly to be safe? If I go back to mine own country, that is prepared for fire and brimstone, and I shall certainly perish there. If I can get to the Celestial City, I am sure to be in safety there. I must venture: to go back is nothing but death, to go forward is fear of death, and life everlasting beyond it. I will yet go forward." So Mistrust and Timorous ran down the Hill, and Christian went on his way.

Now I saw in my dream, that these two men [Christian and Hopeful] went in at the Gate; and lo, as they entered they were transfigured, and they had raiment put on that shone like gold. There was also that met them, with harps and crowns, and gave them to them, the harp to praise withal, and the crowns in token of honour. Then I heard in my dream, that all the bells in the City rang again for joy; and that it was said unto them, *"Enter ye into the joy of your Lord."* I also heard the men themselves, that they sang with a loud voice, saying, *"Blessing, honour, glory, and power, be to him that sitteth upon the throne and to the Lamb for ever and ever."*

Now just as the Gates were opened to let in the men, I looked in after them; and behold, the City shone like the sun, the streets also were paved with gold, and in them walked many men with crowns on their heads, palms in their hands, and golden harps to sing praises withal.

There were also of them that had wings, and they answered one another without intermission, saying, *Holy, Holy, Holy, is the Lord.* And after that, they shut up the Gates: which when I had seen, I wished myself among them.

John Bunyan, *Pilgrim's Progress from this world to that which is to come* (Baltimore: Penguin, 1965) 75-76, 203-204, copyright © Roger Sharrock, 1975. Used by permission of Penguin Books Ltd.

Propers: Artists or Theologians

Hymn of the Day: "All who would valiant be" (498)

Prayers: for courage to set out in quest of spiritual truth
        for strength to endure the pilgrimage
        for grace to win heaven at last
        for writers who explore religious truth and narrative skill

Color: White

September 2

Nikolai Frederik Severin Grundtvig
Bishop, Renewer of the Church, 1872

Together with Kierkegaard, Grundtvig is the most notable figure in Danish theology in the nineteenth century. He was born in a parsonage in Udby, Zeeland, September 8, 1783, the youngest of five children of Johan and Catherine Grundtvig. His father was untouched by the rationalism emanating from Germany at that time; he was a man of quiet, orthodox Lutheran piety. His mother came from a long line of talented and capable people, and she taught her own children well.

At nine years old, Grundtvig left for boarding school at Vejle for six years, after which he enrolled at the gymnasium at Aarhus. In 1800 he entered the University of Copenhagen to study theology and received his degree in theology in three years. At the university Grundtvig had absorbed the spirit of the Enlightenment—its joy, confidence, and optimism. He discovered ancient mythology which opened to him new worlds of thought revealed in the ancient Eddas and Icelandic sagas. His interest in poetry was also reawakened, with the conviction that poetry is the appropriate medium to express the spirit.

After receiving his theological degree, Grundtvig lived with his family doing historical study. In 1805 he was appointed tutor in Langeland, where he fell in love with the twenty-six year old wife of his employer. In 1808 he left the Langeland estate and returned to Copenhagen to publish the *Mythology of the North* in which he argued that ancient myth expresses the spirit of humankind in a way that science cannot do.

Grundtvig's father became ill and asked his son to assist him in the large Udby parish. His first sermon, March 17, 1910, was a scathing attack on the clergy and the Danish church, "Why Has the Lord's Word Disappeared from His House?" For it he was given an official rebuke, and a spiritual crisis followed as he anguished over whether he was awakened and who was he to awaken Denmark. Nonetheless he petitioned for ordination, was ordained in May 1811, and became curate to his father, who died in 1813. From 1813 to 1820 he was in Copenhagen writing, unable to receive a call. He made a version of *Beowulf* (1820) that encouraged research into Anglo-Saxon literature. At last in 1821 he became pastor of Praesto parish in Zeeland. He then moved to Our Savior's Church in Copenhagen 1822-1826 when he resigned following a controversy over his attack upon H. N. Clausen who, Grundtvig said, treated Christianity as a philosophical idea rather than as historical revelation handed down in a living chain of sacramental tradition in Baptism and Holy Communion. He lived as a writer from 1826 to 1839. The first of his five volumes of hymns was published in 1837.

Finally, in 1839 he was appointed chaplain to a home for aged women at Vartov, where he remained for the rest of his life. Here he was able to study and to make use of his reflections and hymns, surrounded by his friends. His writings on education inspired the founding of folk high schools following 1844. He was active in the movement leading to the introduction of parliamentary government in 1849. In 1861 he was given the rank and title of bishop, although without a diocese. He died September 2, 1872, aged 89. He is honored as a scholar and translator; a poet, the father of Danish hymnody (he composed more than a thousand hymns); a champion of political freedom and liberty in church and state; a supporter of popular education to awaken a love of life. There is a church in Copenhagen dedicated to his memory.

Immigrant Danish Lutherans in America eventually formed two separate bodies, reflecting two parties of the Church of Denmark. One group (the "happy Danes") with the more liberal Grundtvigian outlook formed what was to become the American Evangelical Lutheran Church which later merged into the Lutheran Church in America (1962). The other with a more pietistic view (the "gloomy Danes") formed the United Evangelical Lutheran Church (1896), which merged to form the American Lutheran Church in 1960.

G. Everett Arden. Four Northern Lights. Minneapolis: Augsburg, 1964.
Jens Christian Kjaer. History of the Church of Denmark. Blair, NE: Lutheran Publishing House, 1945.
Johannes Knudsen. Danish Rebel. Philadelphia: Muhlenberg, 1955.
_____, ed. N. F. S. Grundtvig: Selected Writings. Philadelphia: Fortress, 1976.
Hal Koch. Grundtvig. tr. Llewellyn Jones. Yellow Springs, O.: Antioch Press, 1952.
P. G. Lindhardt. Grundtvig: An Introduction. London: SPCK, 1951.
Ernest Nielsen. N. F. S. Grundtvig: An American Study. Rock Island, Ill.: Augustana Book Concern, 1955.

Reading

(From a sermon by N. F. S. Grundtvig)

The Spirit of the Son, our Lord Jesus Christ, which proceeds from the Father . . . reflects the glory of God, so that the church feels the real presence of our Lord Jesus Christ, although the world does not see him. He reveals himself spiritually for all those who hold fast his word with proof as plain as when he revealed himself to his friends after the resurrection and spoke to them about matters that pertain to the kingdom of God. He tells us that he can and will dwell in his church and walk in it as the only-begotten Son from eternity in all the regenerated sons and daughters whom the heavenly Father and the Son embrace, sharing his glory.

Then, and only then, God's kingdom comes to us, not so that one can point to it and say: look here or look there, as one points to the great nations, but in such a way that the whole church lives in it, saying and singing: Now we know that God's kingdom is truly righteousness, peace, and joy in the Holy Spirit. It comes as the Spirit proclaims in deeds and truths what is to come through that which is now worked and created in us. Then we cannot for a moment doubt that what now lives in us, a real and joyful power, though concealed, shall be revealed when he who is our life comes again even as he ascended. Thus it follows that the sufferings of this present time are not worth comparing with the glory that is to be revealed to us, just as surely as this glory has descended and rests upon us.

Therefore, Christian friends, we will not be fearful or despondent in the great transition period from darkness to light, from death to life, and from clarity to clarity, for it holds true throughout the lives of all God's children in this world, and not only during their last days, that they shall not fear evil as they walk through the valley of the shadow of death. We who walked in darkness have seen a great light, and he who is the light of the world is with us. . . .

Fourth Sunday after Easter, 1855
N. F. S. Grundtvig. Selected Writings ed. Johannes Knudsen (Philadelphia: Fortress, 1976) 115-116. Used by permission.

344 September 4

Propers: Renewers of the Church
or Renewers of Society

Hymn of the Day: "Built on a rock the church shall stand" (365)
or "O day full of grace" (161). For a translation
of "O day full of grace" which is much closer to
the original text by Grundtvig, see *N.F.S.
Grundtvig, Selected Writings* ed. Johannes Knudsen
(Philadelphia: Fortress, 1976) 121-122.

Prayers: for the Church and people of Denmark
for public schools
for poets and students of theology
for a deeper regard for the church and its sacraments

Color: White

Albert Schweitzer
Missionary to Africa, 1965

Schweitzer, a theologian, philosopher, organist, authority on Bach, physician, and missionary, was born January 14, 1875 at Kaysersberg, Upper Alsace (now France), the eldest son of a Lutheran pastor. The family soon moved to Günsbach, which became Schweitzer's European home until his death. He studied philosophy and theology at Strasbourg and also served as organist. In 1899 he received his doctorate in philosophy and was lecturer in philosophy and preacher at St. Nicholas' Church. He was ordained January 29, 1900 and later that year received his doctorate in theology. He studied organ under Charles-Marie Widor in Paris, who encouraged him to write a study of the life and art of Bach; the book that resulted was published in 1905 and the English translation (*J. S. Bach*) in 1911. His *Quest of the Historical Jesus* (1906, English 1910), in which he suggested that the attitudes of Jesus were shaped by his expectation of the immanent end of the world, established Schweitzer as a leading figure in theological studies.

In 1905 Schweitzer announced his intention to become a mission doctor. He resigned his university appointments and abandoned a promising career. In 1912 he married Helene Bresslau, a scholar and a nurse, and in the following year received his doctorate in medicine. On Good Friday 1913 the husband and wife set out for Lambarene in Gabon Province of French Equatorial Africa, and on the banks of the Ogooue River they built a hospital.

During World War I, he was interned there as an enemy alien and was held as a prisoner in France. While there, he turned his attention to world problems and wrote the two-volume *Philosophy of Civilization* (1923) in which he set forth his "reverence for life" in all its forms, which he believed was essential for the survival of civilization. After his release from the internment camp, he was preacher at St. Nicholas' Church until April, 1921. In 1924 he returned to Africa to rebuild the ruined hospital, which he moved two miles up the river. A leper colony was added. In 1952 Schweitzer won the Nobel Prize for Peace for his work on behalf of the "brotherhood of nations."

Despite his life in Africa, Schweitzer never wholly abandoned his former interests. He continued to write and to lecture throughout Europe, to make recordings, and edit the works of Bach. In 1958 he broadcast from Oslo three appeals called *Peace or Atomic War?* His autobiography, *Out of My Life and Thought,* was published in 1933.

Schweitzer has been criticized as patriarchal and autocratic, primitive in his medical practice. Nonetheless, he remains the century's greatest humanitarian, who by adherence to standards that the world found hard to accept prodded its conscience and inspired generations with his example of sacrifice in response to the gospel parable of the rich man and Lazarus.

Schweitzer died September 4, 1965 in his ninety-first year and was buried at his hospital beside his wife.

James Brabazon. *Albert Schweitzer: A Biography.* New York: Putnams, 1975.
David L. Dungan. "Reconsidering Albert Schweitzer," *Christian Century* XCII, 32 (October 8, 1975), 874-880.
George Seaver. *Albert Schweitzer. The Man and His Mind.* New York: Harper and Row, 1947.

David Livingstone

The famed explorer was born March 19, 1813 at Blantyre, Scotland to a poor family who raised him strictly, with a zeal for education and a sense of mission. He was ordained as a missionary in 1840. He arrived in South Africa in the following year (he had originally intended to go to China but was prevented by the opium wars) and pushed northward in search of converts. By 1849 he acquired some degree of fame as a surveyor and scientist. He saw Christianity, commerce, and civilization as three forces that together would open Africa. He constantly sought the abolition of the slave trade.

In 1853 he began a major expedition to the interior of Africa and discovered the Victoria Falls in 1855. He returned to England in 1856 to find himself, much to his surprise, a national hero.

In 1858 he organized an expedition to the Zambezi, but it did not go well. His wife died. His eldest son, who had gone to the United States was killed in the Civil War. The expedition was eventually recalled.

In 1866 he began his quest for the source of the Nile, which was an object of great fascination to the nineteenth century. Reports of his death circulated, and a newspaper correspondent, Henry M. Stanley was sent by his publisher to find Livingstone. They met in 1871, travelled together for a while.

Livingstone died May 1, 1873 at Chitambo's Village, in what is now Zambia. He was buried in Westminster Abbey April 18, 1874.

Cecil Northcott. *David Livingstone: His Triumph, Decline, and Fall.* Philadelphia: Westminster, 1974
Oliver Ransford. *David Livingstone. The Dark Interior.* London: John Murray, 1978.
George Seaver. *David Livingstone: His Life and Letters.* New York: Harper, 1957.

Reading

The important thing is that we are part of life. We are born of other lives; we possess the capacities to bring still other lives into existence. In the same way, if we look into a microscope we see cell producing cell. So nature compels us to recognize the fact of mutual dependence, each life necessarily helping other lives which are linked to it. In the very fibers of our being, we bear within ourselves the fact of the solidarity of life. Our recognition of it expands with thought. Seeing its presence within ourselves, we realize how closely we are linked with others of our kind. We might like to stop here, but we cannot. Life demands that we see through to the solidarity of all life which we can in any degree recognize as having some similarity to the life that is in us.

To have reverence in the face of life is to be in the grip of the eternal, unoriginated, forward-pushing will, which is the foundation of all being. It raises us above all intellectual knowledge of external objects, and grafts us on to the tree which is assured against drought because it is planted by the rivers of water. All vital religious feeling flows from reverence for life and for the necessity and for the needs for ideals which is implicit in life. In reverence for life religious feeling lies before us in its most elemental and most profound form, in which it is no longer involved in explanations of the objective world, nor has it anything to do with such, but is pure religious feeling founded altogether in implicit necessity and therefore devoid of care about results.

"The Ethics of the Reverence for Life," *Christendom* I, 2 (Winter 1936), 237.
Civilization and Ethics. Part II of *The Philosophy of Civilization* tr. C. T. Campion (New York: Macmillan, 1929) 223.

Propers: Saints
    (or missionaries)

Hymn of the Day: "Hope of the world, thou Christ of great
    compassion" (493)

Prayers: for the spirit of selfless sacrificial service
    for those who relieve suffering
    for strength to share the pain of the world
    for a recognition of the interrelatedness of all life

Color: White

348

John Chrysostom
Bishop of Constantinople, 407

John was born about the year 349 in Antioch, one of the largest and most cosmopolitan cities of the world at that time. His father, who died when John was very young, was a well-to-do army general; his mother Anthusa was a Christian. The name Chrysostom—"golden-mouthed"—first appears in the sixth century and has practically supplanted his given name. (The 1928 Book of Common Prayer calls one prayer "A Prayer of St. Chrysostom.")

John studied for a career in the law under the well-known pagan philosopher Libanius, who regarded him as his most brilliant student. He also came under the influence of the biblical scholar Diodorus, however, and at the age of eighteen he turned away from his proposed career and was baptized a Christian at Easter ca. 368 and ordained a lector in the church. He first thought to become a monk, and for several years he did live an ascetic life as a hermit. He returned to Antioch, however, and served as deacon under the saintly and beloved Bishop Melitius 381-386.

In 386 John was ordained to the priesthood and became an assistant to Melitius' successor, Bishop Flavian of Antioch. John regularly preached in the cathedral, where he became famous for his sermons. He proved himself an excellent expositor of Scripture, able to understand the author's meaning and to make practical application of the message, in opposition to the allegorical interpretation which was then popular. In 387 he preached a dramatic series of sermons "On the Statutes" to the people of Antioch as they awaited the imperial decree of punishment for the rioting in which they had destroyed the statues of the emperor. During the twelve years that he preached in Antioch, his themes included pleas for social justice, opposition to slavery, the equality of women and the sanctity of the home, insistence on the role of laypeople in worship. His sermons were delivered within the framework of the church year, and some of his sermons on particular festivals or occasions are among the most famous. An Easter sermon of his is still read every year in the Easter services of the Eastern Orthodox churches.

In 398 John was unexpectedly selected to be the Bishop of Constantinople, one of the most important posts in the church, and he was consecrated bishop on February 26 of that year. In Constantinople, John of Antioch won the affection and admiration of many by his simple life, his honesty and charity, and the eloquence of his sermons. These same qualities made him many enemies too, and it was especially his attempts to reform the clergy of the capital and his denunciation of corruption in the court that turned powerful people against him. He ousted one deacon for murder, another for adultery.

In 403, the Empress Eudoxia, previously his admirer, conspired with Theophilus of Alexandria to have John condemned on false charges and banished from the city. The uproar among the people caused by this Synod of the Oak, reinforced by an accident in the palace (probably Eudoxia had a miscarriage) which was interpreted by the Empress and others as a sign from God, brought him back. But since he was just as uncompromising as before, he was forbidden to enter his cathedral. When some three thousand catechumens gathered at the Baths of Constantine for baptism, soldiers broke up the service and the waters ran red with blood.

John was exiled to the obscure town of Cucusus in Armenia. He went in exile on June 24, 404, and from there he continued to wield great influence, chiefly through correspondence with friends back in the capital and church leaders in other parts of the world; over two hundred of these letters are still extant. Pope Innocent I supported John and condemned the Synod of the Oak as illegal. The papal envoys to Constantinople were treated rudely, jailed, and then sent back to Rome. The pope broke off communication with all of Chrysostom's chief opponents. Despite support by the people of Constantinople, the pope, and the entire Western church, the Emperor in 407 ordered John moved to a still more isolated spot, Pityus. John Chrysostom died September 14, 407 at Comana in Pontus from the rigors of that journey—he was forced to march on foot, bare-headed in severe weather. His last words were "Glory to God for all things."

St. John Chrysostom was one of the great preachers of Christendom, and he is traditionally regarded as the best preacher in the history of the church. His sermons and other writings, including his best-known book, *On the Dignity of the Priesthood,* have repeatedly been edited and translated; they are available in many languages and different editions today.

On January 27, 438 John Chrysostom's body was brought to Constantinople and placed in the Church of the Apostles, as Emperor Theodosius II did penance for his parents' offenses against him. In 1204 the Venetians plundered the city and sent the remains of Chrysostom to Rome; his grave is still shown in the choir chapel of St. Peter's Basilica. January 27, the date of the moving of his body to Constantinople is the date that has been observed in the Western church for the commemoration of St. John Chrysostom because the date of his death was already a festival, Holy Cross Day. In the East his chief day of commemoration is November 13, but he is remembered on other days as well, including January 27. The new Roman calendar remembers him on September 13; the Episcopal calendar keeps his festival on January 27.

The principal liturgy of the Eastern Orthodox Churches bears the name of St. John Chrysostom, although its main features had developed before his lifetime and it probably reached its final form after his death.

P. Chrysostomos Baur. *John Chrysostom and His Time* tr. M. Gonzaga. 2 vols. Westminster, Md.: Newman, 1960-1961.
Hans von Campenhausen. *The Fathers of the Greek Church* tr. Stanley Godman (New York: Pantheon, 1959) 129-144.

Reading

(From a sermon by St. John Chrysostom)

The waters have risen and severe storms are upon us, but we do not fear drowning, for we stand firmly upon a rock. Let the sea rage, it cannot break the rock. Let the waves rise, they cannot sink Jesus' boat. What are we to fear? Death? *Life to me means Christ, and death is gain.* Exile? *The earth and its fullness belong to the Lord.* The confiscation of our goods? *We brought nothing into this world, and we shall surely take nothing from it.* I have only contempt for the world's threats, I find its blessings laughable. I have no fear of poverty, no desire for wealth. I am not afraid of death nor do I long to live, except for your good. I concentrate therefore on the present situation, and I urge you, my friends, to have confidence.

Do you not hear the Lord saying, *Where two or three are gathered in my name, there am I in their midst?* Will he be absent, then, when so many people united in love are gathered together? I have his promise; I am surely not going to rely on my own strength! I have what he has written; that is my staff, my security, my peaceful harbor. Let the world be in upheaval. I hold to his promise and read his message; that is my protecting wall and garrison. What message? *Know that I am with you always, until the end of the world!*

If Christ is with me, whom shall I fear? Though the waves and the sea and the anger of princes are roused against me, they are less to me than a spider's web. Indeed, unless you, my brothers, had detained me, I would have left this very day. For I always say, *Lord, your will be done;* not what this fellow or that would have me do, but what you want me to do. That is my strong tower, my immovable rock, my staff that never gives way. If God wants something, let it be done! If he wants me to stay here, I am grateful. But wherever he wants me to be, I am no less grateful.

Yet where I am, there you are too, and where you are, I am. For we are a single body, and the body cannot be separated from the head nor the head from the body. Distance separates us, but love unites us, and death itself cannot divide us. For though my body die, my soul will live and be mindful of my people.

You are my fellow citizens, my fathers, my brothers, my sons, my limbs, my body. You are my light, sweeter to me than the visible light. For what can the rays of the sun bestow on me that is comparable to your love? The sun's light is useful in my earthly life, but your love is fashioning a crown for me in the life to come.

Propers

ROMAN	LUTHERAN	EPISCOPAL
Father, the strength of all who trust in you, you made John Chrysostom renowned for his eloquence and heroic in his sufferings. May we learn from his teaching and gain courage from his patient endurance. We ask this through our Lord Jesus Christ, your Son, who lives and reigns with you and the Holy Spirit, one God, for ever and ever.	God of grace and might, we praise you for your servant John Chrysostom, to whom you gave gifts to make the good news known by his eloquence and his courage. Raise up, we pray, in every country, heralds and evangelists of your kingdom, so that the world may know the immeasurable riches of our Savior, Jesus Christ our Lord. Common of Missionaries (i.e. heralds of the kingdom, preachers)	(January 27) O God, who gave to your servant John eloquence to declare your righteousness in the great congregation, and courage to bear reproach for the honor of your Name: Mercifully grant to all bishops and pastors such excellence in preaching and faithfulness in ministering your Word, that your people may be partakers with them of the glory that shall be revealed; through Jesus Christ our Lord, who lives and reigns with you and the Holy Spirit, one God, now and for ever.

ROMAN	LUTHERAN	EPISCOPAL
Common of Pastors or Doctors	Isaiah 62:1-7 Psalm 48 Romans 10:11-17 Luke 24:44-53	Psalm 40:4-11 Jeremiah 1:4-10 Psalm 49:1-8 Luke 21:12-15 Preface of a Saint

Hymn of the Day: "Awake, O Spirit of the watchmen" (382)
    (St. Chrysostom is the name of two tunes in
    SBH: 504 and 507)

Prayers: for the Patriarch of Constantinople
    for preachers of the Gospel
    for strength to endure suffering with Christ

for those who are persecuted for their bold witness to
the Christian life.

Preface: Epiphany

Color: White

HOLY CROSS DAY

In the year 335, the emperor Constantine built two basilicas in Jerusalem. One of the churches was on the supposed site of the Holy
Sepulchre, and in the course of excavating for this church, the story
is, the cross on which Christ was crucified was discovered. Cyril of
Jerusalem—who seems to be reliable—writing in the year 350, says
that the cross of Christ was found at Jerusalem during the time of
Constantine. According to a less reliable tradition, St. Helena, Constantine's mother, was the one who discovered the true cross. Not one
but three crosses were found, it is said, and Helena was able to decide
which one belonged to Christ by applying the three to a dead man.
One brought the dead man to life, and this was declared obviously
to be the cross of Christ.

The relic of the true cross was preserved in a silver receptacle in
the basilica of the Holy Sepulchre after pieces were taken away by
pilgrims and distributed throughout the world. A Spanish pilgrim
lady, Egeria, who made a journey to Jerusalem ca, 385-388 and who
describes the ceremonies of the church there, tells of the practice of
the veneration of the cross on Good Friday and of how the deacons
guarded it so that the pilgrims who kissed it would not bite out
pieces to carry away.

The Festival of the Exaltation of the Holy Cross, first clearly mentioned by Pope Sergius (687-701), commemorates the exposition of
the true cross at Jerusalem in 629 by the emperor Heraclius after he
had recovered it from the Persians who had captured it when they
destroyed the church of the Holy Sepulchre in 614. This exposition
seems actually to have taken place in the spring but it was celebrated

in the fall at the time of the anniversary of the dedication of the church.

There was on May 3 another festival of the cross called the "Invention of the Cross" or the "Finding of the Cross" (from the Latin *invenio*, "I find"). This celebration seems to have originated in Gaul in the seventh century and was celebrated in Rome by the beginning of the eighth century. It recalled the discovery of the cross by St. Helena. It was always treated as a secondary celebration and was suppressed by the Roman Catholic Church in 1960. The Eastern churches originally commemorated the finding of the cross together with the consecration of Constantine's two basilicas.

Holy Cross Day became very popular in northern Europe and remained on Lutheran calendars long after the Reformation. Holy Cross has been a popular name for Lutheran churches in America. The new Roman Catholic calendar calls September 14 "The Triumph of the Cross," and it is a festival of Christ's passion and cross, giving opportunity for a joyous commemoration of his redeeming death with a festal emphasis not appropriate during Holy Week.

Holy Cross Day, the legends of the finding of the true cross and the adoration of the wood of the cross apart, is an occasion for the church to consider what Luther called the "theology of the cross," the divinely-chosen way of humility and service, of death as the path to life and salvation.

Moreover, in the past, and on Episcopal and Roman Catholic calendars still, Holy Cross Day determined the autumnal Ember Days (the Wednesday, Friday, and Saturday following Holy Cross Day). These were originally agricultural festivals kept three, then four times during the year (following Pentecost, Holy Cross, and St. Lucy's Day—December 13; the Wednesday, Friday, and Saturday following the First Sunday in Lent were added later.) The autumn Ember Days were at the occasion of the vintage in Rome and were a time for prayer for the fruits of the earth.

Until the time of Constantine (fourth century) the symbol of the cross was rarely used by Christians because of the need for secrecy and also because of the shame associated with crucifixion. In the fifth century in Syria there is evidence that the cross was placed on the altar during mass, but this use did not appear in the West until much later. During the fifth and sixth centuries the use of a glorified cross is common, studded with jewels. It is portrayed as splendid and royal, a throne for Christ, triumphant over the shame attached to the cross in the first centuries. The first representation of the body of Christ on the cross is found in the fifth century. He is usually seen alive, clothed in the priestly and royal vestments, reigning from the cross. By the sixth century processional crosses were employed and were set up at but not on the altar.

Devotional attention was drawn to the cross, which was treated as a living thing, a tree of life that corresponded to the tree in the Garden by which death entered the world, a creature that could be addressed and asked to bear gently the body of him who hung upon it. (See the hymn, "Sing, my tongue, the glorious battle," 118). Always throughout these centuries, the cross is a sign of salvation and victory. The crucifix increased in popularity during the Middle Ages and the figure of Christ was shown in the agony of death. A "passion mysticism" arose, which emphasized the suffering Servant of God.

The use of the sign of the cross—the tracing of a cross on the forehead with the thumb or forefinger—was already customary in the second century in private devotion. By the fourth century it had come into wider use in the liturgy together with a signing of the breast in addition to the forehead. In the eighth century a signing of the lips was added also.

The making of the sign of the cross with two or three fingers was introduced in the East in the sixth century to combat the Monophysites, who said the Christ had only one nature, or to emphasize belief in the Holy Trinity. The practice passed into the West and was introduced into the Mass in the ninth century.

The large sign of the cross from forehead to breast to shoulders was used in private devotion in the fifth century, in monasteries by the tenth century. In the thirteenth century Innocent III directed that the shoulders be touched from right to left with three fingers (as in the East still); later the direction was changed to left to right and with the whole hand. In the West, the usual accompanying words are "In the name of the father and of the Son and of the Holy Spirit." In the East, there are various formulas such as "Holy God, Holy Mighty One, Holy Immortal one, have mercy on us."

The meaning of the sign is variously interpreted. It is a recalling of the sign made at baptism, it is a sealing with the sign of Christ, it is an invocation of God's grace. George Herbert in his poem "The Crosse" suggests another meaning:

With but four words, my words, *Thy will be done.*
The four words correspond to the four points of the sign of the cross. forehead, breast, and shoulders.

Liturgy: The Holy Cross. Vol. 1, no. 1. Washington: The Liturgical Conference, 1980.
Romano Guardini. *Sacred Signs* tr. Grace Branham. St. Louis: Pio Decimo, 1956.
N. Laliberte and Edward N. West. *The History of the Cross.* New York: Macmillan, 1960.
Patrick Regan. "Veneration of the Cross," *Worship* 52:1 (January 1978) 2-13.

Reading

(From *Centuries* by Thomas Traherne.)

The Cross is the abyss of wonders, the centre of desires, the school of virtues, the house of wisdom, the throne of love, the theatre of joys, and the place of sorrows; It is the root of happiness, and the gate of Heaven.

Of all the things in Heaven and Earth it is the most peculiar. It is the most exalted of all objects. It is an Ensign lifted up for all nations, to it shall the Gentiles seek, His rest shall be glorious: the dispersed of Judah shall be gathered together to it, from the four corners of the earth. If Love be the weight of the Soul, and its object the centre, all eyes and hearts may convert and turn unto this Object: cleave unto this centre, and by it enter into rest. There we might see all nations assembled with their eyes and hearts upon it. There we may see God's goodness, wisdom and power: yea His mercy and anger displayed. There we may see man's sin and infinite value. His hope and fear, his misery and happiness. There we might see the Rock of Ages, and the Joys of Heaven. There we may see a Man loving all the world, and a God dying for mankind. There we may see all types and ceremonies, figures and prophecies. And all kingdoms adoring a malefactor: An innocent malefactor, yet the greatest in the world. There we may see the most distant things in Eternity united: all mysteries at once couched together and explained. The only reason why this Glorious Object is so publicly admired by Churches and

Kingdoms, and so little thought of by particular men, is because it is truly the most glorious. It is the Root of Comforts and the Fountain of Joys. It is the only supreme and sovereign spectacle in all Worlds. It is a Well of Life beneath in which we may see the face of Heaven above: and the only mirror, wherein all things appear in their proper colours: that is, sprinkled in the blood of our Lord and Saviour.

The Cross of Christ is the Jacob's ladder by which we ascend into the highest heavens. There we see joyful Patriarchs, expecting Saints, Prophets ministering, Apostles publishing, and Doctors teaching, all Nations concentering, and Angels praising. That Cross is a tree set on fire with invisible flame, that illuminateth all the world. The flame is Love: the Love in His bosom who died on it. In the light of which we see how to possess all the things in Heaven and Earth after His similitude. For He that suffered on it was the Son of God as you are: tho' He seemed only a mortal man. He had acquaintance and relations as you have, but He was a lover of Men and Angels. Was he not the Son of God; and Heir of the whole World? To this poor, bleeding, naked Man did all the corn and wine, and oil, and gold and silver in the world minister in an invisible manner, even as He was exposed lying and dying upon the Cross.

Here you learn all patience, meekness, self-denial, courage, prudence, zeal, love, charity, contempt of the world, joy, penitence, contrition, modesty, fidelity, constancy, perseverance, contentation, holiness, and thanksgiving: With whatsoever else is requisite for a Man, a Christian, or a King. This Man bleeding here was tutor to King Charles the Martyr: and Great Master to St. Paul, the convert who learned of His activity, and zeal unto all nations. Well therefore may we take up with this prospect, and from hence behold all the things in Heaven and Earth. Here we learn to imitate Jesus in His love unto all.

Thomas Traherne, *Centuries* intro. by John Farrar (New York: Harper, 1960) 28-30.

Propers

ROMAN	LUTHERAN	EPISCOPAL
God our Father, in obedience to you your only Son accepted death on the cross for the salvation of mankind. We acknowledge the mystery of the cross on earth. May we receive the gift of redemption in heaven. We ask this through our Lord Jesus Christ, your Son, who lives and reigns with you and the Holy Spirit, one God, for ever and ever.	Almighty God, your Son Jesus Christ was lifted high upon the cross that he might draw the whole world to himself. Grant that we who glory in his death for our salvation may also glory in his call to take up our cross and follow him; through your Son, Jesus Christ our Lord, who lives and reigns with you and the Holy Spirit, one God, now and forever.	Almighty God, whose Son our Savior Jesus Christ was lifted high upon the cross that he might draw the whole world to himself: Mercifully grant that we, who glory in the mystery of our redemption, may have grace to take up our cross and follow him; who lives and reigns with you and the Holy Spirit, one God, in glory everlasting.

ROMAN

Numbers 21:4-9
   Psalm 78:1-2, 34-38
Philippians 2:6-11
John 3:13-17

LUTHERAN

Isaiah 45:21-25
   Psalm 98:1-5
2 Corinthians 1:18-24
John 12:20-33

EPISCOPAL

Isaiah 45:21-25
   Psalm 98
   or 98:1-4
Philippians 2:5-11
   or Galatians 6:14-18
John 12:31-36a

Preface of Holy Week

Hymn of the Day: "The head that once was crowned with thorns" (173)
   or "We sing the praise of him who died" (344)

Prayers: for grace to choose the way of the Cross
   for humility
   for the knowledge that suffering can be redemptive
   for the gift of hope for all who bear the cross

Preface: Passion

Color: Red

Dag Hammarskjold, Peacemaker, 1961

Dag Hjalmar Agne Carl Hammarskjold was born July 29, 1905 at Jonkoping, Sweden, the son of the Prime Minister. He studied law and economics at the universities of Uppsala and Stockholm and taught political economics at Stockholm, 1933-1936. He joined the Swedish civil service in the Ministry of Finance and subsequently became president of the board of the Bank of Sweden. From 1947 he served in the Ministry of Foreign Affairs and was responsible for dealing with problems of trade. In 1951 he was appointed Minister of State with the functions of deputy Foreign Minister.

In 1951 he was chosen vice-chairman of the Swedish delegation to the United Nations and was made chairman in the following year. On April 10, 1953, following the resignation of Trygve Lie of Norway as Secretary General, Hammarskjold was elected for a five-year term. In September 1957 he was unanimously elected to a second five-year term. During his first term he had to deal with the end of the Korean War, problems in the Middle East, and the crisis over the Suez Canal.

The Belgian Congo became independent June 30, 1960, and civil war followed. Hammarskjold sent a United Nations force to suppress the violence. On a mission to President Moise Tschombe of the province of Katanga to negotiate a cease-fire between the United Nations and Katanga forces, Hammarskjold was killed in a plane crash September 18, 1961, near Ndola, Northern Rhodesia, now Zambia.

Hammarskjold surprised and bewildered the world with the posthumous publication of a devotional notebook, *Markings*. Not until the appearance of that book did people see that he was not only a man of diplomacy but a man with a deep spiritual life as well. He effected in his life a remarkable combination of the contemplative life with a life of action in the world. He was a Christian, the depths of whose spiritual life were entirely unsuspected until the publication of *Markings*. Not all critics were sympathetic with his internal struggle nor with his sense of vocation; it was apparently embarrassing to some to learn that Hammarskjold took Christianity seriously. But the book is a compelling record of Hammarskjold's spiritual wrestling with the reality of the Christian revelation and its implications for his life. He combined secular work, primarily diplomatic service, with a deep desire for personal spirituality, and from that struggle produced a remarkable devotional book. Working out his faith in service of humankind, he strove to learn more about the nature and the work of God. As he wrote in *Markings* (p. 122), "In our era, the road to holiness necessarily passes through the world of action."

Gustav Aulen. *Dag Hammarskjold's White Book.* Philadelphia: Fortress, 1959.
Wilder Foote, ed. *Dag Hammarskjold, Servant of Peace. A Selection of His Speeches and Statements.* New York: Harper, 1962.
Henry P. Van Deusen. *Dag Hammarskjold: The Statesman and His Faith.* New York: Harper and Row, 1966.
Brian Urquhart. *Hammarskjold.* London: Bodley Head, 1973.

Reading

(From Dag Hammarskjold's *Markings*)

God does not die on the day when we cease to believe in a personal deity, but we die on the day when our lives cease to be illumined by the steady radiance, renewed daily, of a wonder, the source of which is beyond all reason.   [1950]

"—Night is drawing nigh—"
For all that has been—Thanks!
To all that shall be—Yes!

Not I, but God in me.   [1953]

I am the vessel. The draught is God's. And God is the thirsty one.

In the last analysis, what does the word "sacrifice" mean? Or even the word "gift"? He who has nothing can give nothing. The gift is God's—to God.

He who has surrendered himself to it knows that the Way ends on the Cross—even when it is leading through the jubilation of Gennesaret or the triumphal entry into Jerusalem.   [April 7, 1953]

Offspring of the past, pregnant with the future, the present moment, nevertheless, always exists in eternity—always in eternity as the point of intersection between time and timelessness of faith, and, therefore, as the moment of freedom from past and future.

Thou who art over us,
Thou who art one of us,
Thou who *art*—
Also within us,
May all see Thee—in me also,
May I prepare the way for Thee,
May I thank Thee for all that shall fall to my lot,
May I also not forget the needs of others,
Keep me in Thy love
As Thou wouldest that all should be kept in mine.
May everything in this my being be directed to Thy glory
And may I never despair,
For I am under Thy hand,
And in Thee is all power and goodness.
Give me a pure heart—that I may see Thee,
A humble heart—that I may hear Thee,
A heart of love—that I may serve thee,
A heart of faith—that I may abide in Thee.   [1954]

Prayer, crystallized in words, assigns a permanent wave length on which the dialogue has to be continued, even when our mind is occupied with other matters.   [1955]

Markings, tr. Leif Sjoberg and W. H. Auden (New York: Knopf, 1964) 56, 89, 90, 91, 100, 106. Used by permission.

Propers: Peace

Hymn of the Day: "O God of love, O King of peace" (414)

Prayers: for the United Nations
            for all who make peace—in families, cities, nations
            for confidence in God's care
            for grace to learn the meaning and the practice of prayer

Color: White

362

ST. MATTHEW, APOSTLE, EVANGELIST

Matthew appears in the gospels as a tax collector for the Roman government in the city of Capernaum. He was probably born in Galilee of a Jewish family, although the Jews of the day despised the tax collectors or "publicans" and generally excluded them from the activities of the Jewish community.

In the gospels of Mark and Luke, Levi, not Matthew, is called to discipleship, but Matthew always appears in the lists of the twelve apostles. In Mark and Luke, Matthew and Levi do not seem to be regarded as the same person (Origen and others distinguished between Matthew and Levi), but it is sometimes suggested that Levi was his original name and that Matthew, the Hebrew for "gift from God", was given to him after he joined Jesus' followers. Mark calls him the son of Alphaeus, a man otherwise unknown and apparently not the Alphaeus who was the father of St. James the Less.

Since the second century the authorship of the first gospel has been attributed to St. Matthew. The name Levi does not appear in this gospel and in the list of the Twelve the name Matthew, who is identified as "the publican," comes after that of Thomas, which it precedes in the other New Testament lists.

Little is known of St. Matthew's life beyond the story of his calling, recounted in the Gospel for the Day, when at the word of Jesus he left his desk and devoted himself to the work of discipleship. Tradition suggests that he was the oldest of the apostles, and there are stories of his preaching in Ethiopia and Persia and dying a martyr's death. Eusebius said that Matthew first evangelized among the Hebrews and then among other people; Clement of Alexandria said that Matthew was a vegetarian. Heracleon says that Matthew died a natural death, but later legend dramatizes his death by fire or sword.

St. Matthew's Day is observed on November 16 in most Eastern churches, but it has always been on September 21 in the West. In year A of the three-year lectionary, when the readings are primarily from Matthew, St. Matthew's Day is an especially appropriate observance. On St. Matthew's Day in 1522 Luther's German translation of the New Testament was published, and there is a woodcut of the time showing Luther as the Evangelist Matthew working on the Bible.

Edgar J. Goodspeed. *Matthew, Apostle, Evangelist.* New York: Winston, 1959.
———. *The Twelve.* New York: Winston, 1957.
Jack Dean Kingsbury. *Matthew.* (Proclamation Commentaries) Philadelphia: Fortress, 1977.

Reading

(From Martin Luther, Lectures on Galatians—1519.)

The Lord is my witness that I am not doing this because of my own inclination or pleasure, since I wish for nothing more ardently than to lie hidden in a corner; but since I am altogether obligated to deal publicly with Holy Writ, I want to render as pure a service as I can to my Lord Jesus Christ. For if Divine Scriptures are treated in such a way as to be understood only with regard to the past and not to be applied to our own manner of life, of what benefit will they be? Then they are cold, dead, and not even divine. For you see how fittingly and vividly, yes, how necessarily, this passage [Galatians 5:26] applies to our age. Because others have not dared this or have not understood it—it is not surprising that the teachers of theology have been hated. To me it is certain that the Word of God cannot have been rightly treated without incurring hatred and danger of death, and that if it gives offense—especially to the rulers and aristocrats of the people—this is the one sign that it has been treated rightly.

Luther's Works vol. 27 Lectures on Galatians, trans. Richard Jungkuntz, pp. 386-387. © 1964 Concordia Publishing House. Used by permission.

Propers

ROMAN	LUTHERAN	EPISCOPAL
God of mercy, you chose a tax collector, Saint Matthew, to share the dignity of the apostles. By his example and prayers help us to follow Christ and remain faithful in your service. We ask this through our Lord Jesus Christ, your Son, who lives and reigns with you and the Holy Spirit, one God, for ever and ever.	Almighty God, your Son our Savior called a despised collector of taxes to become one of his apostles. Help us, like Matthew, to respond to the transforming call of your Son, Jesus Christ our Lord, who lives and reigns with you and the Holy Spirit, one God, now and forever.	We thank you, heavenly Father, for the witness of your apostle and evangelist Matthew to the Gospel of your Son our Savior; and we pray that, after his example, we may with ready wills and hearts obey the calling of our Lord to follow him; through Jesus Christ our Lord, who lives and reigns with you and the Holy Spirit, one God, now and for ever.

(Text from the English translation of the Roman Missal © 1973, International Committee on English in the Liturgy, Inc. All rights reserved.)

(Text from Lesser Feasts and Fasts, Revised Edition, copyright 1973 by Charles Mortimer Guilbert as Custodian of the Standard Book of Common Prayer. All rights reserved. Used by permission.)

ROMAN	LUTHERAN	EPISCOPAL
Ephesians 4:1-7, 11-13 Psalm 19:2-5 Matthew 9:9-13	Ezekiel 2:8—3:11 Psalm 119:33-40 Ephesians 2:4-10 Matthew 9:9-13	Proverbs 3:1-6 Psalm 119:33-40 2 Timothy 3:14-17 Matthew 9:9-13 Preface of Apostles

Hymn of the Day: "Your word, O Lord, is gentle dew" (232)

Prayers: for renewed appreciation of our Jewish heritage
for ethical renewal
for openness to the mystery of the glory of Christ

Preface: Apostles

Color: Red

Sergius of Radonezh
Abbot of Holy Trinity, Moscow, 1392

Sergius, the most popular of all the Russian saints, was born to a once-rich family at Rostov, Russia, May 2, 1314 and was named Bartholomew. The family was driven from their home by civil war and had to make their living by farming at Radonezh, forty miles northeast of Moscow. As a child, Bartholomew avoided lessons in reading and writing until one day a mysterious monk changed his life. He began to read the Bible, books on liturgy, the Fathers; he visited monasteries. But despite his increasing desire for solitude, Bartholomew remained with his parents until their death.

In 1336, with his elder brother Stephen, he went into the forest which surrounded Radonezh and there built a chapel in honor of the Holy Trinity. His brother left him for a monastery in Moscow, but Bartholomew persevered. A neighboring priest-monk gave him the tonsure and the name Sergius; he was ordained a priest when he was thirty. Stephen returned to the now established and flourishing monastery and was honored as co-founder. By 1354, at the request of the Patriarch of Constantinople, this place of retreat had become a monastic center, the Troitskaya Laura or the Troiste-Sergieva Laura. In many ways, Sergius' life was like that of St. Francis of Assisi. He was known for his love of animals, and his detachment from worldy goods. He lived an austere life and was accorded honor throughout Russia. The monastery became a center of religious pilgrimage, a principal center of Russian spirituality. Miracles and visions were attributed to Sergius. He went on numerous missions of peace with various Russian princes with the hope of consolidating the Russian hegemony under the principality of Moscow against the ravages of the Tartars. In 1378 Sergius refused the office of Patriarch of Moscow. He supported Prince Dimitri and urged him to repel the attack of the Mongols in 1380 and so to lay the foundations of independence.

Sergius left no writings, but his teachings were spread by his disciples who founded numerous monasteries. He died at his monastery September 25, 1392 and was buried in the monastery church. Pilgrims continue to flock to his grave. In 1920 the monastery was closed and turned into a museum, but it was later returned to the church and a theological academy was opened there.

Constantin de Grunwold. *Saints of Russia* tr. Roger Capel (New York: Macmillan, 1960) 67-86.
N. Zernov. *Saint Sergius, Builder of Russia.* London: SPCK, 1939.

Reading

(From *The Way of a Pilgrim.*)

. . . Now what is the meaning of sanctity? For the sinner it means nothing else than a return through effort and discipline to the state of innocence of the first man.

I felt, as it were, hungry for prayer, an urgent need to pour out my soul in prayer, and I had not been in quiet nor alone for forty-eight hours. I felt as though there were in my heart a sort of flood struggling to burst out and flow through all my limbs. To hold it back caused me severe, even if comforting, pain in the heart, a pain which needed to be calmed and satisfied in the silence of prayer. And now I saw why those who really practice interior self-acting prayer have fled from the company of man and hidden themselves in unknown places. I saw further why the venerable Isikhi called even the most spiritual and helpful talk mere idle chatter if there were too much of it, just as Ephraim the Syrian says, "Good speech is silver, but silence is pure gold."

. . . the whole salvation of man depends upon prayer, and, therefore, it is primary and necessary, for by it faith is quickened and through it all good works are performed. In a word, with prayer everything goes forward successfully; without it, no act of Christian piety can be done. Thus, the condition that it should be offered unceasingly and always belongs exclusively to prayer. For the other Christian virtues, each of them has its own time. But in the case of prayer, uninterrupted, continuous action is commanded. *Pray without ceasing.* It is right and fitting to pray always, to pray everywhere. True prayer has its conditions. It should be offered with a pure mind and heart, with burning zeal, with close attention, with fear and reverence, and with the deepest humility.

The Way of a Pilgrim and *The Pilgrim Continues His Way.* tr. from the Russian by R. M. French (New York: Seabury, 1965) 45, 98, 189. Used by permission of the publisher, the Seabury Press, New York.

Propers

ROMAN	LUTHERAN	EPISCOPAL
	Lord God, you have surrounded us with so great a cloud of witnesses. Grant that we, encouraged by the example of your servant Sergius, may persevere in the course that is set before us, to be living signs of the Gospel and at last, with all the saints, to share in your eternal joy; through your Son, Jesus Christ our Lord.	O God, whose blessed Son became poor that we through his poverty might be rich: Deliver us from an inordinate love of this world, that, following the example of your servant Sergius, we may serve you with singleness of heart, and attain to the riches of the world to come; through Jesus Christ our Lord, who lives and reigns with you in the unity of the Holy Spirit, one God, now and for ever.

	LUTHERAN	EPISCOPAL
	Common of Saints Micah 6:6-8 Psalm 9:1-10 1 Corinthians 1:26-31 Luke 6:20-23	Common of a Monastic I Psalm 134 Song of Songs 8:6-7 Psalm 139:13-17 Philippians 3:7-15 Luke 12:33-37 or 9:57-62 Preface of a Saint

Hymn of the Day: "Let all mortal flesh keep silence" (198)

Prayers: for a deeper attachment to the things that abide
for an increased love of the natural world
for peace
for the Church in Russia

Preface: All Saints

Color: White

368

ST. MICHAEL AND ALL ANGELS

Christianity, following Judaism (and followed in turn by Islam), speaks of an order of heavenly messengers, the angels, created by God to do his bidding and differing from humans by having a fully spiritual nature and no physical body. They are mentioned by Jesus as watching over children (Matt. 18:10) and rejoicing over penitent sinners (Luke 15:10), and there are numerous references to them in the Scripture. Michael the archangel is mentioned in the books of Daniel (10:13ff; 12:1), Jude (9), and Revelation (12:7-9), as well as in apocryphal literature. Michael is the only angel assigned a liturgical observance before the ninth century. The new Roman Catholic calendar commemorates the three archangels Michael, Gabriel, and Raphael jointly on September 29 (previously they had had separate days). There is also a feast of the Holy Guardian Angels on October 2. At the time of the Reformation the Lutherans and Anglicans retained the feast then called the Dedication of St. Michael, and expanded the commemoration to include not only Michael the Archangel but all the angels.

The cult of Michael originated in Phrygia, where he was venerated as a healer. Hot springs were dedicated to him in Greece and Asia. Beginning in the fourth century churches were dedicated to him, and his popularity spread to the West. He is said to have made an appearance on Mt. Garganus on the southeast coast of Italy in the fifth or sixth century during an invasion by the Goths. This apparition was traditionally commemorated on May 5. Michael, whose name is popularly thought to mean "who is like God?", is usually shown in art as youthful, strong, and clad in armor. He has been regarded as the helper of Christian armies and the protector of individual Christians against the devil, especially in the hour of death.

St. Michael's Day was especially popular in England and in northern Europe, and during the Middle Ages it was one of the three holidays that divided the season after Pentecost. The special calendar function of Michaelmas, as the day is often called in England, has survived in Great Britain and the Commonwealth in marking the fall term at universities and in the courts of law.

Gustav Davidson. *A Dictionary of Angels*. New York: Free Press, 1967.

Reading

(From *Principles of Christian Theology* by John Macquarrie.)

Man is sometimes afflicted with a sense of loneliness on his little planet, the only "existent" upon earth, perhaps just an accident in the cosmos. But if the Christian doctrine of creation is true, then man is no accident, and presumably he is not alone. He must be one of countless races of beings on which the Creator has conferred being, and some of these races must, like man himself, have risen to consciousness and freedom whereby they can gladly cooperate with God. Some must have moved further in the hierarchy of beings, so that they constitute higher orders of creaturely beings. The doctrine of the angels opens our eyes to this vast, unimaginable cooperative striving and service, as all things seek to be like God and to attain fullness of being in him. One may recall here the story of Elisha's servant whose courage was renewed by a vision of supporting angels (2 Kings 6:15-17).

This incident is particularly relevant for understanding the significance of the angels in a contemporary formulation of the doctrine of creation. The doctrine of the angels directs our minds to the vastness and richness of the creation, and every advance of science opens up still more distant horizons. Any mere humanistic creed that makes man the measure of all things or regards him as the sole author of values is narrow and parochial. The panorama of creation must be far more breathtaking than we can guess in our corner of the cosmos, for there must be many higher orders of beings whose service is joined with ours under God.

John Macquarrie, *Principles of Christian Theology* 2nd ed. (New York: Scribner, 1977) 237. Used by permission of Charles Scribner's Sons.

Propers

ROMAN	LUTHERAN	EPISCOPAL
God our Father, in a wonderful way you guide the work of angels and men. May those who serve you constantly in heaven keep our lives safe from harm on earth. Grant this through our Lord Jesus Christ, your Son, who lives and reigns with you and the Holy Spirit, one God, for ever and ever.	Everlasting God, you have ordained and constituted in a wonderful order the ministries of angels and mortals. Mercifully grant that, as your holy angels always serve and worship you in heaven, so by your appointment they may help and defend us here on earth; through your Son, Jesus Christ our Lord, who lives and reigns with you and the Holy Spirit, one God, now and forever.	Everlasting God, you have ordained and constituted in a wonderful order the ministries of angels and mortals: Mercifully grant that, as your holy angels always serve and worship you in heaven, so by your appointment they may help and defend us here on earth; through Jesus Christ our Lord, who lives and reigns with you and the Holy Spirit, one God, for ever and ever.
Daniel 7:9-10, 13-14 or Revelation 12:7-12a Psalm 138:1-5 John 1:47-51	Daniel 10:10-14; 12:1-3 Psalm 103:1-5, 20-22 Revelation 12:7-12 Luke 10:17-20	Genesis 28:10-17 Psalm 103 Revelation 12:7-12 John 1:47-51 Preface of Trinity Sunday

Hymn of the Day: "Praise the Lord! O heavens adore him" (540) or "Stars of the morning" (*SBH* 148)

Prayers: for an enlarged sense of God's creation
for awe before the immensity of the creation
for purity to join the songs of the angels
for an awareness of the unity in praise of heaven and earth

Preface: Weekdays or Sundays after Pentecost

Color: White

Jerome, Translator and Teacher, 420

Eusebius Hieronymus Sophronius, more commonly called Jerome, was born about the year 345 in Stridon, a village near the city of Aquileia in northeast Italy. He came of a moderately well-to-do Christian family. He was educated at home by a tutor until about the age of twelve when he was sent to Rome to study under the famous grammarian Donatus. Jerome from the beginning was an outstanding student, and he acquired a considerable reputation. His moral life was far from blameless, but he remained close to Christianity, and at the close of his studies he was baptized at nineteen.

At the age of twenty Jerome went to Treves, which at that time was the seat of the Imperial Court, and it was there that the religious experience took place which is called his "conversion." In 370 he went to Aquileia where he acquired a circle of friends such as Rufinus, whose names were to recur often in his life. After several years in that city he decided to go to the East, where a great part of his life was to be spent. In 374 he reached Antioch, then one of the great cities of the world, its bishop the patriarch of "all the East." There he continued his studies, but before long his earlier desire to become a hermit was rekindled. Also at this time he had his dream in which God told him "You are a Ciceronian, not a Christian." He was, that is to say, too much concerned with the pagan classics. He withdrew into the desert near Antioch and spent four years there. Letters of his are extant telling of his temptations and hardships and also the joys of his solitary life. He had, moreover, taken his books with him, and during this period he studied Hebrew and wrote several books.

On his return to Antioch Jerome was ordained to the priesthood against his wishes by Bishop Paulinus, but he never exercised this office. He soon left the city and went to Constantinople where he came to know the saintly Bishop Gregory of Nazianzus, and he attended the third Ecumenical Council in 381. The following year he went to Rome and became the secretary of Damasus, the Bishop of Rome, at whose request he made a revision of the Latin version of the gospels in accordance with the Greek text and completed a first revision of the Latin Psalter.

During Jerome's stay in Rome he attacked the luxurious and scandalous life of some of the wealthy Christians and even some of the clergy and so forfeited any hope of succeeding Damasus. He also fostered the growing ascetic movement among the upper class women of Rome and began his association with the Lady Paula and her daughters who were to become his staunch friends. Jerome left Rome in 385 for the East, and after being joined by Paula and her companions in Antioch six months later, he visited Palestine and Egypt, thus acquiring experience in all four of the great cities of the Empire: Antioch, Constantinople, Rome, and Alexandria.

In 386 Jerome established himself in a monastery near the basilica of the Nativity at Bethlehem with communities nearby which had Paula as their abbess. He himself lived and worked there in a large rock-hewn cell for the rest of his life, and representations of the saint working in his hermit's cell are frequent in sacred paintings. Jerome opened a school for boys in Bethlehem, translated a number of historical, philosophical, and theological works into Latin and produced several books of his own, including his valuable collection of Christian biographies *De Viris Illustribus.* He also wrote many letters and engaged in long and bitter theological controversies, including one with his old friend Rufinus over the teachings of Origen. The great work of his life, however, was his Latin translation of the Bible which has remained the standard Latin version for fifteen centuries.

In 404 Paula died, and the last years of Jerome's life were full of troubles—incursions of refugees from the sack of Rome and a Vandal invasion (410-412) and violence on the part of religious opponents. The monastery itself was burned by marauders in 416. Jerome died on September 30, 420, and was buried next to Paula in the Church of the Nativity. His body was later reportedly moved to Rome.

St. Jerome is universally recognized as the most learned man of the age and one of the greatest of biblical scholars. Although he was a violent polemicist and not at his best in theological writings, the wording of his translation of the Bible has had a powerful effect on the thinking of later generations.

Hans von Campenhausen. *The Fathers of the Latin Church* tr. Manfred Hoffman. Stanford University Press, 1964.
J. N. D. Kelly. *Jerome.* London: Duckworth, 1976.
Charles Mierow. *Saint Jerome: The Sage of Bethlehem.* Milwaukee: Bruce, 1959.

F. X. Murphy ed. *A Monument to Saint Jerome.* New York: Sheed and Ward, 1952.

Reading

(From a letter of St. Jerome to Heliodorus, A.D. 374)

My discourse has now sailed clear of the reefs, and from the midst of hollow crags with foaming waves my frail bark has won her way into deep water. Now I may spread my canvas to the wind, and leaving the rocks of controversy astern, like some merry sailor sing a cheerful epilogue. O wilderness, bright with Christ's spring flowers! O solitude, whence come those stones wherewith in the Apocalypse the city of the mighty king is built! O desert, rejoicing in God's familiar presence! What are you doing in the world, brother, you who are more than the universe? How long is the shade of a roof going to confine you? How long shall the smoky prison of these cities shut you in? Believe me, I see something more of light than you behold. How sweet it is to fling off the burden of the flesh, and to fly aloft to the clear radiance of the sky. Are you afraid of poverty? Christ calls the poor blessed. Are you frightened by the thought of toil? No athlete gains his crown without sweat. Are you thinking about food? Faith feels not hunger. Do you dread bruising your limbs worn away with fasting on the bare ground? The Lord lies by your side. Is your rough head bristling with uncombed hair? Your head is Christ. Does the infinite vastness of the desert seem terrible? In spirit you may always stroll in paradise, and when in thought you have ascended there you will no longer be in the desert. Is your skin rough and scurfy without baths? He who has once washed in Christ needs not to wash again. Listen to the apostle's brief reply to all complaints: "The sufferings of this present time are not worthy to be compared with the glory which shall come after them, when shall it be revealed in us." You are a pampered darling indeed, dearest brother, if you wish to rejoice here with this world and to reign with Christ.

The day will come when this corrupt and mortal body shall put on incorruptibility and become immortal. Happy the servant whom the Lord then shall find on the watch. Then at the voice of the trumpet the earth with its peoples shall quake, and you will rejoice. When the Lord comes to give judgment the universe will utter a mournful groan; the tribes of men will beat their breasts; kings once most mighty will shiver with naked flanks; Jupiter with all his offspring will then be shown amid real fires; Plato with his disciples will be revealed as but a fool; Aristotle's arguments will not help him. Then you the poor rustic will exult, and say with a smile: "Behold my crucified God, behold the judge. This is he who once was wrapped in swaddling clothes and uttered baby cries in a manger. This is the son of a working man and a woman who served for wages. This is he who, carried in his mother's arms, fled into Egypt, a God from a man. This is he who was clad in a scarlet robe and crowned with thorns. This is he who was called a magician, a man with a devil, a Samaritan. Behold the hands, ye Jews, that you nailed to the cross. Behold the side, ye Romans, that you pierced. See whether this is the same body that you said the disciples carried off secretly in the night."

O my brother, that it may be yours to say these words and to be present on that day, what labour now can seem hard?

Select Letters of St. Jerome, trans. F. A. Wright, the Loeb Classical Library (Cambridge, Mass.: Harvard, 1963) 49-53. Used by permission of the Harvard University Press.

Propers

ROMAN	LUTHERAN	EPISCOPAL
Father, you gave Saint Jerome delight in his study of the holy scripture. May your people find in your word the food of salvation and the fountain of life. We ask this through our Lord Jesus Christ, who lives and reigns with you and the Holy Spirit, one God, for ever and ever.	God of grace and might, we praise you for your servant Jerome, to whom you gave gifts to make the Holy Scripture understood. Raise up, we pray, in every country, heralds and evangelists of your kingdom, so that the world may know the immeasurable riches of our Savior, Jesus Christ our Lord.	O God, who gave us the Holy Scriptures for a light to shine upon our path: Grant us, after the example of your servant Jerome, so to learn of you according to your holy Word, that we may find the light that shines more and more to the perfect day; through Jesus Christ our Lord, who lives and reigns with you and the Holy Spirit, one God, now and ever.

ROMAN	LUTHERAN	EPISCOPAL
(Text from the English translation of the Roman Missal © 1973, International Committee on English in the Liturgy, Inc. All rights reserved.)		*(Text from Lesser Feasts and Fasts, Revised Edition, copyright 1973 by Charles Mortimer Guilbert as Custodian of the Standard Book of Common Prayer. All rights reserved. Used by permission.)*
Common of Doctors or Pastors *or* 2 Timothy 3:14-17	Common of Missionaries Isaiah 62:1-7 Psalm 48 2 Timothy 3:14-17 Luke 24:44-48	Psalm 119:97-104 Nehemiah 8:1-3, 5-6, 8-9 Psalm 119:105-112 Luke 24:44-48 Preface of the Incarnation

Hymn of the Day: "Father of mercies, in your Word" (240)

Prayers: for an increased love of the Scripture
for students and scholars of the Bible
for translators of the Scripture

Preface: Epiphany

Color: White

October 4

Francis of Assisi
Renewer of the Church, 1226

Giovanni Bernadone was born in Assisi in Umbria, Italy, in 1182, the son of a wealthy cloth merchant. He was baptized Giovanni (John), but soon after his birth he was called Francesco ("French") because of his father's travels in France and admiration of the French. Since his day the name Francis, which was almost unknown before, has become a common name. After a pleasure-seeking youth and work in his father's business, Francis left his comfortable home for a very different life.

His early ambition had been to become a knight, and he took part in the border dispute between Assisi and Perugia. He was captured and imprisoned 1202-1203 and, stricken with a serious fever had to return home. Back in Assisi he underwent a complete change of heart, became increasingly given to self-examination. While preparing to go to war against Apulia, he had a vision of a hall hung with armor. Meeting a leper, he exchanged his clothes for rags, and in 1206 made a pilgrimage to Rome. He rebuilt churches, broke off relations with his father, and finally renounced his possessions.

On the morning of St. Matthias' Day, February 24, 1209, Francis went to the chapel of Portiuncula near Assisi, and as he heard the priest read the words of what was then the gospel for the day, Matthew 10:7-13, he accepted them as divine revelation for himself. (The gospel for St. Matthias' Day has since been changed, first to Matthew 11:25-30—still the Anglican Gospel—and then in the recent revision of the calendar and lectionary to John 15:9-17 for the Roman church; but it was the tenth chapter of Matthew that spoke to Francis that day.) As St. Francis left the church he took off his shoes, staff, cloak, replaced his belt with a piece of rope over his long brown peasant's smock, and began his mission. Ten years later this garb was the uniform of five thousand men.

St. Francis gathered around him a band of men who would follow Jesus' life of poverty, preaching by word and example the Beatitudes of the Sermon on the Mount. This was a new vision of the Christian life, one which combined complete lack of earthly possessions and a rigorous asceticism with a joyful, comradely fellowship, strong sense of humor, and gladness in God's creation. Francis also had a profound respect for the church and its clergy, although he himself never became a priest but remained a deacon until his death. In 1210 St. Francis and some of his disciples went to Rome and obtained the oral permission of Pope Innocent III for their preaching and way of life, thus beginning the Order of Franciscan Friars. Francis presented poverty, chastity, and obedience in the manner of the troubadours and of the courtly love that was popular at the time, and he attracted thousands of followers.

The brothers wandered through Italy preaching, filling their simple physical needs by working or begging. As the brotherhood spread, Francis sent his followers to other parts of the world. He himself attempted a mission to Syria but was shipwrecked in Dalmatia. A projected journey to Morocco was thwarted by an illness in Spain. In 1219-1220 he went to the Holy Land where he attempted to convert the Sultan of Egypt and walked among the towns and shrines of the Holy Land amidst the warring armies of the Fifth Crusade.

On his return to Italy he held a general assembly of the whole order, now grown to vast proportions, to give it a clearer structure and a firmer organization. The assembly met by the chapel of Portiuncula where St. Francis had first been inspired to carry out his mission. Characteristically, he made no provision for food and shelter for the brothers, who had to be provided for by the devotion and generosity of the local people. St. Francis laid down a new rule for the order and retired himself from active administration of it, a task far removed from the simple life he preached and lived.

In the final years of his life, St. Francis withdrew more to himself and turned to the inner mystical devotion which he had always had but which now became much stronger. In August of 1224 he went to Mount La Verna (Alvernia) which had been given to the Franciscans as a place for solitary devotions, and there on September 14 (Holy Cross Day) as he was praying he received the print of the nails and wound in his side which troubled him until his death. The objective reality of those wounds seems well attested, whatever psychological or supernatural origin they may be attributed to, for St. Francis desired to find perfect joy through experiencing the sufferings of his Lord. During the last years of his life he was blind and seriously ill.

St. Francis died on October 4, 1226 in a little hut near the Portiuncula chapel, attended by a few of his closest followers. His last act was the singing of Psalm 142. In two years' time he was recognized formally as a saint, and it has often been said of him that he is "the one saint whom all succeeding generations have agreed in canonizing." His humility, generosity, love of nature, simple and unaffected devotion to God have combined to make him one of the most cherished of all the saints. Pierre Sabatier (1682-1742), a French Calvinist pastor, did much to revive interest in St. Francis by his research into early Franciscan documents.

Edward A. Armstrong. *Saint Francis: Nature Mystic.* Berkeley: University of California Press, 1974.
G. K. Chesterton. *St. Francis of Assisi.* New York: Doubleday, 1924.
Anthony Mockler. *Francis of Assisi. The Wandering Years.* New York: E. P. Dutton, 1976.
John Holland Smith. *Francis of Assisi.* London: Sidgwick and Jackson, 1973 (New York: Scribners, 1974.)

On this day, **Clare** is appropriately remembered with St. Francis. Clare, a noble lady of Assisi, was born in 1194 and in 1212 accepted Francis' ideas and founded a society for women, known as the "Poor Clares," modelled on St. Francis' order. She had a deep sympathy with Francis' ideals of total poverty and absolute renunciation for the sake of Jesus Christ. She died August 11, 1253, and this has become her feast day in the Roman and Episcopal Churches.

Reading

(From a letter written to all the faithful by St. Francis)

O how happy and blessed are those who love the Lord and do as the Lord himself said in the gospel, "You shall love the Lord your God with your whole heart and your whole soul, and your neighbor as yourself." Therefore, let us love God and adore him with a pure heart and mind. This is his particular desire when he says, "True worshippers adore the Father in spirit and truth." For all who adore him must do so in the spirit of truth. Let us also direct to him our praises and prayers saying, "Our Father in heaven," since we "must always pray and never grow slack."

Furthermore, let us produce worthy fruits of penance. Let us also love our neighbors as ourselves. Let us have charity and humility. Let us give alms because these cleanse our souls from the stains of sin. Mortals lose all the material things they leave behind them in this world, but they carry with them the reward of their charity and the alms they give. For these they will receive from the Lord the reward and recompense they deserve. We must not be wise and prudent according to the flesh. Rather we must be simple, humble, and pure. We should never desire to be over others. Instead, we ought to be servants who are submissive to every human being for God's sake. The Spirit of the Lord will rest on all who live in this way and persevere in it to the end. He will permanently dwell in them. They will be the Father's children who do his work. They are the spouses, brothers, and mothers of our Lord Jesus Christ.

Propers

ROMAN	LUTHERAN	EPISCOPAL
Father, you helped Saint Francis to reflect the image of Christ through a life of poverty and humility. May we follow your Son by walking in the footsteps of Francis of Assisi, and by imitating his joyful love. Grant this through our Lord Jesus Christ, your Son, who lives and reigns with you and the Holy Spirit, one God, for ever and ever.	Most high, almighty, and good Lord, you have surrounded us with so great a cloud of witnesses. Grant that we, encouraged by the example of your servant Francis, may joyfully persevere in the course that is set before us, to be living signs of the Gospel and at last, with all the saints, to share in your eternal joy; through your son, Jesus Christ our Lord.*	Most high, almighty, and good Lord, grant your people grace to renounce gladly the vanities of this world; that, after the example of blessed Francis, we may for love of you delight in all your creatures, with perfectness of joy; through Jesus Christ our Lord, who lives and reigns with you and the Holy Spirit, one God, now and for ever.*

Galatians 6:14-18 Matthew 11:25-30 or Common of Saints (for religious)	Common of Saints: Micah 6:6-8 Psalm 9:1-10 *Galatians 6:14-18* *Matthew 11:25-30*	Psalm 148 Galatians 6:14-18 Psalm 131 Matthew 11:25-30 Preface of a Saint

* The address in these two prayers echoes the opening of St. Francis' "Canticle of the Creatures," which is the basis also of the Hymn of the Day.

Hymn of the Day: "All creatures of our God and King" (527)

Prayers: for dedication to the imitation of Christ
for humility to identify with poverty and suffering
for joy in the faith of Christ
for a deeper concern for the natural world of which we
    are a part
for all birds and animals

See also the prayer attributed to St. Francis, "Lord, make us instruments of your peace. . . ."   (#213)

Color: White

Theodor Fliedner, Renewer of Society, 1864

Theodor Fliedner, the founder of the modern institution of deaconesses, was born in Eppstein, Germany, January 21, 1800. He was the fourth of twelve children, and his father, a pastor of limited means, died in 1813. Fliedner attended the gymnasium in Idstein, the universities of Giessen and Göttingen, and a seminary in Herborn. After a brief period as a tutor in a private home at Cologne, he became pastor of the little parish of Kaiserswerth, January 18, 1822.

Pastor Fliedner managed to visit Holland and England in 1823, 1824, and 1832 on tours to collect funds to aid his needy parish, and on these trips he encountered Moravian "deaconesses," who were engaged in several kinds of Christian service. The Moravians had revived the institution in 1745 as it had already existed among their predecessors, the Slavic congregations. But these deaconesses were not full time. Inspired by examples he had seen in England, Fliedner conducted a service of worship in the prison at Düsseldorf in 1825, the first Lutheran service of its kind. In the following year he founded the Rhenish-Westphalian Prison Society. He continued to conduct these services for two years, walking all the way to Düsseldorf every other Sunday, until in 1828 the first regular prison chaplain was appointed. The prison ministry spread in Germany under Fliedner's inspiration and he himself visited prisons throughout the Rheinland and Westphalia as well as in Holland, England, and Scotland. In 1833 he opened the Magdalen home for released women prisoners, and then in 1835 he opened the first nursery school in Düsseldorf. It developed into a large and influential teacher-training college, recognized by the government in 1848.

Gradually Fliedner came to believe that the ancient church order of deaconesses should be revived to help care for the poor and the sick, take care of children, and do prison work. In the early church, widows were commissioned as deaconesses to care for sick and needy women, instruct women catechumens, be present at interviews of women with the clergy, assist at the baptism of women, and in other ways to help in the work of the church. The female diaconate had died out almost everywhere by the seventh century, although some of these tasks were carried out by nuns or charitable orders of various kinds, and there had been some sporadic attempts to revive the institution at the time of the Reformation.

After fruitless attempts to get support for his project, Pastor Fliedner finally decided to open a hospital and deaconess training institute himself in tiny, predominantly Roman Catholic Kaiserswerth. On October 13, 1836 the institute was opened and Gertrude Reichardt, the daughter of a physician, became the first deaconess. Fliedner's wife was the mother superior. Almost immediately the institute received help from all sides, and already in 1838 Fliedner was able to send out deaconesses to serve in the city hospital at Eberfeld. Fliedner's wife, "the first of the deaconesses" he called her, died April 22, 1842. A year later Fliedner married the director of a large hospital in Hamburg.

In 1849 he resigned the pastorate at Kaiserswerth in order to devote himself full time to the deaconess work. He established contact with people in Strassburg, Paris, Switzerland, Holland, and North America. He personally opened a deaconess motherhouse in Pittsburgh in 1849, and he began the extension of the female diaconate to the Middle East with the founding of a motherhouse in Jerusalem in 1851 and a hospital at Constantinople in 1852. Other motherhouses, patterned after Kaiserswerth, spread in Paris, Strassburg, Dresden, Berlin. King Frederik William IV of Prussia silenced critics of the movement by appointing deaconesses to serve in the hospital in Berlin.

In 1856 Fliedner's health gave way, and he spent the year 1856-1857 in Cairo recovering from a serious lung condition. In spite of his physical weakness he visited the deaconess establishments at Jerusalem, Smyrna, and Constantinople on his return trip. When he reached Kaiserswerth he was no longer able to travel, but he kept up active direction and promotion of the work from his study. On the twenty-fifth anniversary in 1861, representatives from deaconess motherhouses in many countries came to Kaiserswerth for the celebration.

In September 1864 he was able to consecrate nineteen sisters and

382 October 4

he was preparing for the second general assembly of deaconess motherhouses when suddenly his strength failed. On October 3 he spoke to his children about his life's work and left his blessings with them and all his "spiritual daughters." On the morning of October 4 he died, leaving his second wife and ten surviving children. His last words are reported to have been, "Conqueror of death—victor!" At the time of his death there were thirty motherhouses, 1600 deaconesses in more than a hundred locations from Pittsburgh to Jerusalem. The motherhouse at Kaiserswerth had 425 sisters and a hundred outer stations on four continents.

Theodor Fliedner wrote a number of works related either to the tasks of deaconesses or their training. These included, besides numerous reports and pamphlets, such works as a songbook for nursery schools (Liederbuch für Kleinkinderschulen), a Christian calendar, and a book of martyrs. His work was carried on at first by his widow and a son-in-law, and it has continued to the present day. The Fliedner diaconate has spread to almost all lands where there are Lutheran churches, and by the mid-twentieth century there were over 35,-000 deaconesses serving parishes, schools, hospitals, and prisons.

Since the commemoration of Fliedner coincided with the day of St. Francis of Assisi, congregations may choose to move this remembrance of the founder of the deaconess movement to another date. October 13, the date of the opening of the Kaiserswerth institute is perhaps a convenient date.

With Fliedner, **William A. Passavant** might also be remembered, for he brought deaconesses to the United States from Germany in 1849 and introduced the diaconate to this continent.

Born in 1821, he was a tireless worker in the cause of relieving human suffering. "I am the servant of all—black as well as white, Catholic and Protestant," he wrote. The need, he said, is for "not merely a witnessing and worshipping church, but a working church, out of love to Christ." He was a pastor, a mission organizer, a founder of hospitals in Milwaukee, Chicago, Pittsburgh, and Jacksonville, Illinois; of orphanages in Mount Vernon (New York), Philadelphia, Boston; of Thiel College and of Chicago Seminary; of the General Council. He died January 3, 1894.

Julie Mergner. *The Deaconess and Her Work* tr. Harriet R. Spaeth. Philadelphia: General Council Publication House, 1915.

Reading

(From William Law, *The Spirit of Prayer*)

All religion is the spirit of love; all its gifts and graces are the gifts and graces of love; it has no breath, no life but the life of love. Nothing exalts, nothing purifies but the fire of love; nothing changes death into life, earth into Heaven, men into angels but love alone. Love breathes the Spirit of God; its words and works are the inspiration of God. It speaketh not of itself, but the Word, the eternal Word of God speaketh in it; for all that love speaketh, that God speaketh, because love is God.

Love is Heaven revealed in the soul; it is light and truth; it is infallible; it has not errors, for errors are the want of love. Love has no more of pride than light has of darkness; it stands and bears all its fruits from a depth and root of humility. Love is of no sect or party; it neither makes nor admits of any bounds; you may as easily enclose the light or shut up the air of the world into one place as confine love to a sect or party. It lives in the liberty, the universality, the impartiality of Heaven. It believes in one, holy, catholic God, the God of all spirits; it unites and joins with the catholic Spirit of the one God, who unites with all that is good, and is meek, patient, well-wishing, and long-suffering over all the evil that is in nature and creature.

Love, like the Spirit of God, rideth upon the wings of the wind, and is in union and communion with all the saints that are in Heaven and on earth. Love is quite pure; it has no by-ends; it seeks not its own; it has but one will, and that is to give itself unto everything and overcome all evil with good.

Lastly, love is the Christ of God; it comes down from Heaven; it regenerates the soul from above; it blots out all transgressions; it takes from death its sting, from the devil his power, and from the serpent his poison. It heals all the infirmities of our earthly birth; it gives eyes to the blind, ears to the deaf, and makes the dumb to speak; it cleanses the lepers and casts out devils, and puts man in Paradise before he dies. It lives wholly to the will of Him of whom it is born; its meat and drink is to do the will of God. It is the resurrection and life of every divine virtue, a fruitful mother of true humanity, boundless benevolence, unwearied patience, and bowels of compassion.

The Selected Mystical Writings of William Law, ed. Stephen Hobhouse (London: Rockliff, 1948) 100-101.

Propers: Renewers of Society

Hymn of the Day: "We give thee but thine own" (410)

Prayers: for deaconesses
　　　　for those in prison
　　　　for the sick and the forgotten
　　　　for the spirit of service

Color: White

William Tyndale, Translator, Martyr, 1536

Tyndale, the translator, humanist, and martyr, was born in Monmouthshire on the border of Wales ca. 1491. He was educated at Oxford, from which he received the M.A. in 1515 and he was ordained the same year. He then went to Cambridge, the best Greek school in England, and there came under the influence of the new learning and revolutionary methods of the study of Scripture. He remained there until 1521. He was for a time a tutor in Gloucestershire and there decided to translate the Bible into English to help revive the church, which he had found in a state of serious decline. He is reported to have said to a clerical opponent of his plan, "If God spare my life, ere many years I will cause a boy that driveth the plough shall know more of the Scripture than thou doest." Tyndale approached the Bishop of London, Cuthbert Tunstall, a distinguished scholar, with his plan but was refused patronage. For a time Tyndale was the preacher at St. Dunstan's-in-the-West, but in May 1524 he moved to Germany and never returned to his own country again. He visited Luther at Wittenberg in 1525.

By 1525 he had completed his translation of the New Testament (from the Greek text of Erasmus). The printing of the book began in Cologne, but Tyndale and his secretary William Roy were forced to flee after their discovery by John Cochlaus, a heretic-hunter, and the printing was completed in Worms. The book was widely distributed in England, "sought by the people to read and by the bishops to burn" according to one commentator. Of the 18,000 copies printed only two remain. In 1534 Tyndale brought out a revised edition. He also worked on a translation of the Old Testament and published the Pentateuch and Jonah, 1530-1536.

In his translation, Tyndale was able to strike a balance between scholarship, simplicity, and grace. The result was the creation of a style of Scripture that was to serve as a model for all future English versions for nearly four hundred years.

Tyndale was forced to live abroad in poverty and danger. In May 1535, he was arrested, tried, and condemned for heresy. He was imprisoned in the castle of Vilvorde, the state prison of the Low Countries, and there on October 6, 1536, he was strangled at the stake and his body burned.

Ironically, while Tyndale was awaiting execution in the Low Countries, the situation in England changed. His most vigorous opponent, Thomas More, himself became a martyr in 1535. In the same year, Miles Coverdale published the first complete English Bible, made up of Tyndale's New Testament and Pentateuch, with the addition of Coverdale's own translation of the rest of the Old Testament and Apocrypha. Although this Bible was printed on the continent, it was allowed to circulate freely in England. The "Matthew Bible," another edition of the Tyndale-Coverdale translation was published with the king's special license in 1537, and in 1540 the second edition of the Great Bible (1539) declared on the title page that it was "appointed to the use of churches" and contained a long preface by Archbishop Cranmer encouraging Bible reading by clergy and laity.

Charles C. Butterworth. *The Literary Lineage of the King James Bible.* Philadelphia: University of Pennsylvania Press, 1941.
David Daiches. *The King James Bible. An Account of Its Development and Sources.* University of Chicago Press, 1941.
J. F. Mozley. *William Tyndale.* London: SPCK, 1937
C. H. Williams. *William Tyndale.* London: Nelson, 1970.

Reading

(From *Foxe's Book of Martyrs*)

Tindall, being in Antwerp, had been lodged about one year in the house of Thomas Pointz, an Englishman, who kept an house of English merchants; about which time came one out of England whose name was Henry Philips, a comely fellow like as he had been a gentleman, having a servant with him; but for what purpose he was sent thither no man could tell. Tindall divers times was desired forth to dinner and supper among merchants; by means whereof Philips became acquainted with him, so that within short space Tindall had great confidence in him and brought him to his lodging, and had him once or twice to dinner and supper, and further entered such friendship with him that through his procurement he lay in the same house; to whom he showed his books and other secrets of his study, so little did Tindall mistrust this traitor.

Then said Philips, "Mr. Tindall, you shall be my guest here this day." "No," said Tindall, "I go forth this day to dinner and you shall go with me and be my guest where you shall be welcome." So when it was dinner-time Tindall went forth with Philips, and at the going forth of Pointz's house was a long narrow entry, so that two could not go in a front. Tindall would have put Philips before him, but Philips would in no wise, but put Tindall before, for he pretended to show great humanity. So Tindall, a man of no great stature, went before, and Philips, a tall person, followed behind him, that the officers might see that it was he whom they should take, as the officers afterwards told Pointz, and said, when they had laid him in prison, that they pitied his simplicity when they took him. Then they took him and brought him to the Emperor's procuror-general, where he dined. Then came the procuror-general to the house of Pointz, and set away all that was there of Tindall's, as well his books as other things; and from there Tindall was had to the castle of Filford, eighteen miles from Antwerp, and there remained till he was put to death.

Thus Pointz for Tindall was sore troubled and long kept in prison; at length, when he saw no other remedy, by night he made his escape and avoided their hands. But Tindall could not escape their hands, but remained in prison still; who being brought unto his answer was offered an advocate and a proctor; for in any criminal cause there it shall be permitted to have counsel, to make answer in the law. But he refused to have any such, saying that he would answer for himself; and so he did.

At last after much reasoning, when no reason would serve, although he deserved no death, he was condemned by virtue of the Emperor's decree made in the Assembly at Ausbrough, and upon the same brought to the place of execution was tied to the stake, and then strangled first by the hangman and afterwards with fire consumed, in the morning, at the town of Filford, *an.* 1536, crying at the stake with fervent zeal and a loud voice, "Lord, open the king of England's eyes."

Such was the power of his doctrine and sincerity of his life that during his imprisonment, which endured a year and a half, it is said that he converted his keeper, his daughter, and other of his household. The rest that were with him in the castle reported of him that if he were not a good Christian man, they could not tell whom to trust. The procuror-general left this testimony of him, that he was *homo doctus, pius,* and *bonus,* a learned, good, and godly man.

Foxe's Book of Martyrs, ed. G. A. Williamson (Boston: Little, Brown, 1966) 125, 127. [John Foxe, Acts and Monuments of these Latter and Perilous Days . . . , 1563.]

Propers

ROMAN	LUTHERAN	EPISCOPAL
	God of grace and might, we praise you for your servant William, to whom you gave courage to make the good news known in the English language. Raise up, we pray, in every country, heralds and evangelists of your kingdom, so that the world may know the immeasurable riches of our Savior, Jesus Christ our Lord.	Give to your people, Lord, grace to hear and keep your Word; that, after the example of your servant William Tyndale, we may not only profess your gospel, but also be ready to suffer and die for it, to the honor of your Name; through Jesus Christ our Lord, who lives and reigns with you and the Holy Spirit, one God, now and for ever.

ROMAN	LUTHERAN	EPISCOPAL

Common of Missionaries:
Isaiah 62:1-7
Psalm 48
Romans 10:11-17
Luke 24:44-53
or Common of Martyrs

Psalm 7:1-7
James 1:21-25
Psalm 19:7-14
John 12:44-50

Preface of a Saint

Hymn of the Day: "Almighty God, your Word is cast" (234)

Prayers: for the renewal of the church
for a love of the scriptures
for those who study English prose and who craft language
of thanksgiving for the English Bible

Color: Red

(The Gospel for today might be read from Tyndale's translation, which is available in libraries, to honor his contribution to the church. It might be also printed out for the congregation with all its (to us) odd spellings and constructions to show how language changes and therefore requires new translations periodically—as does the language of worship also.)

October 7

Henry Melchior Muhlenberg
Missionary to America, 1787

Henry Melchior Muhlenberg, the patriarch of Lutherans in America, was born in Einbeck, Germany in 1711, the seventh of nine children. He graduated from Göttingen University and studied also at Halle, where he served as a schoolmaster.

In 1742 August Hermann Francke, who had made Halle a great center of Pietism, sent Muhlenberg to America. He went first to

London, where he learned from the court chaplain Frederick Ziegen-hagen—also a Halle man—something of the needs of the New World. Also while he was there, Muhlenberg had a gown made that was different from both the German and the Scandinavian style, and this set the pattern for English Lutheran clergy in America.

In the early part of the eighteenth century the Lutheran communities in the New World were scattered over a wide territory and came from various ethnic origins. They had built a few churches, but they were without any kind of general organization, and there was considerable dissention among them. When the three desolate congregations at Philadelphia, New Hanover (Swamp), and New Providence (Trappe) united in sending a commission to London and Halle asking for a pastor to be sent to take charge, Muhlenberg was chosen. He arrived in Charleston, South Carolina on September 23, 1742, and he went to Philadelphia in November. The German-speaking churches soon recognized his authority and the Swedish clergy also cooperated with him.

During the forty-five years he labored in America, Muhlenberg, struggling against schismatics and impostors, travelled incessantly, corresponded widely, and set a course of Lutheranism for coming generations. He preached in German, Dutch, and English, and, it is reported, with a powerful voice. He established the first Lutheran synod in America, the Ministerium of Pennsylvania, which can be dated from Sunday, August 14, 1748, when the delegates met in Philadelphia. At this synod Muhlenberg submitted a liturgy which was ratified and remained the only authorized American Lutheran liturgy for forty years. It was revived and used in many places as part of the bicentennial observance of the United States in 1976. Ultimately this form of the historic Lutheran order developed into the common liturgy of North American Lutherans in the *Common Service Book,* the *Lutheran Hymnal,* the *Service Book and Hymnal,* and the *Lutheran Book of Worship.*

Muhlenberg's concern with questions of stewardship, pastoral care, and education strengthened the church life of Lutheran congregations and aided greatly in the transition from the state churches of continental Europe to the free churches of America; his model congregational constitution of 1762 set the basis for local church government.

Muhlenberg and his sons were also leaders in American public life.

One son, John Peter Gabriel, left his pastorate in Virginia to become a general under Washington, and another, Frederick Augustus Conrad, also a Lutheran pastor, became a member of the Continental Congress and the first speaker of the House of Representatives. A great-grandson, William Augustus Muhlenberg was an outstanding priest of the Episcopal Church and is commemorated on the Episcopal calendar on April 8.

Henry Melchior Muhlenberg died at Trappe, Pennsylvania on October 7, 1787 and was buried there beside the historic church. A Latin inscription on the worn and weathered monument declares confidently, "Who and what he was future ages will know without a stone."

The Journals of Henry Melchior Muhlenberg, tr. T. G. Tappert and J. W. Doberstein. 3 vols. Philadelphia: Muhlenberg Press, 1942-1958.
Helen E. Pfatteicher. *The Ministerium of Pennsylvania.* Philadelphia: Ministerium Press, 1938.
Paul A. W. Wallace. *The Muhlenbergs of Pennsylvania.* Philadelphia: University of Pennslyvania Press, 1950.

Reading

(From the *Journals* of Henry Melchior Muhlenberg)

1748. November 5.

I am worn out from much reading; I am incapacitated for study; I cannot even manage my own household because I must be away most of the time. The Reverend Fathers called me for only three years on trial, but the dear God has doubled the three years and upheld me all this time with forbearance. I write this not out of any discontent of slothfulness, but out of the feeling of spiritual and physical incapacity and a yearning desire to achieve a little more quietude where I could gather my thoughts better, spend more time with my wife and children, and bring them up in the nurture and admonition of the Lord.

1763. August 26.

Alexander Murray, the new missionary of the English in Reading, came to visit me right after my arrival and engaged me in a long conversation concerning the English Church. He deeply regretted that a *coalition* between the German Lutheran congregations and the English Church had not yet been effected. He expressed the opinion that this was just the most suitable period in which to establish a bishop in America. And if this were to come to pass, native German sons of good intelligence and piety could be educated in English academies, ordained, and usefully employed for the best welfare of the church of Christ in both the German and English languages, since, as it is, strife and factiousness prevail in the German Evangelical and Reformed congregations and the people are gradually joining with the Quakers or might even fall back into heathenism if preventive measures are not taken.

I told him that I would think just as he did if I were in his place. I said that one could travel from one pole to the other in the few minutes on a map, but in practice things went much more slowly and laboriously. It is something fondly to be hoped for that all the walls of partition made by human hands may be done away and Christ be all in all.

1777. September 6.

Today I am sixty-six years old and am entering upon my sixty-seventh year.

This summer I beheld a scene or *portrait* at my small dwelling place. A scrawny, unattractive hen, or pullet, laid eleven eggs in a hidden place amid a great cackling. For several weeks the hen sat on the eggs, suffering hunger and thirst and hardly taking a few minutes during the day to search for food in order to preserve life. Finally the little creature came out and brought eleven chicks to my door and asked for feed for her helpless offspring. She broke the bread for her young ones, warmed them at her breast, protected them against storms, warned them when she spied a bird of prey from afar, drew them after her when they wished to stray, fought men and strong beasts who approached too near to her young ones, cut a figure with her wings as if she were wearing a hoop skirt, and brought her young ones to my door or under my window five or six times a day and asked me to feed them. When the young ones had grown enough to help themselves, there was not one among them which showed enough gratitude to bring the mother a kernel of corn or share a chance crumb. Moreover, the mother ceased calling them, became quiet, modest, shy, and timid, and withdrew into solitude.

Let the application be made to poor, aged parents and preachers, children and congregations.

Henry Melchior Muhlenberg, *Notebook of a Colonial Clergyman,* ed. T. G. Tappert and J. W. Doberstein (Philadelphia: Muhlenberg, 1959) 30, 90-91, 176. Used by permission.

Propers: Pastors

Hymn of the Day: "If God himself be for me" (454)

Prayers: for the Lutheran churches in America
for harried administrators and leaders
for a spirit of peace and cooperation
for a concern for orthodoxy
for a deepened piety

Color: White

Ignatius, Bishop of Antioch, Martyr, ca. 115

Ignatius is known primarily through seven letters he wrote while on his way to Rome as a prisoner condemned to die during the reign of Trajan (98-117).

He was apparently born in Syria ca. 35 and was a convert from paganism. He calls himself Theophoros, the bearer of God. It appears that he was the second (or third) bishop of Antioch in Syria—according to some he succeeded St. Peter there. Nothing is known of his life apart from his journey to martyrdom from Antioch to Rome under a guard of ten soldiers. He was received en route with great honor at Smyrna by Polycarp, who attests to his martyrdom at Rome, and by representatives of neighboring Christian communities. While Ignatius was at Smyrna he wrote to the church at Ephesus, Magnesia, Tralles, and Rome. He was then taken to Troas, and from there he wrote to the churches of Philadelphia and Smyrna and to Polycarp. He was from there taken through Macedonia and Illyria to

Dyrrachium and then by ship to Italy, where he was executed doubtless in the Coliseum. Polycarp, writing to the Philippians, says that Ignatius, Zosimus, and Rufus "are now in their deserved place with the Lord, in whose suffering they also shared."

Ignatius' feast day on the old Roman Catholic calendar was February 1; in the Eastern church it was December 20. The new Roman Catholic calendar and the new Episcopal calendar as well have both chosen as Ignatius' feast day the date of his commemoration in the Church of Antioch, October 17, which was observed there as early as the fourth century.

V. Corwin. *Ignatius and Christianity in Antioch*. New Haven: Yale, 1960.
Cyril C. Richardson. *The Christianity of Ignatius of Antioch*. New York: Columbia University Press, 1935.

Reading

(From a letter to the Romans by Ignatius)

May I have the good fortune to meet my fate without interference! What I fear is your generosity which may prove detrimental to me. For you can easily do what you want to, whereas it is hard for me to get to God unless you let me alone. I do not want you to please men, but to please God, just as you are doing. For I shall never again have such a chance to get to God, nor can you, if you keep quiet, get credit for a finer deed. For if you quietly let me alone, people will see in me God's Word. But if you are enamored of my mere body, I shall, on the contrary, be a meaningless noise. Grant me no more than to be a sacrifice for God while there is an altar at hand. Then you can form yourselves into a choir and sing praises to the Father in Jesus Christ that God gave the bishop of [i.e. from] Syria the privilege of reaching the sun's setting when he summoned him from its rising. It is a grand thing for my life to set on the world, and for me to be on my way to God, so that I may rise in his presence.

I am corresponding with all the churches and bidding them all realize that I am voluntarily dying for God—if, that is, you do not interfere. I plead with you, do not do me an unseasonable kindness.

Let me be fodder for wild beasts—that is how I can get to God. I am God's wheat and I am being ground by the teeth of wild beasts to make a pure loaf for Christ. I would rather that you fawn on the beasts so that they may be my tomb and no scrap of my body be left. Thus, when I have fallen asleep, I shall be a burden to no one. Then I shall be a real disciple of Jesus Christ when the world sees my body no more. Pray Christ for me that by these means I may become God's sacrifice. . . .

Even now as a prisoner, I am learning to forego my own wishes. All the way from Syria to Rome I am fighting with wild beasts, by land and sea, night and day, chained as I am to ten leopards (I mean to a detachment of soliders), who only get worse the better you treat them. But by their injustices I am becoming a better disciple. What a thrill I shall have from the wild beasts that are ready for me! I hope they will make short work of me. I shall coax them on to eat me up at once and not to hold off, as sometimes happens, through fear. And if they are reluctant, I shall force them to it. Forgive me— I know what is good for me. Now is the moment I am beginning to be a disciple. May nothing seen or unseen begrudge me making my way to Jesus Christ. Come fire, cross, battling with wild beasts, wrenching of bones, mangling of limbs, crushing of my whole body, cruel tortures of the devil—only let me get to Jesus Christ! Not the wide bounds of earth nor the kingdoms of this world will avail me anything. "I would rather die" and get to Jesus Christ, than reign over the ends of the earth. That is whom I am looking for—the One who died for us. That is whom I want—the One who rose for us. I am going through the pangs of being born. Sympathize with me, my death on me. Do not give back to the world one who wants to be brothers! Do not stand in the way of my coming to life—do not wish death on me. Do not give back to the world one who wants to be God's; do not trick him with material things. Let me get into the clear light and manhood will be mine. Let me imitate the Passion of my God.

From *Early Christian Fathers*, Vol. I, Library of Christian Classics, trans. and ed. by Cyril C. Richardson, 103-105. Published in the U.S.A. by The Westminster Press, 1953. Used by permission.

Propers

ROMAN	LUTHERAN	EPISCOPAL
All-powerful and ever-living God, you ennoble your Church with the heroic witness of all who give their lives for Christ. Grant that the victory of Saint Ignatius of Antioch may bring us your constant help as it brought him eternal glory. We ask this through our Lord Jesus Christ, your Son, who lives and reigns with you and the Holy Spirit, one God, for ever and ever.	Gracious Lord, in every age you have sent men and women who have given their lives for the message of your love. Inspire us with the memory of those martyrs for the Gospel like your servant Ignatius, whose faithfulness led them in the way of the cross, and give us courage to bear full witness with our lives to your Son's victory over sin and death; through Jesus Christ our Lord.	O God, who enabled your blessed bishop and martyr Ignatius to preach your Word and endure steadfastly even to death: Grant us, after his pattern, to be strong in our faith, and to confirm it in our lives by our patient endurance; through Jesus Christ our Lord, who now lives and reigns with you and the Holy Spirit, one God, in glory everlasting.

(*Text from the English translation of the Roman Missal* © *1973, International Committee on English in the Liturgy, Inc. All rights reserved.*)

(*Text from Lesser Feasts and Fasts, Revised Edition, copyright 1973 by Charles Mortimer Guilbert as Custodian of the Standard Book of Common Prayer. All rights reserved. Used by permission.*)

| Philippians 3:17-4:1 John 12:24-26 or Common of Martyrs or Pastors | Common of Martyrs: Ezekiel 20:40-42 Psalm 5 *Romans 8:35-39* *John 12:23-26* | Psalm 43 Romans 8:35-39 Psalm 44:18-26 John 12:23-26 Preface of Holy Week |

Hymn of the Day: "With high delight let us unite" (140) or "Rise again, ye lion-hearted" (*TLH* 470)

Prayers: for courage to face death unafraid
for willingness gladly to give all for Christ
for the Church in Syria and throughout the Near East

Preface: All Saints

Color: Red

396

October 18

ST. LUKE, EVANGELIST

Luke was a Gentile, probably a Greek, and is believed to have come from Antioch in Syria or perhaps Philippi. Not much is known of his life except that he was a physician (Col. 4:14) and was a disciple of Saint Paul and a worker with him. He has traditionally been regarded as one of the seventy disciples commissioned by Jesus, although in his gospel (1:2) he says that he was not an eyewitness of what he writes. A later tradition that he was a painter seems not to be reliable. Luke accompanied St. Paul on some of his journeys and may have been left in charge of the church at Philippi between visits by the Apostle. He is generally believed to have been with Paul during his two imprisonments. "Lucius of Cyrene" (Acts 13:1) and "Lucius my fellow countryman" (Rom. 16:21) may refer to Luke. According to early traditions he wrote his gospel in Greece and preached the faith there and in Bithynia, an important province in northwestern Asia Minor.

St. Luke is said to have died at the age of eighty-four, never having married. Some manuscripts give the place of his death as Boetia and some give Egypt or Bithynia or Achaia. The Emperor Constantinus II had the supposed relics of St. Luke transferred from Thebes in Boeoria to Constantinople with those of St. Andrew and placed in the Church of the Holy Apostles there on March 3, 357. The observance of the feast of St. Luke is probably quite old in the East; it appears on Western calendars only in the eighth century. The date of his commemoration is universally October 18, and this may perhaps be based on the actual date of his death.

St. Luke's day is a traditional time to emphasize the church's ministry of healing by showing concern for hospitals and nursing homes, for doctors and nurses, and by conducting healing services. It is also an important day to observe in Year C of the lectionary cycle, when the readings for that year are drawn largely from the third gospel. It is an especially appropriate time to consider the nature, characteristics, and spirit of the Gospel according to St. Luke and of its sequel, the Acts of the Apostles.

Henry Cadbury. *The Making of Luke-Acts.* New York: Macmillan, 1927.
———. "The Style and Literary Method of Luke," *Harvard Theological Studies* VI, 1919-1920.
Frederick W. Danker. *Luke* (Proclamation Commentaries). Philadelphia: Fortress, 1976.
A. H. N. Green-Armytage. *A Portrait of St. Luke.* Chicago: Regnery, 1955.
Adolf Harnack. *Luke the Physician.* 1907.

Reading

(From *God in Action* by Karl Barth.)

· The "work of an evangelist" does not consist in proclaiming "ideals." It does not consist in criticizing man, his failures, his weaknesses, or his arrogance. It does not consist in the Kierkegaardian critique of the "religious man." It does not consist in *commanding* men to love God and each other, nor in preaching a social hope. It does not consist in giving a description of the evolution of this or that point in dogmatics, even if it is the best dogmatics.

The "work of an evangelist"—while he may make use of every possible material—is in what his name indicates. It consists in proclaiming the Evangel. The proclamation of the gospel is the proclamation of Jesus Christ. If Jesus Christ is the content, if it is "grace, nothing but grace, and the whole of grace," then there is no need of a supporting practical effect of some deed, because it itself is, and does, the one true deed. The church waits upon this deed, and the world awaits the action of this deed from the church. We must learn again to do this work sincerely and thoroughly.

Karl Barth, "The Ministry of the Word of God," *God in Action*, (New York: Round Table Press, 1936) 80-81.

Propers

ROMAN	LUTHERAN	EPISCOPAL
Father, you chose Luke the evangelist to reveal by preaching and writing the mystery of your love for the poor. Unite in heart and spirit all who glory in your name, and let all nations come to see your salvation. Grant this through our Lord Jesus Christ, your Son, who lives and reigns with you and the Holy Spirit, one God, for ever and ever.	Almighty God, you inspired your servant Luke the physician to reveal in his Gospel the love and healing power of your Son. Give your Church the same love and power to heal, to the glory of your name; through your Son, Jesus Christ our Lord, who lives and reigns with you and the Holy Spirit, one God, now and forever.	Almighty God, who inspired your servant Luke the physician to set forth in the Gospel the love and healing power of your Son: Graciously continue in your Church this love and power to heal, to the praise and glory of your Name; through Jesus Christ our Lord, who lives and reigns with you, in the unity of the Holy Spirit, one God, now and for ever.

ROMAN	LUTHERAN	EPISCOPAL
2 Timothy 4:9-17a Psalm 145:10-13b, 17-18 Luke 10:1-9	Isaiah 43:8-13 or Isaiah 35:5-8 Psalm 124 2 Timothy 4:5-11 Luke 1:1-4; 24:44-53	Ecclesiasticus 38:1-4, 6-10, 12-14 Psalm 147 or 147:1-7 2 Timothy 4:5-13 Luke 4:14-21 Preface of All Saints

Hymn of the Day: "Your hand, O Lord, in days of old" (431)

Prayers: for the gift of the Spirit
　　　　　for compassion
　　　　　for the poor and the outcast
　　　　　for all in the healing professions
　　　　　for hospitals and nursing homes

Preface: All Saints

Color: Red

James of Jerusalem, Martyr

James is listed first among the brothers of Jesus (who formed a distinct class, separate from the Apostles) in the lists in Matthew 13:55 and Mark 6:3—James, Joses or Joseph, Simon, Judas. St. Paul in Galatians 1:19 says that he met James the Lord's brother at Jerusalem on his first visit there.

From at least the second century there has been some uncertainty about these "brothers of the Lord" mentioned in the New Testament (Mark 6:3; John 7:3; Acts 1:14; 1 Cor. 9:5.) Helvidius, who claimed the support of Tertullian, said that Jesus was Mary's first child and that the brothers and sisters mentioned in the gospels were children of Mary and Joseph, born after Jesus. Epiphanius in the second century challenged this position and suggested that the "brothers" were sons of Joseph by a former marriage. Their attempt to control Jesus (Mark 3:31; John 7:3-4) may indicate that they were older than Jesus. Moreover, it is argued, Jesus on the cross would not have commended Mary to John if the "brothers" had been her children.

Jerome in the fourth century says that James is the same person as the apostle James the Less (Mark 3:18; 15:40) and that the mother of James and Joses was Mary of Clopas, the younger sister of the Virgin Mary. Jesus and James, therefore, were not brothers but cousins. (The word translated "brother" can sometimes mean "cousin".) Why two sisters would both have the name Mary is not explained.

Jerome's view has prevailed in the West for centuries, but it is rejected by nearly all modern New Testament scholars, partly because there is no evidence in the gospels that James was a disciple during the ministry of Jesus until he became a witness of the resurrection.

James, having seen the risen Jesus (1 Cor. 15:7), is recognized early as a leader in Jerusalem. Although he was not one of the Twelve, he was regarded as an apostle (Gal. 1:19)—perhaps as a replacement for James the son of Zebedee, since James of Jerusalem is not mentioned until after the death of James the Apostle.

James' special vocation was to the Jews (Gal. 2:9). He is traditionally regarded as the first Bishop of Jerusalem, the "bishop of bishops." Jewish Christianity exalted him above Peter and Paul since his ministry was in the principal city of the Holy Land. He remained the most respected and authoritative leader in Jerusalem for most of the first Christian generation, no doubt because of his eyewitness testimony to the risen Jesus. James was, according the secular accounts, put to death by priestly authorities in the mid-sixties. Josephus (ca. 94) says that James "with certain others" was stoned to death in 62 at the instigation of the high priest Annas. Hegesippus says that at Passover "James the Just" claimed that Jesus was the Son of Man and was thrown from the temple and stoned and beaten to death before the siege of A.D. 66.

The Eastern churches commemorate James the brother of the Lord on this date, and it has also been adopted by several Anglican calendars.

J. B. Lightfoot. *St. Paul's Epistle to the Galatians* (1865) 241-274.
J. B. Major. *The Epistle of St. James.* 3rd ed. (1913) i-xlv.
W. Patrick. *James, the Lord's Brother.* 1906.
Bo Reicke. *The Epistles of James, Peter, and Jude.* Garden City, N.Y.: Doubleday, 1964. [Anchor Bible, vol. 37]

Reading

(From *Imitation of Christ.*)

There are two wings that raise a man above earthly things—simplicity and purity. Simplicity must inspire his purpose and purity his affection. Simplicity reaches out after God; purity discovers and enjoys Him. No good deed will prove an obstacle to you if you are inwardly free from uncontrolled desires. And if you are free from uncontrolled desires, and seek nothing but the Will of God and the good of your neighbor, you will enjoy this inner freedom. If your heart be right, then every created thing will become for you a mirror of life and a book of holy teaching. For there is nothing created so small and mean that it does not reflect the goodness of God.

Were you inwardly good and pure, you would see and understand all things clearly and without difficulty. A pure heart penetrates both heaven and hell. As each man is in himself so does he judge outward things. If there is any joy to be had in this world, the pure in heart most surely possess it; and if there is trouble and distress anywhere, the evil conscience most readily experiences it. Just as iron, when plunged into fire, loses its rust and becomes bright and glowing, so the man who turns himself wholly to God loses his sloth and becomes transformed into a new creature.

From *Imitation of Christ*, trans. Leo Sherley-Price (Baltimore: Penguin, 1965) 72. Copyright © 1965, Leo Sherley-Price. Used by permission of Penguin Books Ltd.

Propers

ROMAN	LUTHERAN	EPISCOPAL
	Almighty God, you have raised up faithful bishops and leaders of your church. May the memory of your servant James the Just, brother of our Lord, be a source of joy for us and a bulwark of our faith, so that we may serve you and confess your Name before the world; through your Son, Jesus Christ our Lord.	Grant, O God, that following the example of your servant James the Just, brother of our Lord, your Church may give itself continually to prayer and to the reconciliation of all who are at variance and enmity; through Jesus Christ our Lord, who lives and reigns with you and the Holy Spirit, one God, now and for ever.
		(Text from the Book of Common Prayer [Proposed], copyright 1977 by Charles Mortimer Guilbert as Custodian of the Standard Book of Common Prayer. All rights reserved. Used by permission.)
	Acts 15:15-22a *Psalm 1* *1 Corinthians 15:1-7* *Matthew 13:54-58*	Acts 15:15-22a Psalm 1 1 Corinthians 15:1-11 Matthew 13:54-58 Preface of All Saints

Hymn of the Day: "Rise, O children of salvation" (182)

Prayers: for the Church in Jerusalem
　　　　for the peace of Jerusalem and the Holy Land
　　　　for bishops and others in authority
　　　　for a just and righteous life.

Preface: All Saints

Color: Red

402

October 26

Philipp Nicolai, Hymnwriter, 1608

Nicolai was born August 10, 1556 in Mengeringhausen, Waldeck, Germany, the son of a pastor. He studied theology at the universities of Erfurt and Wittenberg, 1575-1579. In 1583 he became pastor in Herdecke near Dortmund where his father had introduced the Reformation. The town council was Roman Catholic, and, when the Spanish invaded and the Roman Mass was reintroduced, Nicolai was forced to flee. He seems to have served secretly as a pastor in Cologne in 1586 holding services in members' homes. (Gerhardt did the same in Berlin.) At the end of 1586 he was appointed diaconus at Niederwildungen, and in 1587 became pastor there. In November 1588 he was the pastor at Altwildungen, court preacher to the Countess Margaretha of Waldeck, and tutor to her son. In 1594 he at last received his D.D. degree from Wittenberg. The degree had been delayed because of his controversy with the crypto-calvinists.

In October 1596 he became pastor in Unna in Westphalia. It was a time of distress: between July 1597 and January 1598 the plague took 1300 of his parishioners, sometimes thirty in a day, three hundred in July and one hundred seventy in one week in August. The parsonage overlooked the graveyard, and Nicolai could not avoid the constant presence of death. He wrote a series of meditations to comfort his people, *Mirror of Joy*, (the preface was dated August 10, 1598—his forty-third birthday), and to this book, published in 1599, he appended his two chorales. *Wachet Auf* ("Wake, awake, for night is flying"), the "king of chorales" with the title "Of the voice at Midnight, and the wise virgins who meet their heavenly Bridegroom. Mt. 25." The other was *Wie schön leuchtet der Morgenstern* ("How brightly beams the morning star"), the "queen of chorales"; it bore the title, "A spiritual bridal song of the believing soul concerning Jesus Christ, her heavenly Bridegroom, founded on the 45th Psalm of the prophet David." Written in the space of a few hours, it immediately established itself as a favorite in Germany and came to be regarded as an almost indispensable part of the wedding service. Nicolai's fame as a hymnwriter rests entirely on these two hymns.

In December 1598 the Spanish again invaded and Nicolai was forced to flee once more. He returned in April 1599. In 1601 he was made pastor of St. Katherine's Church in Hamburg where he endeared himself to the people with his pastoral concern and won their respect as a courageous and powerful preacher. (He was called a "second Chrysostom.")

In 1596-1597 he had written a two-volume biblical-theological-apocalyptic work on the kingdom of Christ. He also was the author of polemical writings against the crypto-calvinists and the Reformed in his impassioned defense of Lutheran orthodoxy. Nonetheless, personally he was gentle and irenic, with a mystical inclination.

Following an ordination at St. Katherine's October 22, he returned home ill. His illness grew worse and he died October 26, 1608.

Arthur Carl Piepkorn. "Philipp Nicolai (1556-1608)," *Concordia Theological Monthly* XXX, 7 (July-August 1968), 432-461.

Johann Heermann, Hymnwriter, 1647

Heermann was born at Raudten, Silesia, October 11, 1585, his parents' only surviving child. His father was a furrier. The son suffered a severe illness as a child, and his mother vowed that if he recovered he would be educated for the ministry.

After serving as a tutor, he was appointed diaconus at Koeben, a village near Raudten. Within six months he was elevated to the pastorate of the parish (1611). An affliction of the throat in 1634 forced him to stop preaching. For four years his preaching was done by assistants, and in 1638 Heermann retired to Lissa and died there Septuagesima Sunday, February 17, 1647.

He had suffered not only from poor health but also from the deprivations of the Thirty Years' War. Koeben was devastated by fire in 1616, plundered four times between 1629 and 1634, and suffered pestilence in 1631. Heermann was driven from his home and forced to flee again and again, sometimes narrowly escaping death. From this unending affliction, Heermann was able to write hymns of confident faith that have been sung and loved by succeeding generations. As a hymnwriter of his century, he ranks second only to Gerhardt. His hymns mark a transition from the objective hymns of the Reformation to the more subjective type and are characterized by a depth of feeling and tenderness that is unsurpassed.

Paul Gerhardt, Hymnwriter, 1676

Gerhardt, who is perhaps the greatest Lutheran hymnwriter, was born March 12, 1607 at Gräfenhaynichen, near Wittenberg. His father, the mayor of the town, died while his son was still young. Gerhardt studied theology at the University of Wittenberg from 1628 to 1642. The Thirty Years' War was raging, and it was a time of suffering and desolation. Gerhardt went to Berlin as a tutor in the home of Andreas Barthold and in 1655 married Barthold's daughter, Anna Maria. His contact with Johann Crüger, the cantor at St. Nicholas' Church in Berlin, stimulated his poetic gifts, and eighteen of his hymns appeared in the third edition of Crüger's *Praxis pietatis melica*.

When he was forty-four years old, Gerhardt obtained appointment as Probst (chief pastor) at Mittenwalde in Brandenburg, near Berlin, and was ordained November 18, 1651. He became the third assistant at St. Nicholas' Church in Berlin in 1657 and there gained fame as a preacher. In doctrinal debates with the Reformed he maintained the Lutheran position. He refused to sign a pledge not to bring doctrinal discussion into sermons and was deposed by Frederick William of Brandenburg-Prussia in 1666. Although he was restored to his position in the following year, he refused to return and remained without a parish for some years. During this time of trial his wife and a son died (three children had died earlier), and his misery increased. In May 1669 he was appointed archdeacon of Lübben. He lived there with a sister-in-law and his sole surviving son in a somewhat unsympathetic parish. He died June 7, 1676.

Amid affliction and the calamities of the Thirty Years' War and its aftermath, Gerhardt wrote some one hundred and thirty-three hymns of faith and confidence. He was, moreover, able to translate orthodox doctrines in such a way that people could not only know them but could experience them with emotional warmth. In the church at Lübben there is a life-size portrait of Gerhardt with the inscription beneath it, "A Divine sifted in Satan's sieve."

T. B. Hewitt. *Paul Gerhardt as a Hymnwriter and His Influence on English Hymnody*. New Haven and London: Yale University Press, 1919.

Reading

(From Luther's "Preface to the Wittenberg Hymnal.")

That it is good and God pleasing to sing hymns is, I think, known to every Christian; for everyone is aware not only of the example of the prophets and kings in the Old Testament who praised God with song and sound, with poetry and psaltery, but also of the common and ancient custom of the Christian church to sing Psalms. St. Paul himself instituted this in I Corinthians 14 [:15] and exhorted the Colossians [3:16] to sing spiritual songs and Psalms heartily unto the Lord so that God's Word and Christian teaching might be instilled and implanted in many ways.

Therefore I, too, in order to make a start and to give an incentive to those who can do better, have with the help of others compiled several hymns, so that the holy gospel which now by the grace of God has risen anew may be noised and spread abroad.

Like Moses in his song [Exod. 15:2], we may now boast that Christ is our praise and song and say with St. Paul, I Corinthians 2 [:2], that we should know nothing to sing or say, save Jesus Christ our Savior.

. . . Nor am I of the opinion that the gospel should destroy and blight all the arts, as some of the pseudo-religious claim. But I would like to see all the arts, especially music, used in the service of Him who gave and made them.

Martin Luther, "Preface to the Wittenberg Hymnal" (1524) *Luther's Works* vol. 52 (Philadelphia: Fortress, 1965), pp. 315-316.

Propers: Artists

Hymn of the Day: "O morning star, how fair and bright" (Nicolai) (76)
"O God, my faithful God" (Heermann) (504)
"Evening and morning" (Gerhardt) 465)

Prayers: for grace to sing in distress and in joy
for preachers of the gospel
for confidence and faith
for a gentle spirit

Color: White

ST. SIMON AND ST. JUDE, APOSTLES

Simon is called the "Canaanaean" by Matthew and Mark and "the Zealot" by Luke. (The two terms represent the same Aramaic word.) He therefore probably had been associated with the fanatical opponents of Roman rule in Palestine. Nothing further is known of him.

Jude, called "Judas not Iscariot" in John 14:22, is referred to in Luke 6:16 as "Judas, son of James." The phrase can also mean brother of James, and it has generally been so understood in the West. Jude is thought to have been the brother of James, the brother of the Lord, and the author of the Epistle of Jude. He is generally understood to be the same person as Thaddaeus or Lebbaeus of Matthew 10:3 and Mark 3:18—names, like Jude, given to Judas to avoid confusing him with the Judas who betrayed Jesus.

Tradition says that St. Jude preached for ten years in Mesopotamia and that he and St. Simon labored together in Persia and were martyred there on the same day. The Armenian Church regards St. Thaddaeus and St. Bartholomew as the first to preach the gospel among the Armenians and have a joint day of commemoration for them. In the Eastern Orthodox churches the two apostles have separate feast days: St. Simon on May 10 and St. Jude on June 19.

Legendary accounts of St. Jude's miraculous healing of the King of Edessa and the conflicts between two apostles and Zoroastrian magicians in Persia have been handed down with all sorts of embellishments. In recent centuries the Roman Catholic Church has come to regard St. Jude as the saint to turn to for help "in desperate cases."

Reading

(From Luther's "Lectures on Galatians")

Serving another person through love seems to reason to mean performing unimportant works such as the following: teaching the erring; comforting the afflicted; encouraging the weak; helping the neighbor in whatever way one can; bearing with his rude manners and impoliteness; putting up with annoyances, labors, and the ingratitude and contempt of men in both church and state; being patient in the home with a cranky wife and an unmanageable family, and the like. But believe me, these works are so outstanding and brilliant that the whole world cannot comprehend their usefulness and worth; indeed, it cannot estimate the value of even one tiny good work, because it does not measure works or anything else on he basis of the Word of God but on the basis of a reason that is wicked, blind, and foolish.

Therefore men are completely mistaken when they imagine that they really understand the commandment to love. They have it written in their hearts, of course, because by nature they judge that one should do to others what one wants done to oneself (Matthew 7:12). But it does not follow that they understand this. For if they did, they would demonstrate it in their actions and would prefer love to all other works.

Luther's Works, vol. 27 Lectures on Galatians, trans. Jaroslav Pelikan (St. Louis: Concordia, 1964) 56-57. © 1964 Concordia Publishing House. Used by permission.

Propers

ROMAN	LUTHERAN	EPISCOPAL
Father, you revealed yourself to us through the preaching of your apostles Simon and Jude. By their prayers, give your Church continued growth and increase the number of those who believe in you. Grant this through our Lord Jesus Christ, your Son, who lives and reigns with you and the Holy Spirit, one God, for ever and ever.	O God, we thank you for the glorious company of the apostles, and, especially on this day, for Simon and Jude. We pray that, as they were faithful and zealous in their mission, so we may with ardent devotion make known the love and mercy of our Lord and Savior Jesus Christ, who lives and reigns with you and the Holy Spirit, one God, now and forever.	O God, we thank you for the glorious company of the apostles, and especially on this day for Simon and Jude; and we pray that, as they were faithful and zealous in their mission, so we may with ardent devotion make known the love and mercy of our Lord and Savior Jesus Christ, who lives and reigns with you and the Holy Spirit, one God, for ever and ever.

ROMAN	LUTHERAN	EPISCOPAL
Ephesians 2:19-22 Psalm 19:2-5 Luke 6:12-16	Jeremiah 26:(1-6) 7:16 Psalm 11 1 John 4:1-6 John 14:21-27	Deuteronomy 32:1-4 Psalm 119:89-96 Ephesians 2:13-22 John 15:17-27 Preface of Apostles

Hymn of the Day: "Father eternal, ruler of creation" (413)
        or "Awake, my soul, stretch every nerve" (*SBH* 552)

Prayers: for the obscure and the forgotten and the unknown in the
      work of the church
      for the gift of holiness, which is the creation and the
      gift of God
      for faithful continuation of the apostles' preaching
      of the Gospel to all the world

Preface: Apostles

Color: Red

REFORMATION DAY

This celebration is a peculiarly Lutheran festival. Each of the liturgical churches has a day celebrating its central and formative event or experience. Eastern Orthodoxy has a celebration of the Triumph of Orthodoxy, the first Sunday in Lent, commemorating the settling in 843 of the controversy over the use of icons in the church. The Roman Church has the feast of the Chair of Peter (February 22), emphasizing the founding of the church upon Peter the Prince of the Apostles. The Anglican Church commemorates the publication of the First Book of Common Prayer in 1549 as the principal liturgical and theological source for the Anglican Communion. The rubric in the new Prayer Book reads, "The First Book of Common Prayer, 1549, is appropriately observed on a weekday following the Day of Pentecost." The Lutheran Church has its celebration also.

Only six of the several hundred church orders of the sixteenth century make provision for the celebration of the Reformation. The date of the celebration varied: in Pomerania it was celebrated on Luther's birthday; sometimes it was Trinity Sunday (as Pentecost commemorated the birthday of the church so the following Sunday commemorated the rebirth of the church); sometimes it is the Sunday following the day of the Presentation of the Augsburg Confession (June 25). The observances soon died out.

A new anti-Roman spirit was created by the Thirty Years' War in which Roman Catholic princes attempted to eradicate northern European Protestantism. In 1667, John George II, the Elector of Saxony, ordered a Reformation festival to be celebrated on October 31, the anniversary of Luther's posting the Ninety-five Theses on door of the castle church in Wittenberg, questioning abuses in the sale of indulgences. The festival spread and was often moved to the nearest Sunday, whether before or after the date. A more irenic date for the commemoration of the Reformation is June 25, the Presentation of the Augsburg Confession.

Conrad Bergendoff. *The Church of the Lutheran Reformation.* St. Louis: Concordia, 1967.
Werner Elert. *The Structure of Lutheranism,* tr. Walter A. Hansen. St. Louis: Concordia, 1962.

October 31

Wilhelm Pauck. *The Heritage of the Reformation.* Glencoe, Ill.: Free Press, 1961.
Gordon Rupp. *The Righteousness of God.* London: Hodder, 1953.

Reading

(From *English Literature in the Sixteenth Century* by C. S. Lewis.)

. . . In reality Tyndale is trying to express an obstinate fact which meets us long before we venture into the realm of theology; the fact that morality or duty (what he calls 'the Law') never yet made a man happy in himself or dear to others. It is shocking, but it is undeniable. We do not wish either to be, or to live among, people who are clean or honest or kind as a matter of duty: we want to be, and to associate with, people who like being clean and honest and kind. The mere suspicion that what seemed an act of spontaneous friendliness or generosity was really done as a duty subtly poisons it. In philosophical language, the ethical category is self-destructive; morality is healthy only when it is trying to abolish itself. In theological language, no man can be saved by works. The whole purpose of the 'gospel', for Tyndale, is to deliver us from morality. This, paradoxically, the 'puritan' of modern imagination—the cold, gloomy heart, doing as duty what happier and richer souls do without thinking of it—is precisely the enemy which historical Protestantism arose and smote. What really matters is not to obey moral rules but to be a creature of a certain kind.

C. S. Lewis, *English Literature in the Sixteenth Century Excluding Drama* (Oxford: Clarendon, 1954) 187. © Oxford University Press 1954. Used by permission of Oxford University Press.

Propers: Reformation Day

Hymn of the Day: "I trust, O Christ, in you alone" (395)

Prayers: for a renewed sense of the free grace of God
for the living word of God to burn brightly in the church
for a bold, daring, and lively faith
for the unity of the church
for increased love of one another

Color: Red

ALL SAINTS' DAY

The origins of this festival are uncertain. Ephraim of Edessa composed a hymn ca. 359 which suggests that a commemoration of all the martyrs was held on May 13. By 411 in Eastern Syria the commemoration of all the martyrs was held on the Friday after Easter, suggesting a parallel with Good Friday; as Christ died on Friday, so those who follow him in death imitate his passion, but in the light of the resurrection.

From a sermon by John Chrysostom it appears that the church at Antioch commemorated all the martyrs on the Sunday after Pentecost, and Maximus of Turin preached on all the martyrs also on the Sunday after Pentecost. This is still the day of the commemoration of all the saints in the Eastern churches, and it has a logic to it. The birthday of the church, Pentecost, has its parallel in the birthday of the saints—their martyrdom. In the old maxim, the blood of the martyrs is (or waters) the seed of the church. By the seventh century the feast had been extended to include non-martyrs as well. The *Comes* of Wuerzburg calls the day "The Sunday of the Birthday of the Saints." Holiness, we are reminded, is the work of the Holy Spirit.

On May 13, 609 or 610, Boniface IV dedicated the Roman Pantheon to Mary and all the Martyrs. The anniversary of this dedication was kept with great rejoicing—but whether it was because of the martyrs or because of the anniversary of the dedication is unclear. There was a pagan festival to placate the gods (Lemuria) on May 9, 11, and 13; and the Christian celebration on May 13 was probably in part to offset the pagan festival.

Gregory III dedicated an oratory in St. Peter's Basilica to all the saints, but the date is unknown and the chapel is a small one and its principal dedication was to the Virgin Mary.

In England at this time, November 1 is listed as the day of all the Saints. Perhaps Egbert of York, who had been ordained deacon in Rome in 732, carried the celebration of November 1 to England, or the celebration of the day may have originated in Gaul or Ireland. (The Irish often assigned the first day of the month to important feasts, and the oldest Irish martyrology lists November 1 as the feast of all English and Irish saints, April 20 as the day of all the saints of

Europe, and December 23 as the day of all the saints of Africa.)
Moreover, in Celtic lands the mists and frosts of late autumn suggested the visitation and the presence of spirits and made the beginning of November a natural time to remember the departed.

According to John Beleth (died ca. 1165), Gregory IV in 835 transferred the feast from May 13 to November 1 after the harvest so that
there would be sufficient food in Rome for the pilgrims. In the twelfth
century the date of May 13 for all saints disappears from the liturgical
books.

The 1928 proposed English Book of Common Prayer assigned the
octave of All Saints (November 8) to the "Saints, Martyrs, and Doctors of the Church of England." The American *Draft Proposed Book
of Common Prayer* (1976) listed November 8 as the commemoration
of the "Holy Men and Women of the Old Testament," but the commemoration was not carried into the *Proposed Book of Common
Prayer* (1977).

Luther chose the eve of All Saints' Day, October 31, to post his
Ninety-five Theses in Wittenberg because he wanted the crowds who
would come to church on he following day to see them. As the anniversary of the posting of the theses came to be observed as Reformation Day, the ancient and universal celebration of all the saints came
to be overshadowed in Lutheran churches, although All Saints' Day
was preserved on Lutheran calendars.

Reading

(From *Centuries* by Thomas Traherne.)

. . . To delight in the Saints of God is the way to Heaven. One
would think it exceeding easy and reasonable to esteem those whom
Jesus purchased with His precious blood. And if we do so how can
we choose but inherit all things. All the Saints of all Ages and all
Kingdoms are His inheritance, His treasures, His jewels. Shall they
not be yours since they are His whom you love so infinitely?

With all their eyes behold our Saviour, with all their hearts adore
Him, with all their tongues and affection praise Him. See how in all
closets, and in all temples; in all cities and in all fields; in all nations
and in all generations, they are lifting up their hands and eyes unto

His cross; and delight in all their adorations. This will enlarge your Soul and make you to dwell in all kingdoms and ages: strengthen your faith and enrich your affections: fill you with their joys and make you a lively partaker in communion with them. Men do mightily wrong themselves when they refuse to be present in all ages: and neglect to see the beauty in all kingdoms, and despise the resentments of every soul, and busy themselves only with pots and cups and things at home, or shops and trades and things in the street: but do not live to God manifesting Himself in all the world, nor care to see (and be present with Him in) all the glory of His Eternal Kingdom. By seeing the Saints of all Ages we are present with them: by being present with them become too great for our own age, and near to our Saviour.

Thomas Traherne, *Centuries* (Harper: New York, 1960) 41, 43-44.

Propers

ROMAN	LUTHERAN	EPISCOPAL
Father, all-powerful and ever-living God, today we rejoice in the holy men and women of every time and place. May their prayers bring us your forgiveness and love. We ask this through our Lord Jesus Christ, your Son, who lives and reigns with you and the Holy Spirit, one God, for ever and ever.	Almighty God, whose people are knit together in one holy Church, the body of Christ our Lord: grant us grace to follow your blessed saints in lives of faith and commitment, and to know the inexpressible joys you have prepared for those who love you; through your Son, Jesus Christ our Lord, who lives and reigns with you and the Holy Spirit, one God, now and forever.	Almighty God, you have knit together your elect in one communion and fellowship in the mystical body of your Son Christ our Lord: Give us grace so to follow your blessed saints in all virtuous and godly living, that we may come to those ineffable joys that you have prepared for those who truly love you; through Jesus Christ our Lord, who with you and the Holy Spirit lives and reigns, one God, in glory everlasting.

ROMAN	LUTHERAN	EPISCOPAL
Revelation 7:2-4, 9-14 Psalm 24 1 John 3:1-3 Matthew 5:1-12a	Isaiah 26:1-4, 8-9, 12-13, 19-21 Psalm 34:1-10 Revelation 21:9-11, 22-27 (22:1-5) Matthew 5:1-12	Ecclesiasticus 44:1- 10, 13-14 *or* Ecclesiasticus 2:(1- 6) 7-11 Psalm 149 Revelation 7:2-4, 9-17 *or* Ephesians 1:(11- 14) 15-23 Matthew 5:1-12 *or* Luke 6:20-26 (27-36) Preface of All Saints

Hymn of the Day: "For all the saints, who from their labors rest"
(174)

Prayers: for those who waited for the fulfillment of God's promise
for the apostles and heralds of the kingdom
for those who kept the faith through ages of darkness
for missionaries who brought the gospel to our land
for all who recall the church to love and sacrifice
for all who lead the nations to justice and peace

Preface: All Saints

Color: White

At the service on All Saints' Day, gather whatever statues there may
be in the church together with other representations of individual
saints and set them near the altar as a kind of iconostasis, suggesting
the cloud of witnesses that surrounds the church on earth.

November 7

John Christian Frederick Heyer
Missionary to India, 1873

J. C. F. Heyer, the first missionary sent out by American Lutherans,
was born in Helmstedt, Germany on July 10, 1793 to a master furrier
and his wife. When he was thirteen, troops of Napoleon were quar-
tered in the city, and his parents, out of concern about the turmoil
of the time sent their son, after his confirmation in 1807, to stay with
his uncle in America.

Heyer was active in Zion Church, Philadelphia, and at the age of seventeen he decided to enter the ministry. He preached his first sermon, while still a layman, on Trinity Sunday, 1813. He studied theology under two pastors in Philadelphia and returned to Germany in 1814 to continue his education at the University of Göttingen. Upon his return to America he became a licensed home missionary, preaching the gospel in Pennsylvania and the neighboring states as far west as Missouri. In 1819 he married, and in 1820 he was ordained by the Ministerium of Pennsylvania.

For a period of more than twenty years Pastor Heyer travelled extensively not only as a preacher but also as a worker in Christian education, being particularly active in the establishing of Sunday schools in Lutheran parishes and in the work of Gettysburg College and Seminary. In 1839 his wife, who had borne six children, died.

Aged forty-eight, with two dozen years of pastoral experience in six congregations, Heyer began a new phase of his life. He acquired the fundamentals of Sanskrit and a rudimentary knowledge of medicine and was commissioned a foreign missionary on October 5, 1841 at Saint Paulus Church, Philadelphia. Leaving his children (the youngest was thirteen) he sailed from Boston for India, visited the mission fields of Lutherans in Tinnevelly, Tranquebar, and Madras, and on July 31, 1842 he began the mission work in the Telegu-speaking region of Andhra which was to be his life's work. During the next fifteen years he established the mission stations at Guntur, Gurzal, and Rajahmundry, which became the basis of the large Lutheran Church in that area today. On a furlough 1846-1848, he established a church in Baltimore and received his M.D. degree from the University of Maryland (later Johns Hopkins).

In 1857 he returned to America, visiting countries of the Middle East and Germany. Other missionaries had come to carry on the work and his health was for the second time nearly ruined from his strenuous life in the extreme climate of Andhra. Once back in the United States, however, his health revived and the indefatigable planter of churches spent twelve years of active evangelism and reorganization of parishes and schools in Minnesota and neighboring states, culminating in the formation of the Synod of Minnesota in 1860.

In August 1869 Father Heyer, as he was now affectionately called by Indians and Americans (the title was not uncommon in those days for older Lutheran pastors), dramatically volunteered to return to

Andhra where the mission work was in a period of crisis. He stayed two years and by his selfless devotion and ascetic life he infused new spirit in the mission.

He returned to Philadelphia and served as chaplain and house-father at the new Lutheran seminary. He died during the night of November 7, 1873 in his eighty-first year and was buried in Somerset (Pennsylvania) parish beside his wife. He is remembered as a pastor, teacher, missionary, and leader in the church.

E. Theodore Bachmann. *They Called Him Father. The Story of Johann Christian Frederick Heyer.* Philadelphia: Muhlenberg, 1942.
W. A. Lambert. *The Life of Rev. J. C. F. Heyer, M.D.* Philadelphia, 1903.

Reading

(From *Concerning the Inner Life* by Evelyn Underhill.)

A man of prayer is not necessarily a person who says a number of offices, or abounds in detailed intercessions; but he is a child of God, who is and knows himself to be in the deeps of his soul attached to God, and is wholly and entirely guided by the Creative Spirit in his prayer and his work. This is not merely a bit of pious language. It is a description, as real and concrete as I can make it, of the only really apostolic life. Every Christian starts with a chance of it; but only a few develop it. The laity distinguish in a moment the clergy who have it from the clergy who have it not: there is nothing that you can do for God or for the souls of men, which exceeds in importance the achievement of that spiritual temper and attitude.

Evelyn Underhill, *Concerning the Inner Life* (New York: Dutton, 1926), 14

Propers: Missionaries

Hymn of the Day: "O God, send heralds who will never falter" (283)

Prayers: for the church in India
        for colleges and seminaries
        for the schools of the church

for evangelists and those who establish new congregations
for zeal in the Lord's service.

Color: White

Martin, Bishop of Tours, 397

Martin was born about the year 316 in the town of Sabaria in the
Roman province of Pannonia, present day Hungary, of a pagan family, his father a Roman legionary. He spent his boyhood in Pavia in
Lombardy where he came under Christian influence, and at the age
of ten he decided on his own to become a catechumen. When he
was fifteen, being the son of a soldier, he was drafted to serve in
the army. He was apparently a good soldier and popular with his
comrades.

One winter night when he was stationed in Amiens, Martin saw a
poor old beggar at the city gate shivering in the cold, and, having
nothing else to give him, he drew his sword, cut his own cavalryman's
cloak in two, and gave half to the man to wrap himself in. The next
night Martin dreamed of Christ in heaven wearing his half-cloak and
saying, "Martin, still a catechumen, has covered me with his cloak."

The young soldier, however, found it increasingly difficult to combine his own ideal of a Christian life with the duties of the military.
Eventually he decided to be baptized and asked to leave the army,
since he was no longer willing to kill. Like his modern counterparts,
this fourth century "conscientious objector" had difficulty proving he
was not a coward, but finally he was released, now about twenty
years old.

After meeting with Bishop Hilary of Poitiers, the great scholar,
hymnwriter, and defender of Orthodoxy against Arianism, Martin
decided to join him. First, however, he went to Pannonia to convert
his family and friends. On his way back to Hilary he learned that the
bishop had been sent into exile by the Arians, and instead of going
on to Gaul, he stayed a while in Milan and then went to an island
where he lived a hermit's life until Hilary was restored to his see.

The next ten years Martin spent in a hut outside the city of Poitiers in France. Here he was joined by others until the settlement became in effect a monastery and a center of charitable work and missionary activity. (It may have been the first French monastery.) People from the surrounding countryside came to St. Martin for help, and in 371, when the see of Tours became vacant, they got him to the city by a ruse and insisted that Martin become their bishop. Although he finally agreed—he is generally known as St. Martin of Tours—he led a most unusual bishop's life.

Bishop Martin lived in a cave in the cliffs of Marmoutier, two miles from the city. His office space for the work of the diocese was a hut nearby. The new bishop's way of life was quite different from that of his fellow bishops in other cities, but he succeeded in establishing Christianity in rural areas of Gaul; previously it had been limited mostly to the cities. He travelled all over his vast diocese carrying the gospel to peasants and tribesmen, fighting paganism, and setting up centers of Christian life and faith. He was courageous in his dealings with the pagans, and he did not hesitate to speak forcefully to emperors on behalf of his people, but basically he was a gentle and peace-loving man. During the Priscillianist controversies in Spain and Gaul (Priscillian, charged with practicing magic, was executed by Emperor Maxmillian in 386—the first instance of capital punishment for heresy in the history of the church), Martin strongly opposed the sentence and raised important questions concerning the relations between church and state.

St. Martin died on November 8, 397 in a distant post in his diocese, and the date of his commemoration recalls the day of his burial at Tours. He was one of the founders of the great Celtic church which spread the gospel to the British Isles and a great part of what is now France, Germany, and the Low Countries. He is regarded as the patron saint of France, and there are many churches named for him in Britain. During the Middle Ages he was one of the most popular saints in the calendar, and his tomb at Tours was for several centuries an important center of pilgrimage. After the Reformation many Lutherans continued to observe St. Martin's Day, possibly in part because Luther was born on St. Martin's Eve and bore the name of the saint on whose feast day he was baptized. In the United States there are about fifty Lutheran churches named for St. Martin. He was one of the greatest figures in the history of the Western church, and his life, summed up in his motto *Non recuso laborem* "I do not turn back from work," has been an inspiration to missionaries and Christian workers since his day.

The feast day of Hilary of Poitiers on the Roman and Episcopal calendars is January 13.

Christopher Donaldson. *Martin of Tours: Parish Priest, Mystic and Exorcist.* London: Routledge and Kegan Paul, 1980.

L. Foley. *St. Martin of Tours. The Greatest Saint of France.* New York: Morehouse, 1931.

Reading

(From a letter of Sulpicius Severus)

Martin knew long in advance the time of his death and he told his brethren that it was near. Meanwhile, he found himself obliged to make a visitation of the parish of Candes. The clergy of that church were quarreling, and he wished to reconcile them. Although he knew that his days were few, he did not refuse to undertake the journey for such a purpose, for he believed that he would bring his virtuous life to a good end if by his efforts peace was restored in the church.

He spent some time in Candes, or rather in its church, where he stayed. Peace was restored, and he was planning to return to his monastery when he suddenly began to lose his strength. He summoned his brethren and told them he was dying. All who heard this were overcome with grief. In their sorrow they cried to him with one voice, "Father, why are you deserting us? Who will care for us when you are gone? Savage wolves will attack your flock, and who will save us from their bite when our shepherd is struck down? We know you long to be with Christ, but your reward is certain and will not be any less for being delayed. You will do better to show pity for us, rather than forsake us."

Thereupon he broke into tears, for he was a man in whom the compassion of our Lord was continually revealed. Turning to our Lord, he made this reply to their pleading: "Lord, if your people still need me, I am ready for the task; your will be done."

Here was a man words cannot describe. Death could not defeat him nor toil dismay him. He was quite without a preference of his own; he neither feared to die nor refused to live. With eyes and hands raised to heaven he never withdrew his unconquered spirit from prayer. It happened that some priests who had gathered at his bedside suggested that he should give his poor body some relief by lying on his other side. He answered, "Allow me, brothers, to look toward heaven rather than at the earth, so that my spirit may set on the right course when the time comes for me to go on my journey to the Lord." As he spoke these words, he saw the devil standing near. "Why do you stand there, you bloodthirsty brute?" he cried. "Murderer, you will not have me for your prey. Abraham is welcoming me into his embrace."

With these words, he gave up his spirit to heaven. Filled with joy, he left this life a poor and lowly man and entered heaven rich in God's favor.

From the English translation of the Office of Readings from the Liturgy of the Hours © 1974, the International Committee on English in the Liturgy, Inc. All rights reserved.

Propers

ROMAN	LUTHERAN	EPISCOPAL

Father, by his life and death Martin of Tours offered you worship and praise. Renew in our hearts the power of your love, so that neither death nor life may separate us from you. Grant this through our Lord Jesus Christ, your Son, who lives and reigns with you and the Holy Spirit, one God, for ever and ever.

(Text from the English translation of the Roman Missal © 1973, Interna-

Heavenly Father, shepherd of your people, we thank you for your servant Martin, who was faithful in the care and nurture of your flock; and we pray that, following his example and the teaching of his holy life, we may by your grace grow into the full stature of our Lord and Savior Jesus Christ.

O God, who by your Holy Spirit enabled your servant Martin to withstand the temptations of the world, the flesh, and the devil: Give us grace, with pure hearts and minds, to follow you, the only God; through Jesus Christ our Lord, who lives and reigns with you and the Holy Spirit, one God, now and for ever.

(Text from Lesser Feasts and Fasts, Revised Edition, copyright 1973 by Charles Mortimer Guilbert as Custodian of the Standard Book of Common Prayer. All rights reserved. Used by permission.)

Søren Kierkegaard 421

ROMAN	LUTHERAN	EPISCOPAL
tional Committee on English in the Liturgy, Inc. All rights reserved.) Common of Pastors or Saints (for Religious) or Matthew 25:31-40	Common of Pastors: Ezekiel 34:11-16 Psalm 84 1 Peter 5:1-4 *Matthew 25:31-40*	Psalm 15 Isaiah 58:6-12 Psalm 16:5-11 Matthew 25:34-40 Preface of a Saint

Hymn of the Day: "Jesus, thy boundless love to me" (336)

Prayers: for a spirit of generosity to the poor
for those who courageously make their witness for peace
for strength to support those under attack for their faith
for the church in France.

Preface: All Saints

Color: White

November 11

Soren Aabye Kierkegaard, Theologian, 1855

Søren Aabye Kierkegaard, the father of modern existentialism, was born in Copenhagen on May 5, 1813, the seventh and last child of an elderly couple. The mother and five of her children died within two years (the eldest and the youngest survived), and the desolate father became deeply melancholy.

As a theological student Kierkegaard learned of the secret guilt of his father who had once cursed God, and this knowledge, "the great earthquake," convinced the son that God's curse hung over the family. He became estranged from his father and for a time led a life of dissipation. Later he experienced a religious conversion and became reconciled with his father, who died in 1838 and left his sons a considerable fortune. Kierkegaard, a brilliant student, took his degree in theology but never sought ordination.

In 1840 he became engaged to Regine Olsen, a seventeen-year old girl. After great emotional distress, he broke the engagement and in the years immediately following this harrowing experience he published (not under his own name) a number of significant books:

Either-Or (1843), *Fear and Trembling* (1843), *The Concept of Dread* (1844), *Philosophical Fragments* (1844), *Concluding Unscientific Postscript* (1846). These writings often assume the character of works of the imagination, employing imaginary characters and dramatic narratives. His productivity slackened as he became engaged in a bitter feud with a radical Danish satirical paper, *The Corsair*. His subjection to ridicule in cartoons in that publication led to a feeling of martyrdom and the publication in 1849 of *Sickness Unto Death*.

In 1854 the eulogy of the Primate of Denmark by his successor set off Kierkegaard's last and most violent battle, a conflict with the Danish church in which he attacked the sterility of "official Christianity." In the midst of this conflict, lonely, with hardly a single follower, Kierkegaard collapsed on the street October 2, 1855 and died at Frederikshospital in Copenhagen on November 11, 1855 at the age of forty-two. His sickness was vaguely diagnosed as a disease of the spinal marrow. He was buried November 18 from the Cathedral Church of Our Lady, the largest church in the city, with only two priests present (his brother Peter and the dean of the cathedral). He was buried in the family plot in a long-unmarked grave.

Kierkegaard's highly personal philosophy was opposed to the objective certainty of truth which led the church of his time to an unjustified security, deprived, Kierkegaard thought, of personal choice, risk, will. The state church (or as Grundtvig preferred to call it, the National Church) institutionalized and killed the essential spirit of Christianity, Kierkegaard charged, and obscured the necessarily "troubled truth." Kierkegaard's notion of truth was revolutionary. In his view truth was not something to be observed by a detached thinker, but rather something to be experienced by a participant in the risks of life and faith. A "poet of faith," he realized that truth could come in ways other than through intellect, and his writings often exhibit remarkable literary qualities as they require readers to search their hearts and to know themselves.

Melville Channing-Pierce. "Kierkegaard." *Modern Christian Revolutionaries* ed. Donald Attwater. London: J. Clarke, 1947.
T. Haeckar. *Soren Kierkegaard*, tr. A. Dru. Oxford: Clarendon Press, 1937.
Walter Lowrie. *Kierkegaard*. London: Oxford University Press, 1938.
———. *A Short Life of Kierkegaard*. Princeton University Press, 1942.
P. Rhode. *Soren Kierkegaard: An Introduction to His Life and Philosophy*. New York: Humanities Press, 1963.

Reading

(From *Sickness Unto Death* by Søren Kierkegaard.)

There is so much said now about people being offended at Christianity because it is so dark and gloomy, offended at it because it is so severe, etc. It is now high time to explain that the real reason why man is offended at Christianity is because it is too high, because its goal is not man's goal, because it would make of a man something so extraordinary that he is unable to get it into his head. A perfectly simple psychological investigation of what offense is will explain this, and at the same time it will show how infinitely silly their behavior has been who defended Christianity by taking away the offense. . . .

If I were to imagine to myself a day-laborer and the mightiest emperor that ever lived, and were to imagine that this mighty Emperor took a notion to send for the poor man, who never had dreamed . . . that the Emperor knew of his existence, and who therefore would think himself indescribably fortunate if merely he was permitted once to see the Emperor, and would recount it to his children and children's children as the most important event of his life—but suppose the Emperor sent for him and informed him that he wished to have him for his son-in-law . . . what then? Then the laborer, humanly, would become somewhat or very much puzzled, shame-faced, and embarrassed, and it would seem to him, quite humanly (and this is the human element in it), something exceedingly strange, something quite mad, the last thing in the world about which he would say a word to anybody else, since he himself in his own mind was not far from explaining it by supposing (as his neighbors would be busily doing as soon as possible) that the Emperor wanted to make a fool of him. . . .

And now for Christianity! Christianity teaches that this particular individual, and so every individual, whatever in other respects this individual may be, man, woman, serving-maid, minister of state, merchant, barber, student, etc.—this individual exists *before God*—this individual who perhaps would be vain for having once in his life talked with the King, this man who is not a little proud of living on intimate terms with that person or the other, this man exists before God, can talk with God any moment he will, sure to be heard by Him; in short, this man is invited to live on the most intimate terms with

God! Furthermore, for this man's sake God came into the world, let himself be born, suffers and dies; and this suffering God almost begs and entreats this man to accept the help which is offered him! Verily, if there is anything that would make a man lose his understanding, it is surely this! Whosoever has not the humble courage to dare to believe it, must be offended at it.

Excerpts from Søren Kierkegaard, *Fear and Trembling* and *The Sickness Unto Death*, trans. Walter Lowrie (copyright 1941, 1954 by Princeton University Press), 214-216. Reprinted by permission of Princeton University Press.

Propers: Theologians

Hymn of the Day: "Through the night of doubt and sorrow" (355)
　　　　　　　　　　(by the Danish hymnwriter Bernhardt Severin
　　　　　　　　　　Ingemann)

Prayers: for grace to search our souls and to know ourselves
　　　　　　for courage to reject false security in the search for truth
　　　　　　for courage to risk all for the sake of Christ

Also these prayers drawn from Kierkegaard's writings:

Father in heaven! Reawaken conscience in our breast. Make us bend the ear of the spirit to your voice, so that we may perceive your will for us in its clear purity as it is in heaven, pure of our false worldly wisdom, unstifled by the voice of passion; keep us vigilant so that we may work for our salvation with fear and trembling; oh, but grant also that when the Law speaks most strongly, when its seriousness fills us with dread, when the thunder booms from Sinai— Oh grant that we may hear also a gentle voice murmuring to us that we are your children, so that we will cry with joy, Abba, Father. *(The Prayers of Kierkegaard,* ed. Perry D. LeFevre [Chicago: University of Chicago Press] 1956) 37.

O Lord Jesus Christ, the birds have their nests, the foxes their holes, and you did not have a place to lay your head, were homeless upon earth, and yet a hiding-place, the only one, where a sinner could flee. And so today you are still the hiding-place; when the sinner flees to you, hides himself in you, is hidden in you—

then he is eternally defended, then "love" covers a multitude of sins. (Ibid. 85).

Color: White

Elizabeth of Thuringia
Princess of Hungary, 1231

Elizabeth, the daughter of King Andrew of Hungary, was born in the summer of 1207 at Saros Patak, Hungary. In order to seal a political alliance she was betrothed at the age of one to Ludwig, the young son of the Landgrave of Thuringia, and when she was four she was taken to the castle of the Wartburg near Eisenach to be raised with her future husband. Elizabeth was a serious child, generous to those who had less than she had, and a devout Christian. Some of the people at the Thuringian court disapproved of her as the future duchess, but Ludwig was very fond of her.

In 1216 Ludwig succeeded his father as Landgrave, and in 1221 when he was twenty-one and Elizabeth was fourteen, the marriage took place. In the course of the next few years they had three children, a boy and two girls, and the marriage was a happy one. Elizabeth in her new position was even more generous to the poor. On one occasion, in 1225, when there was a severe local famine she gave away most of her own fortune and supply of grain to the poor of the area. She was criticized for this, but her husband upon his return gave his approval to her action.

Elizabeth founded two hospitals during this period, one at the foot of the steep rock on which the Wartburg was located. She regularly tended the patients in these hospitals herself and gave money for the care of children, especially orphans. In helping the poor she and her husband also tried to find suitable jobs for those who had no way of earning a living. In 1221, when the Franciscans entered Thuringia, Elizabeth put herself under the spiritual direction of Brother Rodeger, who guided her in the spirit of St. Francis of Assisi. Her kindness extended to all kinds of unfortunate people, and there is a well-known story of her lodging a leper in the house. The Landgrave was startled and repelled to find him in their bed, but he almost immediately realized that in helping the leper his wife was serving the crucified Lord.

On September 11, 1227 Ludwig died of the plague while on a journey to join a crusade. During that winter Elizabeth left the castle —some accounts say that her brother-in-law expelled her—and went to live in Eisenach. She was rejected by the townspeople and suffered great hardship until she received the protection of her uncle the Bishop of Bamberg. On Good Friday in 1228, she formally renounced her worldly cares, adopted coarse garments for clothing, and devoted herself as a follower of St. Francis. After the care of her children was assured, she built a small house near Marburg and with it a hospice for the sick, the aged, and the poor, and devoted her life to their care.

St. Elizabeth in her last years lived a life of unnatural austerity and isolation from her friends, partly out of obedience to her confessor, who seems to have been almost sadistic in his treatment of her. Her health broke, and on November 17, 1231 she died, at the age of twenty-four. Four years later the church began annual commemoration of her. Her traditional feast day was November 19, since November 17 already had several saints assigned to it and November 18 was the commemoration of the dedication of the basilicas of St. Peter and St. Paul. The new Roman calendar has moved her commemoration to the day of her death, November 17, but the Episcopal Church remembers her on November 19 since the 17th is the day of Hugh, Bishop of Lincoln (1200) and the 18th is the day of Hilda, Abbess of Whitby (680). She is known either as St. Elizabeth of Hungary or St. Elizabeth of Thuringia. Since her time countless hospitals have been named for her in Europe, America, and other parts of the world.

The Wartburg, in which Elizabeth lived for most of her brief life, was the same castle in which, some three hundred years later, Luther completed his translation of the New Testament into German. The town of Eisenach where Elizabeth took her vows was Luther's childhood home and the birthplace of Johann Sebastian Bach. Marburg, where St. Elizabeth is buried in the beautiful Gothic church that bears her name, is also the site of the first Protestant university, founded by Philip of Hesse, her descendant.

William Canton. *The Story of Saint Elizabeth of Hungary.* London: Herbert and Daniel, 1912.

J. Ancelet-Hustache. *St. Elizabeth de Hongrie.* Paris, 1947 English tr. P. J. Oligny and V. O'Donnell, *Gold Tried by Fire.* Chicago: Franciscan Herald Press, 1963.

Anne G. Seesholtz. *Saint Elizabeth, Her Brother's Keeper.* New York: Philosophical Library, 1948.

Reading

(From *Light of Christ* by Evelyn Underhill.)

But there is the essence of the spiritual life. Profound submission to the mysterious Will of God declared in circumstance. And being what we are and the world what it is, that means for most of us Gethsemane and the Cross and the darkness of the Cross. Lots of the saints have been through that. We don't begin to understand the Passion till we see what it was in their lives. For union with Christ means accepting the dread fact of human nature, that only those willing to accept suffering up to the limit are capable of giving love up to the limit; and that this is the kind of love which is the raw material of the redeeming life. Only those who place themselves in the hands of God without reserve and without fear are going to be used by Him to save. We want a lot of practice before we can manage this. It will not come out of an easy-going religion.

To look at the Crucifix—"the supreme symbol of our august religion" —and then to look at our own hearts; to test the Cross by the quality of our love—if we do that honestly and unflinchingly we don't need any other self-examination than that, any other judgment or purgation. The lash, the crown of thorns, the mockery, the stripping, the nails—life has equivalents of all these for us and God asks a love for Himself and His children which can accept and survive all that in the particular way in which it is offered to us. It is no use to talk in a large vague way about the love of God; *here* is its point of insertion in the world of men.

Evelyn Underhill, *Light of Christ* (London: Longmans, Green and Co., 1945) 82-83.

Propers

ROMAN	LUTHERAN	EPISCOPAL

ROMAN

Father,
you helped Elizabeth
of Hungary
to recognize and
honor Christ
in the poor of this
world.
Let her prayers help
us to serve our
brothers and
sisters
in time of trouble and
need.
We ask this through
our Lord Jesus
Christ, your Son,
who lives and reigns
with you and the
Holy Spirit,
one God, now and for
ever.

(Text from the English translation of the Roman Missal © 1973, International Committee on English in the Liturgy, Inc. All rights reserved.)

LUTHERAN

Lord God, your Son came
among us to serve and not
to be served, and to give
his life for the world. Lead
us by his love and the example of Elizabeth to serve
all those to whom the world
offers no comfort and little
help. Through us give hope
to the hopeless, love to the
unloved, peace to the troubled, and rest to the weary;
through Jesus Christ our
Lord.

EPISCOPAL

(November 19)
Almighty and everlast-
ing God, who kindled
the flame of your love
in the heart of your
servant Elizabeth:
Grant to us, your hum-
ble servants, a like
faith and power of
love; that, as we re-
joice in her triumph,
we may profit by her
example; through Je-
sus Christ our Lord,
who lives and reigns
with you and the Holy
Spirit, one God, now
and for ever.

(Text from Lesser Feasts and Fasts, Revised Edition, copyright 1973 by Charles Mortimer Guilbert as Custodian of the Standard Book of Common Prayer. All rights reserved. Used by permission.)

Common of Saints
(for those who work
for the disadvantaged
or for religious)
Tobit 12:6-13
   or Isaiah 58:6-11
Matthew 25:31-46

Common of Renewers of
   Society
Hosea 2:18-23
   Psalm 94:1-14
Romans 12:9-21
Luke 6:20-36

Psalm 34:1-7
Philippians 4:6-13
Psalm 146
Matthew 25:31-40

Preface of a Saint

Hymn of the Day: "O God of mercy, God of light" (425)

Prayers: for the poor
for the sick and suffering
for the unemployed
for self-sacrificing service

Preface: All Saints

Color: White

Clement, Bishop of Rome, ca. 100

The biographical details of Clement's life are meager. He is perhaps the Clement referred to in Philippians 4:3. He was probably the fourth bishop of Rome (some say the third). In later centuries he became the subject of numerous legends. He was, it is said, banished to the Crimea during the reign of Trajan and forced to work in the mines. Nonetheless his missionary efforts there met with success. On another occasion he was tied to an anchor (which has now become his emblem) and was thrown into the Black Sea. His tomb, the legends continue, was built by angels and was shown once a year to the faithful of that region by a miraculous ebbing of the tide.

Despite the lack of any certain knowledge of Clement's life, he is of considerable importance as an apostolic father. His fame rests on a letter sent by the church at Rome to the church at Corinth ca. 96. The letter, with the exception of the New Testament writings, the earliest Christian document extant, was written to oppose the factious spirit which had divided the Corinthian church when some dissatisfied younger members deposed the bishop-presbyters and deacons. First Clement, as the letter is known, is a pastoral letter of advice and warning, written anonymously but is the work, all agree, of Clement. It gives a valuable picture of early Roman Christianity. It was well received in Corinth and was in fact so honored there that it was read in the Corinthian church along with the Scripture ca. 170. Several manuscripts of the New Testament include it among the books of the New Testament.

Second Clement is not a letter but a sermon and while its authorship is not certain, all agree it is not by Clement.

W. W. Jaeger. *Early Christianity and Greek Paideia.* Cambridge, Mass.: Harvard, 1961.

Reading

(From the First Letter of Clement)

. . . Let us fix our eyes on the Father and Creator of the universe and cling to his magnificent and excellent gifts of peace and kindness to us. Let us see him in our minds and look with the eyes of our souls on his patient purpose. Let us consider how free he is from anger toward his whole creation.

The heavens move at his direction and peacefully obey him. Day and night observe the course he has appointed them, without getting in each other's way. The sun and the moon and the choirs of stars roll on harmoniously in their appointed courses at his command, with never a deviation. By his will and without dissension or altering anything he has decreed the earth becomes fruitful at the proper seasons and brings forth abundant food for men and beasts and every living thing upon it. The unsearchable, abysmal depths and the indescribable regions of the underworld are subject to the same decrees. The basin of the boundless sea is by his arrangement conducted to hold the heaped up waters, so that the sea does not flow beyond the barriers surrounding it, but does just as he bids it. For he said, "Thus far shall you come, and your waves shall break within you." The ocean which men cannot pass, and the worlds beyond it, are governed by the same decrees of the Master. The seasons, spring, summer, autumn, and winter, peacefully give way to each other. The winds from their different points perform their service at the proper time and without hindrance. Perennial springs, created for enjoyment and health, never fail to offer their life-giving breasts to men. The tiniest creatures come together in harmony and peace. All these things the great Creator and Master of the universe ordained to exist in peace and harmony. Thus, he showered his benefits on them all, but most abundantly on us who have taken refuge in his compassion through our Lord Jesus Christ, to whom be glory and majesty forever and ever. Amen.

Early Christian Fathers, from Vol. I, Library of Christian Classics, trans. and ed. by Cyril C. Richardson, 53-54. Published in the U.S.A. by The Westminster Press, 1953. Used by permission.

Propers

ROMAN	LUTHERAN	EPISCOPAL
All-powerful and ever-living God, we praise your power and glory revealed to us in the lives of all your saints. Give us joy on this feast of Saint Clement, the priest and martyr who bore witness with his blood to the love he proclaimed and the gospel he preached. We ask this through our Lord Jesus Christ, your Son, who lives and reigns with you and the Holy Spirit, one God, for ever and ever.	Almighty God, you have raised up Clement as a faithful bishop in your Church. May the memory of his life be a source of joy for us and a bulwark of our faith, so that we may serve you and confess your name before the world; through your Son, Jesus Christ our Lord.	O God, who enlightened your Church by the teaching of your servant Clement: Enrich us evermore with your heavenly grace, and raise up faithful witnesses who by their life and doctrine will set forth the truth of your salvation; through Jesus Christ our Lord, who lives and reigns with you and the Holy Spirit, one God, now and for ever.

(Text from the English translation of the Roman Missal © 1973, International Committee on English in the Liturgy, Inc. All rights reserved.)

Common of Martyrs or Pastors (for a Pope)

Common of Pastors:
Acts 20:17-35
Psalm 84
Ephesians 3:14-21
Matthew 24:42-47

(Text from Lesser Feasts and Fasts, Revised Edition, copyright 1973 by Charles Mortimer Guilbert as Custodian of the Standard Book of Common Prayer. All rights reserved. Used by permission.)

Psalm 78:1-4
2 Timothy 2:1-7
Psalm 34:11-18
Luke 6:37-45

Preface of a Saint

Hymn of the Day: "Nature with open volume stands" (119)
("The day you gave us, Lord, has ended" [274] is to the tune *St. Clement)*

Prayers: for peace in the church
for the stilling of passions
for the impatient
for the natural world

Preface: All Saints

Color: White

432

Isaac Watts, Hymnwriter, 1748

English hymnody is said to have begun with Caedmon, the first singer of Christian songs in England. He was a herdsman who entered the monastery at Whitby at an advanced age. According to Bede, one night Caedmon was inspired in a dream to compose a hymn on the creation, and after entering the monastery he made other paraphrases of biblical narratives. Others in later centuries continued the tradition: George Herbert (d. 1633), Samuel Crossman (d. 1683), Richard Baxter (d. 1691), Thomas Ken (d. 1711), Joseph Addison (d. 1719). But it is Isaac Watts who is regarded as "the Father of the English Hymn."

Watts was the eldest of nine children of a Nonconformist minister, who had been twice imprisoned for his dissenting ideas. He was born at Southampton July 17, 1674. He showed great promise as a student (at age seven he amused his parents with his rhymes), and several friends in the town offered him an education at a university leading to ordination in the Church of England. Refusing the offer, Watts entered the Nonconformist Academy at Stoke Newington in 1690. He left when he was twenty and spent the next two years at home writing. He was dissatisfied with the poor quality of the verified psalms then in use and began to try to do better. Most of his *Hymns and Spiritual Songs* seem to have been written during this period. He served as tutor to the son of an eminent Puritan at Stoke Newington and engaged in intense study.

When he was twenty-four he began preaching. He was ordained in 1702 and became pastor of an independent congregation in Mark Lane of which many distinguished Independents were members, including Cromwell's granddaughter. His health began to fail soon after and he was forced to spend the last thirty-six years of his life in the house of Sir Thomas Abney, preaching and teaching only occasionally.

He nonetheless earned considerable theological and philosophical fame. His *Logic* was long a text at Oxford; *The World to Come* (1745) was a favorite devotional work; *Improvement of the Mind* (1741) and *Speculations on the Human Nature of the Logos* increased his fame. A book of poems and hymns *Horae Lyricae* was published 1706-1709 and his *Hymns and Spiritual Songs*, although written earlier, was published 1707-1709—the first hymnbook in English. His versified *Psalms of David* "in the language of the New Testament and applied to the Christian state and worship" was printed in 1719. His sermons appeared in 1721-1724. His *Divine Songs Attempted in Easy Language for Children* was popular enough to be satirized more than a century later in *Alice in Wonderland*. Other works of Watts were used as texts in religious education—his Catechisms and his *Scriptural History*. In 1721 he put out *The Art of Reading and Writing English*. In 1728 he was awarded the D.D. by the University of Edinburgh.

At last, after years of suffering, Watts died November 25, 1748 and was buried in the Puritan burial ground at Bunhill Fields not far from the grave of John Bunyan. He had never married. He has been called the Melanchthon of his day because of his learning, gentleness, and devotion. There is a monument to him in Westminster Abbey.

Louis F. Benson. *The English Hymn*. New York, 1915.
Arthur P. Davis. *Isaac Watts. His Life and Works*. New York: Dryden. 1943.
Harry Escott. *Isaac Watts. Hymnographer*. London: Independent Press, 1962.
Norman Victor Hope. *Isaac Watts and His Contribution to English Hymnody*. Papers of the Hymn Society of America XIII. Springfield, OH, 1947.
Bernard L. Manning. *The Hymns of Wesley and Watts*. London: Epworth, 1942.
Eric Routley. "The Eucharistic Hymns of Isaac Watts," *Worship* 48: 9 (November 1974), 526-535.

With Isaac Watts, the Father of the English Hymn, it would be appropriate also to remember the ancient hymnwriters whose work helped establish the tradition of hymn singing in the Christian church and whose hymns still appear in modern hymnals.

Anatolius (d. 458)
Andrew of Crete (ca. 660-732)
Clement of Alexandria (ca. 200)
Venantius Fortunatus (530-609)
Germanus (ca. 634-734)
Joseph the Hymnographer (d. 883)
Aurelius Clemens Prudentius (d. 413)
Coelius Sedulius (d. ca. 450)

Synesius of Cyrene (ca. 375-430)
Theodolph of Orleans (ca. 760-821)

An alternate date for their commemoration—although it comes in the summer when services are often reduced—is July 1, the commemoration of John Mason Neale, who translated many of these Greek and Latin hymns into English.

Reading

(From *Voices and Instruments in Christian Worship* by Joseph Gelineau.)

If the word holds such a predominant position in Christian worship, does it not render music superfluous? And is it not best to strip words of special sacredness from all melodic ornament so that their message may come through with more certainty? If anyone were to draw that conclusion he would show that he is laboring under a serious misconception of the nature of human language. Also, he would have overlooked several important meanings which pertain to the mystery of song. . . .

The word which is merely spoken is a somewhat incomplete form of human language. It suffices for ordinary utilitarian communications. But as soon as the word becomes charged with emotion, as soon as it is filled with power, as soon as it tends to identify itself with the content of its message—when, in fine, it has to signify the sacredness of actions being performed—then it calls for number and melos, that is, for a musical form. . . . The complete word, the fully developed word, has the nature of song.

Joseph Gelineau, *Voices and Instruments in Christian Worship* tr. Clifford Howell, S.J. (Collegeville, Minn.: Liturgical Press, 1964) 44. Copyrighted by The Order of St. Benedict, Inc. Collegeville, Minnesota. Used by permission.

Propers: Artists

Hymn of the Day: "O God our help in ages past" (320)

Prayers: for the spirit of joy in worship
for those who help the church to sing

for theological perception on the part of hymnwriters

for those in frail health

Color: White

ST. ANDREW, APOSTLE

Andrew (the name means "manly"), brother of Peter, was born in Bethsaida, a village in Galilee. He was the first apostle to follow Christ (John 1:35-40), and his name regularly appears near the head of the lists of the apostles. Perhaps his greatest work was to bring his brother Simon Peter to the Lord. After Pentecost he is said to have preached in Palestine, Scythia, Epirus, and Thrace. A late and rather unreliable tradition says that he was martyred on November 30, ca. 70 at Patras in Achaia, Greece. The tradition that he was crucified on an X-shaped cross was popular in the fifteenth century; the earliest examples are from the tenth century. He was martyred, legend has it, for defying the proconsul Aegeas who ordered Andrew to stop preaching and to sacrifice to the gods.

St. Andrew's body is said to have been taken, together with that of St. Luke, to the Church of the Holy Apostles in Constantinople in 357, and later removed to the cathedral of Amalfi, Italy. The church at Constantinople claimed St. Andrew as its first bishop. The churches in Greece and Russia in particular hold him in high honor. Also, quite early certain of his relics were taken to St. Andrew's Church, Fife, and he became a patron saint of Scotland; the cross of St. Andrew in the Union Jack represents Scotland.

The feast of St. Andrew was observed as early as the fourth century by the Eastern church and in the sixth century in Rome and elsewhere; it is a national holiday in Scotland. St. Andrew's Day determines the beginning of the church year, since the First Sunday in Advent is the Sunday nearest to St. Andrew's Day. In many liturgical books, therefore, the list of saints begins with Andrew.

F. Dvornik. *The Idea of Apostolicity in Byzantium and the Legend of the Apostle Andrew.* Cambridge, Mass.; Harvard, 1958.

Reading

(From *The Quest of the Historical Jesus* by Albert Schweitzer.)

. . . He was not a teacher, not a casuist; He was an imperious ruler. It was because He was so in His inmost being that He could think of Himself as the Son of Man. That was only the temporarily conditioned expression of the fact that He was an authoritative ruler. The names in which men expressed their recognition of Him as such, Messiah, Son of Man, Son of God, have become for us historical parables. We can find no designation which expresses what He is for us.

He comes to us as One unknown, without a name, as of old, by the lake-side, He came to those men who knew Him not. He speaks to us the same word: "Follow thou me!" and sets us to the tasks which He has to fulfill for our time. He commands. And to those who obey Him, whether they be wise or simple, He will reveal Himself in the toils, the conflicts, the sufferings, which they shall pass through in His fellowship, and, as an ineffable mystery, they shall learn in their own experience Who He is.

Albert Schweitzer, *The Quest of the Historical Jesus,* trans. W. Montgomery (New York: Macmillan, 1968) 403. Used by permission of Adam and Charles Black Publishers Ltd.

Propers

ROMAN	LUTHERAN	EPISCOPAL
Lord, in your kindness hear our petitions. You called Andrew the apostle to preach the gospel and guide your Church in faith. May he always be our friend in your presence to help us with his prayers. We ask this through	Almighty God, as the apostle Andrew readily obeyed the call of Christ and followed him without delay, grant that we, called by your holy Word, may in glad obedience offer ourselves to your service; through your Son, Jesus Christ our Lord, who lives and reigns with you and	Almighty God, who gave such grace to your apostle Andrew that he readily obeyed the call of your Son Jesus Christ, and brought his brother with him: Give us, who are called by your Holy Word, grace to follow him without delay, and to bring those near to us into his gracious presence; who

ROMAN	LUTHERAN	EPISCOPAL
our Lord Jesus Christ, your Son, who lives and reigns with you and the Holy Spirit, one God, for ever and ever.	the Holy Spirit, one God, now and forever.	lives and reigns with you and the Holy Spirit, one God, now and for ever.

(Text from the English translation of the Roman Missal © 1973, International Committee on English in the Liturgy, Inc. All rights reserved.)

(Text from the Book of Common Prayer [Proposed], copyright 1977 by Charles Mortimer Guilbert as Custodian of the Standard Book of Common Prayer. All rights reserved. Used by permission.)

Romans 10:9-18
Psalm 19:2-5
Matthew 4:18-22

Ezekiel 3:16-21
Psalm 19:1-6
Romans 10:10-18
John 1:35-42

Deuteronomy 30:11-14
Psalm 19 or 19:1-6
Romans 10:8b-18
Matthew 4:18-22

Preface of Apostles

Hymn of the Day: "Jesus calls us; o'er the tumult" (494)

Prayers: for obedience to God's command
for a sense of mission
for those on spiritual pilgrimage
for the church in Scotland
for the church in Greece
for those who minister to their own families

Preface: Apostles

Color: Red

December 3

Francis Xavier
Missionary to Asia, 1552

Francis Xavier (in Spanish Francisco do Yasu y Javier), the Apostle of India and Japan and one of the greatest missionaries in the history of the church, was born in the castle of Xavier near Sanguesa, Navarre, Spain on April 7, 1506. He studied in Spain, went to

Paris in 1525 and there met Ignatius Loyola and Pierre Favre. These three friends, with three others, on August 15, 1534 bound themselves to the service of God with a vow at Montmartre. Francis received his M.A. in 1530 and served as regent at Beauvais College, 1530-1534. For the next two years he studied theology. He and Ignatius were ordained June 24, 1537.

They left Paris for Venice, November 15, 1537, expecting to sail from there to Palestine. Their plans did not work out, and Francis spent the fall and winter in Bologna, Italy. In April 1538 he went to Rome and participated in a conference which led to the formation of the Society of Jesus.

He was called to Lisbon in 1540, and in the following year King John III of Portugal appointed him nuncio in the East, and Francis sailed for India. After a difficult thirteen-month voyage, he landed in Goa, May 6, 1542, and immediately set about learning the language and writing a catechism. In September 1542 he visited the coast opposite Sri Lanka (Ceylon) where the fishing people had been baptized as a condition for receiving help from the King of Portugal against northern robbers but for whom little had in fact been done. He met with huge success there. He wrote on January 15, 1543 that he was so exhausted administering baptism that he could hardly lift his arms. There was also, however, local hostility and the new Christians were attacked, some were killed and some were carried off to slavery.

In August 1543 Francis went to Malacca, the easternmost Portugese port, in what is now Indonesia, for further work and there met a Japanese who interested him in Japan. On August 15, 1549 he landed at Kagoshima in southern Japan. The first European to live in the area, he learned the language and wrote a catechism. Unaccustomed to winter, he suffered greatly from the cold. A year later Francis went on to the center of Japan and the then capital of the empire, Kyoto. It was a time of civil strife and Francis failed in his attempt to see the Mikado. He came to recognize what he described as the noble quality of the Japanese people, their intelligence, and the excellence of their civilization.

Francis returned to Malacca, and at the end of 1551 was appointed provincial of the Province of India. At length, he turned his attention to China. He sailed to the island of Chang-Chuen (Sancian) near the China coast in August 1522 and waited there while arranging a means of entering China. He was seized by a fever in November, weakened, and died December 3, 1552. He was buried there temporarily; later his remains were taken to Goa where they have been enshrined ever since.

J. Broderick. *Saint Francis Xavier (1506-1552)*. London: Burns, Oates, & Washbourne, 1952.
H. J. Coleridge. *The Life and Letters of St. Francis Xavier*. 2 vols. London, 1886.
Madhur Jaffrey. "The Last Chance, Probably, to View a Saint's Remains," *Smithsonian* VI, 2 (May 1975), 42-49. With photographs.
Edith A. Robertson. *Francis Xavier: Knight Errant of the Cross*. London: SCM, 1930.
Georg Schurhammer, S. J. *Francis Xavier. His Life, His Times*. Rome: Jesuit Historical Institute, 1976—

On this day also might be remembered three Protestant missionaries to China. **Robert Morrison** (1782-1834) was the first Protestant missionary to the people of China. A Congregationalist minister, he reached Canton in 1807. Through twenty-seven years of extreme hardship he engaged largely in Bible translation and literary activity. His translations were imperfect but nonetheless began the work of putting the Bible into the language of China.

Karl Guetzlaff (1803-August 9, 1851) was the first Lutheran missionary to China, a country then closed to outsiders. He met Morrison and worked with him. Known sometimes as "the father of the German branch of the China Inland Mission," he aroused European interest in the work in China, and through him Hudson Taylor received his missionary call.

James Hudson Taylor (1832-1905), a man of intense dedication, landed at Shanghai in 1854 and founded the China Inland Mission to work in the interior of the country. It was an interdenominational effort that was remarkable in that it accepted men and women as missionaries without formal college training. Taylor sought identification with the Chinese; he adopted native dress and he sought the growth of indigenous churches.

In addition, **Johann Flierl** (1858-1947) is appropriately remembered as a missionary to the East. He was born into a peasant family in Buchof, Bavaria and was educated at the mission seminary at Neuendettelsau. In 1878 he was sent to Australia and for seven years did mission work among the aborigines in the interior of that continent. On July 12, 1886 he landed at Finschafen, Papua New Guinea, the capital of the German colony of Kaiser-Wilhelmsland, the first Lutheran missionary on that island. Only after fourteen years was he able to baptize his first converts. For nearly half a century he worked among the Papuans and was a champion of the rights of the natives against government oppression. He retired in 1930 and died September 30, 1947. On the calendar of the Evangelical Lutheran Church of Papua New Guinea, July 12 is the birthday of their church, and it is sometimes also observed in Australia.

Reading

(From the letters by Francis Xavier to Ignatius Loyola)

Many, many people hereabouts are not becoming Christians for one reason only: there is nobody to make them Christians. Again and again I have thought of going round the universities of Europe, especially Paris, and everywhere crying out like a madman, riveting the attention of those with more learning than charity: "What a tragedy: how many souls are being shut out of heaven and falling into hell, thanks to you!"

I wish they would work as hard at this as they do at their books, and so settle their account with God for their learning and the talents entrusted to them.

This thought would certainly stir most of them to meditate on spiritual realities, to listen actively to what God is saying to them. They would forget their own desires, their human affairs, and give themselves over entirely to God's will and his choice. They would cry out with all their heart: *Lord, I am here! What do you want me to do?* Send me anywhere you like—even to India!

Propers

ROMAN	LUTHERAN	EPISCOPAL

God our Father,
by the preaching of
Francis Xavier
you brought many
nations to yourself.
Give his zeal for the
faith to all who
believe in you,
that your Church may
rejoice in continued
growth
throughout the world.
Grant this through our
Lord Jesus Christ,
your Son,
who lives and reigns
with you and the
Holy Spirit,
one God, for ever and
ever.

God of grace and might,
we praise you for your servant Francis, to whom you
gave gifts to make the good
news known to the Indian
and Asian people. Raise up,
we pray, in every country,
heralds and evangelists of
your kingdom, so that the
world may know the im-
measurable riches of our
Savior, Jesus Christ.

*(Text from the English
translation of the Roman
Missal © 1973, Interna-
tional Committee on Eng-
lish in the Liturgy, Inc.
All rights reserved.)*

Common of Pastors
(for Missionaries)
especially
1 Corinthians 9:16-19,
22-23
Mark 16:15-20

Common of Missionaries
Isaiah 62:1-7
Psalm 48
1 Corinthians 9:16-19, 22-23
Mark 16:15-20

Hymn of the Day: "Hail to the Lord's anointed" (87)
see also "O God, I love thee" (491)

Prayers: for the church in China and Japan
for the church in the East Indies
for the church in India and Sri Lanka
for the spirit of service
for courage to share the lot and life of the poor

Preface: Epiphany

Color: White

Nicholas, Bishop of Myra, ca. 342

Although Nicholas has become one of the most popular saints of the Christian calendar, nearly nothing is known about his life. He was a bishop of Myra on the south-west coast of Asia Minor (Turkey) during the fourth century. Beyond those bare facts nothing else is certain.

In the absence of facts, legends abound. Nicholas as an infant, it is said, refused to nurse on the ancient fast days of Wednesday and Friday. He aided the poor and once saved three daughters of a poor man from a life of prostitution by putting three purses through the window of their home for their dowries. (So he is the patron of virgins.) He wonderfully reconstituted three boys who had been murdered and hidden in a pickling tub. He saved three unjustly condemned men from death. He aided sailors who were in distress off the coast of his diocese and once went to the Holy Land and showed courage on board ship during a storm. (So he is patron of sailors.) He attended the Council of Nicaea and gave the heretical bishop Arius a resounding box on the ear. He is the patron of Russia and of Greece; the guardian of virgins and poor maidens; the protector of children, travellers, sailors, and merchants, as well as guardian against thieves and volence. He is patron of many towns and cities including Bari, Venice, Freiburg, and Galway.

Because of his enormous popularity, he was impersonated by a man with a white beard, in the vestments of a bishop, who was kind to children. In Holland, even after the Reformation, Sinter Klaas in bishop's vestments and on a white horse visits children on the eve of his feast day. This popular figure was brought to New York by the Dutch and combined with the English Father Christmas. His day was moved from December 6 to December 25, his bishop's vesture was replaced by secular clothing, but he retained his cheerful colors, the name Santa Claus, and the traditional association with gift-giving. With the added features of the Nordic "Christmas Man," he was given a home and factory at the North Pole and a sleigh and reindeer. (In northern Europe Thor was the god of peasants and common people, who is represented as an old man, jovial, friendly, stout, with a long white beard, whose element is fire and whose color hence is red. He fought with the giants of ice and snow and so became the Yule god.)

In 560 the Emperor Justinian dedicated a church to Nicholas in Constantinople. Since then, there have perhaps been more churches and chapels dedicated to St. Nicholas than to any other saint.

The remains of St. Nicholas are said to be in the crypt of the basilica of San Nicola in Bari, Italy. In 1087, three ships sailed from the seaport of Bari to Myra on an expedition to bring the bones of Nicholas to their town. They returned to Bari on May 9, 1097 with the relics that were temporarily housed in a church dedicated to San Giovanni a Mare until a basilica could be built in honor of St. Nicholas. The relics were transferred to their present resting place in 1089 by Pope Urban II, and May 9 has been a day of celebration in honor of St. Nicholas in Bari since that time.

Eric Crozier. *The Life and Legends of Saint Nicholas, Patron Saint of Children*. London: Duckworth, 1949.

Charles W. Jones. *Saint Nicholas of Myra, Bari, and Manhattan: Biography of a Legend*. Chicago and London: University of Chicago Press, 1978.

Reading

(From *The Practice of the Presence of God* by Brother Lawrence.)

He told me . . . that God always gave us light in our doubts when we had no other design than to please Him, and to act for His love.

That our sanctification did not depend upon *changing* our works, but in doing that for God's sake which commonly we do for our own. That it was lamentable to see how many people mistook the means for the end, addicting themselves to certain works, which they performed very imperfectly, by reason of their human or selfish regards.

That the most excellent method he had found of going to God was that of *doing our common business* without any view of pleasing men, and (as far as we are capable) *purely for the love of God*.

That it was a great delusion to think that the times of prayer ought to differ from other times; that we are as strictly obliged to adhere to God by action in the time of action as by prayer in the season of prayer.

That his view of prayer was nothing else but a sense of the Presence of God, his soul being at that time insensible to everything but Divine Love; and that when the appointed times of prayer were past, he found no difference, because he still continued with God, praising and blessing Him with all his might, so that he passed his life in continual joy; yet hoped that God would give him somewhat to suffer when he should have grown stronger.

That we ought not to be weary of doing little things for the love of God, who regards not the greatness of the work, but the love with which it is performed.

Brother Lawrence (Nicholas Herman), *Conversations and Letters on the Practice of the Presence of God*. Fourth Conversation. November 25, 1667. (Cincinnati: Forward Movement Publications, 1941) 15-16.

Propers

ROMAN

Father,
hear our prayers for mercy,
and by the help of Saint Nicholas
keep us from all danger,
and guide us on the way of salvation.
Grant this through our Lord Jesus Christ, your Son,
who lives and reigns with you and the Holy Spirit,
one God, for ever and ever.

(Text from the English translation of the Roman Missal © 1973, International Committee on English in the Liturgy, Inc. All rights reserved.)
Common of Pastors

LUTHERAN

Heavenly Father, shepherd of your people, we thank you for your servant Nicholas, who was faithful in the care and nurture of your flock; and we pray that, following his example and the teaching of his holy life, we may by your grace grow into the full stature of our Lord and Savior Jesus Christ.
Common of Pastors

EPISCOPAL

Heavenly Father, shepherd of your people, we thank you for your servant Nicholas, who was faithful in the care and nurture of your flock; and we pray that, following his example and the teaching of his holy life, we may by your grace grow into the full manhood and stature of our Lord and Savior Jesus Christ, who lives and reigns with you and the Holy Spirit, one God, for ever and ever.

(Text from Lesser Feasts and Fasts, Revised Edition, copyright 1973 by Charles Mortimer Guilbert as Custodian of the Standard Book of Common Prayer. All rights reserved. Used by permission.)

ROMAN	LUTHERAN	EPISCOPAL
	Isaiah 10:33-11:9	Psalm 78:1-7
	Psalm 84	1 John 4:7-14
	1 John 4:7-14	Psalm 34:11-15
	Mark 10:13-16	Mark 10:13-16
		Preface of a Saint

Hymn of the Day: "Comfort, comfort now my people" (29)

Prayers: for the spirit of generosity
     for children
     for sailors and travellers
     for the church in Greece

Preface: All Saints

Color: White

December 7

Ambrose, Bishop of Milan, 397

Ambrose is the first Latin church father to be born, raised, and educated not as a pagan but as a Christian. He was born about 339 in the city of Treves (Trier) in what is now France, where his father was Prefect of Gaul, the governor of a large part of Europe. He studied the classics and the law at Rome and before he was thirty-three was named governor of Liguria and Aemilia, with headquarters at Milan, which was at that time the seat of the imperial court. When the Arian bishop of that city died, Ambrose settled the violence that broke out between the Arians and the Catholics. Both sides unanimously insisted that Ambrose become their bishop, even though at that time he had not been baptized. (It was a custom of the time to delay baptism until late in life so that one might be cleansed close to the time of death.) Ambrose finally bowed to pressure from church and state authorities, and on December 7, 374, was baptized, ordained priest, and consecrated bishop.

He gave a portion of his family wealth to the poor and set an example of strict asceticism. Although the Roman Empire was in decline, Ambrose by his preaching, writing, organizing, and administration made Milan one of the most important centers of learning and Christian activity, in some ways surpassing even Rome itself. He was a powerful preacher, and his sermons affected many, including Augustine, whom he baptized at Milan at Easter, 387.

The Empress Justina, mother of Valentinian, jealous of the growing importance of Ambrose, organized a coalition against the bishop and at the beginning of Lent, 385, demanded that one basilica in Milan be given to the Arians. Ambrose refused and a riot broke out in the city. Just before Easter, Justina demanded the bishop's own cathedral. On Palm Sunday there were a series of clashes between the imperial troops and Ambrose's congregations. On Maundy Thursday the court abandoned its attempt to seize and hold a church. The struggle, however, continued. An edict against the Catholics was promulgated in June, 386, and Ambrose was summoned to appear before the Emperor. He refused and took refuge in his basilica, which was surrounded by imperial troops. Inside, Ambrose and his people spent the time singing Psalms and hymns of their bishop's own composition. At length the court was forced to rescind the edict.

Ambrose was a zealous defender of orthodoxy and one of the most important Latin authors of his day. At the request of the Emperor Gratian he wrote *On the Christian Faith*. He is also the author of a work of pastoral concern, *On the Duties of the Clergy*. One comes closest to the saintly bishop, perhaps, through his hymns. He was one of the first to write metrical Latin hymns, and many of them are still sung in Christian churches. St. Augustine says, addressing God,

> The tears flowed from me when I heard your hymns and canticles, for the sweet singing of your church moved me deeply. The music surged in my ears, truth seeped into my heart, and my feelings of devotion overflowed, so that the tears streamed down. But they were tears of gladness. *(Confessions, IX, 6-7)*.

Ambrose is the only church father of whom we possess a portrait —idealized to be sure—but an authentic portrait nonetheless. It is a mosaic with his name that adorns a chapel of the basilica dedicated to his brother Satyrus, made at the beginning of the fifth century, shortly after his death.

Ambrose died at Milan on Easter Eve, April 4, 397. Some Anglican calendars have commemorated him on that day, but the traditional date for his remembrance in the Roman Catholic and Eastern Orthodox churches (now also adopted by the Episcopal and Lutheran churches) is the date of his baptism-ordination-consecration as bishop. It seems a more convenient date, since April 4 usually falls near Easter, which requires its celebration to be delayed.

Hans von Campenhausen. *The Fathers of the Latin Church,* tr. Manfred Hoffman. Stanford University Press, 1964.
F. H. Dudden. *The Life and Times of St. Ambrose* 2 vols. Oxford University Press, 1935.
Early Latin Theology, ed. S. L. Greenslade. Philadelphia: Westminster, 1956.
A. Paredi. *St. Ambrose,* tr. J. Costello. Notre Dame, Ind.: Notre Dame Press, 1963.

Reading

(From the *Confessions* of St. Augustine)

In Milan I found your devoted servant the bishop Ambrose, who was known throughout the world as a man whom there were few to equal in goodness. At that time his gifted tongue never tired of dispensing the richness of your corn, the joy of your oil, and the sober intoxication of your wine. Unknown to me, it was you who led me to him, so that I might knowingly be led by him to you. This man of God received me like a father and, as bishop, told me how glad he was that I had come. My heart warmed to him, not at first as a teacher of the truth, which I had quite despaired of finding in your Church, but simply as a man who showed me kindness. I listened attentively when he preached to the people, though not with the proper intention; for my purpose was to judge for myself whether the reports of his powers as a speaker were accurate, or whether eloquence flowed from him more, or less, readily than I had been told. So while I paid the closest attention to the words he used, I was quite uninterested in the subject-matter and was even contemptuous of it. I was delighted with his charming delivery, but although he was a more learned speaker than Faustus, he had not the same soothing and gratifying manner. I am speaking only of his style for, as to content, there could be no comparison between the two. Faustus had lost his way among the fallacies of Manicheism, while Ambrose most surely taught the doctrine of salvation. But *your mercy is unknown to sinners* such as I was then, though step by step, unwittingly, I was coming closer to it.

For although I did not trouble to take what Ambrose said to heart, but only to listen to the manner in which he said it—this being the only paltry interest that remained to me now that I had lost hope that man could find the path that led to you—nevertheless his meaning, which I tried to ignore, found its way into my mind together with his words, which I admired so much.

Saint Augustine, *Confessions* trans. R. S. Pine-Coffin (Baltimore: Penguin, 1961) 107-108. Copyright © R. S. Pine-Coffin. Reprinted by permission of Penguin Books Ltd.

Propers

ROMAN	LUTHERAN	EPISCOPAL
Lord, you made Saint Ambrose an outstanding teacher of the Catholic faith and gave him the courage of an apostle. Raise up in your Church more leaders after your own heart to guide us with courage and wisdom. We ask this through our Lord Jesus Christ, your Son, who lives and reigns with you and the Holy Spirit, one God, for ever and ever.	Almighty God, you have raised up for your Church faithful bishops like your servant Ambrose. May the memory of his life be a source of joy for us and a bulwark of our faith, so that we may serve you and confess your name before the world; through your Son, Jesus Christ our Lord. Common of Pastors:	O God, who gave to your servant Ambrose grace eloquently to declare your righteousness in the great congregation, and fearlessly to bear reproach for the honor of your Name: Mercifully grant to all bishops and pastors such excellence in preaching, and faithfulness in ministering your Word; that your people may be partakers with them of the glory that shall be revealed; through Jesus Christ our Lord, who lives and reigns with you and the Holy Spirit, one God, in glory everlasting.

Common of Pastors or Doctors

ROMAN	LUTHERAN	EPISCOPAL
	Ezekiel 34:11-16	Psalm 27:1-8
	Psalm 84	Ecclesiasticus 2:7-11, 16-18
	1 Peter 5:1-4	Psalm 27:9-17
	John 21:15-17	Luke 12:35-37, 42-44
		Preface of a Saint

Hymn of the Day: "O Splendor of the Father's light" (271)

Prayers: for lawyers
   for preachers of the Word of God
   for a joyful confidence in God's care
   for all leaders of the church that they may show by
    their lives the love of God for the world

Preface: All Saints

Color: White

December 11

Lars Olsen Skrefsrud, Missionary to India, 1910

Lars Olsen Skrefsrud, the Apostle of the Santals, was born in Lysgaard, Norway, February 4, 1840. He grew up in poverty and received little formal education. After studying at the parish school and being confirmed, he was apprenticed to a coppersmith in the town of Skrefsrud and mastered that trade.

He was repeatedly frustrated in his ambitions: he could not afford the education to become a pastor, his poems were rejected by the local publisher, and his companions ridiculed his desire to be a drummer in the army. Increasingly he turned to alcohol for comfort, following in the footsteps of his father, generally a sturdy, hard-working farmer and carpenter, but given to bouts of drinking. Under the influence of his companions, he robbed a bank and when he was apprehended, refused to name his associates, was found guilty and sentenced to four years in prison.

Once in jail the nineteen-year-old began to read religious books, became an exemplary prisoner, and was assigned to the infirmary where he tended the sick. One day, after a talk with a visiting pastor, he began to study in earnest to become a pastor. Although he was rejected by his family and former friends, one girl, Anna Onsum, visited him in prison and had faith in him. When he left prison in 1861, penniless, he worked his way to the Gossner Missionary Society in Berlin where he told of his past and of his desire to become a missionary. He was accepted and began a life of single-minded devotion to his goal. He worked, studied, fasted, and prayed, attended church services daily and lived on little more than bread, cheese, and water.

In the fall of 1863 Skrefsrud left for India. He had to work to pay his passage and slept on the deck and lived with the mixed crew of Europeans, Africans, and Indians, whose languages and ways of life he began to learn. In 1864 the young missionary reached Calcutta, and the following year a Danish co-worker, Father Børresen, his wife, and Anna Onsum joined him. He and Anna were married, and the group of four went off on their own, without help from European sources, joining the Baptist E. C. Johnson to preach the gospel among the Santals, an oppressed tribe in northern India who had never seen a Christian missionary.

Skrefsrud, as the leader, worked day and night studying the Santali language and learning the ways of the people. Soon he could preach in the language, and in a little over a year the first converts were baptized. The work spread from "Ebenezer," the first mission station they built, until at Skrefsrud's death there were nearly twenty thousand baptized Santal Christians. Skrefsrud wrote a grammar and dictionary of Santali, translated the Gospels and Luther's Small Catechism, and compiled textbooks and hymnals. He defended the Santals from their traditional oppressors and pled their cause with the British government, and he taught them agriculture, irrigation, carpentry, and other useful arts. His aim was an indigenous Santal church; he said, "We came to the Santals to bring them Christianity and not to take away their nationality." He was a social reformer as well as a missionary and helped to raise their standard of living.

There were hardships and severe blows—no support from home, opposition from local groups, the death of his wife, and his own serious illness. But in 1873, on a trip back to Europe to take the ailing Mrs. Børresen home, Skrefsrud was received with acclaim in Germany, Great Britain, and Scandinavia. The Church of Norway at last ordained the successful missionary, and he returned with renewed zeal to his work in Santalistan.

In his sixty-ninth year Skrefsrud had a stroke, but he recovered sufficiently to write with his left hand and kept busy with correspondence, translating, and writing. On December 11, 1910 he died and was buried in the cemetery of Ebenezer, beside his wife, Father Børresen, and other missionaries and Santal Christians. The Santal Church, started through the work of Skrefsrud and his associates, is now a flourishing member church of the Federation of Evangelical Lutheran Churches in India. In the town of Skrefsrud in Norway his parents' home is kept as a memorial to this modern saint, and a nearby museum houses articles related to his life and work.

O. Hodne. *L. O. Skrefsrud: Missionary and Social Reformer Among the Santals of Santal Parganas.* Oslo, 1966.

Reading

(From Augustine's *Confessions.*)

I have learnt to love you late, Beauty at once so ancient and so new! I have learnt to love you late! You were within me, and I was in the world outside myself. I searched for you outside myself and, disfigured as I was, I fell upon the lovely things of your creation. You were with me, but I was not with you. The beautiful things of this world kept me far from you and yet, if they had not been in you, they would have had no being at all. You called me; you cried aloud to me; you broke my barrier of my deafness. You shone upon me; your radiance enveloped me; you put my blindness to flight. You shed your fragrance about me; I drew breath and now I gasp for your sweet odour. I tasted you, and now I hunger and thirst for you. You touched me, and I am inflamed with love of your peace.

Saint Augustine, *Confessions* trans. R. S. Pine-Coffin (Baltimore: Penguin, 1961) 231-232. Copyright © R. S. Pine-Coffin. Reprinted by permission of Penguin Books Ltd.

Propers: Missionaries

Hymn of the Day: "Your kingdom come! O Father hear our prayer"
(376)

Prayers: for those in prison and those who minister to them
        for alcoholics
        for those near despair
        for single-minded devotion
        for the Santal church

Preface: Epiphany

Color: White

John of the Cross
Renewer of the Church, 1591

Juan de Ypres y Alvarez was born at Fontiveros, Spain on the day of John the Baptist, June 24, 1542, the third son of a disowned silk merchant, who was probably Jewish and who died shortly after his son was born. The son was placed in an institution for the poor. He displayed a remarkable incapacity for manual work and was returned by all to whom he was apprenticed. At seventeen he worked in a hospital in Medina to support himself in the Jesuit College in which he had enrolled.

He was a small man, less than five feet tall, who led a life of extraordinary struggle. Yet he was one whose ambition was only to spend his life in prayer and meditation. In 1563 he entered the Order of the Blessed Virgin (Carmelites) and took the name Fray Juan de San Matias. He studied theology at the University of Salamanca, 1564-1567. He was ordained in 1567, and at Medina, where he went to sing his first mass, he met Teresa of Avila, who had begun a reform of the Carmelite Order to restore the austere and predominantly contemplative primitive rule and who wanted to extend the austerity to monks of the order as well. The followers of this reform wore sandals instead of shoes and so were known as "Discalced"—barefoot—Carmelites. Juan promised to adopt this way of life and in token of his promise, changed his name to Juan de la Cruz (John of the Cross).

John was appointed sub-prior and master of novices at Duruelo and then rector of the house of studies at Alcala. In 1571 Teresa got John appointed confessor to the Convent of the Incarnation, where she was a sister.

Jealousies within the order led to a suspension of the reform. On December 2, 1577, the Carmelites seized John, took him to Toledo, and demanded that he renounce the reform. He refused and was imprisoned for nine months in a six-foot by ten-foot nearly dark cell. He managed to escape—miraculously, some say—in August, 1578 and made his way to a Discalced monastery in southern Spain.

He spent his next years in administration of various sorts, writing, and guiding the laity in the spiritual life. He was able to complete works begun in the darkness of the prison—poems and commentaries on them. He is, many claim, the greatest Spanish poet. Notable are the *Ascent of Mt. Carmel—the Dark Night,* a treatise on how to reach perfection; *The Spiritual Canticle,* a commentary on the poem dealing with love between the soul and Christ; and *The Living Flame of Love,* a song of a transformed soul.

In 1591 controversy again emerged over the control of the reform, and John was banished to a "desert house" in Andalusia in southern Spain. There he was seized with a fever and went to Ubeda for medical attention because he thought that he was not known there. The prior of the monastery complained of the added expense of an additional monk. John died during the night of December 13-14, 1591, with the words of the Psalm of Compline on his lips, "Into your hands, O Lord, I commend my spirit."

He is remembered as a supreme lyric poet and as a mystical spiritual writer. Salvador Dali's painting of the crucifixion as seen from above the cross is based on a drawing by John of the Cross of a vision he had.

Gerald Brennan. *St. John of the Cross. His Life and Poetry* with a translation of the poetry by Lynda Nicholson. Cambridge University Press, 1973.

Eric W. T. Dicken. *The Crucible of Love: a Study of the Mysticism of St. Theresa of Jesus and St. John of the Cross.* New York: Sheed and Ward, 1963.

E. A. Peers. *Spirit of Flame. A Study of St. John of the Cross.* New York: Morehouse, 1944.

———. *Handbook to the Life and Times of Saint Teresa and Saint John of the Cross.* Westminster, Md.; Newman, 1954.

Reading

(From a spiritual canticle by St. John of the Cross)

Though holy teachers have uncovered many mysteries and wonders, and devout souls have understood them in this earthly condition of ours, yet the greater part still remains to be unfolded by them,
and even to be understood by them.

We must then dig deeply in Christ. He is like a rich mine with
many pockets containing treasures: however deep we dig we will
never find their end or their limit. Indeed, in every pocket new
seams of fresh riches are discovered on all sides.

For this reason the apostle Paul said of Christ, *In him are hidden
all the treasures of the wisdom and knowledge of God.* The soul cannot enter into these treasures, nor attain them, unless it first crosses
into and enters the thicket of suffering, enduring interior and exterior
labors, and unless it first receives from God very many blessings in
the intellect and in the senses, and has undergone long spiritual
training.

All these are lesser things, disposing the soul for the lofty sanc-
tuary of the knowledge of the mysteries of Christ: this is the highest
wisdom attainable in this life.

Would that mortals might come at last to see that it is quite impossible to reach the thicket of the riches and wisdom of God except
by first entering the thicket of much suffering, in such a way that the
soul finds there its consolation and desire. The soul that longs for
divine wisdom chooses first, and in truth, to enter the thicket of the
cross.

Saint Paul therefore urges the Ephesians *not to grow weary in the
midst of tribulations, but to be rooted and grounded in love, so that
they may know with all the saints the breadth, the length, the height,
and the depth—to know what is beyond knowledge, the love of Christ,
so as to be filled with all the fullness of God.*

The gate that gives entry into these riches of wisdom is the cross;
because it is a narrow gate, while many seek the joys that can be
gained through it, it is given to few to desire to pass through it.

Teresa of Avila, Renewer of the Church, 1582

Teresa de Cepeda y Ahumada was born in Avila, Spain, March 28, 1515 of an old Spanish family. Her mother died when Teresa was fifteen, leaving the father with ten children. Teresa went to a convent school, where she read the letters of Jerome and decided to become a nun. Her father refused permission, and she ran away. On November 2, 1535, she entered the Carmelite monastery of the Incarnation at Avila. The community was large and open, freely associating with the world outside. There Teresa fell seriously ill, worsened, and lapsed into a deep coma. She revived, but her legs were paralyzed for three years. Despite her recovery, she remained rather lax in her spiritual life. She began to experience visions, and at age thirty-nine she experienced a vivid sense of God's presence within her. She wrote of such experiences rather matter-of-factly, but finally she was converted to a life of intense devotion. On November 15, 1572 she experienced "spiritual marriage with Christ" while receiving Holy Communion.

In 1560 she resolved to reform the monastery that had, she thought, departed from the order's original intention and had become insufficiently austere. In August 1562, in the face of strong opposition in the town and in the older monastery, a new monastery in Avila was dedicated to St. Joseph. A series of lawsuits resulted as the struggle continued. At length Teresa, who had taken the name Teresa of Jesus, was given permission to establish other reformed monasteries and she travelled throughout Spain founding seventeen monasteries. They were small, poor, disciplined, and strictly enclosed. After great difficulties and deprivations, she fell ill and died at Alba, October 4, 1582.

Teresa was a most attractive person, witty, frank, affectionate. She

is remembered for her practical achievements and ceaseless activity
in reforming the Carmelite Order and also for her mystic contemplation. An activist who nonetheless explored the spiritual life, she was
the first to indicate the existence of states of prayer between the dis-
cursive meditation and the final state of ecstasy, and she gave a careful
description of the entire life of prayer from meditation to mystic
marriage. Her *Life* is her autobiography to 1562; *The Way of Perfection* for the instruction of her sisters; the *Book of Foundations* tells
of her establishment of convents; and *The Interior Castle* deals with
the spiritual life. She is known to many from Bernini's sculpture de-
picting her ecstatic vision of an angel who came to her with a long
golden spear, burning at the tip. She wrote:

With this he seemed to pierce my heart several times so that it penetrated to my entrails. When he drew it out, I thought he was drawing
them out with it, and he left me completely afire with a great love for
God. The pain was so sharp that it made me utter several moans; and so
excessive was the sweetness caused me by this intense pain that one can
never wish to lose it, nor will one's soul be content with anything less than
God.

Her feast day in the Roman Catholic Church is October 15.

M. Auclair. *Saint Teresa of Avila,* tr. K. Pond. New York: Pantheon, 1953.
H. J. Coleridge. *The Life and Letters of Saint Teresa.* 3 vols. London,
    1881-1888.
E. Allison Peers. *The Complete Works of St. Teresa.* 3 vols. London: Sheed
    and Ward, 1946.
———. *Studies of the Spanish Mystics.* 3 vols. London; SPCK, 1951-1960.
———. *Mother of Carmel: A Portrait of St. Teresa of Jesus.* New York: More-
    house, 1946.
William Thomas Walsh. *St. Teresa of Avila.* Milwaukee: Brice, 1943.
Robert Peterson. *The Art of Ecstasy. Teresa, Bernini,* and *Crashaw.* New
    York: Athenaeum, 1970.

Reading

(From the *Life* of St. Teresa of Avila)

Beginners in prayer, we may say, are those who draw the water
from the well; this, as I have said, is very hard work, for it will
fatigue them to keep their senses recollected, which is extremely dif-

ficult because they have been accustomed to a life of distraction. Beginners must accustom themselves to pay no heed to what they see or hear, and they must practise this during hours of prayer; they must go away by themselves and in their solitude think over their past life—and we must all do this, in fact, whether we are at the beginning of the road or near its end. There are differences, however, in the extent to which it must be done, as I shall show later. At first it causes distress, for beginners are not always sure that they have repented of their sins (though clearly they have, since they have determined to serve God so faithfully). Then they have to endeavour to meditate upon the life of Christ, which fatigues their minds. Thus far we can make progress by ourselves—with the help of God, of course, for without that, as is well known, we cannot think a single good thought.

That is what is meant by beginning to draw water from the well—and God grant there may be water in it! But that, at least, does not depend on us: our task is to draw it and to do what we can to water the flowers. And God is so good that when, for reasons known to His Majesty, perhaps to our great advantage, He is pleased that the well should be dry, we, like good gardeners, do all that in us lies, and He keeps the flowers alive without water and makes the virtues grow. By water here I mean tears—or at least, if there are no tears, tenderness and an interior feeling of devotion.

What, then, will a person do here who finds that for many days he experiences nothing but aridity, dislike and distaste, and has so little desire to go and draw water that he would give it up entirely did he not remember that he is pleasing and serving the Lord of the garden; if he were not anxious that all his service should not be lost, to say nothing of the gain which he hopes for from the hard work of continually lowering the bucket into the well and then drawing it up without water? It will often happen that, even for that purpose, he is unable to lift his arms—unable, that is, to think a single good thought, for working with the understanding is of course the same as drawing water from the well.

What, then, as I say, will the gardener do here? He will rejoice and take new heart and consider it the greatest of favours to work in the garden of so great an Emperor; and as he knows that he is pleasing Him by doing so (and his purpose must be to please, not himself, but Him), let him render Him great praise for having placed such confidence in him, because He sees that, without receiving any recompense, he is taking such great care of that which He had entrusted to him; let him help Him to bear the Cross and remember how He lived with it all His life long; let him not wish to have his kingdom on earth or ever cease from prayer; and so let him resolve, even if this aridity should persist his whole life long, not to let Christ fall with His Cross.

E. Allison Peers trans. *The Mystics of Spain* (London: Allen and Unwin, 1951), pp. 81-83. Used by permission of George Allen & Unwin Ltd. (See the English carol, "King Jesus hath a garden full of divers flowers.")

Propers

ROMAN

St. John of the Cross
(December 14)
Father,
you endowed John of
   the Cross with a
   spirit of self-denial
and a love of the
   cross.
By following his
   example,
   may we come to
   the eternal vision of
   your glory.
We ask this through
   our Lord Jesus
   Christ, your Son,
who lives and reigns
   with you and the
   Holy Spirit, one
   God, for ever and
   ever.

(From the English translation of the Roman Missal © 1973, International Committee on English in the Liturgy, Inc. All rights reserved.)

Common of Pastors
   or Doctors
especially
1 Corinthians 2:1-10a

LUTHERAN

Almighty God, we praise you for the men and women you have sent to call the Church to its tasks and renew its life, such as your servants John and Teresa. Raise up in our own day teachers and prophets inspired by your Spirit, whose voices will give strength to your Church and proclaim the reality of your kingdom; through your Son, Jesus Christ our Lord.

Common of Renewers of
   the Church or
Jeremiah 1:4-10
   Psalm 46
1 Corinthians 2:1-10a
Mark 10:35-45

EPISCOPAL

ROMAN	LUTHERAN	EPISCOPAL

St. Teresa of Avila
(October 15)
Common of Virgins
or Saints
or Romans 8:22-27

Father,
by your Spirit you
raised up Saint
Teresa of Avila
to show your Church
the way to perfec-
tion.
May her inspired
teaching
awaken in us a long-
ing for true
holiness.
Grant this through our
Lord Jesus Christ,
your Son,
who lives and reigns
with you and the
Holy Spirit,
one God, for ever and
ever.

Hymn of the Day: "Come down, O Love divine" (508)

Prayers: for the love of the cross of Christ
for patience in suffering
for the gift of love that overcomes opposition and persecution
for intensity of the spiritual life

Preface: All Saints

Color: White

ST. THOMAS, APOSTLE

Practically all the information about "Thomas called Didymus" is found in the Fourth Gospel. "Thomas" seems not to be a personal name but rather an epithet meaning "twin"; Didymus is the Greek and Teoma (Thomas) is the Aramaic for "twin." There is a tradition that he was the twin of Jesus, at least in appearance. He is portrayed as something of a plodding literalist who is nonetheless an earnest searcher for truth. After Jesus' resurrection Thomas doubted and sought convincing proof that Jesus was in fact alive. His confession of faith went beyond what he saw with his eyes and what he touched with his hands to a statement of the belief of Johanine Christians: "My Lord and my God."

Later legend associates St. Thomas with Bartholomew, Matthew, Simon, and Jude—the five "Apostles of the East"—and tells of his evangelization of the lands between the Caspian Sea and the Persian Gulf and of his missionary travels to India. He is said by the *Acts of Thomas* to have entered India as a carpenter, preached the gospel, performed miracles, and died a martyr at Mylapore near Madras. One of the greatest of the early basilicas (fourth century) was the Church of St. Thomas in Edessa, Syria, and his body is said to have been buried there, but the stories of his work in India claim that he was buried at St. Thomas Mount near Madras. The third-century *Acts of Thomas* contains not only the earliest accounts of his work in India but the beautiful Syriac poem called the *Hymn of the Soul* as well.

It is possible, although most modern scholars think it unlikely, that St. Thomas reached India. There is a body of Christians, the "Christians of St. Thomas," along the Malabar coast in southern India who claim spiritual descent from St. Thomas and who were in India at least a thousand years before the coming of European missionaries in the sixteenth century.

Eastern churches have commemorated Thomas since the sixth century and the Roman observance dates from the ninth century. The date of his commemoration in the East is October 6. The Roman Catholic Church has moved the festival of St. Thomas out of Advent to July 3, the date of his commemoration in the Syrian Church. The new Episcopal calendar keeps the commemoration on the traditional Western date, December 21.

In art, St. Thomas is usually shown holding a carpenter's square and rule.

The Acts of Thomas, tr. B. Pick. Chicago, 1909.
J. N. Farquhar. "The Apostle Thomas in North India," *Bulletin of the John Rylands Library* X (1926), 80-111; XI (1927), 20-50.
G. E. Medlycott. *India and the Apostle Thomas.* 1905.
H. E. W. Turner and H. Montefiore. *Thomas and the Evangelists.* London: Allenson, 1962.
R. McL. Wilson. *Studies in the Gospel of Thomas.* London: Mowbray, 1960.

Reading

(From a sermon by Kaj Munk for the First Sunday after Easter)

And now, this is the Gospel for you, my Christian friend, who struggles with doubt and faith, with anxiety and denial. This is the Gospel that does not come to catechise you and force upon you certain dogmas, or to condemn you, but comes only to listen to the heartbeat of your soul. If it leans toward Jesus no matter what happens because it has chosen Him and wants to belong to Him, then the Gospel says to you: Be faithful, continue in the faith.

It is great to have assurance of faith, but perhaps you do not belong to those who can always take this for granted. However, the Master is also able to use the Thomas type. Such people have a place in His group of disciples. And let me tell you that when the time is at hand, Jesus himself will come and bring an end to your uncertainty and your timid spirit. You will understand that it is not what you fail to understand that matters. Christ has had disciples who did not understand the Virgin Birth and the Resurrection of the body and the Sacraments. Do not just stare blindly at them. Let not the devil fool you into thinking that unless you understand these things, you cannot be a disciple of Christ.

Abstain from empty and morbid speculation about whether you believe or not. This will get you no place except downwards. But be faithful to your inner soul, which once and for all has made its choice. Practice Christianity and at the proper time, even though the doors be ever so tightly closed, Christ himself will appear before you and show you the hands that were pierced for your sin; and you will bow down in prayer, crying out to Him in repentance and joy, "My Lord and my God!"

And after you have first addressed Him with so great a name, other things will no longer seem unintelligible. Perhaps it will then come to pass that the things you could not accept before will become dearest to you and your common sense.

But our Gospel for today goes much farther. It embraces those who do not even suspect that it is for them. There are those who deny Christianity because of the worldliness of the Christians, and because of the weakness and sin of the Church. These people, as far as they themselves can tell, deny Christ; but He dwells in their humility of heart and in their search for truth. They may experience the same "Thomas week" of despair. It pains them that what is genuinely good is trodden down with an iron heel, and that the struggle for justice seems hopeless. Yet they are faithful, and they prevail. To them it should be said that at the end of the week Christ will appear before them just as He really is, the guest of their hearts and the final conqueror of death and all its works and all its ways; and each one will greet Him saying, "My Lord and my God!"

Kaj Munk, *By the Rivers of Babylon*. Fifteen Sermons trans. J. M. Jensen (Blair, NE: Lutheran Publishing House, 1945) 23-25.

Propers

ROMAN	LUTHERAN	EPISCOPAL
(July 3) Almighty Father, as we honor Thomas the apostle, let us always experience the help of his prayers. May we have eternal life by believing in Jesus, whom Thomas acknowledged as Lord, for he lives and reigns with you and the Holy Spirit, one God, for ever and ever.	Almighty and ever-living God, you have given great and precious promises to those who believe. Grant us that perfect faith which overcomes all doubts; through your Son, Jesus Christ our Lord, who lives and reigns with you and the Holy Spirit, one God, now and forever.	Everliving God, who strengthened your apostle Thomas with firm and certain faith in your Son's resurrection: Grant us so perfectly and without doubt to believe in Jesus Christ, our Lord and our God, that our faith may never be found wanting in your sight; through him who lives and reigns with you and the Holy Spirit, one God, now and for ever.

ROMAN	LUTHERAN	EPISCOPAL
Ephesians 2:19-22 Psalm 117:1-2 John 20:24-29	Judges 6:36-40 Psalm 136:1-4, 23-26 Ephesians 4:11-16 John 14:1-7	Habakkuk 2:1-4 Psalm 126 Hebrews 10:35—11:1 John 20:24-29 Preface of Apostles

Hymn of the Day: "Lo! He comes with clouds descending" (27)

Prayers: for a healthy skepticism
for a renewal in us of the Easter faith
for grace to receive Christ

Preface: Apostles

Color: Red

ST. STEPHEN, MARTYR

St. Stephen, who, Luke reports, was "full of grace and power and did great wonders among the people," was the first of the band of martyrs to follow Christ and is therefore sometimes called "Proto-martyr." His devotion to the faith, his love for his persecutors, and his dramatic death by stoning that is reported in detail in Acts 6-7 make this deacon and martyr a much-revered figure among the saints.

The feast of St. Stephen was established very early in the history of the church, and it is possible that the date of his commemoration recalls the actual day of his death. In the Eastern church December 26 is the feast of the God-bearer, Mary the Theotokos, and St. Stephen is remembered on the 27th. In the Western church St. Stephen's Day is the first of the succession of three festivals immediately following Christmas—St. Stephen, St. John, and Holy Innocents—which associate the three "heavenly birthdays" with the birthday of Christ: as he was born into this world from that, so they were born into that world from this.

In some Lutheran churches December 26 has been celebrated as the Second Christmas Day, replacing St. Stephen's Day. In Finland it is the custom to ride a horse or horsedrawn vehicle on St. Stephen's Day; this observance is probably connected with the Scandinavian legend of Stephen as the stable boy of King Herod.

M. Simon. *St. Stephen and the Hellenists in the Primitive Church*. London: Longmans, 1958.
M. H. Scharlemann. "Stephen: a Singular Saint," *Analecta Biblica* XXXIV. Rome, 1958.

Reading

(From a sermon for St. Stephen's Day by Kaj Munk)

The Christ Child is the world's Savior and Prince of Peace because He is the world's greatest war Lord. Apparently there is the most glaring contrast between the Christmas gospel and that for St.

Stephen's Day—between the Christ Child and the first Christian martyr. But in reality there is the closest connection.

The pagan Christmas with eating and drinking and parties and family joy may well be contained in the Christian celebration, but it can never take the place of it. Jesus Himself took an interest in family life, and He attended parties; but He was, nevertheless, ever on the way to the cross. Let us sing Ingemann songs and eat goose and play with our children about the glittering Christmas tree; but we must never forget that the coming of Christ to earth means dauntless struggle against evil. And if we kneel by the manger in other than sentimental moods, we shall become aware that one hand of the little Child is open and kindly, the other clenched in blood.

We wish one another Merry Christmas. And we mean: may your Christmas goose be delicious—or your meatballs, if that is the best you can afford this year; may you have fuel to keep your house warm; may you have friends and loved ones about you; may your tree glitter in its wonted beauty and the hymns sound with their old power. And may there, through it all, be one song in your heart: "My Jesus, I want to be where Thou alone wilt have me." Yes, but there are so many doubts and questions that spoil my Christmas joy.

Well, but who promised you joy? It may be better that you have a poor Christmas. Don't be like a spoiled child and think of God as a great Santa Claus who has in His bag some sort of electromagnet with which to give your brain cells such a shot that everything becomes gloriously clear to you, and that you can be happy, in harmony with yourself and the world. My friend, perhaps your doctor can do that for you with a stimulant that will send the blood to the brain and clarify your mind so you see things in bright perspective. This has nothing to do with real joy. True Christmas joy, no matter how much or how little of it you may comprehend, means that you have Christ, and that you go where He wants you to go.

Kaj Munk, *Four Sermons* trans. J. M. Jensen (Blair, NE: Lutheran Publication House, 1944) 20-22.

Propers

ROMAN	LUTHERAN	EPISCOPAL
Lord, today we celebrate the entrance of Saint Stephen into eternal glory. He died praying for those who killed him. Help us to imitate his goodness and to love our enemies. We ask this through our Lord Jesus Christ, your Son, who lives and reigns with you and the Holy Spirit, one God, for ever and ever.	Grant us grace, O Lord, that like Stephen we may learn to love even our enemies and seek forgiveness for those who desire our hurt; through Jesus Christ our Lord, who lives and reigns with you and the Holy Spirit, one God, now and forever.	We give you thanks, O Lord of glory, for the example of the first martyr Stephen, who looked up to heaven and prayed for his persecutors to your Son Jesus Christ, who stands at your right hand; where he lives and reigns with you and the Holy Spirit, one God, in glory everlasting.

ROMAN	LUTHERAN	EPISCOPAL
Acts 6:8-10; 7:54-59 Psalm 31:3cd-4, 6ab, 7b, 8a, 17, 21ab Matthew 10:17-22	2 Chronicles 24:17-22 Psalm 17:1-9, 16 Acts 6:8-7:2a, 51-60 Matthew 23:34-39	Jeremiah 26:1-9, 12-15 Psalm 31 or 31:1-5 Acts 6:8-7:2a, 51c-60 Matthew 23:34-39 Preface of the Incarnation

Hymn of the Day: "The Son of God goes forth to war" (183) or "Let us now our voices raise" (*SBH* 546) sung to *Tempus adest floridum* as in the *Hymnal 1940,* since "Good King Wenceslaus looked out on the Feast of Stephen."

Prayers: for courage to explore the mysteries of both birth and death
for our enemies
for the gift of love
for courageously effective preachers

Preface: Christmas

Color: Red

ST. JOHN, APOSTLE, EVANGELIST

John the son of Zebedee, was one of the inner circle of the Twelve along with his brother James and Peter. He was a fisherman, and he is often assumed to be the "disciple whom Jesus loved" of the Fourth Gospel.

St. John is traditionally regarded as the author of the Fourth Gospel and the three epistles that bear his name and also the book of Revelation. Especially in connection with Revelation he is called St. John "the Divine", i.e. the Theologian. After a period of exile on the island of Patmos, where tradition says he wrote Revelation, St. John is said to have lived at Ephesus, where he died about the year 100 at an advanced age. In extreme old age, St. Jerome tells us, he would be carried into the church to say to the congregation, "My little children, love one another." He is believed to be the only one of the twelve Apostles who did not die a martyr's death, and is sometimes called a "martyr in will but not in deed." (Stephen was a martyr in will and deed; the Holy Innocents were martyrs in deed but not in will.)

In the fourth century a church was dedicated to St. John at Constantinople, and it is possible that the date of his feast day is based on the date of that dedication. Some Eastern calendars have December 27 as a day of commemoration of St. John and St. James, the brother of the Lord, but the Western church ever since it accepted the feast has made it for St. John alone.

An interesting custom on St. John's Day in northern Europe and England during the Middle Ages was the blessing and drinking of wine, called the "love of St. John." (According to legend, John once drank poisoned wine and was unharmed—hence his symbol of a chalice with a serpent in it.) This blessed wine was then used ceremonially throughout the year, especially by the bride and groom after weddings. (It is St. John's gospel that tells of Jesus' changing water into wine at the wedding at Cana in Galilee.)

Raymond E. Brown. *The Gospel According to St. John.* 2 vols. Garden City, N.Y.: Doubleday, 1966, 1970.

H. P. V. Nunn. *The Son of Zebedee and the Fourth Gospel.* New York: Macmillan, 1927.

J. N. Sanders. "Who was the Disciple whom Jesus Loved?" *Studies in the Fourth Gospel,* ed. F. L. Cross (London: Mowbray, 1957) 72-82.

D. Moody Smith. *John* (Proclamation Commentaries). Philadelphia: Fortress, 1976.

Reading

(From *Revelations of Divine Love* by Julian of Norwich.)

It was at this time that our Lord showed me spiritually how intimately he loves us. I saw that he is everything that we know to be good and helpful. In his love he clothes us, enfolds and embraces us; that tender love completely surrounds us, never to leave us. As I saw it he is everything that is good.

And he showed me more, a little thing, the size of a hazel-nut, on the palm of my hand, round like a ball. I looked at it thoughtfully and wondered, "What is this?" And the answer came, "It is all that is made." I marvelled that it continued to exist and did not suddenly disintegrate; it was so small. And again my mind supplied the answer, "It exists, both now and for ever, because God loves it." In short, everything owes its existence to the love of God.

Propers

ROMAN	LUTHERAN	EPISCOPAL
God our Father, you have revealed the mysteries of your Word through John the apostle. By prayer and reflection may we come to understand the wisdom he taught. Grant this through our Lord Jesus Christ, your Son, who lives and reigns with you and the Holy Spirit, one God, for ever and ever.	Merciful Lord, let the brightness of your light shine on your Church so that all of us, instructed by the teachings of John, your apostle and evangelist, may walk in the light of your truth and attain eternal life; through your Son Jesus Christ our Lord, who lives and reigns with you and the Holy Spirit, one God, now and forever.	Shed upon your Church, O Lord, the brightness of your light, that we, being illumined by the teaching of your apostle and evangelist John, may so walk in the light of your truth, that at length we may attain to the fullness of eternal life; through Jesus Christ our Lord, who lives and reigns with you and the Holy Spirit, one God, for ever and ever.

ROMAN	LUTHERAN	EPISCOPAL
1 John 1:1-4 Psalm 97:1-2, 5-6, 11-12 John 20:2-8	Genesis 1:1-5, 26-31 Psalm 116:10-17 1 John 1:1-2:2 John 21:20-25	Exodus 33:18-23 Psalm 92 or 92:1-4, 11-14 1 John 1:1-9 John 21:19b-24 Preface of the Incarnation

Hymn of the Day: "O Word of God incarnate" (231)

Prayers: for the work of the new creation in us
        for the spirit of awe and reverence in the presence of God
        for a glimpse of the glory of God in Jesus Christ
        for increased knowledge of the Incarnation

Preface: Christmas or Apostles

Color: White

THE HOLY INNOCENTS, MARTYRS

The Holy Innocents were the children of Bethlehem (numbered 14,000 on Eastern calendars) who were slaughtered by order of King Herod in his attempt to eliminate the infant Jesus. There is no record of this event outside Matthew's gospel, but it is not impossible, given Herod's character. He drowned his sixteen-year old brother-in-law, the high priest; killed his uncle, aunt, and mother-in-law, with several members of his brother-in-law's family, his own two sons and some three hundred officials he accused of siding with his sons.

Although the Holy Children, as they are called in Eastern Orthodox churches, were not believers and were unaware of the reason for their fate, they were killed for the sake of Christ, and in a sense in place of him, and the church by the beginning of the third century recognized them as martyrs. The feast dates from the fourth century in North Africa; it was universal by the sixth century. It has been suggested that in early times the festival commemorated all newly baptized infants tying baptism not only to Easter and Pentecost but to Christmas as well.

The fifth century Latin hymn of Prudentius *Salvete flores martyrum* ("Sweet flowerets of the martyr band"—*TLH* 273) is the traditional office hymn celebrating the children, the buds of martyrs killed by the frost of persecution as soon as they appeared.

The day is an appropriate time to remember children and to hold Christmas parties for them.

On this day one might also choose to remember, as the prayer of the day suggests, the innocents of all ages killed in the slaughters of history, such as:

- Sand Creek, Colorado (November 29, 1864), a slaughter of 450 unarmed Cheyenne men, women, and children;
- Wounded Knee, South Dakota (December 29, 1890), a slaughter of nearly three hundred Sioux men, women, and children;
- the massacre by the Turks of the Armenians who lived in the Turkish part of Armenia (April 24, 1915);
- Guernica (April 26, 1937), destruction of a Spanish town by German and Italian aircraft in the first mass bombing of an urban community;

- Latvia (June 13-14, 1941), over fourteen thousand Latvians departed to slave labor camps;
- Lidice (June 10, 1942), obliteration of a village by the Nazis in reprisal for the death of Reinhard Heydrich;
- Oradour (June 10, 1944), obliteration of a French town and all but ten of its inhabitants by the Nazis;
- Dachau, Auschwitz, and the extermination camps (1939-1945);
- Dresden (February 13, 1945), fire bombed by the Allies;
- Hiroshima (August 6, 1945) and Nagasaki (August 9, 1945), the first and second atomic bombs used in warfare;
- the martyrs behind the Iron Curtain.

For propers for the observance of the Holocaust (cf. the Jewish observance of Yom Hashoah), see the Day of Penitence in the *Lutheran Book of Worship*.

Lucy S. Dawidowicz. *The War against the Jews 1933-1945*. New York: Holt, Rinehart, Winston, 1975.
Dying We Live, ed. Helmut Gollwitzer, Kathe Kuhn, Reinhold Schneider. New York: Pantheon, 1956.

Reading

(From an article by Elie Wiesel.)

I admit it sadly: I feel threatened. For the first time in many years I feel that I am in danger. For the first time in my adult life I am afraid that the nightmare may start all over again, or that it has never ended, that since 1945 we have lived in parentheses. Now they are closed.

Could the Holocaust happen again? Over the years I have often put the question to my young students. And they, consistently, have answered yes, while I said no. I saw it as a unique event that would remain unique. I believed that if mankind had learned anything from it, it was that hate and murder reach beyond the direct participants; he who begins by killing others, in the end, will kill his own. Without Auschwitz, Hiroshima would not have been possible. The murder of one people inevitably leads to that of mankind.

In my naivete I thought, especially in the immediate postwar period, Jews would never again be singled out, handed over to the executioner. That anti-Semitism had received its deathblow long ago, under the fiery skies of Poland. I was somehow convinced that—paradoxically—man would be shielded, protected by the awesome mystery of the Event.

I was wrong. What happened once, could happen again. Perhaps I am exaggerating. Perhaps I am oversensitive. But then I belong to a traumatized generation. We have learned to take threats more seriously than promises.

. . . I have chosen until now to place the Holocaust on a mystical or ontological level, one that defies language and transcends imagination. I have quarreled with friends who built entire theories and doctrines on an event which, in my view, is not to be used or approached casually. If I speak of it now, it is only because of my realization that Jewish survival is being recalled into question.

Hence the fear in me. All of a sudden, I am too much reminded of past experiences. The enemy growing more and more powerful, more and more popular. The aggressiveness of the blackmailers, the permissiveness of some leaders and the total submissiveness of others. The overt threats. The complacency and diffidence of the bystanders. I feel as my father must have felt when he was my age.

Not that I foresee the possibility of Jews being massacred in the cities of America or in the forests of Europe. Death-factories will not be built again. But there is a certain climate, a certain mood in the making. As far as the Jewish people are concerned, the world has remained unchanged: as indifferent to our fate as to its own.

And so I look at my young students and tremble for their future; I see myself at their age surrounded by ruins. What am I to tell them?

I would like to be able to tell them that in spite of endless disillusionments one must maintain faith in man and in mankind; that one must never lose heart. I would like to tell them that, notwithstanding the official discourses and policies, our people does have friends and allies and reasons to advocate hope. But I have never lied to them, I am not going to begin now. And yet . . .

Despair is no solution, I know that. What is the solution? Hitler had one. And he tried it while a civilized world kept silent.

I remember. And I am afraid.

Propers

ROMAN	LUTHERAN	EPISCOPAL
Father, the Holy Innocents offered you praise by the death they suffered for Christ. May our lives bear witness to the faith we profess with our lips. We ask this through our Lord Jesus Christ, your Son, who lives and reigns with you and the Holy Spirit, one God, for ever and ever.	We remember today, O God, the slaughter of the holy innocents of Bethlehem by order of King Herod. Receive, we pray, into the arms of your mercy all innocent victims, and by your great might frustrate the designs of evil tyrants and establish your rule of justice, love, and peace; through Jesus Christ our Lord, who lives and reigns with you and the Holy Spirit, one God, now and forever.	We remember today, O God, the slaughter of the holy innocents of Bethlehem by King Herod. Receive, we pray, into the arms of your mercy all innocent victims; and by your great might frustrate the designs of evil tyrants and establish your rule of justice, love, and peace; through Jesus Christ our Lord, who lives and reigns with you, in the unity of the Holy Spirit, one God, for ever and ever.

ROMAN

1 John 1:5-2:2
Psalm 124:2-5, 7b-8
Matthew 2:13-18

LUTHERAN

Jeremiah 31:15-17
Psalm 124
1 Peter 4:12-19
Matthew 2:13-18

EPISCOPAL

Jeremiah 31:15-17
Psalm 124
Revelation 21:1-7
Matthew 2:13-18

Preface of the Incarnation

Hymn of the Day: "Your little ones, dear Lord, are we" (52)
or "Sweet flowerets of the martyr band" (*TLH* 273)

Prayers: for children
for sensitivity to the suffering of others
for courage to resist oppression and to share the lot of
the oppressed
for repentance for brutality and repression, especially
that committed in the name of Christ, the Holy Child

Preface: Christmas
Color: Red

Other Observances

Certain other days have been observed with some frequency in various congregations and therefore might also be appropriate to the new Lutheran calendar.

The *Beheading of St. John the Baptist* (August 29), sometimes called from the Latin title of the day the "Decollation" of John, is on the Roman calendar but not on the new Episcopal calendar. It has appeared on European Lutheran calendars at various times. There is some question as to whether John can be understood as a Christian martyr since he died before the ministry of Jesus was completed (although the Holy Innocents are on the calendar). In any case, the celebration of John's birth, which was closely associated with the birth of Jesus, has been the more popular celebration both because of its relationship to the summer solstice and because of its relationship to the Incarnation.

Gustavus Adolphus, the Lutheran king, who died November 6, 1632, is remembered particularly in Germany and the Baltic countries, and there are a number of Lutheran churches in North America named for him. His exploits and fame are entirely military. He saved large parts of Europe for Protestantism, but this was part of his expansionist policies. The wars of the counter-reformation offer little edification for today. Churches named for him, however, might appropriately keep his day.

The Rev. *Jehu Jones Jr.* was ordained by the New York Ministerium on October 24, 1832 in St. Matthew's Church, New York City. He is the first black person to be ordained a Lutheran pastor. He was jailed upon his return to his native South Carolina, and he was urged by a Lutheran pastor in Philadelphia to join the Methodist, Presbyterian, or Baptist church. He founded St. Paul's Church in Philadelphia. The Synod of Pennsylvania, when the church encountered financial difficulties, took title to the building and failed to assist him. (The building is now the property of the Mask and Wig Club of the University of Pennsylvania.) The New York Ministerium rejected his appeal for funds. Disillusioned, Jones disappeared from the scene and was heard from no more. The melancholy story of his ministry is told by Douglas Strange in *Una Sancta* XXIV, 2 (Pentecost 1967) 52-55.

Joseph of Arimathea is on the Episcopal calendar (July 31) but not on the Roman one. He is remembered in England largely because of the legends of his arrival there with the Holy Grail, the chalice used at the Last Supper.

Lutherans of Swedish ancestry remember *Jenny Lind* with affection. She was born October 6, 1820 in Stockholm and was a devout Christian and benefactor. She died November 2, 1887 in London and is buried next to Handel in Westminster Abbey. Her generosity endeared her to many Americans when she appeared in the United States on a concert tour in 1851.

St. Lucy or *Lucia* (December 13) was an early martyr at Syracuse, probably during the Diocletian persecution, ca. 304. She is listed on the Roman calendar but not on the Episcopal calendar. Little is known of her life, but because of her early popularity her name is included in the list of saints in the Roman Canon of the Mass. She is remembered with great affection by the people of Sicily and southern Italy, and in the Roman Catholic Church she is regarded as a patron saint of the laboring poor and a protector against diseases of the eye.

In medieval Europe before the Gregorian reform of the calendar, St. Lucy's Day was the shortest day of the year (John Donne has a poem on the theme), and this day was celebrated especially in Scandinavia where it marked the turning from the long cold nights to the increase in daylight. It was originally a time for celebrating light in order to encourage the strengthening of the light of the sun and to prevent the decline into total darkness. (The name Lucia means "light.") Swedish communities, including many in America, still have special festivities for this day. In private homes one of the young girls of the household, dressed in white and wearing a crown of lighted candles, awakens the family in the morning and offers them cakes and coffee from a tray. For the whole day she is then called Lucia or "Lussi" instead of her own name. Now that the solstice occurs on December 21 or 22, the purpose of celebrating St. Lucy's Day as a festival of light has been largely removed, and of her life only the barest details are known.

The Martyrs of Uganda are commemorated on the Roman and Episcopal calendars on June 3. During 1885-1887 King Mwanga of Uganda, who feared white domination of his country, killed many Christians, some of whom had been court officials and personal aides to the king. On June 3, 1886, some thirty-two young men, both Anglican and Roman Catholic, were burned at the stake. They were canonized in 1964 at a ceremony in St. Peter's Basilica at which the Archbishop of Canterbury was an honored guest. J. F. Faupel in *African Holocaust* (London: Geoffrey Chapman, 1965) erroneously calls the non-Romans Lutherans.

The Episcopal Church on October 29 remembers *James Hannington*, Bishop of Eastern Equatorial Africa and his companions, who were martyred in 1885 in Uganda under King Mwanga.

Chronological List of Names

First Century: Andrew, Barnabas, Bartholomew, Dorcas, Holy Innocents, James the Elder, James of Jerusalem, James the Less, John, John the Baptist, Joseph, Jude, Lazarus, Luke, Lydia, Mark, Mary, Mary of Bethany, Mary Magdalene, Matthew, Matthias, Michael, Paul, Peter, Philip, Phoebe, Silas, Simon, Stephen, Thomas, Timothy, Titus

Second Century: Clement, Ignatius, Justin, Polycarp

Third Century: Irenaeus, Lawrence, Perpetua

Fourth Century: Ambrose, Athanasius, Basil, Gregory Nazianzus, Gregory of Nyssa, Martin, Monica, Nicholas

Fifth Century: Augustine, Chrysostom, Jerome, Patrick

Sixth Century: Benedict, Columba

Seventh Century: Aidan, Gregory the Great

Eighth Century: Bede, Boniface

Ninth Century: Ansgar, Cyril, Methodius

Tenth Century: Dustan, Olga

Eleventh Century: Olaf, Vladimir

Twelfth Century: Anselm, Bernard, Erik, Henry

Thirteenth Century: Elizabeth, Francis, Thomas Acquinas

Fourteenth Century: Birgitta, Catherine, Sergius

Fifteenth Century: Hus

Sixteenth Century: Agricola, Calvin, Copernicus, Duerer, Francis Xavier, John of the Cross, Las Casas, Luther, Martyrs of Japan, Melanchthon, Michaelangelo, the Petris, Teresa, Tyndale

Seventeenth Century: Bunyan, Donne, Eliot, Fox, Gerhardt, Heermann, Herbert, Jensen, Nicolai, Schuetz, Tranovsky

Eighteenth Century: Bach, Edwards, Euler Handel, Muhlenberg, Seattle, Watts, the Wesleys, Ziegenbalg

Nineteenth Century: Fliedner, Grundtvig, Hauge, Heyer, Kierkegaard, Loehe, Neale, Wallin, Winkworth

Twentieth Century: Berggrav, Bonhoeffer, Fedde, Hammarskjold, John XXIII, Kagawa, King, Maass, Munk, Nightingale, Nommensen, Onesimos, Schweitzer, Skrefsrud, Söderblom

476

Geographical Distribution

Africa—North Africa: Athanasius, Augustine, Monica, Perpetua. *Sub-Sahara:* Onesimos, Schweitzer

The Americas—North: Edwards, Eliot, Fedde, Jensen, King, Maass, Muhlenberg, Seattle. *Central and South:* Las Casas

British Isles—Ireland: Patrick. *Britain:* Aidan, Anselm, Bede, Bunyan, Columba, Donne, Dunstan, Fox, Handel, Herbert, Knox, Neale, Nightingale, Tyndale, Watts, the Wesleys, Winkworth

Eastern Europe—Czechoslovakia: Cyril, Hus, Methodius, Tranovsky *Hungary:* Elizabeth *Poland:* Copernicus *Russia:* Euler, Olga, Sergius, Vladimir

Asia—India: Heyer, Skrefsrud, Ziegenbalg *Indonesia:* Nommensen *Japan:* Francis Xavier, Kagawa, Martyrs of Japan

Near and Middle East—Palestine: the biblical saints, Jerome *Asia Minor:* Basil, Chrysostom, Gregory Nazianzus, Gregory of Nyssa, Ignatius, Nicholas, Polycarp

Scandinavia—Denmark: Ansgar, Grundtvig, Kierkegaard, Munk *Finland:* Agricola, Henry *Norway:* Berggrav, Hauge, Olaf *Sweden:* Birgitta, Erik, Hammarskjold, the Petris, Söderblom, Wallin

Western Europe—France: Bernard, Calvin, Irenaeus, Martin *Germany:* Bach, Bonhoeffer, Boniface, Duerer, Fliedner, Gerhardt, Heermann, Loehe, Luther, Melanchthon, Nicolai, Schuetz *Italy:* Ambrose, Benedict, Catherine, Clement, Francis, Gregory, John XXIII, Justin, Lawrence, Michaelangelo, Thomas Aquinas *Spain:* John of the Cross, Teresa

Denominations Represented

Eastern Church: Basil, Chrysostom, Cyril, Gregory Nazianzus, Gregory of Nyssa, Ignatius, Methodius, Nicholas, Olga, Polycarp, Sergius, Vladimir

Western Church (to the Reformation): Aidan, Ambrose, Anselm, Ansgar, Athanasius, Augustine, Bede, Benedict, Bernard, Birgitta, Boniface, Catherine, Clement, Columba, Dunstan, Elizabeth, Erik, Francis, Gregory, Henry, Irenaeus, Jerome, Justin, Lawrence, Martin, Monica, Olaf, Patrick, Perpetua, Thomas Aquinas

Roman Catholic: Copernicus, Duerer, Francis Xavier, John of the Cross, John XXIII, Las Casas, Michaelangelo, Seattle, Teresa

Lutheran: Agricola, Bach, Berggrav, Bonhoeffer, Fedde, Fliedner, Gerhardt, Grundtvig, Hammarskjold, Hauge, Heermann, Heyer, Jensen, Kierkegaard, Loehe, Luther, Melanchthon, Muhlenberg, Munk, Nicolai, Nommensen, Onesimos, the Petris, Schuetz, Schweitzer, Skrefsrud, Söderblom, Tranovsky, Wallin

Anglican: Donne, Herbert, Neale, Nightingale, Winkworth

Calvinist: Calvin, Edwards, Eliot, Euler

Other Protestant: Bunyan, Fox, Handel, Hus, Kagawa, King, Tyndale, Watts, the Wesleys

Distribution of Propers

Martyrs: Bonhoeffer, Erik, Hus, Ignatius, Justin, Lawrence, Martyrs of Japan, Munk, Perpetua, Polycarp. (Boniface, Olav, Tyndale)

Saints: Bede, Benedict, Birgitta, Catherine, Dorcas, Dunstan, Francis, Joseph, Lazarus, Lydia, Martha, Mary of Bethany, Monica, Olav, Olga, Phoebe, Seattle, Schweitzer, Sergius, Vladimir. (Bernard, Erik)

Pastors: Ambrose, Berggrav, Clement, Gregory the Great, Herbert, Irenaeus, James of Jerusalem, Jensen, John XXIII, Loehe, Martin, Muhlenberg, Nicholas, Söderblom, Wallin.

Missionaries (and Preachers and Translators): Aidan, Ansgar, Boniface, Chrysostom, Columba, Cyril, Donne, Eliot, Francis Xavier, Henry, Jerome, Heyer, Las Casas, Methodius, Nommensen, Onesimos, Patrick, Skrefsrud, Silas, Timothy, Titus, Tyndale, Ziegenbalg. (Edwards, Schweitzer)

Theologians: Anselm, Athanasius, Augustine, Basil, Bernard, Edwards, Gregory Nazianzen, Gregory of Nyssa, Kierkegaard, Thomas Aquinas. (Bonhoeffer, Bunyan)

Renewers of the Church: Agricola, Calvin, Grundtvig, Hauge, John of the Cross, Luther, Melanchthon, the Petris, Teresa, the Wesleys. (Catherine, Hus)

Renewers of Society: Elizabeth, Fedde, Fliedner, Fox, Kagawa, King, Maass, Nightingale. (Catherine, Las Casas, Grundtvig)

Peace: Hammarskjold

Artists and Scientists: Copernicus, Bach, Bunyan, Duerer, Euler, Gerhardt, Handel, Heermann, Michaelangelo, Nicolai, Neale, Schuetz, Tranovsky, Watts, Winkworth. (Donne, Wallin)

Bibliography

(* Major resources)

*Attwater, Donald *Penguin Dictionary of Saints.* Baltimore: Penguin, 1965.

Bainton, Roland H. *Women of the Reformation in Germany and Italy.* Minneapolis: Augsburg, 1971.

Burghardt, Walter J. *Saints and Sanctity.* New York: Prentice-Hall, 1965.

Butler's Lives of the Saints ed., rev., and supplemented by Herbert Thurston, S. J. and Donald Attwater. 4 vols. New York: Kenedy, 1956.

Chavchavadze, Marina, ed. *Man's Concern with Holiness.* London: Hodder and Stoughton, 1970.

Deen, Edith. *Great Women of the Christian Faith.* New York: Harper and Row, 1959.

Flannery, Austin, et al. *The Saints in Season. A Companion to the Lectionary.* Collegeville, MN: Liturgical Press, 1977.

Fox, Adam; Gareth and Georgina Keene, eds. *Sacred and Secular.* Grand Rapids, MI: Eerdmans, 1976.

Freemantle, Anne. *Saints Alive!* Garden City, NY; Doubleday, 1978.

Kalberer, Augustine. *Lives of Saints.* Chicago: Franciscan Herald Press, 1976.

*McClendon, James William, Jr. *Biography as Theology: How Life Stories Can Remake Today's Theology.* Nashville: Abingdon, 1975.

McGinley, Phyllis. *Saint-Watching.* New York: Viking, 1969.

Martindale, Cyril Charles. *What Are Saints? Fifteen Chapters in Sanctity.* London: Sheed and Ward, 1932.

The New Catholic Encyclopedia. 15 vols. New York: McGraw-Hill, 1967.

The Oxford Dictionary of the Christian Church, ed. F. L. Cross. 2nd ed. London: Oxford, 1974.

The Oxford Dictionary of Saints, ed. D. H. Farmer. London: Oxford, 1978.

Payne, Robert. *Fathers of the Western Church.* New York: Viking, 1951.

———. *The Holy Fire. Fathers of the Eastern Church.* New York: Harper, 1957.

Prayer Book Studies XVI: The Calendar and the Collects, Epistles, and Gospels for the Lesser Feasts and Fasts. New York: the Church Pension Fund, 1963.

See also Studies IX, XII, and XIX.

Saint of the Day. A Life and Lesson for Each of the 173 Saints of the New Missal. ed. Leonard Foley, O.F.M. 2 vols. Cincinnati: St. Anthony Messenger Press, 1974.

Saints for All Seasons ed. John J. Delaney. Garden City, NY: Doubleday, 1978.

Index of Readings